QUANTUM COMPUTING

The Vedic Fabric of the Digital Universe

Thomas J. Routt, PhD

Dear Barbara,
Enjoy this expression of
Maharishi's Vedic Science.
Jai Guru Dev
Tom Routt

Quantum Computing
The Vedic Fabric of the Digital Universe
by Thomas J. Routt, PhD

Published by 1st World Publishing
1100 North 4th St. Suite 131
Fairfield, Iowa 52556
Tel: 641-209-5000 • Fax: 641-209-3001
www.1stworldpublishing.com

Author's web site: www.vediccomputing.com

First Edition
LCCN: 2005903597
ISBN: 978-1-59540-941-6

Design and layout by Aaron & Heather Lyon, monkeymatic.com.

About The Author Thomas J. Routt, PhD, has 25 years experience in computer network architecture, design, commercialization and executive management. Dr. Routt has guided Fortune 500 clients in acquisition of US$1 billion in computer network systems.

Dr. Routt's areas of professional expertise include quantum computing and networking, optical computing and networking, relational databases, broadband and mobile network architecture, information security, storage networks, predictive modeling, service level agreements, systems management, and enterprise IT integration.

Dr. Routt holds a PhD, *Computer Science*, Maharishi European Research University (MERU), Switzerland; MBA, *Information Systems* (*Beta Gamma Sigma* Honors), Southern Illinois University, USA; and BSc, *Environmental Science* (Research Honors), Western Washington University, USA.

Dr. Routt is a frequent keynote speaker, chair and presenter at science and technology conferences worldwide, having addressed over one million computing and networking professionals on six continents.

Dr. Routt holds two pending patents in quantum computation, and has published over 80 papers in computer network technology and business journals (including *Business Communications Review*, *Network World*, and *Data Communications* / McGraw-Hill).

As President & CEO, Vedacom® Corporation, Dr. Routt leads teams providing broadband, mobile computing, information security, and systems management solutions to Fortune 500 clients.

As President, Safetystream™ Ltd, Dr. Routt co-leads a firm that develops, patents and commercializes hardware-software systems enabling secure management of fixed and mobile assets.

Dr. Routt previously was Director, F5 Networks, Inc., a firm that develops and commercializes Web and Internet traffic load balancing and management technologies that optimize and scale network applications.

As Manager, Boeing Network Architecture, The Boeing Company, Dr. Routt co-pioneered Boeing Network Architecture and directed Boeing's worldwide network application resource. Previously, as Senior Systems Analyst, Dr. Routt led a team that developed a manufacturing database, ensuring just-in-time, in-budget aircraft design-to-delivery cycles.

As Research Scientist, MERU and UCLA, Dr. Routt was responsible for integration of electroencephalographic (EEG) and cardiopulmonary systems on the team that created the world's first research laboratory studying the neurophysiology of enlightenment. Dr. Routt participated in development of computer-based Coherence Spectral Array (COSPAR) tools that graphically summarize human brain inter-hemispheric EEG coherence during practice of the Transcendental Meditation® Technique.

Dr. Routt pioneered physiological research comparing TM Technique practitioners and non-meditators as part of an undergraduate thesis published in 1977—"Low Normal Heart and Respiration Rates in Individuals Practicing the Transcendental Meditation Technique," *Scientific Research on the Transcendental Meditation Program: Collected Papers, Volume I.*

HIS HOLINESS MAHARISHI MAHESH YOGI

Here is the
Guiding Light
for all future research
in the field of
Computer Science

– Maharishi

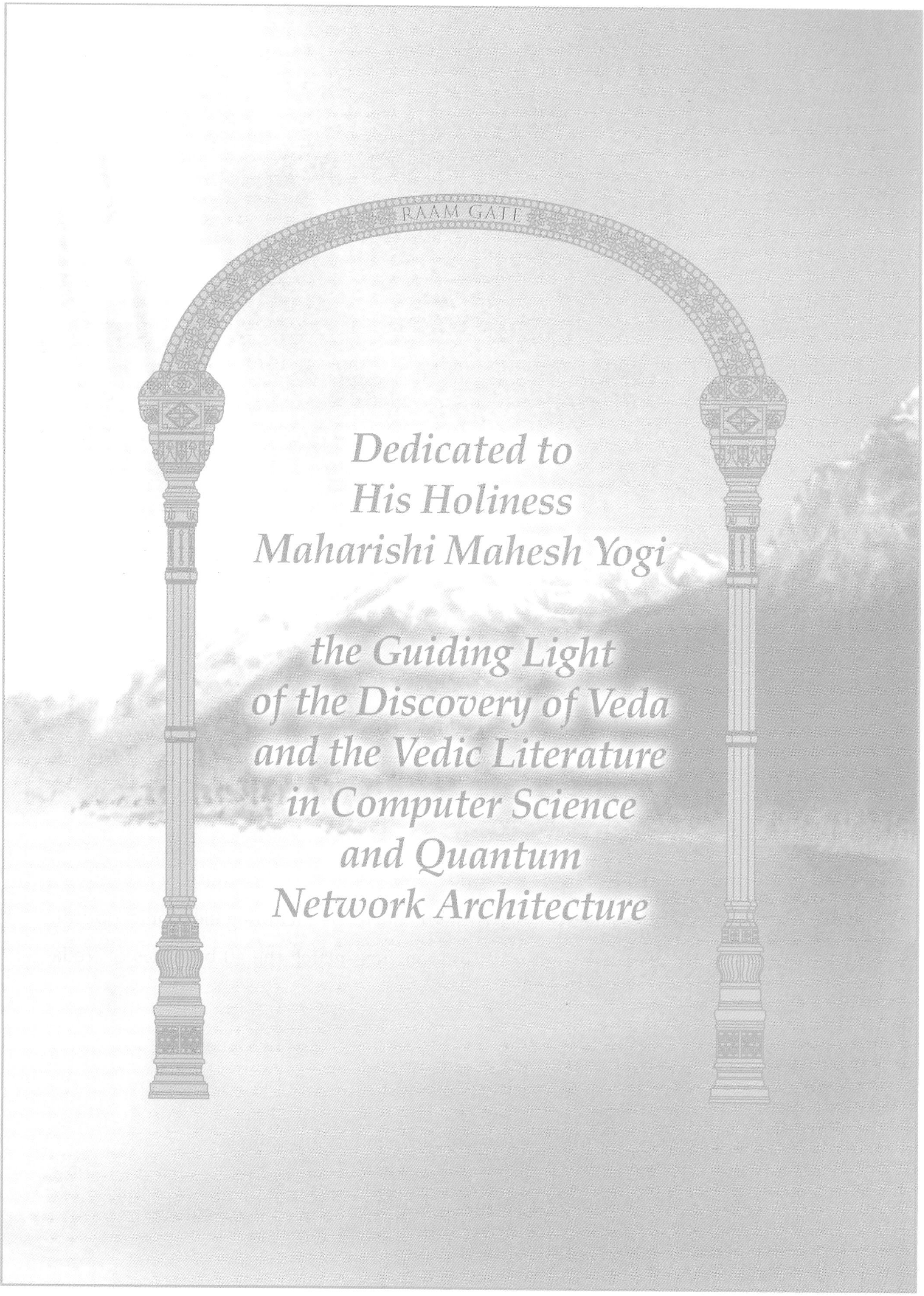

Dedicated to
His Holiness
Maharishi Mahesh Yogi

the Guiding Light
of the Discovery of Veda
and the Vedic Literature
in Computer Science
and Quantum
Network Architecture

Summary

Quantum computing and quantum networking establish the holistic foundation of the Global Internetwork and complete expression of Information Science and Technology. Networked information presides as the nucleus of today's interconnected world. At any given moment, a billion people interact with hundreds of millions of applications, through a trillion interconnected, intelligent devices.

The Global Internetwork embodies the physical, logical, and ubiquitous confluence of the Internet; the World Wide Web; and hundreds of thousands of intranets, extranets, and private computer networks. It functions as a global nervous system, or self-referral conscious superfabric, that collects, interprets, processes, interconnects, and integrates enterprise and personal data throughout the world on an exponentially increasing scale.

Profound insights into the ancient Vedic Literature, brought to light by His Holiness Maharishi Mahesh Yogi over the past 50 years, ushered in the discovery that the laws that shape the structure and function of quantum computing and networking—Quantum Network Architecture™—are identical to those that give rise to the syllables, verses, chapters, and books of the Vedic (Sanskrit term that means pertaining to knowledge) Literature and to the administering intelligence of Natural Law described in the Vedic Literature as Vedic *Devatā.*

Quantum computation—including the quantum algorithms and gates at its core—has the same structure and function as the holistic, self-sufficient, self-referral reality expressed in Ṛk Veda. The information units, network processing units, and topology units of both classical and quantum network architecture—including electronic, optical, and quantum systems, subsystems, and components—match the 40 branches of Veda and the Vedic Literature on a one-to-one basis, both in structure and function.

Quantum computing and networking synthesizes quantum information theory; sampling theory; quantum physics; classical space-time physics; computer science; electrical, electronic, optical, video, and voice engineering; data communications; telecommunications; wireless technology; analytic queueing theory; simulation; linear programming; and mathematical programming.

Quantum computation is the natural outcome of an oceanic scale of inexorable trends, both at the component level and throughout the Global Internetwork. In order to sufficiently enhance computer and network throughput to continually meet worldwide networked information throughput and availability requirements, the following conditions must be met:

- Computing and networking components and systems must be driven at increasingly higher clock frequencies within shrinking chip geometries and diminishing memory latencies.
- Computing and networking components and systems must be increasingly integrated due to the speed of light limitation while remaining within classical space-time symmetries.
- Increasingly miniaturized components and systems need to be continually more energy efficient, while avoiding serial architecture (Von Neumann) bottlenecks and resistance-capacitance delays. These issues are only temporarily delayed within parallel processing platforms.

When we extrapolate the exponential trend of miniaturization, which has held since 1950 under Moore's Law, we attain a limit of one atom per bit and Single Electron Transistor (SET) by 2010–2020. Prior to the one-atom-per-bit level, it becomes necessary to use quantum effects to read bits from and write bits to the memory registers of nano-, pico-, femto-, or atto-scale computers and network nodes.

Of all candidate technologies that continue to scale beyond the Very Large Scale Integration (VLSI) era, quantum logic has one unique feature—it is not contained by classical space-time physics. Moore's Law is exponential; any classical approach demands exponential increases in space or time. Even the Avogadro's number of elements in a molecular computer is quickly limited by the size of the exponential problem. Quantum computing and networking accesses Hilbert space, the one exponential resource that had been untapped for computation.

There are two essential bases to quantum computer and network systems:

1 Fermions, which have 1/2-integer spin and cannot be in the same state due to the

Pauli exclusion principle (no two electrons/fermions can simultaneously occupy the same single-particle quantum state on the same atom), and

2 Bosons, which have integer spin and can share the same state.

Electrons are fermions; photons are bosons. Electronic computing and networking is ultimately fermion-based, where N_8 must be either 0 or 1 because there cannot be more than one fermion in a single state. Optical computing and networking is ultimately boson-based, where, for bosons, the sum over N_8 runs from 0 to infinity.

Bosons (the ultimate basis of optical computing and networking) are particles whose spin is a whole number. Fermions (the ultimate basis of electronic computing and networking) are particles whose spin is half of a whole (odd) number, and tend to give canceling quantum-mechanical contributions. When the quantum jitters of a boson are positive, those of a fermion tend to be negative, and vice versa. Since supersymmetry ensures that bosons and fermions occur in pairs, substantial cancellations occur from the outset—cancellations that ultimately calm the apparently frenzied quantum effects.

Quantum information researchers initially attempted to understand how the basic operations of a conventional computer (a computer constrained to operation within classical space-time symmetries) could be accomplished while using quantum mechanical interactions. It is now clear however, that by exploiting quantum phenomena that have no classical analogs, it is possible to perform certain computational tasks far more efficiently than can be done by any classical space-time symmetry-bound computer or network node.

The quantum phenomena associated with quantum computing and networking enable the rapid accomplishment of the following previously unprecedented results:

- Quantum information teleportation
- Generation of true random numbers
- Factoring of complex polynomials
- Quantum searching to extract statistics, such as the minimal element, from an unordered data set, far more quickly and efficiently than on a classical computer

- Quantum search of an unstructured database
- Quantum counting, where the number of solutions, M, to an N-item search problem can be found if M is not known in advance, far more quickly and efficiently than on a classical computer
- Quantum Fast Fourier Transform (QFFT), that can be used to solve discrete logarithm and factoring problems, and find a hidden subgroup (a generalization of finding the period of a periodic function)
- Breaking heretofore classically unbreakable cryptosystems
- Communicating with messages that reveal the presence of eavesdropping

When we consider a quantum computational system of n quantum bits (qubits), we find the computational basis states of this system to be of the form $|\chi_1, \chi_2, \ldots, \chi_n\rangle$. Therefore, a quantum state of such a system is specified by 2^n amplitudes. For n greater than 300, this number is larger than the estimated number of atoms in the known physical universe.

The Cosmic Computer and Cosmic Switchboard, revealed by His Holiness Maharishi Mahesh Yogi, are perpetually processing far greater than 2^n amplitudes, even for systems that contain only a few hundred atoms, to say nothing of the massively parallel infinity-point calculations that are eternally proceeding behind the scenes to evolve and maintain all the Laws of Nature on every level of creation. We extrapolate that Nature maintains greater than 2^{300} calculations for every few hundred atoms throughout the entire universe.

The scale of Natural Law calculations of the Cosmic Computer and Cosmic Switchboard are further estimated to extend exponentially beyond the atomic level when we shift our attention to the scales of the fundamental force particles (photons for the Electromagnetic Force; weak gauge bosons for the Weak Force; gluons for the Strong Force; gravitons for the Gravitational Force). The fundamental force computational density of the Cosmic Computer and Cosmic Switchboard is again eclipsed hyper-exponentially at the superstring dimensions that pervade sub-Planck scales of less than 10^{-33} centimeter and less than 10^{-43} second.

The entire structure of the Cosmic Computer and Cosmic Switchboard is pure, cosmic intelligence and has been identified by His Holiness Maharishi Mahesh Yogi as integral to his Vedic Science and Technology as the infinity-within-all-points and all points-within-infinity cosmic computational foundation for perfection of evolution.

We locate the Cosmic Computer and Cosmic Switchboard both within the self-luminous junction point of the Hardware-Software Gap™ and throughout every point of manifest creation. It is here that we discover that intelligence which is at the same time numeric and also with boundaries, where physical digits are connected to numeric digits, where the physical is expressed in terms of numbers. It is also here that we reveal the Digital Fabric of Consciousness™ at the very basis of computational creation.

It is my fulfillment, under the guidance of His Holiness Maharishi Mahesh Yogi, to bring to light the one-to-one correspondence between Information Science and Technology, and Maharishi's Vedic Science and Technology in terms of the inner intelligence of Quantum Network Architecture, the Cosmic Computer and Cosmic Switchboard, whose impulses are available in the form of the sounds of Veda and the Vedic Literature.

Thomas J. Routt, PhD

Table of Contents

List of Figures

1: Modern Science and Ancient Vedic Science

His Holiness Maharishi Mahesh Yogi has brought to light and revitalized the ancient Veda and Vedic Literature by identifying a single, universal source of all orderliness in Nature. This universal source of orderliness has within itself all the diverse Laws of Nature, governing life at every level of the manifest universe. The entire spectrum of creation—ranging from the cosmological scale at the outermost reaches of the observable universe to the Planck and sub-Planck scales of the superstring fabric of the Unified Field—is based on these laws and their sequential unfoldment.

Veda is a Sanskrit term that means knowledge; *Vedic* means pertaining to Veda. *Nature* is used in its broadest sense to include all that exists in the entire universe, from its unmanifest, unified level, to all its expressions, forms, and phenomena. *Laws of Nature* refers to all the laws of Quantum Computation, Quantum Network Architecture™, computer science, classical physics, quantum physics, unified field physics, and mathematics, including the laws that structure life at the individual and social levels and that maintain order within the infinite diversity of the universe.

Natural Law refers to the integrated, balanced, and holistic functioning of all the Laws of Nature. National laws and international laws are creations of human beings—they can be close to or far from Natural Law, depending on the degree to which the awareness of the human beings or societies that create them is in tune with Natural Law. Maharishi's Vedic Science and Technology offers a practical, scientifically validated procedure to apply this most fundamental and powerful level of Natural Law for the benefit of mankind.

Sounds of Veda refers to the sound value in the texts of Veda. A word has two aspects: sound and meaning. When one hears a foreign language, one hears the sound but does not comprehend the meaning. In Veda and the Vedic Literature, the sound value of the Vedic Chanting or Recitation is given importance independent from its meaning level. The sounds of Veda, which have been recited for generation after generation in the tradition of the Vedic Families, have been described by Maharishi as "...the Laws of Nature murmuring to themselves. They are Natural Law describing itself and its own structure and function—eternally the same total potential of Natural Law on that self-referral level of intelligence."

Maharishi's Vedic Science and Technology is organized into 40 branches (refer to Figure 2-8 on page 32), with each branch specializing in a particular field or aspect of knowledge. The first branch of the Vedic Literature is called Ṛk Veda, and its specialty is Wholeness, the *Saṁhitā,* or holistic aspect of total knowledge. In this book, Ṛk Veda, Sāma Veda, Yajur Veda, and Atharva Veda will often be simply referred to as Veda, while the other 36 branches will be referred to collectively as the Vedic Literature. Veda and the Vedic Literature provide the means to achieve perfect harmony with Natural Law.

Throughout this book, we present and emphasize central points of Maharishi's Vedic Science and Technology in Sanskrit, the language of Natural Law and the Veda. Sanskrit *(Samskṛta)* means "perfected," or "put together." Sanskrit is divided into two principal parts—Vedic Sanskrit and Classical Sanskrit. The older language is Vedic Sanskrit, or Vedic, the language of the *Saṁhitā* and *Brāhmaṇa,* the two principal parts of the Veda. The script of Sanskrit is called *devanāgarī* (city of the immortals). Appendix A ("Sanskrit Alphabet, Pronunciation, Transliteration") presents the Sanskrit alphabet, rules of pronunciation, and transliteration.

Natural Law in Quantum Network Architecture™— The Cosmic Computer and Cosmic Switchboard

During the past 200 years, modern science has systematically revealed ever-deeper levels of order in Nature, from the molecular and atomic to the nuclear and subnuclear levels. Recent discoveries in quantum and superstring physics have revealed even more fundamental levels of Nature's functioning, where the diverse forces and Laws of Nature are unified, ultimately leading to one Unified Field of all the Laws of Nature.

Figure 1-1 (on pages 4–6) shows how the whole range of Quantum Network Architecture has its source in the Unified Field of all the Laws of Nature. The Unified Field gives rise to the fundamental force and matter fields, which then generate the optical and electronic bases to computing and networking. The Unified Field also gives rise to the Cosmic Computer and Cosmic Switchboard, which in turn provide the basis to quantum computing and networking. The Unified Field portion of Figure 1-1 is authored by Dr. John Hagelin, one of the preeminent quantum physicists of our time and responsible for multiple breakthroughs in Unified Field physics.

The Routt Addressable Absolute Memory Gate™ (RAAM Gate™) provides the quantum window and computational superfabric through which the source, course, and goal of the Cosmic Computer and Cosmic Switchboard are known. The Unified Field creates and governs the flow of network computational intelligence within the levels of applied Quantum Network Architecture. The Global Internetwork is the confluence of all aspects of computer network architecture, acting as a global, self-referral, celestial nervous system that collects, processes, interconnects, and integrates enterprise and personal data throughout nations, governments, and the Global Country of World Peace.

Electronic computing and networking is ultimately fermion-based; optical computing and networking is ultimately boson-based; and quantum computing and networking has its basis directly in the supersymmetry of the Unified Field. When we extrapolate the exponential trends of computer network miniaturization and power, we can project the attainment of a limit of single-atom bits and Single Electron Transistors (SETs) in the years 2010–2020. Beyond this point no further inward progress in computing and networking can be experienced while remaining within the confines of classical space-time physics.

Prior to efficient attainment of the single-atom bit and single-electron transistor scales, quantum effects will be necessary to read quantum bits (qubits) from and write qubits to the memory registers of nano- and pico- (and soon thereafter, femto-, atto-, zepto-, and yocto-) scale computers and network nodes (refer to Appendix B, "Units of Measurement

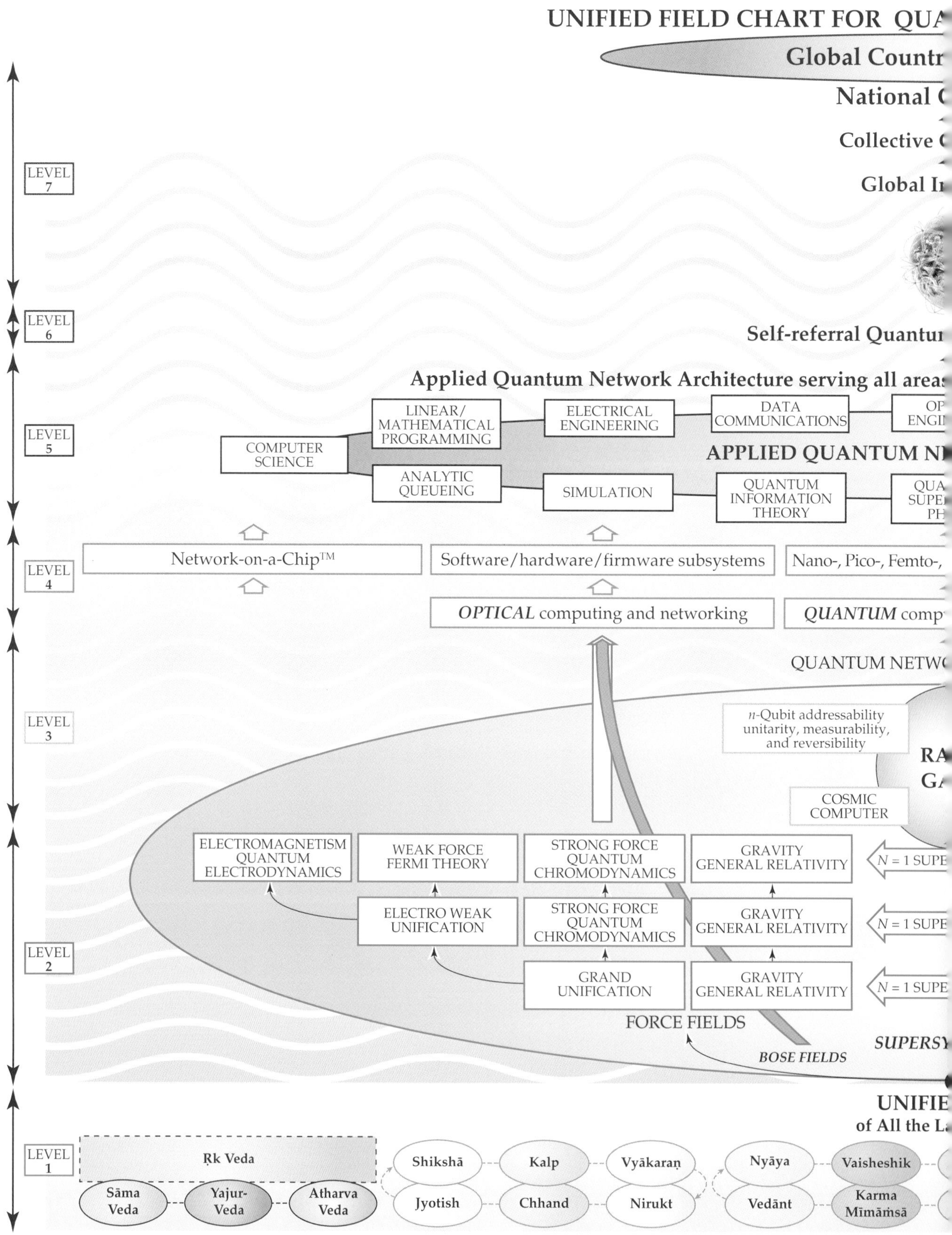
UNIFIED FIELD CHART FOR QUA
Global Countr
National
Collective
Global I
Self-referral Quantu
Applied Quantum Network Architecture serving all area
LEVEL 7
LEVEL 6
LEVEL 5
LEVEL 4
LEVEL 3
LEVEL 2
LEVEL 1
COMPUTER SCIENCE
LINEAR/ MATHEMATICAL PROGRAMMING
ELECTRICAL ENGINEERING
DATA COMMUNICATIONS
APPLIED QUANTUM N
ANALYTIC QUEUEING
SIMULATION
QUANTUM INFORMATION THEORY
Network-on-a-Chip™
Software/hardware/firmware subsystems
Nano-, Pico-, Femto-,
OPTICAL computing and networking
QUANTUM comp
QUANTUM NETW
n-Qubit addressability unitarity, measurability, and reversibility
COSMIC COMPUTER
ELECTROMAGNETISM QUANTUM ELECTRODYNAMICS
WEAK FORCE FERMI THEORY
STRONG FORCE QUANTUM CHROMODYNAMICS
GRAVITY GENERAL RELATIVITY
ELECTRO WEAK UNIFICATION
STRONG FORCE QUANTUM CHROMODYNAMICS
GRAVITY GENERAL RELATIVITY
GRAND UNIFICATION
GRAVITY GENERAL RELATIVITY
FORCE FIELDS
BOSE FIELDS
SUPERS
UNIFIE
of All the L
Ṛk Veda
Sāma Veda
Yajur-Veda
Atharva Veda
Shikshā
Kalp
Vyākaraṇ
Jyotish
Chhand
Nirukt
Nyāya
Vaisheshik
Vedānt
Karma Mīmāṁsā

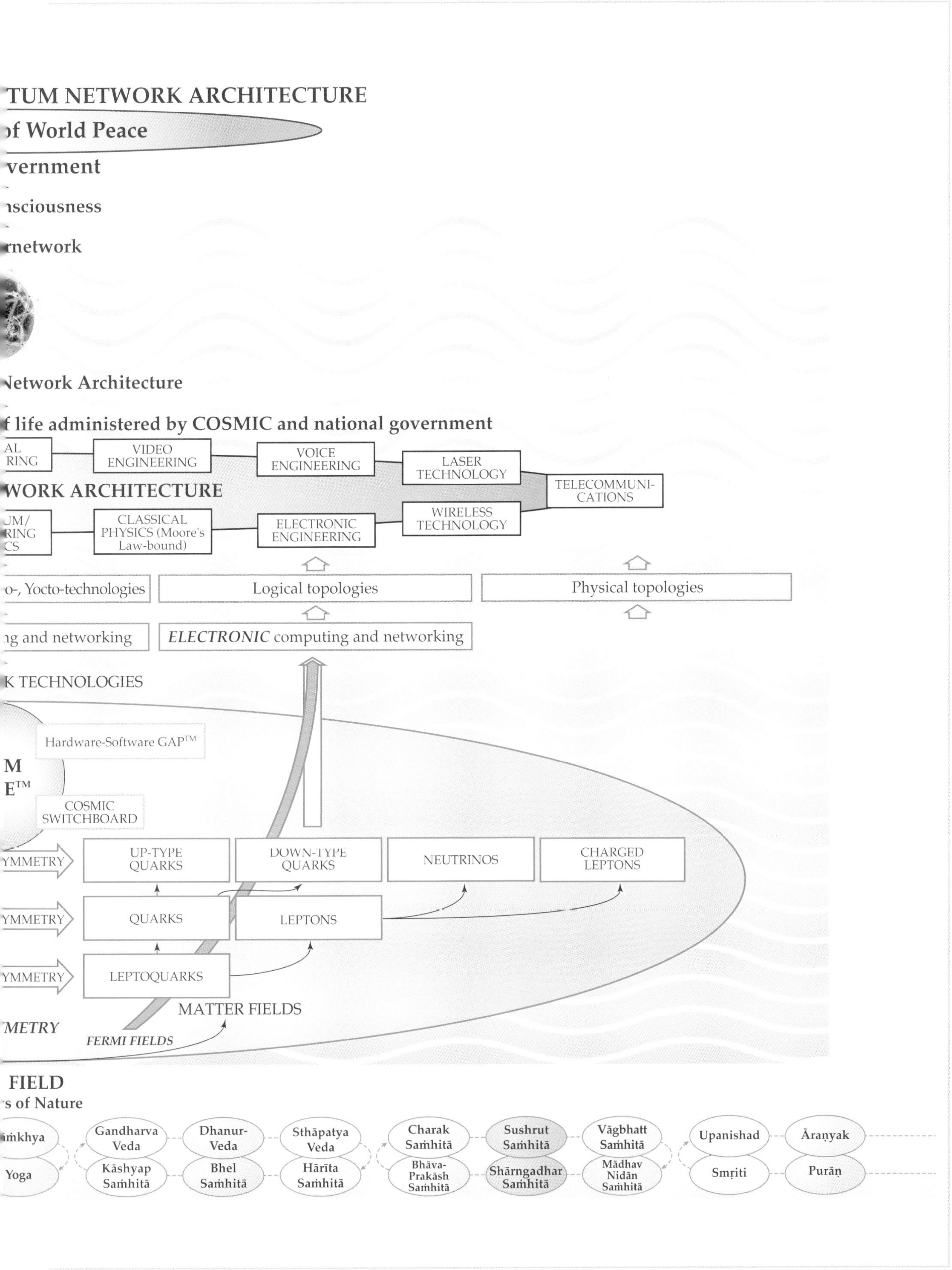
TUM NETWORK ARCHITECTURE
of World Peace
vernment
nsciousness
rnetwork
Network Architecture
f life administered by COSMIC and national government
AL RING
VIDEO ENGINEERING
VOICE ENGINEERING
LASER TECHNOLOGY
TELECOMMUNI-CATIONS
WORK ARCHITECTURE
UM/ RING CS
CLASSICAL PHYSICS (Moore's Law-bound)
ELECTRONIC ENGINEERING
WIRELESS TECHNOLOGY
o-, Yocto-technologies
Logical topologies
Physical topologies
ng and networking
ELECTRONIC computing and networking
K TECHNOLOGIES
Hardware-Software GAP™
M
E™
COSMIC SWITCHBOARD
YMMETRY
UP-TYPE QUARKS
DOWN-TYPE QUARKS
NEUTRINOS
CHARGED LEPTONS
YMMETRY
QUARKS
LEPTONS
YMMETRY
LEPTOQUARKS
MATTER FIELDS
METRY
FERMI FIELDS
FIELD
s of Nature
mkhya
Yoga
Gandharva Veda
Kāshyap Saṁhitā
Dhanur-Veda
Bhel Saṁhitā
Sthāpatya Veda
Hārīta Saṁhitā
Charak Saṁhitā
Bhāva-Prakāsh Saṁhitā
Sushrut Saṁhitā
Shārngadhar Saṁhitā
Vāgbhatt Saṁhitā
Mādhav Nidān Saṁhitā
Upanishad
Smṛiti
Āraṇyak
Purāṇ

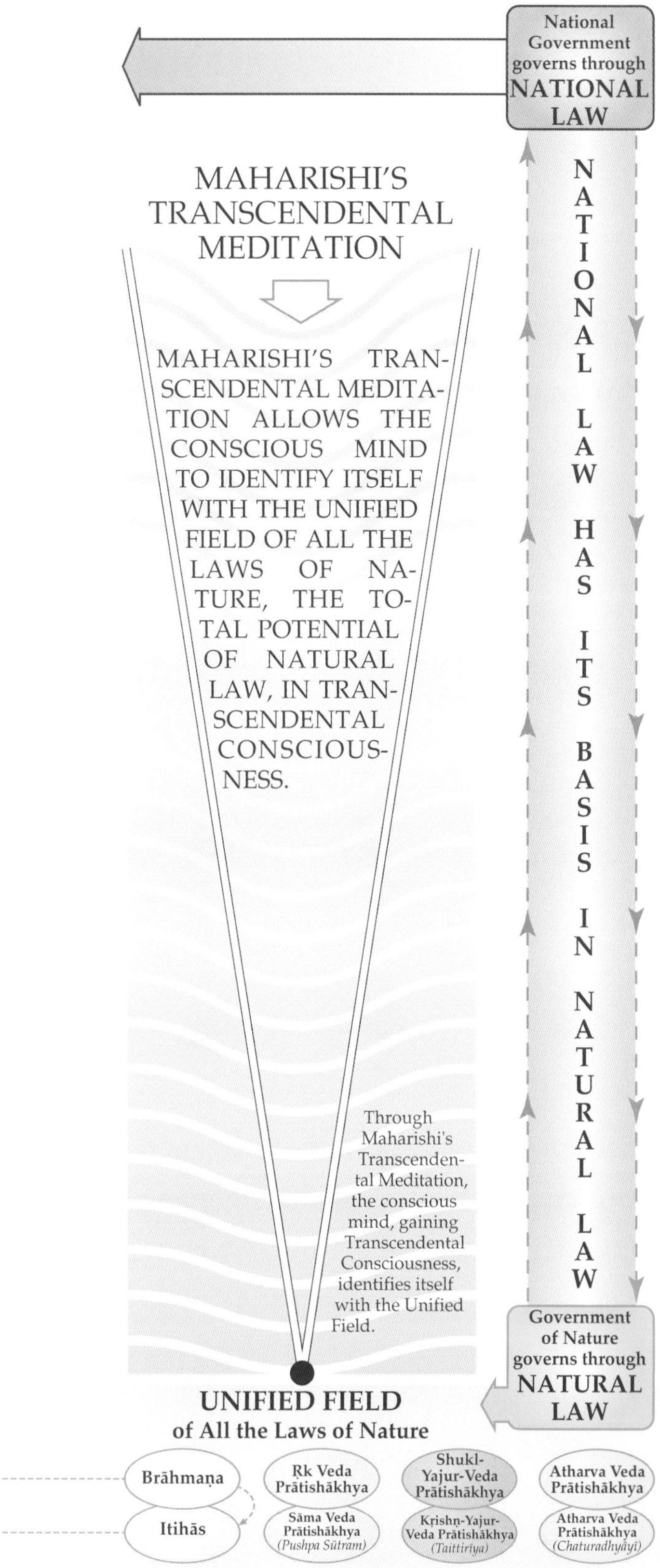
National Government governs through NATIONAL LAW
MAHARISHI'S TRANSCENDENTAL MEDITATION
MAHARISHI'S TRANSCENDENTAL MEDITATION ALLOWS THE CONSCIOUS MIND TO IDENTIFY ITSELF WITH THE UNIFIED FIELD OF ALL THE LAWS OF NATURE, THE TOTAL POTENTIAL OF NATURAL LAW, IN TRANSCENDENTAL CONSCIOUSNESS.
NATIONAL LAW HAS ITS BASIS IN NATURAL LAW
Through Maharishi's Transcendental Meditation, the conscious mind, gaining Transcendental Consciousness, identifies itself with the Unified Field.
Government of Nature governs through NATURAL LAW
UNIFIED FIELD
of All the Laws of Nature
Brāhmaṇa
Itihās
Ṛk Veda Prātishākhya
Sāma Veda Prātishākhya (Pushpa Sūtram)
Shukl-Yajur-Veda Prātishākhya
Krishṇ-Yajur-Veda Prātishākhya (Taittirīya)
Atharva Veda Prātishākhya
Atharva Veda Prātishākhya (Chaturadhyāyī)

Figure 1-1: Unified Field Chart for Quantum Network Architecture™

The Unified Field of all the Laws of Nature is an unmanifest field at the source of all manifestation. It is a single, universal source of all orderliness in Nature—the home of all the Laws of Nature maintaining balance and order in every aspect of the universe.

This chart illustrates how the technologies of Maharishi's Vedic Science contribute to modern Quantum Network Architecture™ by providing a new, integrated approach in which the whole range of Quantum Network Architecture can be appreciated from its source in the Unified Field.

The chart also shows how the Unified Field gives rise to the fundamental force and matter fields, which then generate the optical and electronic bases (respectively) to computing and networking.

The chart further illustrates how the Unified Field gives rise to the supersymmetric basis of the Routt Addressable Absolute Memory Gate™ (RAAM Gate™)—a quantum computer and network gate comprising the Cosmic Computer and Cosmic Switchboard, *n*-qubit addressability, unitarity, measurability, and reversibility, and the Hardware-Software Gap™—the quantum computing and networking expression of the Unified Field, which creates and governs the flow of network computational intelligence within the various levels of applied Quantum Network Architecture.

The sequential expression of knowledge and organizing power from the Unified Field is displayed in seven hierarchical levels:

- **Level 1**—The Unified Field
- **Level 2**—The fundamental force and matter fields
- **Level 3**—The RAAM Gate, comprising the Hardware-Software Gap, the Cosmic Computer and Cosmic Switchboard, and *n*-qubit addressability, unitarity, measurability, and reversibility
- **Level 4**—Quantum Network Technologies, including the optical, electronic, and quantum computer networking expressions of the force fields, matter fields, and the quantum RAAM Gate (respectively), as well as the expressed levels of computer network organizations (Network-on-a-Chip™; software/hardware/firmware subsystems; nano-, pico-, femto-, atto-, zepto-, and yocto-technologies; logical topologies; and physical topologies).
- **Level 5**—Applied Quantum Network Architecture
- **Level 6**—Self-referral Quantum Network Architecture
- **Level 7**—The Global Internetwork as the physical, logical, and ubiquitous confluence of the Internet, World Wide Web, intranets, extranets, and private computer networks, acting as a global, celestial nervous system, or self-referral, conscious superfabric that collects, interprets, processes, and interconnects enterprise and personal data throughout national governments and the Global Country of World Peace.

This vision of all levels of Quantum Network Architecture at a glance helps connect any one level with the Unified Field of all the Laws of Nature, which the individual experiences through Maharishi's Vedic Science and Technology as his own simplest state of awareness, Transcendental Consciousness.

The names of the 40 aspects of Veda and the Vedic Literature are written inside the blue band at the bottom of the chart. This illustrates that Veda and the Vedic Literature reside in their unmanifest form in the Unified Field.

and Orders of Magnitude—Powers of Ten and Two," for an explanation of large and small scales with accompanying scientific notation). At that juncture or earlier, the entire spectrum of computing and computer networking—including designing algorithms, loading programs, loading network configurations, running programs and configurations, and reading results—will be dominated by quantum effects.

Of all the candidate technologies to continue scaling beyond the Very Large Scale Integration (VLSI) era, quantum logic has one unique feature: It is not contained by classical space-time physics. Moore's Law is exponential; any classical approach demands exponential increases in space or time. Even the Avogadro's number of elements in a molecular computer is quickly limited by the size of the exponential problem. Quantum computing and networking accesses Hilbert space, the one exponential resource that has been untapped for computation.

The Cosmic Computer and Cosmic Switchboard embody the infinity-within-all-points and all-points-within-infinity cosmic computational foundation for perfection of evolution within the human neuroanatomy and neurophysiology, as well as for the universal automation of administration within our Cosmic Counterparts. The one-to-one correspondence between human physiology and our Cosmic Counterparts has been brilliantly brought to light by Professor Tony Nader, MD, PhD (coronated by Maharishi on 12 October 2000 as His Majesty Raja Nader Rām, *Vishwa Prashāsak*, Sovereign Ruler of the Global Country of World Peace), under Maharishi's guidance, in his book *Human Physiology: Expression of Veda and the Vedic Literature*.

The Cosmic Computer and Cosmic Switchboard, integral to Maharishi's Vedic Science and Technology, are expressed at every point within the cosmic spectrum of creation from the cosmological to sub-Planck scales. They are eternally computing and fathoming the farthest ends of the universe, while processing all of the innumerable Laws of Nature behind the scenes and in a perfectly flawless fashion. The entire range of creation simultaneously and sequentially computes infinities of possibility through the divine fabric of the Cosmic Computer and Cosmic Switchboard. As we elaborate in Chapter 8, the RAAM Gate is a quantum computer network gate that supports *n*-qubit superpositionality, addressability, unitarity, measurability, and reversibility. It operates at the *Atyanta-Abhāva* and *Anyonya-Abhāva* of the Hardware-Software Gap™ of the Cosmic Computer and Cosmic Switchboard.

Natural Law in Maharishi's Vedic Science

Maharishi's Vedic Science describes the source of all the Laws of Nature as an unmanifest state of absolute pure Being that is self-referral and self-sufficient. *Self-referral* means that it is conscious of itself—pure consciousness, devoid of any object outside of itself. All the Laws of Nature in their unmanifest state are found in the dynamics of self-referral consciousness—consciousness knowing itself. These eternal dynamics are embodied in the very structure of the sounds of Ṛk Veda and the entire Vedic Literature, as we summarize in Figure 2-8 on pages 32 and 33 ("Quantum Network Architecture According to Veda and the Vedic Literature") and Figure 2-9 on pages 34 and 35 ("The 40 Aspects of Veda and the Vedic Literature and Their Corresponding Aspects in Quantum Network Architecture").

Confirmation of Natural Law Through Quantum Network Architecture

This book reveals that the descriptions of Quantum Network Architecture provided by modern science and the description of Veda and the Vedic Literature provided by Maharishi's Vedic Science correspond exactly. These two great traditions of knowledge—objective and subjective, modern and ancient—uphold one another and provide basic and timely knowledge of Natural Law. Natural Law alone is competent to eliminate all problems and raise the quality of life in society to the level of *Heaven on Earth*.

Maharishi's *Apaurusheya Bhāshya* (refer to Figure 2-2 on pages 22–23, "Maharishi's Commentary on Ṛk Veda Saṁhitā—*Apaurusheya Bhāshya*") finds that Veda extends from the smallest point value to the largest infinite value of the ever-expanding universe. This range is completely covered in a perfect, sequential order of expressions, in such a way that the whole universe is very clearly available as the structure of Veda. This truth, revealed by Maharishi's Commentary, has fashioned the entire structuring dynamics of creation available in Ṛk Veda and the Vedic Literature.

Complete knowledge of Natural Law provided by Maharishi's Vedic Science and Technology is now open to scientific confirmation through the most recent discoveries of the structure and function of computer networks. These discoveries include classical and quantum physical/logical topologies and algorithmic execution through classical and quantum gates and circuits, both at the Central Processing Unit (CPU) and Network-on-a-Chip™ levels and throughout the self-referral Global Internet and Internetwork. The following chapters describe how the structure of Veda and the Vedic Literature is reflected in Quantum Network Architecture in its completely expressed breadth and depth. Information Science and Technology—through its expression in Quantum Network Architecture—is found to have a one-to-one correspondence to Maharishi's Vedic Science and Technology.

All 40 aspects of Veda and the Vedic Literature have been found to correspond in structure and function to Quantum Network Architecture indicating that Quantum Network Architecture expresses the Vedic blueprint of creation. This blueprint is *Nitya* (eternal) and *Apaurusheya* (uncreated), and it evolves into logical and physical network computational creation.

Practical Significance of Natural Law

Maharishi's Vedic Science and Technology not only provides a detailed intellectual understanding of Natural Law, but also provides a highly practical, scientifically validated technology for applying this most fundamental and powerful level of Natural Law for the benefit of mankind. Over 600 scientific studies conducted at more than 200 universities and research institutes in 30 countries throughout the world have verified the immense practical benefits of this simple technology—Maharishi's Transcendental Meditation, TM-Sidhi Programme, and Yogic Flying—which develops full human potential in all areas of mind, body, and behavior. The total potential of Natural Law on the self-referral level of individual intelligence is fully enlivened by the attention of the conscious mind through the applied technologies of Maharishi's Vedic Science. The full enlivenment of mental potential through Maharishi's Vedic Science and Technology provides the necessary foundation to continue exponential classical and quantum developments in computer network architecture.

Supreme Understanding of Creation and Evolution

Insights into the parallels between the structure of classical and quantum computer network architecture and the structure of Veda reveal the absolute order that prevails throughout the universe. The self-referral, unmanifest level of intelligence assumes its object-referral, manifest quality and administers the infinitely diverse multiplicity of all the objective values of its own expressions—the entire universe. This is possible because all the manifest objective values eternally maintain their connectedness with their unified source—the unmanifest level of intelligence. The order in creation and evolution is eternal and can never be disturbed because there is no second element to pure intelligence—it is all that there is.

Every grain in creation is itself infinity. The smallest point value is itself unbounded, unlimited: अणोरणीयान् महतो महीयान् *Aṇoraṇīyān Mahato-mahīyān*—"The smaller than the smallest is bigger than the biggest."

Every individual has a cosmic status as does the quantum foundation of every subcomponent, component, subsystem, and system of the Global Internetwork. Everyone is the embodiment of total Natural Law:

वेदोऽसि *Vedo 'si:* Thou art the Veda;

वेदोऽहम् *Vedo 'ham:* I am Veda;

अयम् आत्मा ब्रह्म *Ayam Ātmā Brahm:* The Self is Totality—Wholeness;

अहं ब्रह्मास्मि *Ahaṁ Brahmāsmi:* I am Totality—Wholeness;

सर्वं खलु इदं ब्रह्म *Sarvaṁ Khalu Idaṁ Brahm:* All this is Totality—Wholeness.

Realization of Total Knowledge brings fulfillment to all the functional subsets of applied Quantum Network Architecture as well as to human physiology, education, economics, and all other fields, raising them to perfection. This theme of perfection will be realized by Maharishi's Perfect System of Education available in Maharishi Open University and Maharishi Vedic Universities, and Maharishi's Perfect Management available in

Maharishi Universities of Management. In the field of administration, it is available in the training programs of Maharishi's Global Administration through Natural Law.

Supreme understanding of creation and evolution has been verified as a scientific truth through our comparative study of the structure of Veda and the structure of Quantum Network Architecture.

2: The Correspondence of Quantum Network Architecture to the Veda and Vedic Literature

In this and the following chapters we unfold both classical and Quantum Network Architecture™ as a precise one-to-one expression of the 40 branches of Veda and the Vedic Literature revealed and presented to the world by His Holiness Maharishi Mahesh Yogi. We also develop the Routt Addressable Absolute Memory Gate™ (RAAM Gate™)—a quantum network computational superfabric—that reveals the computational and connection basis states of the Cosmic Computer and Cosmic Switchboard.

Maharishi has predicted the Cosmic Computer and Cosmic Switchboard to be that quantum computational network system eternally computing at every cosmic moment and point within the *Atyanta-Abhāva* and *Anyonya-Abhāva* of the *Sandhi* (the self-referral, massively parallel nexuses of infinity-within-all-points, all-points-within-infinity) throughout the universe.

We find the quantum network computational density for the Cosmic Computer and Cosmic Switchboard to be on the order of 10^{1068} calculations at each cosmic moment and point throughout the observable universe as a precise expression of the Veda and the Vedic Literature (refer to Chapter 8, "PRĀTISHĀKHYA in Quantum Network Architecture"). Therefore, all that is expressed in Quantum Network Architecture—ranging from the massively parallel quantum and superstring networked computations of the Cosmic Computer and Cosmic Switchboard to the Global Internetwork—is the reflection of the structuring dynamics of Nature.

The most fundamental aspect of the Cosmic Computer and Cosmic Switchboard resides in the self-referral dynamics of consciousness knowing itself. That pure level of consciousness is the source of pure knowledge, which also structures all thought and action within the human neurophysiology. These principles were brought to light under Maharishi's guidance by Professor Tony Nader, MD, PhD (His Majesty Raja Nader Rām) in his groundbreaking work, *Human Physiology: Expression of Veda and the Vedic Literature*.

Human physiology has the ability to be conscious and to know itself. It can also, as demonstrated by Maharishi's Transcendental Meditation and TM-Sidhi Programme, experience finer levels of consciousness until the finest level is transcended, and a pure level of infinite unbounded consciousness is attained. Pure knowingness is the inner Self—the *Ātmā*—of everyone. It is pure knowledge, wakefulness devoid of any thought, image, or fluctuation. It is unbounded, pure silence.

Physics has also discovered the silent, unbounded level of Nature. It is called the Unified Field of all the Laws of Nature within unified quantum field theories. The Unified Field is an unmanifest field that underlies all the manifest expressions of the universe—from elementary particles to cosmic structures.

Quantum Network Architecture Framework

Quantum Network Architecture encompasses a wide range of subfields. In its complete theoretical and expressed breadth and depth, it synthesizes the following core competencies:

- Quantum information theory
- Quantum information logic and algorithms
- Computer science
- Electrical engineering
- Electronic engineering
- Data communications
- Telecommunications
- Optical engineering
- Laser technology
- Video engineering
- Voice engineering
- Wireless technology
- Bandwidth engineering
- Quantum and superstring physics
- Classical physics
- Linear programming
- Mathematical programming
- Analytic queueing
- Simulation

Quantum Network Architecture, in its most essential expression as the quantum-to-cosmological superfabric of the Cosmic Computer and Cosmic Switchboard, is found to be identical to the non-changing Unified Field of Natural Law called the *Ātmā* in Veda and the Vedic Literature. Since *Ātmā* is the source of the structure and dynamism of the universe, it must contain structure and dynamism within itself. The structure contained in *Ātmā* is Veda, the blueprint of creation.

The One-to-Three Elaboration in Maharishi's Vedic Science

Maharishi Vedic Science describes the process through which diversity unfolds from Unity. The one unbounded, non-changing field of pure Being—absolute pure existence, intelligence, and consciousness—is the Unified Field. The Unified Field is self-referral—it does not have any reference outside of itself. These qualities of the Unified Field are also fundamental to the Cosmic Computer and Cosmic Switchboard.

Emergence of diversity through the self-referral quality of intelligence creates a stir within the Absolute by raising a question: Since the Absolute is pure consciousness, what is it conscious of? Maharishi points out that the Absolute can only be conscious of itself, because it alone exists as that state of pure singularity. Even though there is nothing but pure consciousness, when we say it is conscious of itself, we distinguish among the observer *(Ṛishi),* the process linking the observer to the observed *(Devatā),* and the observed *(Chhandas).* As one leads to three, the interaction between the three leads to an infinite number of possibilities.

Perfect order as expressed in the universe and displayed in Quantum Network Architecture is the expression of the perfect order present within Veda. It is displayed in terms of its constituents: *Ṛishi* (the knower), *Devatā* (the process of knowing), *Chhandas* (the known), and *Saṁhitā* (the togetherness of *Ṛishi, Devatā,* and *Chhandas*). Similarly, all the functions of Quantum Network Architecture follow the scheme of four separate values of *Ṛishi, Devatā, Chhandas,* and *Saṁhitā:*

- *Ṛishi* is represented by all the classical and quantum computer network self-referral and feedback, sensory, knowledge-based, and input functions;

- *Devatā* is represented by all the classical and quantum computer and network processing, transforming, and transformational functions;
- *Chhandas* is represented by all the nodal Input/Output (I/O), scaling, hiding, terminating, and output functions; and
- *Saṁhitā* is represented by the holistic functioning of network computational systems, which operates as both the classical and quantum Global Internetwork.

Four Main Levels of Manifestation

Maharishi describes in his Vedic Science that the unmanifest structure of Natural Law becomes, through the breaking of infinite symmetry, progressively more expressed and manifest. There are four levels of consciousness or manifestation:

1. परा *Parā* is the totally unmanifest level of life—pure Being—the transcendental level of the structuring dynamics of Natural Law. In Quantum Network Architecture, *Parā* is the structureless structure of the *Atyanta-Abhāva* and *Anyonya-Abhāva* within the Hardware-Software Gap™ (refer to Chapter 3, "The Four Veda in Quantum Network Architecture").
2. पश्यन्ती *Pashyantī* is the finest level of the intellect—intuition—that corresponds to the finest level of manifestation. In Quantum Network Architecture, it is the inherent superpositionality, network computational reversibility, unitarity, measurability, and universality found in superposed qubit states (refer to Chapter 8, "Prātishākhya in Quantum Network Architecture").
3. मध्यमा *Madhyamā* is the thinking level—the structure of Natural Law available on the level of the mind and the structuring dynamics of thought, speech, and action—corresponding to a more expressed level of creation. In Quantum Network Architecture, it is the set of classical and quantum network computational gates, circuits, and algorithms (refer again to Chapter 8).
4. बैखरी *Baikharī* is the level of speech that corresponds to the more manifest structure of Natural Law available to us on the sensory level in the structure of the universe as a whole. In Quantum Network Architecture, it is the Global Internetwork—the

physical, logical, and ubiquitous confluence of the Internet, World Wide Web, intranets, extranets, and private computer networks. The global Internetwork functions as a global celestial nervous system, or self-referral superfabric, that collects, interprets, processes, interconnects, and integrates enterprise and personal data throughout the world. It is also the entire set of pico-, nano-, micro-, and macro-instructions integral to network computing systems.

Veda and the Vedic Literature

Another name for Natural Law and its structuring dynamics is Veda and the Vedic Literature. Veda is total Natural Law, and the structure of Veda is the structure of Natural Law. Veda exists on all levels, from the *Parā* level, where it is unmanifest Natural Law, to the *Baikharī* level, where it is the collection of subcomponents, components, subsystems, and systems that comprise the Global Internetwork.

Traditionally, Veda and the Vedic Literature are held to be the total knowledge of life and creation, transmitted in the oral tradition of the Vedic Families of India for countless thousands of years. In more recent times, Veda and the Vedic Literature have been recorded in written form. Many commentators over the centuries have analyzed Veda and the Vedic Literature from different perspectives, depending on their interests and their level of knowledge, experience, and understanding.

During the past 50 years, the complete knowledge of Veda, its structuring dynamics in the Vedic Literature, and its infinite organizing power have been discovered by His Holiness Maharishi Mahesh Yogi. Maharishi received the supreme wisdom of Veda from his master, His Divinity Brāhmaṇanda Saraswati, Jagad-Guru, Shankaracharya of Jyotir Math, Himalayas, a shining light in the line of the great teachers of the Holy Tradition of Masters, including Vasishtha, Vyasa, Shankara, and their disciples.

Maharishi has explained that Veda is uncreated *(Apaurusheya)* and eternal *(Nitya)*. Veda is the infinite set of fluctuations of pure consciousness. In the Vedic Literature, pure consciousness is called *Ātmā*. *Ātmā* is a state of pure Being, an unmanifest reality of pure existence, unboundedness, and singularity. It is the totality of all possibilities, infinite silence and infinite dynamism, unboundedness and point values.

Veda is a self-sufficient and self-referral state, and all manifestations in creation emerge from it and submerge into it. This emergence and submergence, creation and dissolution, as well as all possible interactions in the physical universe, are conducted by the Laws of Nature. All the Laws of Nature are contained in pure consciousness, *Ātmā*.

Maharishi has discovered Veda to be the collectedness of all the Laws of Nature. He discovered the self-referral, invincible structure of Veda, which provides from within itself—and through the sequence of sounds *(Mantras)* and Gaps *(Sandhi)* within itself—its own uncreated commentary *(Apaurusheya Bhāshya)*. Maharishi explains that the structure of Veda and the Vedic Literature corresponds to the structure of all the Laws of Nature, which are the source of all expressions and laws of the entire creation—from the quantum mechanical level to all the manifest levels of elementary particles, atoms, molecules, biological systems, planetary and cosmic life, and the entire universe.

Maharishi describes the human body and mind as the embodiment of Veda, the living replica of Natural Law, emerging from the self-referral quality of pure consciousness. Maharishi also describes the Cosmic Computer and Cosmic Switchboard to be the central computer and switchboard, respectively, of Natural Law. In order to understand the relationship of Quantum Network Architecture to Veda and the Vedic Literature, we will first consider the structure of Veda itself.

Ṛk Veda—Dynamism and Silence in Natural Law

Ṛk Veda, the most fundamental aspect of the Vedic Literature, represents the eternal, self-referral dynamics of consciousness knowing itself. The very structure of the sounds of Ṛk Veda (syllables, verses, chapters, and the Gaps between each syllable, phrase, verse, section, and chapter) is the embodiment of the eternal dynamism and silence at the basis of the infinite organizing power of Natural Law.

Ṛk Veda means Veda of ऋक् (Ṛk)—knowledge of ऋक् (Ṛk). As Figure 2-1 indicates, ऋक् (Ṛk) is a word whose pronunciation displays dynamism from infinity to a point—ऋऋऋऋऋ (ṚṚṚṚṚ) displays dynamism, and क् (K) displays the stop of dynamism. The pronunciation of क् (K) stops the flow of speech; क् (K) stands for stop or point value.

The relationship between ऋृऋृऋृऋृ (ṚṚṚṚṚ) and क् (K) displays the collapse of dynamism to a point. Decreasing dynamism means increasing silence. Just as silence stands for the unmanifest, so dynamic silence means that the unmanifest is dynamic. Ṛk Veda is the knowledge of the dynamism of the silent, unmanifest reality, the field of Transcendental Consciousness.

This aspect of knowledge is the subject matter of *Yoga*—silence (expressed in Quantum Network Architecture as *Logical Network Topology and Associations*)—and *Karma Mīmāṁsā*—dynamism (expressed in Quantum Network Architecture as the *Backbone Network System*). In their togetherness, neutralizing each other, the reality of the unmanifest collapse of dynamism and silence arises.

Flow of ऋृ (R) into क् (K) sequentially gives rise to Sāma Veda (expressed in Quantum Network Architecture as *Network Self-referral and Feedback Systems*) and Yajur-Veda (expressed in Quantum Network Architecture as *Network Processing Systems*). Transformation of क् (K) into अ (A) structures Atharva Veda (expressed in Quantum Network Architecture as *Nodal Input/Output Systems*).

Figure 2-1: Ṛk Veda—Infinity to a Point

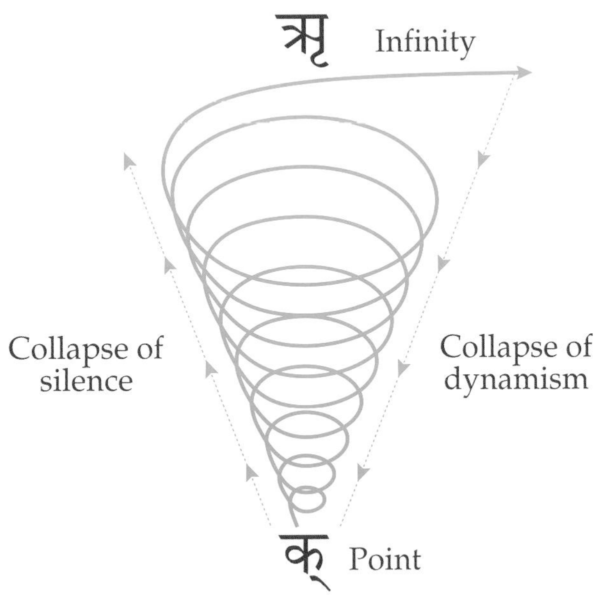

On the one hand, the syllable ऋक् (Ṛk) contains pure knowledge (theory); on the other hand, it contains the organizing power of pure knowledge (applied aspect). It is therefore clear that ऋक् (Ṛk) is the one-syllable expression of the science and technology of the Ultimate Reality—pure wakefulness, pure consciousness—the Self. This is unfolded in Vedānt (expressed in Quantum Network Architecture as *Integrated Functioning of the Backbone Network System*).

The Self, both on the individual level *(Ātmā)*, and on the cosmic level *(Brahm)*, is self-referral—pure wakefulness, pure consciousness. ऋक् (Ṛk) is the one-word expression of the total value of science and technology and, therefore, of Quantum Network Architecture. The full value of ऋक् (Ṛk) enlivened in individual consciousness makes the individual an embodiment of all knowledge and the infinite organizing power of pure knowledge. This reality of the Self is *Brahm*—अयम् आत्मा ब्रह्म *Ayam Ātmā Brahm (Māṇḍūkya Upanishad, 2)*, "This *Ātmā* (Self) is *Brahm* (Totality)."

The knower of ऋक् (Ṛk) is the knower of reality—*Brahm*—about which the Bhagavad-Gītā says:

> एषा ब्राह्मी स्थितिः पार्थ नैनां प्राप्य विमुह्यति
>
> *Eshā Brāhmī sthitiḥ Pārtha naināṁ prāpya vimuhyati*
>
> *(Bhagavad-Gītā, 2.72)*
>
> *This is Brahman Consciousness—Unity Consciousness. Once achieved it is never lost—life in enlightenment—life of the individual a lively field of all possibilities—achievement of anything through mere desiring.*

Unity Consciousness is life in fulfillment—the goal of all life enjoyed in the practicalities of daily living. This is Maharishi's vision of ऋक् (Ṛk): full revival of complete knowledge—the unfoldment of total science and technology. This revival after thousands of years is Maharishi's contribution to everyone for all generations to enjoy full enlightenment—Heaven on Earth.

Maharishi's Commentary on Ṛk Veda

Figure 2-2 (on pages 22 and 23) presents Maharishi's Commentary on Ṛk Veda Saṁhitā, his *Apaurusheya Bhāshya.* Maharishi's Vedic Science and Technology reveals this Vedic level of reality that is competent to create perfection in all areas of life, because life is an expression of unified Wholeness of reality, the eternal dynamic silence.

According to Maharishi's *Apaurusheya Bhāshya,* the structure of Veda provides its own commentary that is contained in the sequential unfoldment of Veda in its various stages of expression. The precise sequence of sounds in Ṛk Veda is highly significant. The true meaning and content of Veda resides within the sequential progression of sound and silence, and not in the meaning of the words of Veda in its multifarious translations. Vedic sounds incorporate syllables *(Akshara),* words *(Shabdas),* phrases *(Pādas),* verses *(Richās),* hymns *(Sūktas),* and chapters *(Maṇdals);* the silence resides within the Gaps *(Sandhi)* between the *Akshara, Shabdas, Pādas, Richās, Sūktas,* and *Maṇdals.*

The first *Akshara* of Ṛk Veda, अक् (Ak), describes the collapse of fullness of consciousness अ (A) within itself to is own point value क् (K). This collapse, which represents the eternal dynamics of consciousness knowing itself, occurs in eight successive stages. Subsequent stages of unfoldment of Veda elaborate eight stages of collapse within the eight *Akshara* of the first *Pāda.* The first Pāda, in turn, emerges from and provides a further commentary on अक् (Ak). As shown in Figure 2-2, these eight *Akshara* correspond to the eight *Prakṛiti,* or eight fundamental qualities of intelligence that constitute the divided nature of pure consciousness.

The first *Richā* of Ṛk Veda, comprising 24 *Akshara,* provides a further commentary on अक् (Ak) where the eight-*Akshara* structure of the first *Pāda* now appears three times. The first *Pāda* expresses the eight *Prakṛiti* with respect to the *Ṛishi* (observer) quality of pure consciousness. The second *Pāda* expresses the eight *Prakṛiti* with respect to the *Devatā* (process of observation) quality of pure consciousness. The third *Pāda* expresses the eight *Prakṛiti* with respect to the *Chhandas* (known, observed) quality of pure consciousness. Together, these three *Pādas* comprise the first *Richā* of Veda, which represents another complete stage in the sequential unfoldment of knowledge.

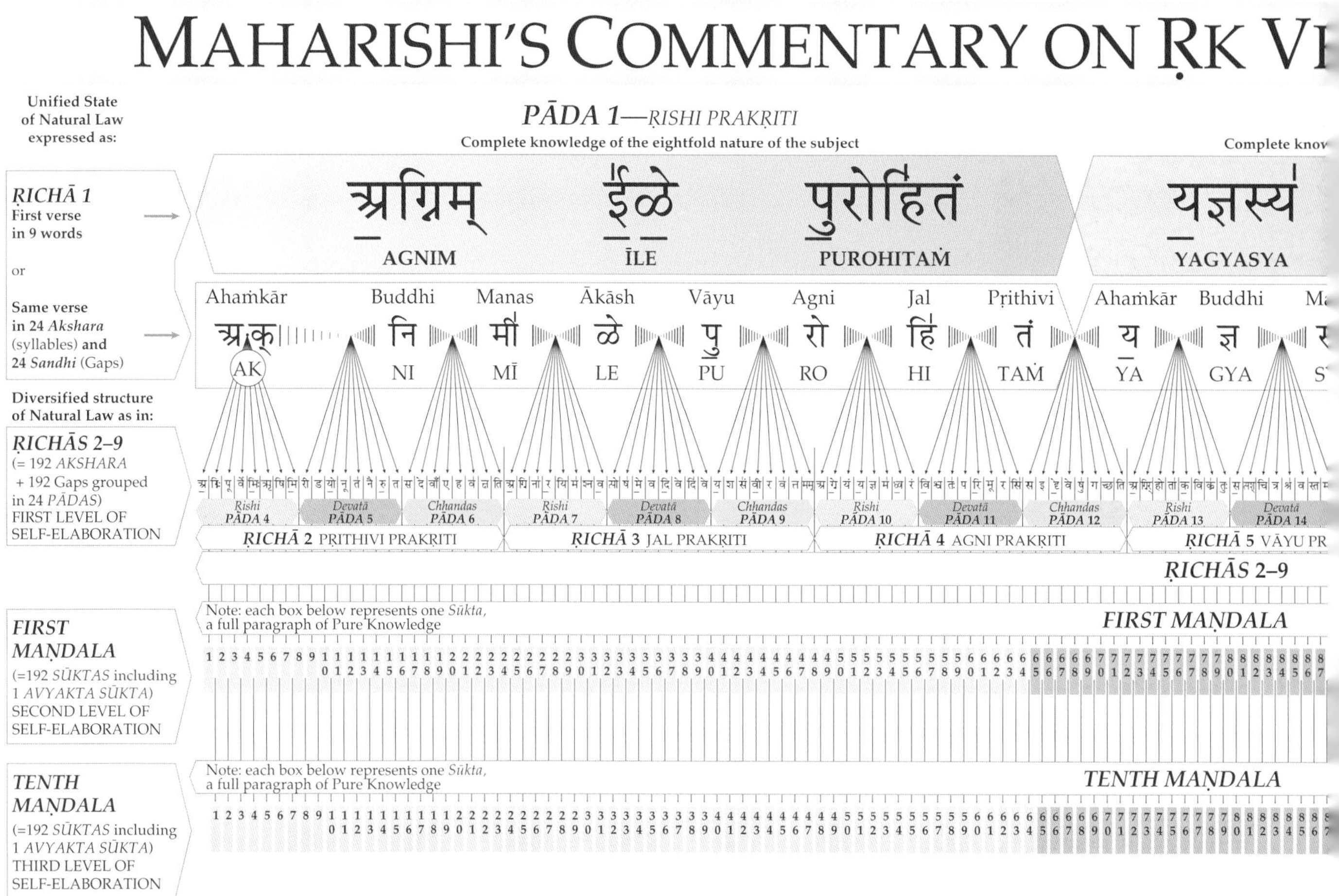

Figure 2-2: Maharishi's Commentary on Ṛk Veda

Maharishi's timeless commentary on Ṛk Veda, the *Apaurusheya Bhāshya,* shows that the structure of Veda is composed of syllables and Gaps (refer to second line of illustration, *Ṛichā* or verse one, split into 24 *Akshara* or syllables, and 24 *Sandhi* or Gaps). The center of the Gap is the unmanifest point of pure intelligence into which one syllable dissolves and from which the next syllable emerges. In this process of transformation of one syllable into the next is the liveliness of the dynamism of Veda, pure knowledge. In the middle of the Gap is the silent state of Veda, a state of intelligence that is unmanifest and dynamic. This quality of dynamism within the silent state of Veda is called *Anyonya-Abhāva,* which is the self-referral state of intel-ligence. *Anyonya-Abhāva* is the liveliness of the unmanifest state of Veda present within the manifest state of Veda. This unmanifest state of Veda is the abstract structure of Veda; it is that level of intelligence—Creative Intelligence—which is fully awake within itself. It is that self-referral level of intelligence which is the *Saṁhitā* of *Ṛishi, Devatā,* and *Chhandas.*

Total Knowledge of Natural Law Within the Gap

Self-referral intelligence is the liveliness of both unity and diversity. Since this liveliness of self-referral intelligence is the nature of the Gap, it is from the Gap that the total potential of Veda is available. The cognition of this value of the Gap is the cognition of the total potential of Veda—total knowledge of Natural Law lively in its full potential. The sequence of the Gaps between the syllables of *Ṛichā* (verse) one (see above illustration of *Ṛichā* one split into 24 syllables and 24 Gaps) clearly shows that the structure of Veda is in terms of syllables and Gaps. The sequential unfoldment of the structure of Ṛk Veda, which is orderly and symmetrical, displays the total potential of Natural Law within the structure of Veda and is the source of order and symmetry in the whole universe.

Significance and Value of the Transformation of One Syllable into Another Through The Gap

So far whatever commentaries are available on Veda, they are a commenting on the *Akshara,* or syllables; the *Shabdas,* or words; th *Pādas,* or phrases; the *Ṛichās,* or verses; the *Sūktas,* or hymns; etc. The commentaries do not bring to light the value and meaning of th Gaps, which actually contain the mechanics of transformation—th Brāhmaṇa—the intelligence that transforms the previous expressic into the following.

Creation is a phenomenon of constant transformation. Transform tion, or evolution, is the reality of existence. The mechanics transformation takes place in the unmanifest field; that is why whe this field of transformation, within the reality of the Gap, was n brought to light by the commentators, the whole field of pure know edge and its infinite organizing power remained **out of sight**; insig into the mechanics of the sequential progression of pure knowledg and the signifiance of its structuing dynamics remained **out of sigh** Veda and its utility remained **out of sight**; Law, Natural Law, and i ordering intelligence remained **out of sight**; how creation emerg from Veda—how Veda structures itself into *Vishwa* (creatio —remained **out of sight**; the relationship of the unmanifest with th manifest, and how unmanifest consciousness, self-referral consciou ness, Transcendental Consciousness, structures itself into th structure of Veda remained **out of sight**; how Veda is the who universe remained **out of sight;** how *Ātmā*—Transcendent Consciousness—has the whole universe within it remained **out c sight**; how the part is the whole remained **out of sight**; how point i infinity remained **out of sight**; how mortality is essentially immorta ity remained **out of sight**; how mortality expresses immortalit remained **out of sight**; how the infinite, unbounded nature of life ca become the living reality of daily life remained **out of sight**. Tota potential, freedom, and bliss were lost—ignorance and sufferin became real.

A SAṀHITĀ—*APAURUSHEYA BHĀSHYA*

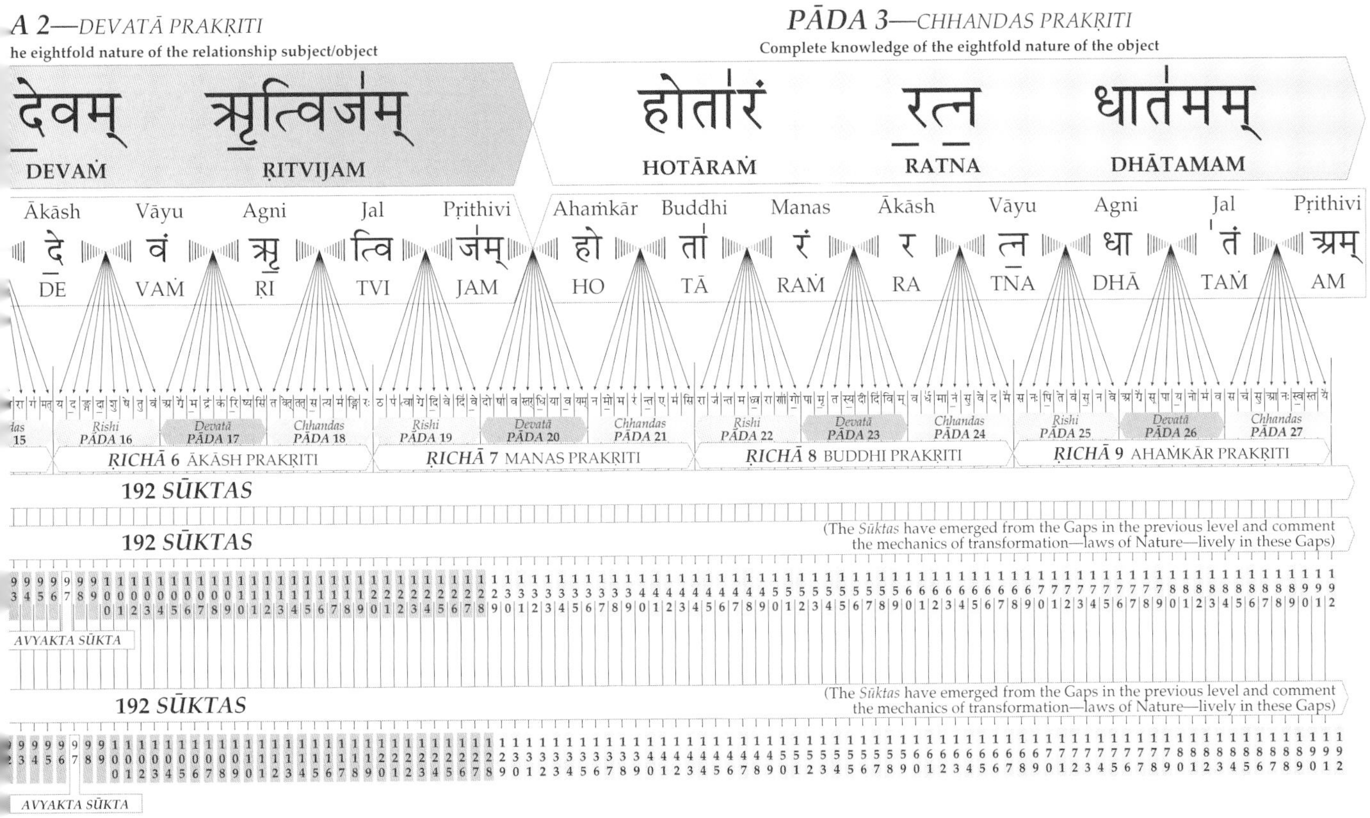

Total Knowledge of Natural Law Available to Everyone

ow, with the cognition of the reality of the GAPS, all that was out of ght becomes a concrete vision. This is the time when full enlighten- ıent is available to everyone, and now everyone can be, and actually ıould be, at home with the total potential of Natural Law so that ıey can enjoy perfection in daily life. With Maharishi's Vedic Science ıd Technology, the Age of Enlightenment is available to everyone, verywhere. This unique cognition identifies the structuring dynam- s of Veda to be the structuring dynamics of consciousness, of the hysiology, and of the entire creation. It explains that total knowl- dge (the *Saṁhitā* of *Ṛishi, Devatā,* and *Chhandas*) and its infinite rganizing power are completely contained, expressed, and demon- rated in the sequential unfoldment of the structure of Ṛk Veda. This rderly, sequential unfoldment of Ṛk Veda is available to anyone at ny time, intellectually in Maharishi's *Apaurusheya Bhāshya,* and xperientially in one's own Transcendental Consciousness through Iaharishi's Transcendental Meditation.

Constitution of the Universe

'he different levels of elaboration shown in the illustration above ive a holistic vision of Nature's total intelligence, which eternally esides at the unmanifest basis of creation and is continuously giving ise to its own self-elaborating structure of complete knowledge. This tructure is the Constitution of the Universe, which ensures flawless dministration of the universe and upholds its evolutionary process.

Inherent Dynamism of अक् (Ak),One-Word Expression of Total Veda

'he total range of knowledge and infinite organizing power lively vithin *Ātmā*—the self-referral consciousness of everyone—initially xpresses itself in a highly compactified, one-syllable version of total 'eda, the single *Akshara,* अक् (Ak), denoting the balanced state of ure wakefulness that has to exist between the opposite values of nfinity (अ [A]) and point (क् [K]), lest they neutralize each other. The nherent dynamics of this seed form of Veda are seen sequentially progressing into a single straight line of pure knowledge, the first *Ṛichā,* or verse, of Ṛk Veda, which carries the characteristics of absolute order and thereby serves as a precise index for the entire structure of Ṛk Veda to arise.

Four Levels of Self-Elaboration Illustrated Above

From the 24 *Sandhi* (unmanifest Gaps) of the first *Ṛichā* (verse) emerge the corresponding 24 *Pādas* (phrases) of the next eight *Ṛichās* (*Ṛichās* two through nine), which provide the **first level of self-elaboration** of Ṛk Veda. *Ṛichās* two through nine are a precise commentary on the mechanics of transformation present within the 24 Gaps of the first *Ṛichā.*

The **second level of self-elaboration** arises from the 192 *Sandhi* (GAPS) between the 192 *Akshara* (syllables) of *Ṛichās* two through nine . They give rise to the corresponding 192 *Sūktas* (hymns) of the first *Maṇḍala* of Ṛk Veda, a circular, cyclical, and eternal structure that comments upon the mechanics of transformation inherent in the 192 GAPS of *Ṛichās* two through nine.

In the **third level of self-elaboration** the 192 *Sandhi* (GAPS) between the 192 *Sūktas* (hymns) of the first *Maṇḍala* give rise to the corresponding 192 *Sūktas* of the tenth *Maṇḍala,* which again is a circular, cyclical, and eternal structure that precisely fills the GAPS of the first *Maṇḍala* and serves as a commentary on the mechanics of transformation between the *Sūkta* of the first *Maṇḍala.*

In the **fourth level of self-elaboration** the GAPS between all the nine *Ṛichās* of the first *Sūkta* are elaborated in *Maṇḍals* two through nine of Ṛk Veda. Now the total Ṛk Veda with all its ten *Maṇḍals* has unfolded.

It should be noted that the whole structuring dynamics of Ṛk Veda emerges from one syllable, अक् (Ak). This shows that Natural Law, which is managing the ever-expanding universe, manages by virtue of its total presence in every grain of creation: in *Aṇoraṇīyān Mahato-mahīyān,* which is lively in the seat of transformation —*Atyanta-Abhāva* expressed in *Anyonya-Abhāva.*

The subsequent eight *Richās* of Ṛk Veda complete the first *Sūkta,* the next stage of sequential unfoldment of knowledge in Veda. These eight *Richās* consist of 24 *Pādas,* comprising 192 *Akshara* (8 × 24 = 192). According to Maharishi's *Apaurusheya Bhāshya,* these 24 *Pādas* of eight *Akshara* each elaborate the unmanifest eight-fold structure of the 24 *Sandhi* (Gaps) between the *Akshara* of the first *Richā*. Each *Richā* consists of three *Pādas* which, as in the first *Richā,* present the structure of self-interaction with respect to the *Ṛishi, Devatā,* and *Chhandas* qualities of pure consciousness respectively.

Ultimately, 192 *Akshara* of *Richās* two through nine of the first *Sūkta* are elaborated in the 192 *Sūktas* that constitute the first *Maṇdala* (circular, cyclical, eternal structure) of Ṛk Veda, and the 192 *Sūktas* of the tenth *Maṇdala* emerge from the Gaps between these 192 *Sūktas*. The remaining *Maṇdals, Maṇdals* two through nine (corresponding to the eight *Prakṛiti*), emerge sequentially from the Gaps between the *Richās* of the first *Sūkta,* giving rise to the rest of Veda and the entire Vedic Literature.

Significance of the Gap in Veda and the Vedic Literature

Maharishi, in his *Apaurusheya Bhāshya,* locates the fundamental significance of Veda and the Vedic Literature as emerging from the dynamics of the Gaps *(Sandhi).* Veda and the Vedic Literature are profoundly significant because they are the expression of the Laws of Nature, which continuously transform one state into another, maintaining order and evolution on the basis of their eternal, immortal, self-referral reality. These mechanics of transformation are located in the Gaps. It is in the full understanding of the dynamics of the Gaps that the understanding of the holistic, all-inclusive character of Veda and the Vedic Literature resides.

As Figure 2-3 indicates, the Gap has four values:

1 Silent point value of all possibilities called *Atyanta-Abhāva*

2 Structuring dynamics of what occurs in the Gap, called *Anyonya-Abhāva*

Figure 2-3: Dynamics of the Gap

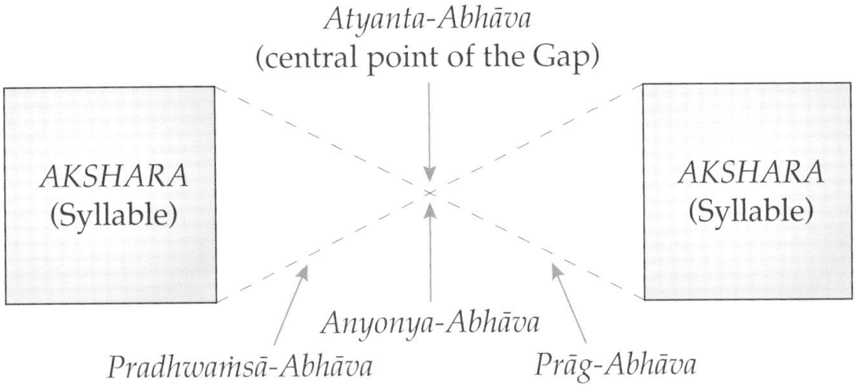

3 Mechanics by which a sound or a syllable (or a hardware-software interface) collapses into the point value of the Gap—sound becomes silence. This is called *Pradhwaṁsā-Abhāva*.

4 Mechanics by which a sound (or a hardware or software expression, such as a classical network bit or a quantum network qubit) emerges from the point value of the Gap (i.e., the emergence of the following *Akshara*). This is called *Prāg-Abhāva*.

It is revealing to see how the state of *Atyanta-Abhāva*—the absolute state of abstraction, the state of pure wakefulness—just by virtue of being awake, knows itself. Therefore, it has four qualities within its self-referral singularity: 1) knower, 2) process of knowing, 3) known, and 4) unity of knower, process of knowing, and known—*Saṁhitā* of *Ṛishi, Devatā,* and *Chhandas*.

Figure 2-4 (on page 26) depicts these four qualities of the three-in-one structure of *Atyanta-Abhāva*. This reality of four emerging and four submerging in the fully awake state of self-referral consciousness presents eight values of self-referral Unity Consciousness *(Brahmi Sthiti* or *Brahmi Chetana)*. The figure indicates that the eight changing values of *Prakṛiti* and one non-changing value of *Prakṛiti* present nine qualities of *Prakṛiti* within *Atyanta-Abhāva*. The eight changing values are called *Aparā Prakṛiti,* and the one non-changing value is called *Parā Prakṛiti*. This state of many values within *Atyanta-Abhāva* is called *Anyonya-Abhāva*.

Figure 2-4: Eight Values of Self-Referral Unity Consciousness

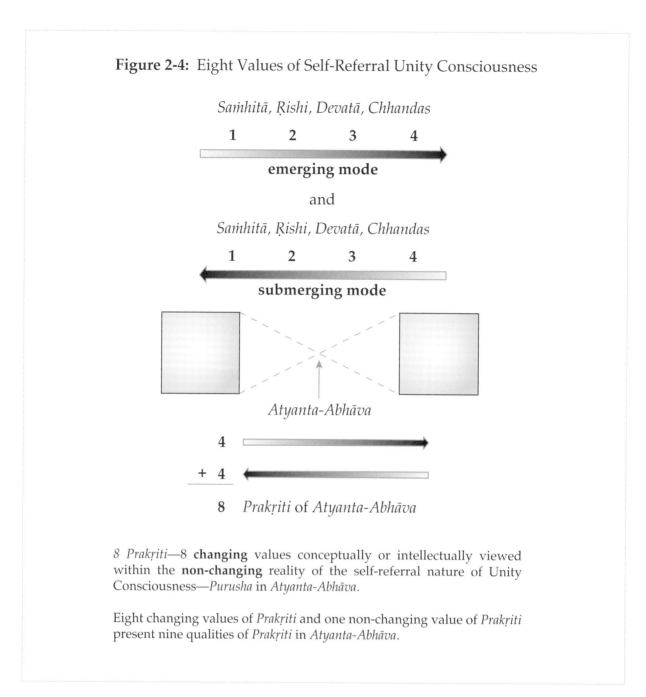

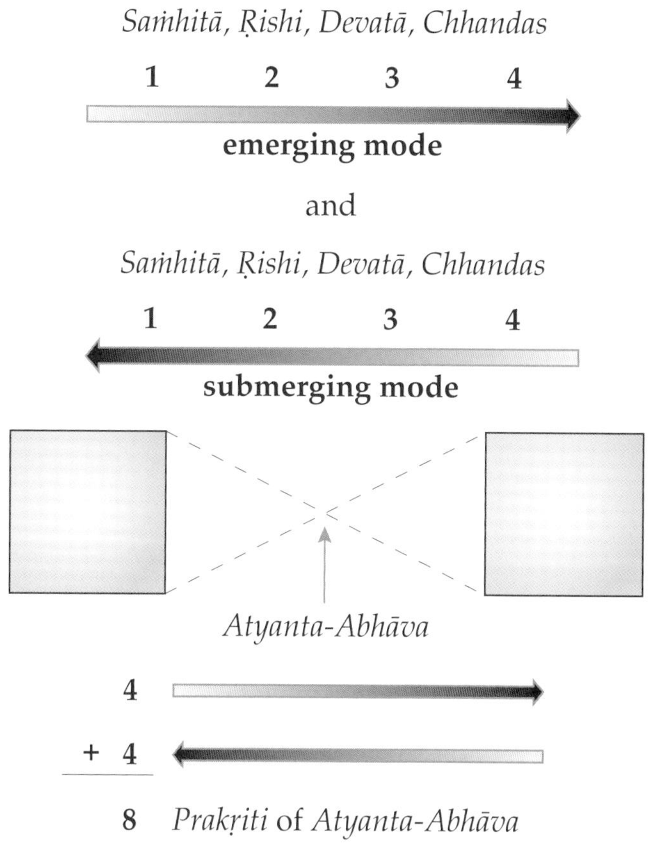

8 Prakṛiti—8 **changing** values conceptually or intellectually viewed within the **non-changing** reality of the self-referral nature of Unity Consciousness—*Purusha* in *Atyanta-Abhāva.*

Eight changing values of *Prakṛiti* and one non-changing value of *Prakṛiti* present nine qualities of *Prakṛiti* in *Atyanta-Abhāva.*

The nature of the Ultimate Reality is the unmanifest *Atyanta-Abhāva* in its self-referral singularity, uninvolved wakefulness—*Purusha.* Coexistence of silence and dynamism structures the mechanics of how singularity is duality—how pure wakefulness is both singularity and duality. This presents the mechanics of singularity evolving into duality without losing its essential nature, singularity. This level of intelligence is the source of creation as revealed by the Cosmic Computer and Cosmic Switchboard.

Self-referral intelligence, or self-referral consciousness, with its self-interacting dynamics forms the basis of creation. At the common basis of all these processes of creation there is a flat field of silence. This silent field of intelligence, being fully awake, is silently witnessing the performance of the eight active *Prakṛiti* and the non-performance of the ninth. Silent witnessing is the tenth quality of intelligence—*Purusha*—expressed in the tenth *Maṇḍala* of Ṛk Veda.

We therefore locate ten qualities of intelligence within the singularity of *Atyanta-Abhāva*—the eight *Aparā Prakṛiti,* ninth *Parā Prakṛiti,* and tenth *Purusha*—the unmanifest state of the supreme level of abstraction. These ten values of intelligence constitute the structure of *Atyanta-Abhāva* and the self-interacting dynamics of its functioning intelligence—*Anyonya-Abhāva.*

There is an expression in Ṛk Veda:

> दशमे युगे यतीनां ब्रह्मा भवति सारथिः
>
> *Dashame yuge yatīnāṁ Brahmā bhavati sārathiḥ*
>
> *(Ṛk Veda, 1.158.6)*

Dashame yuge means evolution arriving at its supreme level, leading individual intelligence to function on the level of Cosmic Intelligence. This can be counted as the tenth and final state of evolution of the Vedic Structure, after nine cycles of transformation, where all the eight active *Prakṛiti* and the silent ninth *Prakṛiti* are together supported by a Wholeness—the tenth quality of intelligence—*Purusha.*

The ten *Maṇḍals* of Ṛk Veda contain all knowledge of the sequential evolution of Veda (*Anupurvi* of Veda)—sequentially evolving *Mantra, Sūkta,* and *Maṇḍals* one to ten. The tenth *Maṇḍala* displays *Purusha,* the supreme state of evolution, structuring the complete display of the evolution of Natural Law, from point to infinity. Figure 2-5 (on page 28) indicates that the ten *Maṇḍals* constitute the dynamics of *Anyonya-Abhāva* in the silent nature of *Atyanta-Abhāva.*

Figure 2-6 (on page 28) shows that the point of *Atyanta-Abhāva* within the Gap is the self-referral field of all possibilities in which all 40 values of the Veda and the Vedic Literature are fully awake. The ten *Maṇḍals* of Ṛk Veda are lively at a point, which is

Figure 2-5: The Emergence of *Anyonya-Abhāva* in *Atyanta-Abhāva*

In the center of the Gap is the indestructible force that spontaneously promotes the sequential evolution of the unmanifest field of consciousness into its expression—the Laws of Nature.

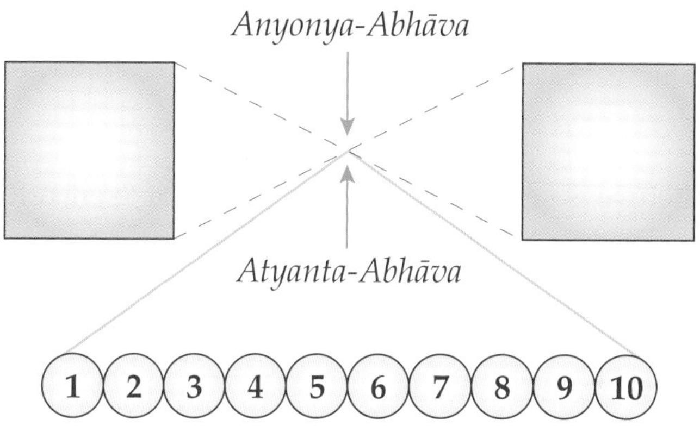

Ten *Maṇdals* of Ṛk Veda constitute the dynamics of *Anyonya-Abhāva* in the silent nature of *Atyanta-Abhāva*. By virtue of the *Maṇdala* (circular) structure, this structure (the field of all possibilities—the self-referral source of all creation) is indestructible—Natural Law is indestructible, invincible; that is why the expression of Natural Law, the universe, is an eternal continuum.

Figure 2-6: *Parame Vyoman*

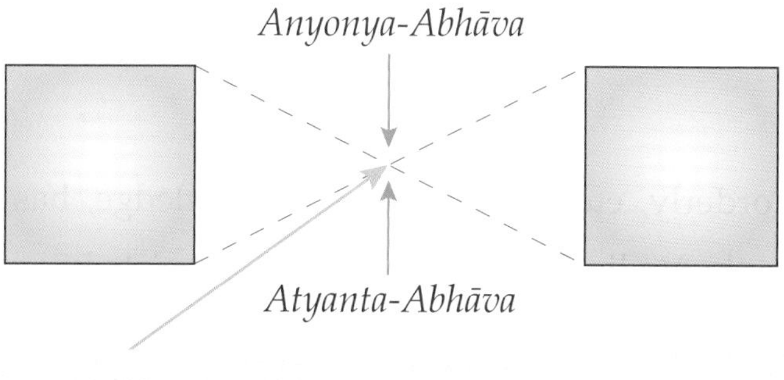

Here at the point, in the unmanifest Transcendental Field—

परमे व्योमन् यस्मिन् देवा अधि विश्वे निषेदु

Parame vyoman yasmin Devā adhi vishwe nisheduḥ (Ṛk Veda, 1.164.39)

—is the self-referral field of all possibilities, the total value of Natural Law fully awake within itself—all the ten *Maṇdals* of Ṛk Veda (and also all the 40 values of Vedic Literature) fully awake.

Anyonya-Abhāva within *Atyanta-Abhāva*, the unmanifest field. The secret of this lies in the invincible nature of Veda.

Invincibility of the Looping Structure

Invincibility of the Vedic Structure is due to the self-referral quality of consciousness in which the Veda is structured. The self-referral quality of consciousness is expressed in the phrase, *"Saṁhitā* of *Ṛishi, Devatā, Chhandas"* (top portion of Figure 2-7 on page 30). This three-in-one structure is self-looping. This quality of "self-referral looping" renders the structure invincible. The self-referral quality of *Saṁhitā* maintains itself as *Saṁhitā* even when it is expressed in the sequentially evolving ten *Maṇḍals* of Ṛk Veda.

Figure 2-7 also illustrates the indestructibility of the Vedic Structure—each *Maṇḍala* (circle) loops onto itself and thereby maintains its individual indestructibility. Sequential evolution of each *Maṇḍala* also maintains its indestructibility by continuing to maintain its connectedness with all others through the looping phenomenon. The *Purusha* (tenth *Maṇḍala*) quality of consciousness is absolute silence beyond which there is no dynamism. Similarly, looping structures also pervade associated subfields in Quantum Network Architecture, imparting the self-referral basis to its indestructibility.

One-to-One Relationship Between Maharishi's Vedic Science and Quantum Network Architecture

Veda, the perfectly orderly, eternal structure of knowledge, has been preserved over thousands of years in the Vedic Tradition of India. Complete knowledge of Veda and its profound significance for life has been revived and understood in a scientific framework by Maharishi Mahesh Yogi in his Vedic Science and Technology. The breadth of the field of Information Science and Technology—the basis of Quantum Network Architecture—corresponds to this perfectly orderly, eternal structure of knowledge because Veda is the blueprint of creation. Figure 2-8 (on pages 32 and 33) presents the entire range of Maharishi's Vedic Science and Technology and shows the one-to-one correspondence with Quantum Network Architecture.

Figure 2-7: Self-Referral, Self-Looping, Invincible Nature of Ṛk Veda

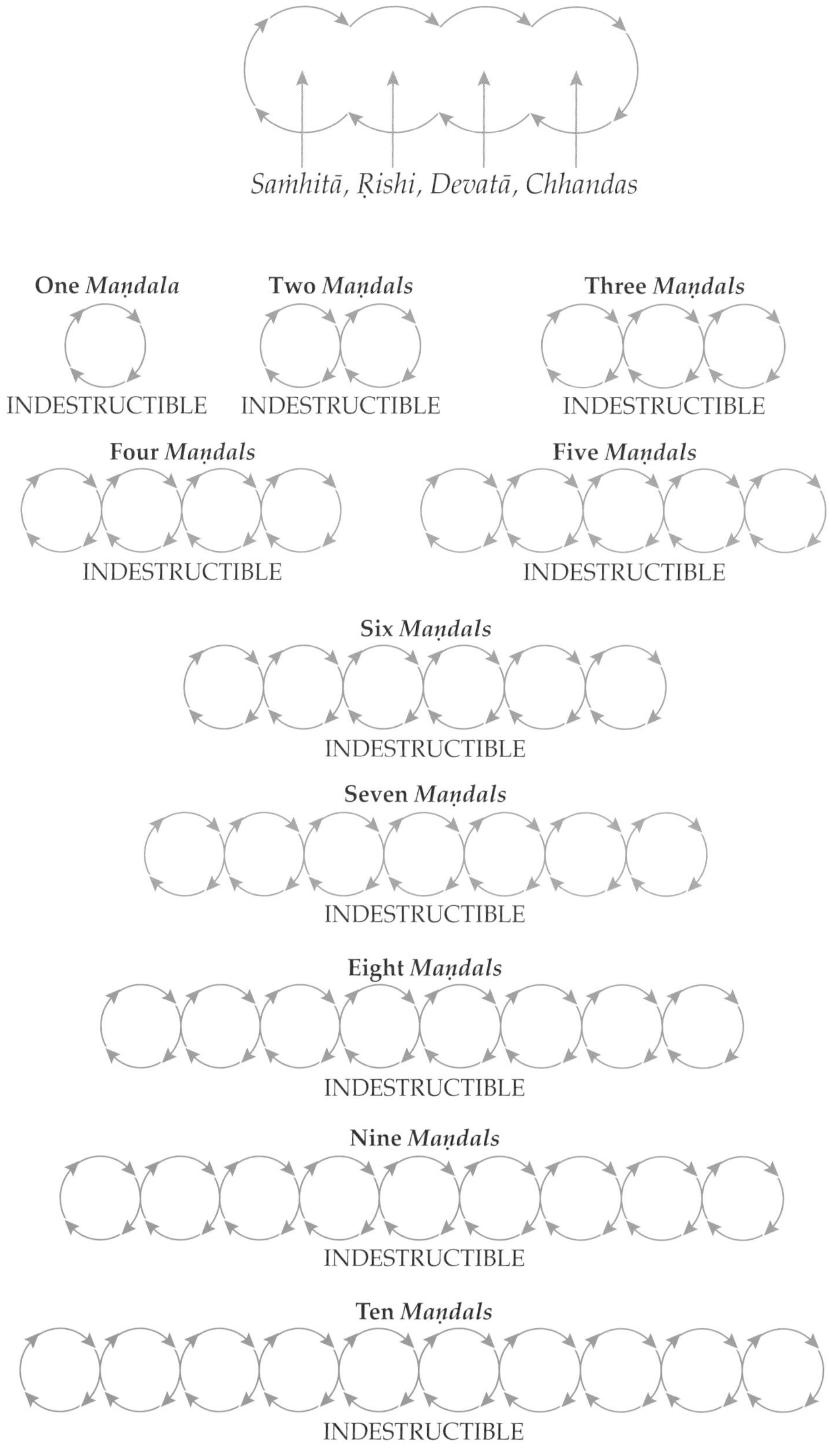

As shown in Figure 2-8 (on pages 32 and 33), Ṛk Veda is expressed in Quantum Network Architecture as the Cosmic Network of Consciousness—Holistic Functioning of the Cosmic Computer and Cosmic Switchboard. As Ṛk Veda has a structure that is an eternal, holistic, all-time reality on its own level, the structuring dynamics of Ṛk Veda have to be self-referral. Therefore, all the other 39 aspects of Veda and the Vedic Literature are self-referral.

Although each of the 40 aspects of Veda and the Vedic Literature is self-referral, each assumes one predominant quality as its specialty. For example, Sāma Veda expresses *Saṁhitā* quality of consciousness with a predominantly *Ṛishi* value. Sāma Veda is all that is pertaining to *Ṛishi*. It is *Flowing Wakefulness* and is expressed in Quantum Network Architecture as *Network Self-referral and Feedback Systems*. Each aspect of Veda and the Vedic Literature and its correspondence to Quantum Network Architecture is illustrated in Figure 2-8. Chapters 3 through 8 unfold the one-to-one correspondence between Maharishi's Vedic Science and Technology and Quantum Network Architecture in terms of Veda (Chapter 3), Vedānga (Chapter 4), Upānga (Chapter 5), Upa-Veda (Chapter 6), Brāhmaṇa (Chapter 7), and Prātishākhya (Chapter 8).

Figure 2-8 illustrates the fundamental looping structure of Veda and the Vedic Literature, with the exception of the four principal Vedas and the six Prātishākhyas. Vedic loops signify the process of emergence from and submergence to the source and the invincible nature of the Veda and the Vedic Literature. Ultimately, the entire 40 branches of Veda and the Vedic Literature form a loop with Veda emerging from *Ātmā* as unity and diversity (Wholeness and all its point values integrated together), and with the Prātishākhyas submerging into the self-sufficient, self-referral, omnipresent, holistic value of Totality—*Brahm*. अयम् आत्मा ब्रह्म *Ayam Ātmā Brahm*. "This *Ātmā* is *Brahm*".

These one-to-one relationships between Veda, the Vedic Literature, and Quantum Network Architecture are also presented in a different format in Figure 2-9 (on pages 34 and 35). This format emphasizes the correspondence among the qualities, names, and manifestation in Quantum Network Architecture of each of the 40 aspects of Veda and the Vedic Literature.

Figure 2-8: Quantum Network Architecture™ According to Veda and the Vedic Literature

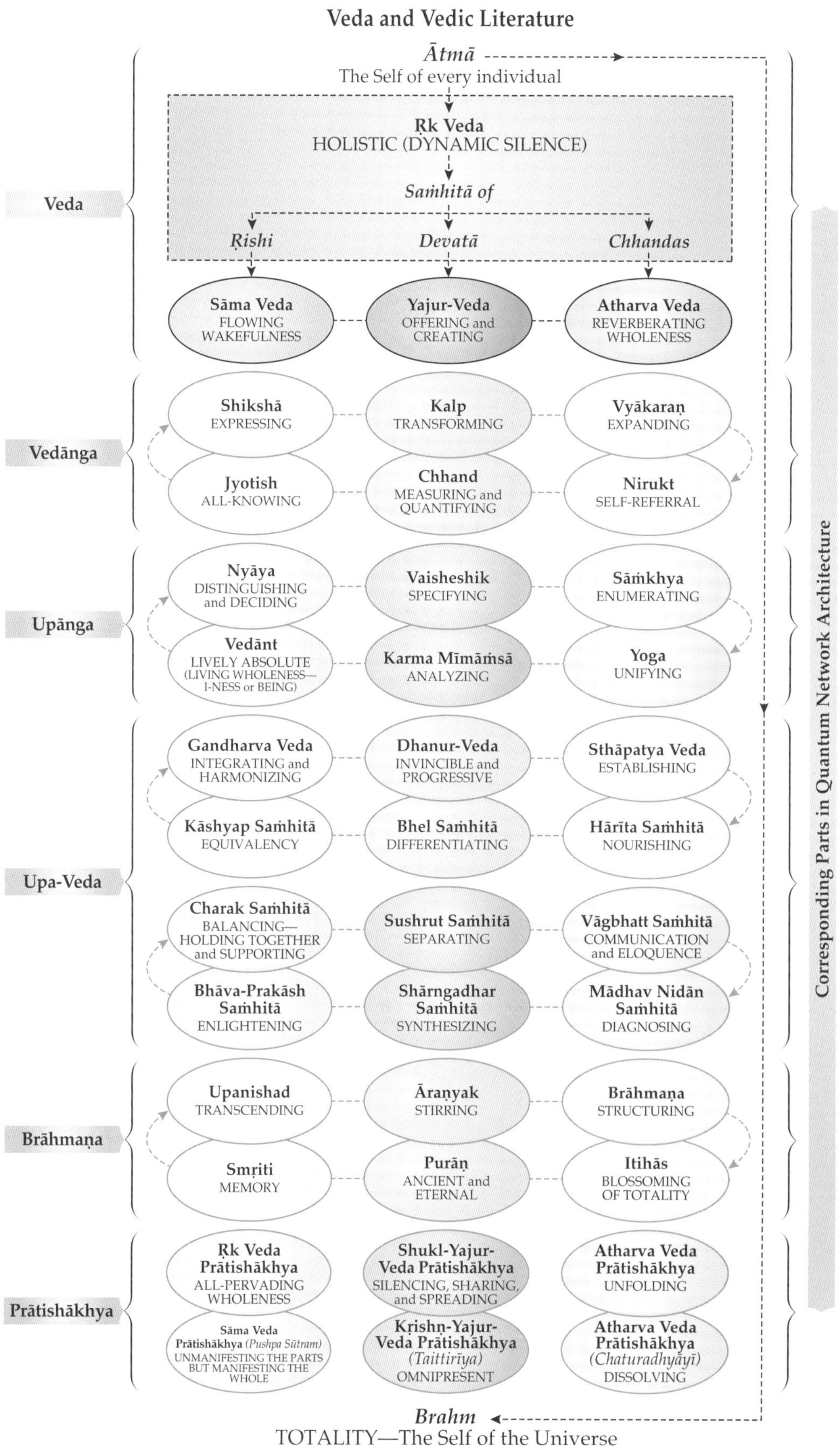

Figure 2-8 (continued): Quantum Network Architecture™
According to Veda and the Vedic Literature

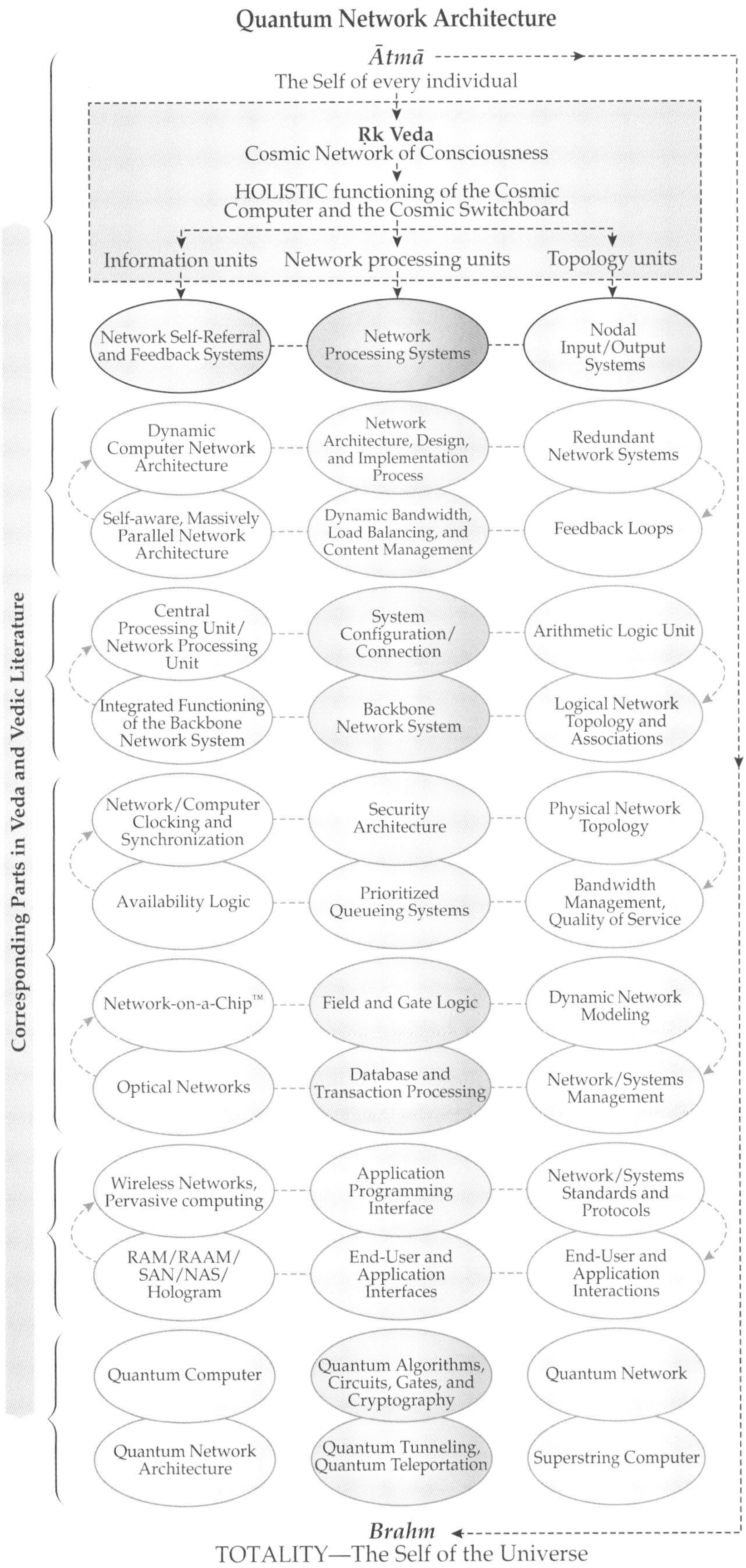

Figure 2-9: The 40 Aspects of Veda and the Vedic Literature and Their Corresponding Aspects in Quantum Network Architecture™

Impulses of Consciousness—Structures and Structuring Dynamics of the Laws of Nature

their Qualities .... Qualities of Intelligence		.... *their Names* .... Terminology of Vedic Literature		.... *their Forms* Terminology of Quantum Network Architecture
1. *HOLISTIC (DYNAMIC SILENCE)* quality of intelligence	fully expressed in	**Ṛk Veda**	which in turn expresses itself in	**HOLISTIC functioning of the Cosmic Computer and the Cosmic Switchboard**
2. *FLOWING WAKEFULNESS—FLOWING* quality of intelligence	fully expressed in	**Sāma Veda**	which in turn expresses itself in	**Network Self-Referral and Feedback Systems**
3. *OFFERING* and *CREATING* quality of intelligence	fully expressed in	**Yajur-Veda**	which in turn expresses itself in	**Network Processing Systems**
4. *REVERBERATING WHOLENESS—REVERBERATING* quality in every point of holistic intelligence	fully expressed in	**Atharva Veda**	which in turn expresses itself in	**Nodal Input/Ouput systems**
5. *EXPRESSING* quality of intelligence	fully expressed in	**Shikshā**	which in turn expresses itself in	**Dynamic Computer Network Architecture**
6. *TRANSFORMING* quality of intelligence	fully expressed in	**Kalp**	which in turn expresses itself in	**Network Architecture Design and Implementation Process**
7. *EXPANDING* quality of intelligence	fully expressed in	**Vyākaraṇ**	which in turn expresses itself in	**Redundant Network Systems**
8. *SELF-REFERRAL* quality of intelligence	fully expressed in	**Nirukt**	which in turn expresses itself in	**Feedback Loops**
9. *MEASURING* and *QUANTIFYING* quality of intelligence	fully expressed in	**Chhand**	which in turn expresses itself in	**Dynamic Bandwidth, Load Balancing, and Content Management**
10. *ALL-KNOWING* quality of intelligence	fully expressed in	**Jyotish**	which in turn expresses itself in	**Self-Aware, Massively Parallel Network Architecture**
11. *DISTINGUISHING* and *DECIDING* quality of intelligence	fully expressed in	**Nyāya**	which in turn expresses itself in	**Central Processing Unit/ Network Processing Unit**
12. *SPECIFYING* quality of intelligence	fully expressed in	**Vaisheshik**	which in turn expresses itself in	**System Configuration/ Connection**
13. *ENUMERATING* quality of intelligence	fully expressed in	**Sāṁkhya**	which in turn expresses itself in	**Arithmetic Logic Unit**
14. *UNIFYING* quality of intelligence	fully expressed in	**Yoga**	which in turn expresses itself in	**Logical Network Topology and Associations**
15. *ANALYZING* quality of intelligence	fully expressed in	**Karma Mīmāṁsā**	which in turn expresses itself in	**Backbone Network System**
16. *LIVELY ABSOLUTE (LIVING WHOLENESS—I-NESS* or *BEING)* quality of intelligence	fully expressed in	**Vedānt**	which in turn expresses itself in	**Integrated Functioning of the Backbone Network System**
17. *INTEGRATING* and *HARMONIZING* quality of inteligence	fully expressed in	**Gandharva Veda**	which in turn expresses itself in	**Network/Computer Clocking and Synchronization**
18. *INVINCIBLE* and *PROGRESSIVE* quality of intelligence	fully expressed in	**Dhanur-Veda**	which in turn expresses itself in	**Security Architecture**
19. *ESTABLISHING* quality of intelligence	fully expressed in	**Sthāpatya Veda**	which in turn expresses itself in	**Physical Network Topology**
20. *NOURISHING* quality of intelligence	fully expressed in	**Hārīta Saṁhitā**	which in turn expresses itself in	**Bandwidth Management, Quality of S?ervice**

Figure 2-9 (continued): The 40 Aspects of Veda and the Vedic Literature and Their Corresponding Aspects in Quantum Network Architecture

Impulses of Consciousness—Structures and Structuring Dynamics of the Laws of Nature

their Qualities ... Qualities of Intelligence		... *their Names* ... Terminology of Vedic Literature		... *their Forms* Terminology of Quantum Network Architecture
21. *DIFFERENTIATING* quality of intelligence	fully expressed in	**Bhel Saṁhita**	which in turn expresses itself in	**Prioritized Queueing Systems**
22. *EQUIVALENCY* quality of intelligence	fully expressed in	**Kāshyap Saṁhitā**	which in turn expresses itself in	**Availability Logic**
23. *BALANCING—HOLDING TOGETHER* and *SUPPORTING* quality of intelligence	fully expressed in	**Charak Saṁhitā**	which in turn expresses itself in	**Network-on-a-Chip™**
24. *SEPARATING* quality of intelligence	fully expressed in	**Shushrut Saṁhitā**	which in turn expresses itself in	**Field and Gate Logic**
25. *COMMUNICATION and ELOQUENCE* quality of intelligence	fully expressed in	**Vāgbhatt Saṁhitā**	which in turn expresses itself in	**Dynamic Network Modeling**
26. *DIAGNOSING* quality of intelligence	fully expressed in	**Mādhav Nidān Saṁhitā**	which in turn expresses itself in	**Network/Systems Management**
27. *SYNTHESIZING* quality of intelligence	fully expressed in	**Shārngadhar Saṁhitā**	which in turn expresses itself in	**Database and Transaction Processing**
28. *ENLIGHTENING* quality of intelligence	fully expressed in	**Bhāva-Prakāsh Saṁhitā**	which in turn expresses itself in	**Optical Networks**
29. *TRANSCENDING* quality of intelligence	fully expressed in	**Upanishad**	which in turn expresses itself in	**Wireless Networks, Pervasive Computing**
30. *STIRRING* quality of intelligence	fully expressed in	**Āraṇyak**	which in turn expresses itself in	**Application Programming Interface**
31. *STRUCTURING* quality of intelligence	fully expressed in	**Brāhmaṇa**	which in turn expresses itself in	**Network/Systems Standards and Protocols**
32. *BLOSSOMING OF TOTALITY* quality of intelligence	fully expressed in	**Itihās**	which in turn expresses itself in	**End-User and Application Interactions**
33. *ANCIENT* and *ETERNAL* quality of intelligence	fully expressed in	**Purāṇ**	which in turn expresses itself in	**End-User and Application Interfaces**
34. *MEMORY* quality of intelligence	fully expressed in	**Smṛiti**	which in turn expresses itself in	**RAM/RAAM/SAN/ NAS/Hologram**
35. *ALL-PERVADING WHOLENESS* quality of intelligence	fully expressed in	**Ṛk Veda Prātishākhya**	which in turn expresses itself in	**Quantum Computer**
36. *SILENCING, SHARING,* and *SPREADING* quality of intelligence	fully expressed in	**Shukl-Yajur-Veda Prātishākhya**	which in turn expresses itself in	**Quantum Algorithmns, Circuits, Gates, and Cryptography**
37. *UNFOLDING* quality of inteligence	fully expressed in	**Atharva Veda Prātishākhya**	which in turn expresses itself in	**Quantum Network**
38. *DISSOLVING* quality of intelligence	fully expressed in	**Atharva Veda Prātishākhya** *(Chaturadhyāyi)*	which in turn expresses itself in	**Superstring Computer**
39. *OMNIPRESENT* quality of intelligence	fully expressed in	**Kṛishṇ-Yajur-Veda Prātishākhya** *(Taittirīya)*	which in turn expresses itself in	**Quantum Tunneling, Quantum Teleportation**
40. *UNMANIFESTING THE PARTS BUT MANIFESTING THE WHOLE* quality of intelligence	fully expressed in	**Sāma Veda Prātishākhya** *(Pushpa Sūtram)*	which in turn expresses itself in	**Quantum Network Architecture**

Figure 2-10 presents the 40 aspects of Maharishi's Vedic Science and Technology in Sanskrit, the language of Natural Law and the language of Veda.

This chapter has introduced the range of Maharishi's Vedic Science and Technology and its expression in Quantum Computing and Quantum Network Architecture. Chapter 3 explores in more detail the one-to-one correspondence between Ṛk Veda and Quantum Network Architecture, and unfolds the Hardware-Software Gap as central to network computing.

Figure 2-10: Vision of Maharishi's Vedic Science
Expressed in Sanskrit, the Language of Nature

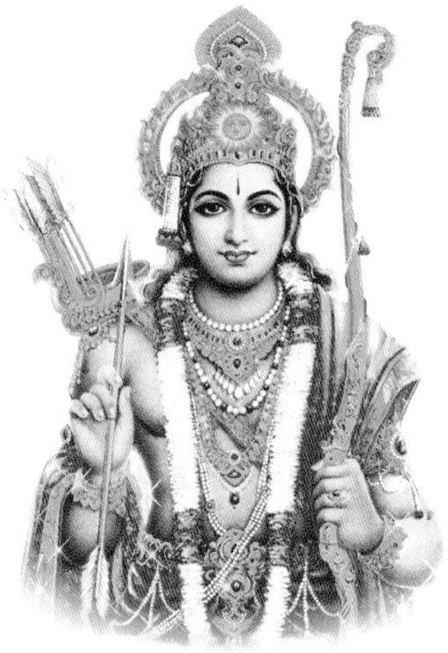

3: The Four Veda in Quantum Network Architecture

All Theories of Information Science and Technology Contained in One Verse of Ṛk Veda

Veda is Total Knowledge, the Constitution of the Universe. In this chapter, we precisely map the entire structure and function of Ṛk Veda—its *Akshara* (syllables), *Shabdas* (words), *Pādas* (phrases), *Richās* (verses), *Sūktas* (hymns), *Maṇdals* (chapters), and *Sandhi* (Gaps)—into the entire structure and function of Information Science and Technology as revealed in Quantum Network Architecture™. This discovery of Veda in Quantum Network Architecture makes the study and knowledge of Information Science and Technology a study and understanding of Veda, the Computational Constitution of the Universe.

Chapter 1 presented theoretical and applied aspects of Quantum Network Architecture in terms of direct expressions of the Unified Field. We have also seen that the Unified Field contains within itself the whole field of Veda and the Vedic Literature. Figure 3-1 (on pages 41–43) illustrates how all the major theories of Information Science and Technology are directly related, without reference to the Unified Field, to the dynamics of consciousness as displayed in one key verse of Ṛk Veda:

ऋचो अक्षरे परमे व्योमन् यस्मिन् देवा अधि विश्वे निषेदुः
यस्तन्न वेद किमृचा करिष्यति य इत् तद् विदुस् त इमे समासते

Ṛicho ak-kshare Parame vyoman yasmin Devā adhi vishwe nisheduḥ.
Yastanna veda kim Ṛichā karishyati. Ya it tad vidus ta ime samaste.
(Ṛk Veda, 1.164.39)

The verses of the Veda exist in the collapse of fullness (the kshara of अ [A]) in the transcendental field in which reside all the Devās, the impulses of Creative Intelligence, the Laws of Nature responsible for the whole manifest universe. He whose awareness is not open to this field, what can the verses accomplish for him? Those who know this level of reality are established in evenness, wholeness of life.

This direct relationship between Quantum Network Architecture and Ṛk Veda indicates that there is a level of consciousness—Transcendental Consciousness—which everyone can enliven within himself; all can gain the benefit of studying all disciplines of Information Science and Technology as well as all disciplines of modern science. It also indicates that all the Laws of Nature have one common basis in *Parame vyoman*—the transcendental, unmanifest field.

Pure intelligence, endowed with the infinite organizing power of Natural Law, is available in unbounded infinity (expressed by अ [A], the first holistic expression of Ṛk Veda). The infinite organizing power of Natural Law is also available in every point of infinity (expressed by the syllable क् [K], the syllable following अ [A]).

Ṛk Veda Saṁhitā—*Holistic (Dynamic Silence)*—Holistic Functioning of the Cosmic Computer and Cosmic Switchboard

Ṛk Veda, as introduced in Chapter 2, is the most fundamental aspect of Vedic Literature and represents the eternal, self-referral dynamics of consciousness knowing itself. The very structure of the sounds of Ṛk Veda is the embodiment of the eternal dynamism and silence at the basis of the infinite organizing power of Natural Law. We find the structuring dynamics of the Gap to be central to Maharishi's *Apaurusheya Bhāshya,* in which the structure of Veda provides its own commentary that is self-contained in its sequential unfoldment in various stages of expression through *Akshara* and Gaps (refer to Figure 2-2 on pages 22 and 23, "Maharishi's Commentary on Ṛk Veda Saṁhitā *(Apaurusheya Bhāshya),*" and Figure 2-3 on page 25, "Dynamics of the Gap").

Elaboration of the one-to-one correspondence between Ṛk Veda and Quantum Network Architecture presented in this chapter is based on two perspectives: one that considers the

Figure 3-1: All Theories of INFORMATION SCIENCE AND TECHNOLOGY in One Verse of Ṛk Veda—*Ṛk Veda 1.164.39*

VEDIC SCIENCE → MODERN SCIENCE ↓ (Information Science and Technology)	ऋचो अक्षरे ṚICHO AK-KSHARE The verses of the Veda exist in the collapse of fullness (the *kshara* of अ (A))...	परमे व्योमन् PARAME VYOMAN ...in the transcendental field,...
CLASSICAL INFORMATION THEORY	Classical digital information flow (*Ṛichā*) is generated through transitions (*kshara* of 'A') of binary digits (bits). Classical analog information flow (*Ṛichā*) is generated through transitions (*kshara* of 'A') relative to reference amplitudes, where any waveform can be accurately represented as a summation (*kshara* of 'A') of sine waves (Fourier).	Classical computation and networking find their transcendental bases in the state of *Atyanta-Abhāva*—the absolute state of abstraction within the *Sandhi* of the Hardware-Software Gap™, expressed as Compiler-Assembler, Assembler-Linker, Assembler-Machine Language, Linker-Loader, and analog-digital signaling Gaps.
SAMPLING THEORY	Sampling is the process (*Richā*) of representing a continuous-time signal by a collapsed series of discrete samples (kshara of 'A'). Reconstruction is the process (*Richā*) of recreating associated continuous-time signals (*kshara* of 'A') from discrete samples.	Signaling sine waves have a characteristic wavelength (λ, distance between crests), velocity (v, rate at which the wave propagates), and frequency (f, number of crests that pass per unit of time), where the waveform is based in transcendental, self-referral Wholeness, and each division of Wholeness is Wholeness itself.
ELECTRONIC NETWORK ENGINEERING	Electronic computer networks enable information flow (*Ṛichā*) through inband information processing of source and destination address, sequence number, channel number, parity checking, and multiplexing, collapsed as a set of nonlinear operations (*kshara* of 'A').	Communication signals and circuits represent the peak amplitude and phase of sine waves (trigonometric sine or cosine curves) using complex numbers that are actually a pair of numbers consisting of real and imaginary (transcendental) counterparts.
OPTICAL NETWORK ENGINEERING	Optical computer networks provide information flow (*Ṛichā*) through photonic routing and switching functions in the optical domain, collapsed as a set of linear operations (*kshara* of 'A').	Optical network architecture is a two-level environment, where the optical physical topology is imbued with specific knowledge about the traffic (lightpaths) supported over it. The virtual topology, while presenting lightpath requirements to and receiving constraints from the physical topology, transcends physical constraints.
WIRELESS NETWORK ENGINEERING	Wireless computer networks provide information flow (*Ṛichā*) through radio frequency (RF) signal oscillations in the power and signal (time and frequency) domains, collapsed as a set of time-based phase constellations (*kshara* of 'A').	Wireless systems represent information using constant amplitude phase modulation, where the carrier phase is shifted depending on the data to be sent, and the signal amplitude remains constant during phase and amplitude transition decision points at their transcendental basis in the Hardware-Software Gap.
INFORMATION SECURITY ARCHITECTURE	Secure flow of information (*Ṛichā*) presumes security policies, architecture, guidelines, trusted third-party user identification, and authentication. Information theory defines the amount of information in a message as the minimum (collapsed) number of bits/qubits (*kshara* of 'A') needed to encode all possible meanings of the message.	The key to achieving perfect classical or quantum information secrecy is a crytosystem in which the ciphertext yields no possible information about the plaintext. The cornerstone to secrecy is found in the transcendental basis to crypto-algorithms, where the number of possible keys is always as large as the number of possible messages.
ANALYTIC QUEUEING THEORY	Optimal performance, reliability, and flow of network computational information (*Ṛichā*) is based upon predictive probabilistic and statistical workloads containing random service intervals, determined through analytic queueing (collapsed state space and non-state space) and collapsed discrete-event simulation models (*kshara* of 'A').	The information contained in a random variable, X ,that can assume all values in the interval, $[a, b]$, where $-\infty$ $a < b$ $+\infty$ is a continuous random variable. It provides the transcendental basis for its cumulative distribution function and specifies the probability that X assumes values less than or equal to x, for every x.
QUANTUM INFORMATION THEORY	Quantum information flow (*Ṛichā*) is generated through quantized probability amplitudes of superposed transitions resulting from the summation (collapse) over all possible computational trajectories achievable in time t (*kshara* of 'A') into qubits.	The Cosmic Computer and Cosmic Switchboard eternally vibrate as the lively, transcendental Cosmic Network of Consciousness and are inextricably linked in a multi-tier, full-mesh fashion, where the cosmic nodal interconnection topology is specified by 10^n probability amplitudes.

Figure 3-1: All Theories of INFORMATION SCIENCE AND TECHNOLOGY in One Verse of Ṛk Veda—*Ṛk Veda 1.164.39 (continued)*

	यस्मिन् देवा YASMIN DEVĀ ...in which reside all the *Devas*, the impulses of Creative Intelligence, the Laws of Nature...	अधि विश्वे निषेदुः ADHI VISHWE NISHEDUḤ ...responsible for the whole manifest universe.	यस्तन्न वेद YASTANNA VEDA He whose awareness is not open to this field...
CLASSICAL INFORMATION THEORY	Classical information processing proceeds through a set of electrical or optical circuits containing wires and logic gates *(Devas)* that execute classical algorithms. Classical network computational logic gates include AND, NAND, OR, XOR, NOR, FANOUT, CROSSOVER, and combinational processing.	The universe of classical information-theoretic entropies is deduced from an entropy Venn diagram integrating $H(X)$ and $H(Y)$ as $H(X\|Y)$, $H(X{:}Y)$, and $H(Y\|X)$, where H is Shannon entropy. Binary entropy exhibits concavity properties, yielding the deepest and most complete results in both classical and quantum information theory.	Shannon entropy and the noiseless channel encoding theorem are associated with a classical probability distribution and measure the degree of uncertainty about X prior to learning its value. System architects who do not represent an information source with sufficient bits encounter high probabilities of error when the information is decompressed.
SAMPLING THEORY	Signal processing and sampling are orchestrated through stochastic gradient (least mean squares), least squares, multipath equalization, cross-relation, direct symbol estimation, space-time signal processing, and orthogonally anchored algorithms; signal models; audio and video compression; and Analog/Digital (A/D) sampling logic *(Devas)*.	The universe of signal sampling theory incorporates Maxwell's equations, Hertz's proofs, Shannon Theory (source coding, channel coding, and multiple-access coding), Moore's Law (the number of integrated circuit components per unit area doubles every 18 months), and Metcalfe's Law (a network value grows as the square of the number of network users).	Network signal processing components and systems that do not integrate the fundamental relations between velocity, wavelength, and frequency ($v = \lambda f$) in all sinusoidal waves and associated conversion logic are not able to properly sample, filter, or reconstruct analog and/or digital information.
ELECTRONIC NETWORK ENGINEERING	Electronic signal bandwidth is the range of sinusoidal components whose frequencies *(Devas)* span a given frequency range. Logical network design incorporates Boolean algebra and logic *(Devas)* for which outputs are related to inputs by any specified Boolean function.	Electronic and opto-electronic system design methodology optimizes the universe of modulation, sidebands, encoding, multiplexing, signal power, signal sampling, frequency, frequency shifting, entropy, inverse square law, distortion, capacity, digital versus analog decision, switching, blocking, routing, throughput, and performance.	Electronic and opto-electronic network systems deployed in a design methodology vacuum experience signal loss, signal processing errors, circuit failures, switch blocking conditions, queueing system delay degradations, spatial and temporal incoherence, and unacceptably high frequency/time domain sampling error thresholds.
OPTICAL NETWORK ENGINEERING	Light is an electromagnetic wave, and its propagation through any medium is governed by Maxwell's equations *(Devas)*. Light propagation can be described by specifying the evolution of associated electric and magnetic field vectors in space and time.	Optical system design optimizes the universe of analog versus digital decision, sensitivity analysis (source intensity noise, fiber noise, receiver noise, time jitter, intersymbol interference, and bit error rate), optical signal-to-noise ratio, optical regeneration, modulation schemes, rise-time budget, link loss budget, dispersion, and cost/performance tradeoffs.	Optical network systems deployed without design methodology experience major loss mechanisms that include material absorption, Rayleigh scattering, chromatic dispersion, intersymbol interference, chirped gaussian pulses, nonlinear effects (proportional to the square of the field amplitude), wave division multiplexing, and cross-phase modulation.
WIRELESS NETWORK ENGINEERING	Digital wireless data is modified in standard high-or-true and low-or-false voltage levels prior to modulation on the final RF carrier. Wireless digital intelligence is based to a great extent upon AND, OR, XOR, Inverter and Shift Register Gates, and algorithms *(Devas)*.	Wireless (cellular, satellite) system design optimizes the universe of link budget, RF passive components, wireless logic, software radio, hybrid circuitry, modulation, signal propagation, component design (amplifier, oscillator, frequency synthesizer, filter, mixer, support circuit and antenna), power, EIRP, illumination, noise, loss, telemetry, and tracking.	Wireless network systems deployed in a design methodology vacuum experience link budget issues, component and system noise, electromagnetic interference, board design issues, RF software issues, speech processing issues, and poor cost/performance ratios.
INFORMATION SECURITY ARCHITECTURE	Cryptographic algorithms and logic gates *(Devas)* account for message entropy (uncertainty). Shannon (classical information) entropy measures the degree of uncertainty about X prior to learning its value. Von Neumann (quantum information) entropy is non-negative and zero if the state is pure; in a d-dimensional Hilbert space, the entropy is at most $\log d$.	The universe of information security integrates perimeter security; access control and services; authentication, authorization, and auditing; content and liability management (application security control, e-mail filtering, content control, and virus protection); VPN services; PKI; intrusion detection and response services; user management; and policy enforcement.	E-business and mobile commerce (m-commerce) applications that do not integrate comprehensive information security policies/procedures, architecture/design, implementation standards, operations/management guidelines, disaster recovery, and audit enforcement mechanisms are increasingly vulnerable to data compromise over time.
ANALYTIC QUEUEING THEORY	The probability density function (pdf) $f_X^{(x)}$ can be used in place of the cumulative distribution function provided pdf is differentiable. The density function of a continuous random variable is analogous to the probability mass and distribution functions of discrete random variables, including Bernoulli, binomial, geometric, and Poisson variables *(Devas)*.	Continuous random variable distributions in the universe of analytic queueing theory include exponential (the most important distribution function, where interarrival times and service times are represented exactly or approximately), hyperexponential, Erlang-k, hypoexponential, gamma, generalized Erlang, Cox (branching Erlang), Weibull, and lognormal.	Network system architects who do not incorporate predictive network performance methodologies (including analytic queueing, discrete-event simulation, linear programming, and mathematical programming models) into the design process are not able to optimize existing network systems or validate/verify future network systems against requirements.
QUANTUM INFORMATION THEORY	Quantum computing accesses Hilbert space, which contains quantum-mechanical network computational operators and gate logic *(Devas)*. 2^n-dimensional Hilbert space is an inner-product space, existing in infinite dimensions, where the inner product of two vectors is equal to the vector inner product between two matrix representations of those vectors.	Quantum information state sources are described by a Hilbert space H, and a density matrix ρ on that Hilbert space. The state ρ is, in turn, a subset of a larger system that exists in a pure, universal state, where the mixed nature of ρ is due to quantum entanglement between H and the remainder of the quantum information system.	Quantum computation and entanglement are not accessible classically. The No-Cloning Theorem disallows copying an unknown quantum information state. The Holevo bound establishes the upper bound on accessible quantum information. If state ρ_X does not have orthogonal support, the receiver cannot determine with certainty which state the sender prepared.

Figure 3-1: All Theories of INFORMATION SCIENCE AND TECHNOLOGY in One Verse of Ṛk Veda—*Ṛk Veda 1.164.39 (continued)*

	किमृचा करिष्यति KIM ṚICHĀ KARISHYATI ...what can the verses accomplish for him?	य इत् तद् विदुस् YA IT TAD VIDUS Those who know this level of reality...	त इमे समासते TA IME SAMĀSTE ...are established in evenness, wholeness of life.
CLASSICAL INFORMATION THEORY	Computational complexity dictates that classical models require differential resources (polynomial versus exponential) to solve the same problem. Primality decision problems that are not stated in formal languages become intractable in worst-case polynomial time.	The fundamental results of classical information theory are Shannon's noiseless channel coding theorem (which quantifies the number of bits required to store information emitted by an information source) and noisy channel coding theorem (which quantifies how much classical information can be reliably transmitted through a noisy communication channel).	Shannon entropy—the central concept of classical information theory—quantifies how much information is gained, on average, upon discovering the value of X. Concavity properties of Shannon entropy yield the deepest results in both classical and quantum information theory and measure the uncertainty associated with a classical probability distribution.
SAMPLING THEORY	Signals that are improperly sampled generate significant and disruptive errors in modulation; multiplexing; channel fading; spectral, temporal, and spatial diversity; coherence-time scaling; linear interference; adaptive algorithms; attenuation; shadowing; delay; coding; timing recovery; power control; and non-uniform quality of service.	The Nyquist Sampling Theorem enables distortion-free reconstruction of a continuous-time signal, given that the signal is bandlimited and that the samples are sufficiently close enough in time.	Sampling rates greater than twice the maximum frequency present in the input signal ($2W$, Nyquist rate) accommodate the entire range of spectral diversity (spread-spectrum system based), temporal diversity (yielding time-varying multipath propagation), and spatial diversity (receiver multi-element antenna arrays).
ELECTRONIC NETWORK ENGINEERING	Electronic processing is ideal for complex nonlinear operations. However, the limited speed of electronic and opto-electronic devices (i.e., electronic switches, processing units, and memory devices) and the high processing load and penalties imposed on broadband network electronics generate 1000-fold bottlenecks within transit optical networks.	Electronics is ideal for networks that switch a high number of information units per unit of time (yielding relatively high switch processing loads and low switch throughput) and for inband processing (yielding a high degree of virtual connectivity relative to end-to-end optical clear channels).	Electronic properties are complementary to those of optics and are ideal for complex nonlinear operations in environments. Opto-electronic designs are optimal for wide area networks which must handle both large and small information units.
OPTICAL NETWORK ENGINEERING	Nonlinear network operations (including signal detection, regeneration, buffering, and logic functions) are difficult to perform in the optical domain because non-linearities make the signal path opaque rather than transparent.	Optical networks that incorporate Native Optical Logic™ (including optical AND gates and soliton-trapping AND gates) are able to perform complex network computational operations at very high speeds, relative to electronic and opto-electronic networks.	Purely optical networks (comprised of all-optical sources, logic devices, storage elements, transmissions, routers, switches, receiving components, and systems) effectively transfer nonlinear operations native to electronics to the optical level and yield data rates that are infeasible within relatively throughput-bound electronic or opto-electronic interfaces.
WIRELESS NETWORK ENGINEERING	Improperly designed wireless networks encounter mixer-generated spurious responses, externally generated noise, transmitter interference with wireless and non-RF electronics, harmonic outputs, wideband noise, phase noise, and two-tone intermodulation products created by two or more frequency components mixing together in any nonlinearities.	Knowledgeable terrestrial and celestial wireless network engineers recognize that the most challenging design element is the receiver. Therefore, they architect low noise figures, low group delay variation and IMD, high dynamic range, appropriate RF and IF gain, stable AGC, low phase noise, negligible in-band spurs, sufficient selectivity, and suitable BER.	Stable wireless system designs optimize receiver frequency plan, cost, and link budgets (transmitter power, antenna gain, equivalent isotropically radiated power, illumination level, free space path loss, system noise temperature, receiver figure-of-merit, carrier-to-thermal noise ratio, carrier-to-noise-density ratio, and carrier-to-noise ratio).
INFORMATION SECURITY ARCHITECTURE	There are three Internet characteristics that encourage cyberspace attacks and e-business /m-commerce compromise: automation (enabling attacks with a minimal rate of profitable return), action at a distance (endpoints are logically adjacent), and technique propagation. Vulnerable infrastructures lack comprehensive security policies, protocols, and procedures.	Provably secure key and data distribution proceeds through non-orthogonal quantum information states and by properties of quantum information pure-state-entanglement distillation and dilution. Channel eavesdropping causes a detectable increase in error rate due to the fact that information gain implies disturbance; high fidelity implies low entropy.	Quantum cryptography ensures provably secure distribution of private information and transmits non-orthogonal qubits over a public channel. Information reconciliation and privacy amplification distill a shared secret key string with security of the resulting key ensured by the properties of quantum information superposition.
ANALYTIC QUEUEING THEORY	Computer networks—the global knowledge repositories of corporations, governments, universities, and individuals—implemented without reference to requirements yield sub-optimal end-system and server throughput, erratic performance, and unpredictable traffic bottlenecking and downtime.	Current system states embody probabilistic memory of the process back into the infinite past. Markov processes are defined with discrete or continuous states and time. They provide flexible, powerful and efficient means to predict performance and dependability of dynamic system properties.	Markov random processes constitute the fundamental theory underlying queueing systems in which any future state depends only on its current state. Markov chains exhibit transition behaviors that reflect a memoryless property that neither depend on the history that led to the present state, nor on the state sojourn time.
QUANTUM INFORMATION THEORY	Non-quantum network system components simultaneously reach physical limits encountered within classical space-time symmetries. Non-quantum wires cannot be thinner than a single atom; classical memories cannot have less than one electron; and multiple classical classes of algorithmic and computational complexity are intractable in worst-case polynomial time.	The quantum information state of 1-to-n qubits requires association of a complex amplitude coefficient with each superposed computational basis state. Quantum network computation proceeds through qubit representation, controllable unitary evolution, preparation of initial qubit states, and measurement of final qubit states.	Quantum Information Theory presents a profound holistic vision in which all the diverse expressions of Natural Law are found to be embodied within the Computational Constitution of the Universe, the foundation for n-partite quantum entanglement and transformation within the structureless structure of the entire spectrum of 2-to-n information states.

dynamism value available in *Prakṛiti* (fundamental qualities of intelligence), and a second that considers the silence value of *Purusha* (silently witnessing intelligence). The first perspective is dominated by the dynamic network computational processes that orchestrate the flow of information. The focus in the second perspective is the basic structural organization of Information Science and Technology. We will see that both perspectives lead to the same conclusion: Quantum Network Architecture (as is true of human physiology) is organized and expressed on the basis of the inner intelligence of Natural Law as available in Veda.

Hardware-Software Gap™

Figure 3-2 presents a generalized view of the Hardware-Software Gap™ as central to the network computational process. The Hardware-Software Gap corresponds to the structure of the Gap between the syllables in Veda and the Vedic Literature. The figure also indicates that the Hardware-Software Gap contains a lively Virtual Operand Instruction Set™ functioning as the structural and functional interface between a given software instruction set and hardware registers (primitives used in hardware design). Virtual Operands™ and the Virtual Operand Instruction Set are elaborated in this chapter within the context of Gap *Prakṛiti* qualities and are the Digital Fabric of Consciousness™.

Bi-directional, sequential expression of software instructions into hardware primitives and hardware primitives into software instructions occurs through a process of collapse *(Pradhwaṁsā-Abhāva)* onto its point value *(Atyanta-Abhāva)*. The structuring dynamics of

Figure 3-2: The Hardware-Software Gap™—
Generalized Hardware-Software Interface

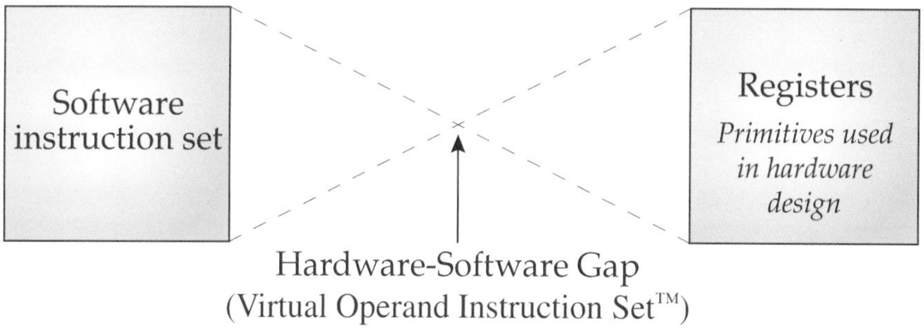

the Hardware-Software Gap *(Anyonya-Abhāva)* are elaborated from the point value, leading to the emergence of the next software instruction or hardware primitive *(Prāg-Abhāva)*. Sequential evolution of *Pradhwaṁsā-Abhāva* to *Atyanta-Abhāva, Anyonya-Abhāva,* and *Prāg-Abhāva,* is shown for the emergence of each syllable in Ṛk Veda through the gaps between two consecutive syllables in Figure 2-3 (on page 25), "Dynamics of the Gap."

At each of the individual Gaps between software instructions and hardware primitives or between specific software and memory instances, there are eight factors that determine the accuracy and completeness of collapse, silence, and re-emergence through the Gap. The integrity of these eight Gap factors is crucial to ensure precise and orderly progression of computer network information. It also ensures the quality and wholeness of the emerging network computational step on the egress side of that particular Gap. Otherwise, the software instruction or hardware primitive could be distorted and result in an inappropriate and partial experience of the signal, diminishing or preventing proper network computational flow. The eight Gap factors are as follows:

1 ***Ahaṁkār* (cosmic ego)** structures the status of the Gap as a whole in terms of its general structure, its feedback loops integral to its activation and deactivation, and its readiness to respond. *Ahaṁkār* also corresponds to the Self of the Gap—the ego quality—and to network computational self-awareness.

2 ***Buddhi* (intellect)** determines the ability of the Gap to differentiate between various possible inputs of software instruction set and hardware primitives, and it orchestrates the sorting out and appropriate discrimination between their qualities. The quality of the Hardware-Software Gap depends on its discriminating intellect. *Buddhi* also corresponds to network computational decision logic.

3 ***Manas* (mind)** enables the Gap to accommodate the passage of software instructions and hardware primitives without disturbing their integrity and structure, and it depends on the Virtual Operands present in the Gap junction. *Manas* also corresponds to network computational processing logic.

4 ***Ākāsh* (space),** the space of the Gap, is crucial for intra-Gap Virtual Operand processing. *Ākāsh* also corresponds to computer network logical topology and associations.

5 ***Vāyu* (air),** the medium of transmission within the Gap space, is also crucial and it depends on the proper exchanges of protocols and logic that maintain the liveliness of the Gap junction. *Vāyu* also corresponds to computer network protocol and logic exchange.

6 ***Agni* (fire)** is expressed as the excitability of the Gap junction and its ability to transmit electronic and optical impulses and integrate them properly. It depends on feedback-loop logic. *Agni* also corresponds to optical network components, logic, and processes.

7 ***Jal* (water)** corresponds to the structure and integrity of the Virtual Operand Instruction Set, permeates all of the components of the Hardware-Software Gap, and depends on virtual logic interoperability. *Jal* also corresponds to computer network system and component interoperability.

8 ***Pṛithivī* (earth)** represents the physical structure of all Gap junction components and their number, position, and relationships. It is crucial and it depends on a variety of factors related to previous activation sequences. *Pṛithivī* also corresponds to chip substrate and network physical topology.

Hardware-Software Gap Instances

Figure 3-3 presents specific instances of the generalized Hardware-Software Gap introduced in Figure 3-2. These include the following:

- *Compiler Gap,* between instances of a C program and an assembly language program
- *Assembler Gap,* between instances of an assembly language program and objects (machine language module and library routine)
- *Linker Gap,* between instances of machine language module or library routine, and an executable (machine language program)
- *Loader Gap,* between instances of an executable and memory

Figure 3-4 (on page 48) provides a more detailed elaboration of the Hardware-Software Gap. In this example, a routine has been written in the C programming language to compute and print the sum of the squares of integers between 0 and 100 (left side of the figure). A Compiler Gap is depicted that converts the C code to assembly language with no labeled registers, memory locations, or comments. Alternatively, and with relatively significant effort, a programmer could use opcode and instruction format tables to translate the instructions into a symbolic program.

Figure 3-4 also depicts a Compiler Gap that converts the C routine into assembly language containing labels, but no comments, which is an assembler format that is generally preferred over the former case. Names beginning with a period—`.data` and `.globl` for example—are directives that instruct the assembler how to translate a program, yet do not generate machine-level instructions. Names followed by a colon—including `str:` and `main:`—are labels that name the next memory location.

Figure 3-4 further illustrates an Assembler Gap that can generate Millions of Instructions Per Second (MIPS) computer machine language. Assemblers translate files of assembly language statements into files of binary machine instructions and binary data. The translation process within the Assembler Gap is comprised of two major steps: (1) Memory locations with labels are found to ensure that the relationship between symbolic names and addresses is known; and (2) Each assembly statement is translated by combining the numeric equivalents of opcodes, register specifiers, and labels into a legal instruction. The illustrated MIPS language output from the Assembler Gap is called an object file.

Figure 3-3: The Hardware-Software Gap™—
Compiler-Assembler-Linker-Loader Cases

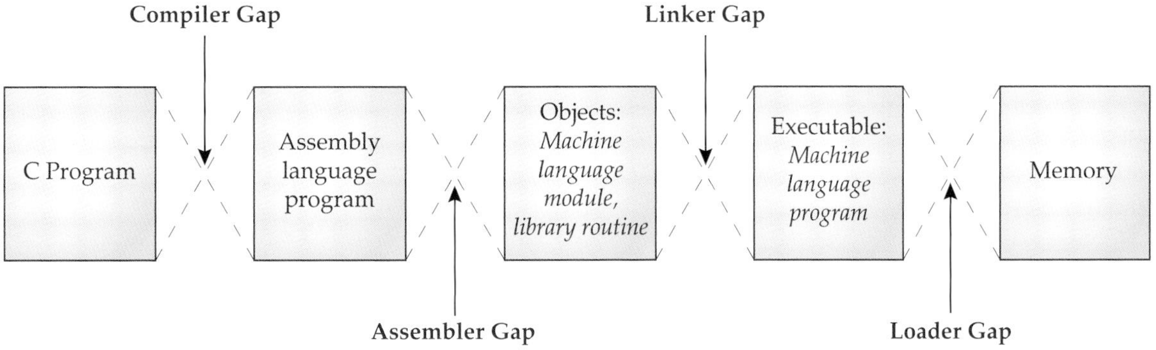

Figure 3-4: The Hardware-Software Gap™—C, Assembly Language, and Machine Language Example

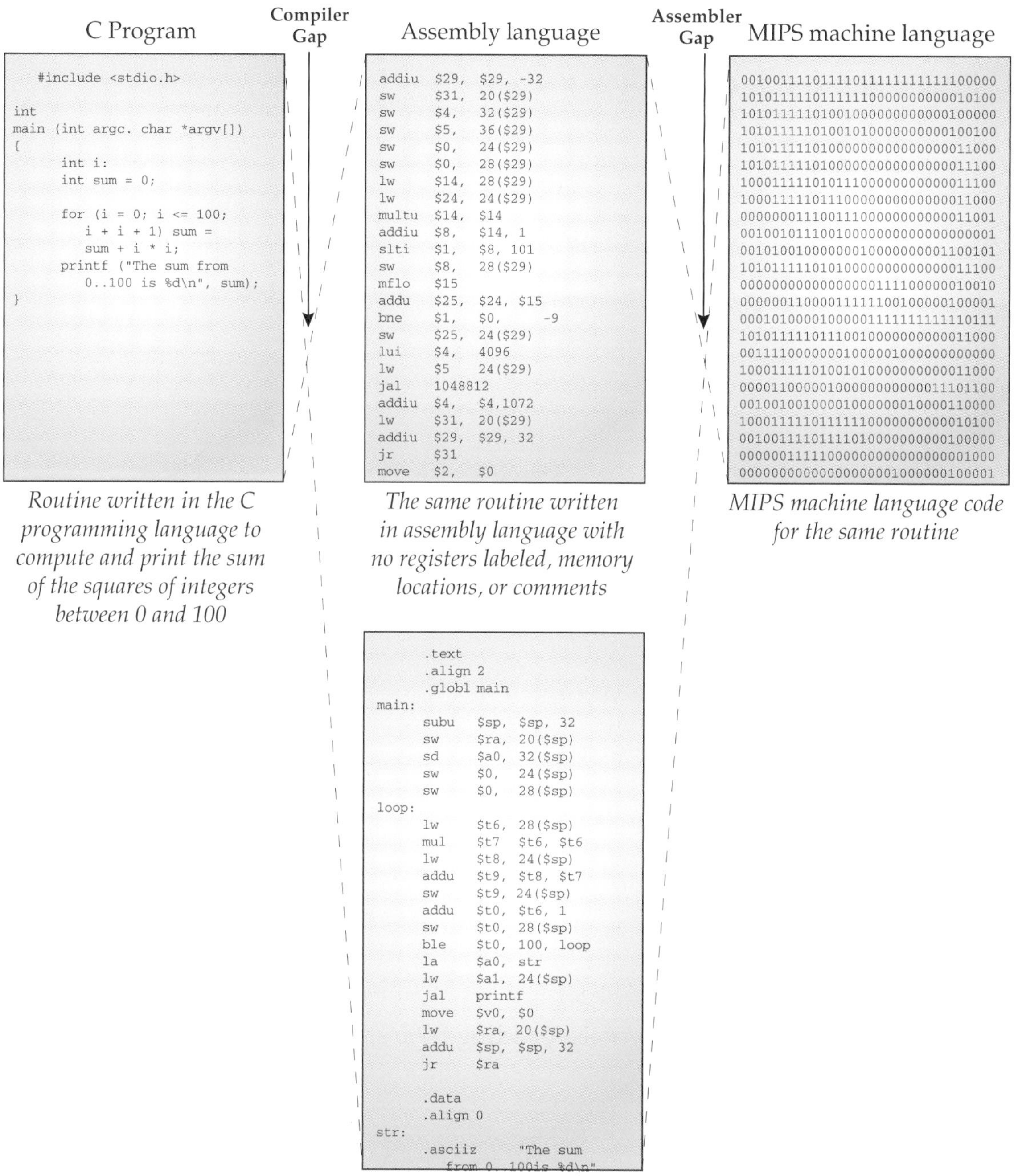
C Program
Compiler Gap
Assembly language
Assembler Gap
MIPS machine language
#include <stdio.h>
int
main (int argc. char *argv[])
{
int i:
int sum = 0;
for (i = 0; i <= 100;
i + i + 1) sum =
sum + i * i;
printf ("The sum from
0..100 is %d\n", sum);
}
addiu $29, $29, -32
sw $31, 20($29)
sw $4, 32($29)
sw $5, 36($29)
sw $0, 24($29)
sw $0, 28($29)
lw $14, 28($29)
lw $24, 24($29)
multu $14, $14
addiu $8, $14, 1
slti $1, $8, 101
sw $8, 28($29)
mflo $15
addu $25, $24, $15
bne $1, $0, -9
sw $25, 24($29)
lui $4, 4096
lw $5 24($29)
jal 1048812
addiu $4, $4,1072
lw $31, 20($29)
addiu $29, $29, 32
jr $31
move $2, $0
00100111101111011111111111100000
10101111101111110000000000010100
10101111101001000000000000100000
10101111101001010000000000100100
10101111101000000000000000011000
10101111101000000000000000011100
10001111101011100000000000011100
10001111101110000000000000011000
00000001110011100000000000011001
00100101110010000000000000000001
00101001000000010000000001100101
10101111101010000000000000011100
00000000000000000111100000010010
00000011000011111100100000100001
00010100001000001111111111110111
10101111101110010000000000011000
00111100000001000001000000000000
10001111101001010000000000011000
00001100000100000000000011101100
00100100100001000000010000110000
10001111101111110000000000010100
00100111101111010000000000100000
00000011111000000000000000001000
00000000000000000001000000100001
.text
.align 2
.globl main
main:
subu $sp, $sp, 32
sw $ra, 20($sp)
sd $a0, 32($sp)
sw $0, 24($sp)
sw $0, 28($sp)
loop:
lw $t6, 28($sp)
mul $t7 $t6, $t6
lw $t8, 24($sp)
addu $t9, $t8, $t7
sw $t9, 24($sp)
addu $t0, $t6, 1
sw $t0, 28($sp)
ble $t0, 100, loop
la $a0, str
lw $a1, 24($sp)
jal printf
move $v0, $0
lw $ra, 20($sp)
addu $sp, $sp, 32
jr $ra
.data
.align 0
str:
.asciiz "The sum
from 0..100is %d\n"

Routine written in the C programming language to compute and print the sum of the squares of integers between 0 and 100

The same routine written in assembly language with no registers labeled, memory locations, or comments

MIPS machine language code for the same routine

The same routine written in assembly language containing labels, but no comments

Assembly languages are often preferred in place of high-level languages in computers and/or network nodes when the speed or size of a program is critically important. Embedded computers and network nodes, for example, need to respond rapidly and highly predictably to external and asynchronous events, and they often prefer assemblers over compilers because the latter introduce uncertainties regarding time and cost of operations. On the other hand, assembly languages are inherently machine-specific and must be completely rewritten to run on different computer architectures. Assembly language programs are generally more code-intensive than equivalent programs written in a high-level language.

In each of these general or specific cases of the Hardware-Software Gap, the state of abstraction within the Gap—*Atyanta-Abhāva*, the state of pure wakefulness and fully awake intelligence—knows itself and integrates the qualities of *Saṁhitā* of *Ṛishi, Devatā,* and *Chhandas*. The *Atyanta-Abhāva* of the Gap is the self-referral field of all possibilities of the sequential unfoldment and evolution of network computation within both classical and quantum computer network architecture. As we discuss in Chapter 2, the ten *Maṇḍals* of Ṛk Veda are lively at a point, which is *Anyonya-Abhāva* within the *Atyanta-Abhāva* of *Sandhi,* the unmanifested field.

Analog/Digital Signaling Gap

Figure 3-5 (on page 50) presents a sampling mechanism (signaling Gap) to digitize and convert an analog voice signal, generating Analog/Digital (A/D) and Digital/Analog (D/A) conversions. The example selects a simplified three-bit (eight-level) code with 125 microsecond (μsec) sampling intervals, yielding 8000 samples per second.

Pulse Code Modulation (PCM, pioneered in the 1940s and 1950s), was the first international digital standard speech-encoding algorithm which became International Telecommunications Union Telecommunications Group (ITU, formerly CCITT) recommendation G.711 in 1972. PCM samples speech (or any analog waveform) at 125 μsec intervals, or 8000 samples per second. The volume, or amplitude, of each of these 8000 samples is measured, and the resulting value is stored as an eight-bit digital number—one of 256 possible "volumes"—then transmitted digitally. The PCM transmission rate is

Figure 3-5: Signaling Gap (Three-Bit, Eight-Level Code Example)

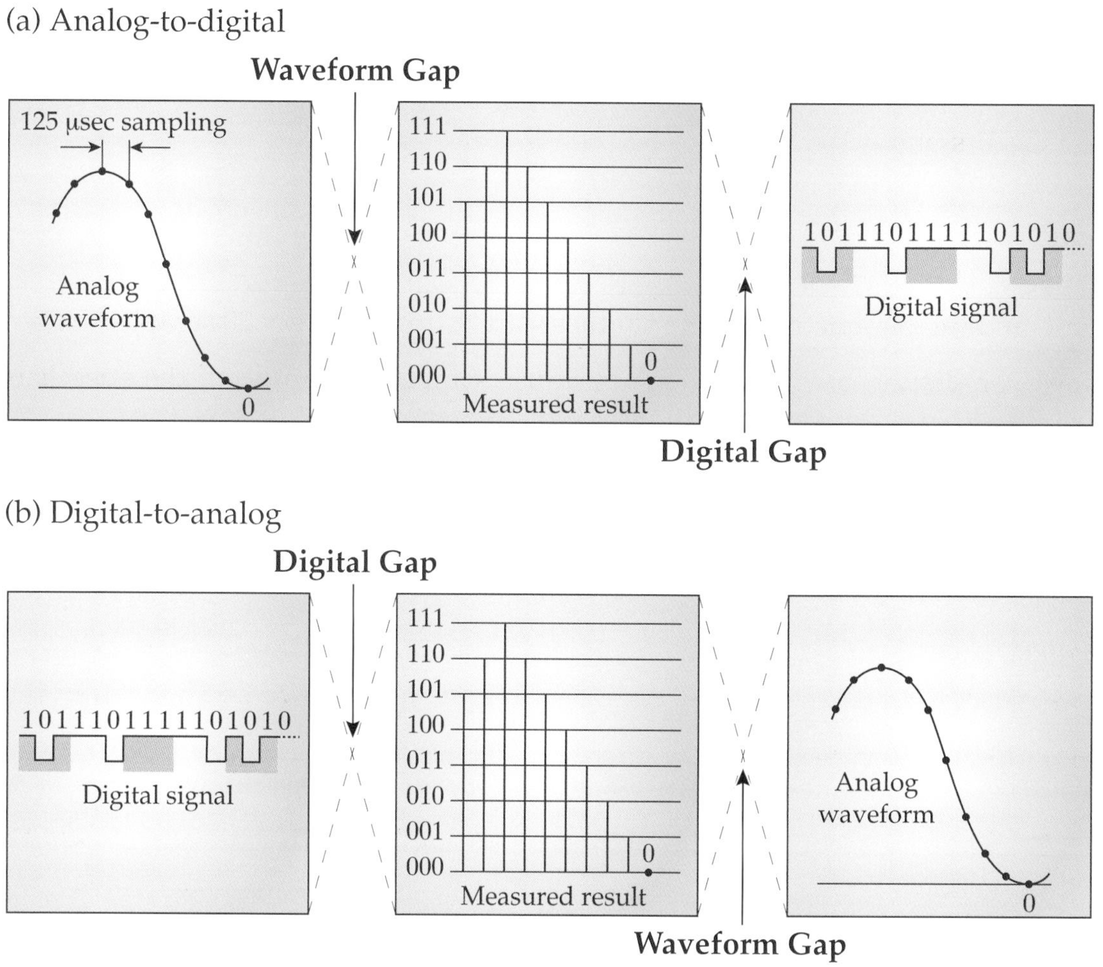

64 kilobits per second (Kbps) (calculated as 125 µsec sample intervals yielding 8000 samples per second × 8 bits per sample = 64,000 bits per second, or 64 Kbps). Refer to Appendix C ("Mathematical and Quantum Information Symbols, Notations, and Operations") for an explanation of mathematical and physics symbols, notations, and operations as they appear throughout this book, especially in Chapters 3 and 8.

The PCM basic transmission rate of 64 Kbps was much higher than common data transmission rates available at its 1972 inception, and was several hundred times higher than that of the linguistic information content of speech. As a result, several alternative bit-rate-reducing encoding algorithms were developed, driven by the requirement to maintain tonal speech quality. Speech sampling, encoding, and synthesis algorithmic developments have included the following:

- *Linear Predictive Coding (LPC),* which predicts the current sample from a linear combination of past samples using a least mean squares criterion. LPC achieves high efficiency but has poor tone quality.
- *Adaptive Differential PCM (ADPCM) algorithm,* which operates at 32 Kbps and became the G.721 standard in 1983.
- *Low Delay Code-Excited Linear Prediction (LD-CELP) algorithm,* which is the G.728 standard and has a bit rate of 16 Kbps. LD-CELP synthesizes speech using a five-sample unit, and the parameters for the synthesis are refreshed every 20 samples. In general, linear prediction computes the succeeding sample amplitude of the speech waveform as a weighted sum of the preceding sample amplitudes.
- *Conjugate Structure Vector Quantizer Code-Excited Linear Prediction (CS-CELP) algorithm,* developed by Nippon Telecommunications and Telegraph (NTT) in 1992.
- *Conjugate Structure Asynchronous Code-Excited Linear Prediction (CS-ACELP) 8 Kbps speech-encoding algorithm,* which yields speech quality equivalent to 32 Kbps ADPCM in error-free conditions.

AT&T developed T-carrier ("T" is Time-Division Multiplexing-based) trunking networks to address exponentially increasing A/D signaling and bandwidth requirements. Figure 3-6 (on page 52) summarizes the major digital hierarchies used to multiplex voice, data, and video onto network backbones. The basic unit of T-carrier is the digitized voice channel, which generates a stream of bits at the rate of 64 Kbps. The 64 Kbps digitized-voice channel is designated Digital Signal-0 (DS-0), where "0" indicates the lowest level of the T-carrier hierarchy. No carrier is involved in DS-0 because this basic signal is not multiplexed with anything else.

Maharishi's *Apaurusheya Bhāshya* Reflected in Digital Signal Hierarchies

Twenty-four DS-0 signals combine to yield a DS-1, where the "1" indicates the first level of the T-carrier hierarchy. DS-1 specifies the structure of binary 0s and 1s from input DS-0s, and T-1 specifies the transmitters, receivers, and wiring requirements to transport the DS-1 signal. DS-1 is organized into frames distinguished in time, not frequency;

Figure 3-6: Plesiochronous Digital Hierarchy

Digital Level	Channels	North America (Mbps)[a]	Europe (Mbps)	Japan (Mbps)	ISDN[b]	SDH Signal[c]
0	1	0.064	0.064	0.064	—	—
1	24	1.544	—	1.544	H-11	C-11
	30	—	2.048	—	H-12	C-12
	48	3.152	—	3.152	—	—
2	96	6.312		6.312	—	C-2
	120	—	8.448		—	—
3	480	—	34.386	32.064	H31	C-3
	672	44.736	—	—	H31	C-3
	1344	91.053	—	—	H32	C-3
	1440	—		97.726	—	—
4	1920	—	139.264		H4	C-4
	4032	274.176	—	—	—	—
	5760	—	—	397.200	—	—
5	7680	—	565.148	—	—	—

a. Mbps Megabits per second
b. ISDN Integrated Services Digital Network
c. SDH Synchronous Digital Hierarchy

therefore, T-carrier trunking is based on Time Division Multiplexing (TDM). The DS-1 frame structure is calculated as:

DS-0 = 125 microsecond (μsec) sample intervals = 8000 samples/second
× 8 bits/sample
= 64,000 bits/second, or 64 Kbps

DS-1 = 24 DS-0s × 8 bits/frame = 192 bits/frame
× 8000 frames/second = 1,536,000 bits/second = 1.536 Mbps of data
+ 1 framing/delimiter bit/DS-1 frame × 8000 frames/second
= 1,544,000 bits/second, or 1.544 Mbps

The 24 DS-0 signals in the fundamental DS-1 signal correspond to the 24 syllables *(Akshara)* of the first verse *(Richā)* of Ṛk Veda and to the 24 Gaps between these 24 *Akshara*. The 192 bits per DS-1 frame correspond to the 192 *Akshara* of *Richās* two through nine of the first hymn *(Sūkta)* of Ṛk Veda.

The first chapter *(Maṇḍala)* of Ṛk Veda arises as the second level of self-elaboration from the 192 Gaps between the 192 *Akshara* of the first *Sūkta* of Ṛk Veda. The tenth *Maṇḍala* of Ṛk Veda arises as the third level of self-elaboration of the 192 Gaps between the 192 *Sūktas* of the first *Maṇḍala* of Ṛk Veda.

Figure 3-6 summarizes three regional digital signal hierarchies for North American, European, and Japanese digital networks. Their signals are not synchronous, but are quasi-synchronous in most cases. They form the Plesiochronous Digital Hierarchy (PDH), where North American digital hierarchy is the T-carrier, European digital hierarchy is the E-carrier, and Japanese digital hierarchy is the J-carrier.

Figure 3-7 (on page 54) provides a subset of the Synchronous Optical Network (SONET) digital hierarchy. The baseline Optical Carrier (OC) level is OC-1, and the baseline electrical level is Synchronous Transport Signal-1 (STS-1). The STS-1 frame consists of 810 bytes, sampled at a 125 μsec rate (transmitted 8000 times per second, or once every 125 μsec), generating a signal rate of 51.84 Mbps (calculated as follows: 810 bytes per frame [arranged as 9 rows of 90 columns] × 8 bits per byte × 8000 frames per second = 51.84 Mbps). OC-*N* equals 51.84 Mbps × *N;* therefore, OC-192 is approximately 10 Gigabits per second (Gbps). SONET also interoperates frame synchronization timing of existing asynchronous digital signaling network standards (i.e., DS-1, E-1, and DS-3).

Digital signal hierarchies are structural and functional subsets of classical and quantum computer network architecture, which are, in turn, the major structural and functional subset of Information Science and Technology. We will see in Figures 3-10 through 3-13 how Maharishi's *Apaurusheya Bhāshya* is also perfectly reflected in Quantum Network Architecture as a whole.

Optical Wavelength and Waveband Gap

Optical wavelength-routed networks partition and greatly enhance the bandwidth-carrying efficiency of the optical spectrum using Wavelength Division Multiplexing (WDM)

Figure 3-7: SONET[a] Digital Hierarchy

Optical Level	Electrical Level	Line Rate (Mbps)[b]	Payload Rate (Mbps)	Overhead Rate (Mbps)	SDH[c] Equivalent
OC-1[d]	STS[e]-1	51.84	50.112	1.728	—
OC-3	STS-3	155.52	150.336	5.184	STM[f]-1
OC-12	STS-12	622.08	601.344	20.736	STM-4
OC-48	STS-48	2488.32	2405.376	82.944	STM-16
OC-192	STS-192	9953.28	9621.504	331.776	STM-64
OC-768	STS-768	39,813.12	38,486.016	1327.104	STM-256
OC-3072	STS-3072	159,252.48	153,944.060	5308.416	STM-1024

a. SONET Synchronous Optical Network
b. Mbps Megabits per second
c. SDH Synchronous Digital Hierarchy
d. OC Optical Carrier
e. STS Synchronous Transport Signal
f. STM Synchronous Transport Module

algorithms. The general technique is to first divide the optical spectrum into wavebands, and then to subdivide the wavebands into wavelength-specific channels (λ-channels). The assigned wavelengths of the λ-channels must be spaced sufficiently far apart to prevent overlap and interchannel cross-talk of neighboring spectra.

Optical wavelength, λ, and frequency, f, are related by $f\lambda = c$, where c is the velocity of light in the transmission medium, yielding the relation

$$\Delta f \approx -\frac{(c\Delta\lambda)}{\lambda^2} \qquad (3.1)$$

between small changes in frequency, Δf, and small changes in wavelength, $\Delta\lambda$. Therefore, correspondence exists at optical wavelength and frequency intervals of 100 gigahertz (GHz) ≅ 0.8 nanometers (nm) in the range of 1550 nm, where the majority of lightwave networks operate. The total optical bandwidth occupied by modulated laser signals is designed to be less than the Equation 3.1 frequency spacing yield in order to leave sufficient "guardbands" to accommodate imprecision and drift in laser transmitter tuning.

Figure 3-8 presents an optical wavelength conversion Gap using coherent effects based on wave-mixing. Wave-mixing has the following attributes:

- Arises from the nonlinear optical response of a medium when multiple waves are present,

- Preserves both phase and amplitude information,

- Enables simultaneous conversion of a set of multiple input wavelengths to a different set of multiple output wavelengths,

- Provides complete transparency, and

- Accommodates signals exceeding 100 Gbps.

Optical receivers can support close channel spacings (10 GHz), yet λ-channel spacings in switched multiwavelength networks are generally greater than 100 GHz and yield a full order of magnitude mismatch between the spacings required in the λ-channel layer and the optical path layer. Spacing λ-channels to 100 GHz permits individual wavelengths to

Figure 3-8: Optical Wavelength Gap

Coherent wave-mixing Gap

Input signal

λ_s

Continuous wave
λ_p (unmodulated pump signal)

Coherent wave-mixing

$\chi^{(n)}$

$f_c = (n-1)f_p - f_s$

Converted signal

λ_c

Wavelength conversion Gap

Legend

f	frequency	λ_c	converted wavelength
c	speed of light in the medium	$n = 2$	corresponds to Difference Frequency
λ_s	input signal wavelength		Generation (DFG)
λ_p	pump wavelength	$n = 3$	corresponds to Four-Wave Mixing (FWM)

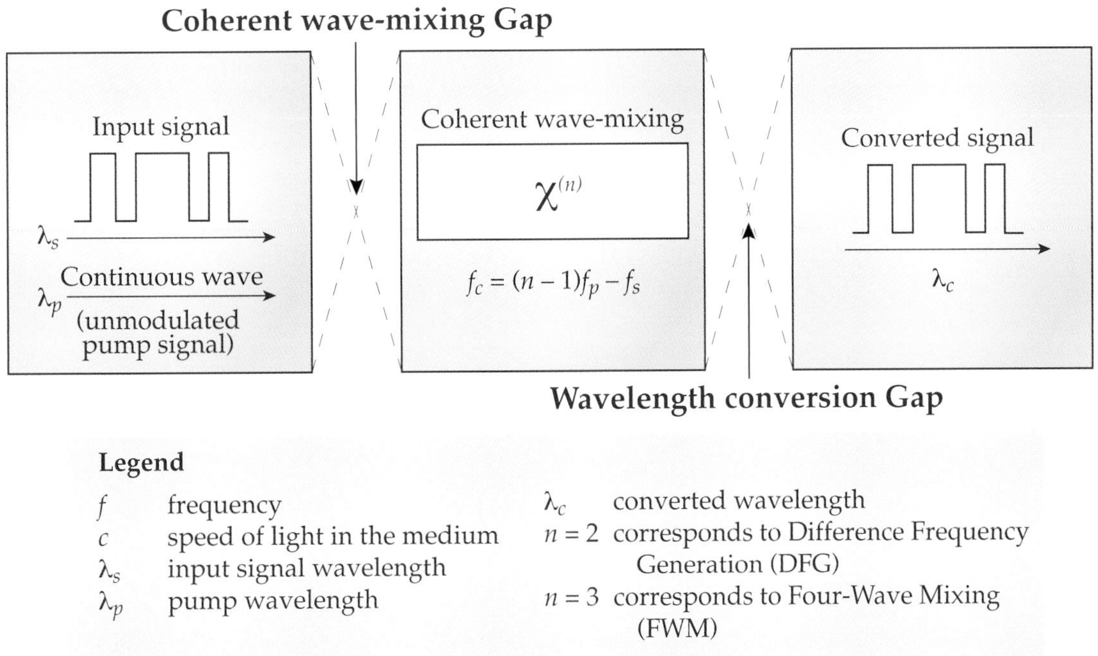

be routed independently, therein reducing channel density (and therefore throughput) by a factor of 10. Alternative solutions to the λ-channel layer/optical path layer mismatch include the following:

- Refine the optical switching node technology to generate an order of magnitude resolution improvement.
- Partition the optical spectrum into two tiers where a waveband is defined as the smallest segment of the spectrum that is resolvable in the node optical path, rather than the λ-channel, which is the smallest unit resolvable in the optical access node by a tunable receiver.

Figure 3-9 depicts an optical waveband-routed Gap that generates the two-tier, waveband-routed alternative described above. In this example, 100 GHz spectral-width optical wavebands are placed at intervals of 200 GHz, separated by 100 GHz guardbands. The Gap logic generates three possible outputs from this input:

1. All λ-channels share a single copy of the resulting network topology.
2. A multiwavelength network with λ-channels on *m* wavelengths, λ1, λ2,..., λ*m,* is spaced sufficiently far apart to be switched independently (wavelength-routed network) and contains *m* copies of one network, each with the same physical topology.
3. A two-tiered partitioning is selected in which there are as many copies of the network as there are wavebands, with multiple λ-channels sharing each copy of the network.

The Gap output expresses the third alternative as a waveband-routed multi-tier topology, the highest throughput compromise between exclusive and no wavelength switching/routing.

Figure 3-9: Optical Waveband Gap

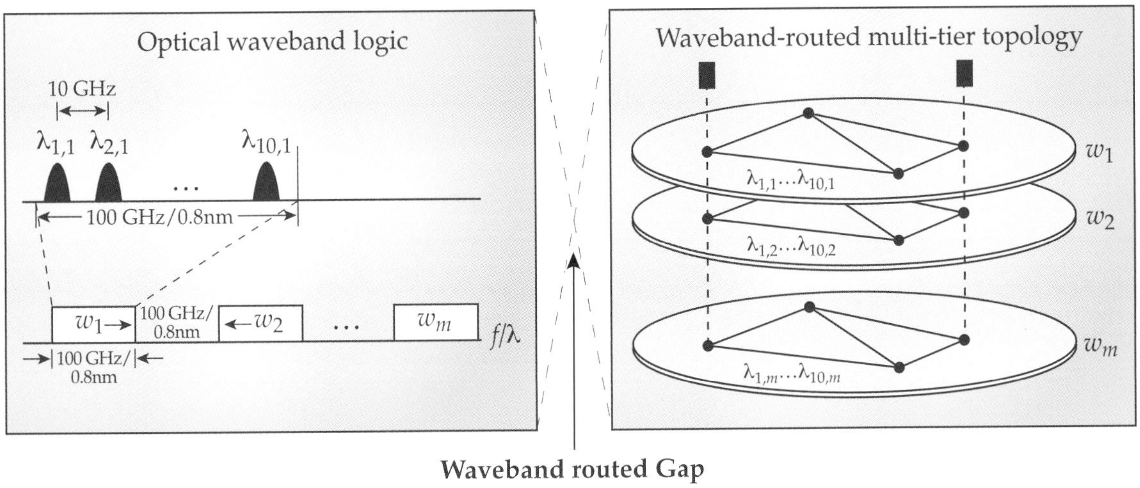

Maharishi's *Apaurusheya Bhāshya* Reflected in Quantum Network Architecture

Network computation and transmission lies at the heart of Information Science and Technology and is orchestrated by the rules (algorithms), structure (physical topology), and function (logical topology) of quantum and classical computer network architecture. Figures 3-10 through 3-13 elaborate the one-to-one structural and functional correspondence between Ṛk Veda *Saṁhitā* and Quantum Network Architecture. We find in Figure 2-2 (on pages 22 and 23), "Maharishi's Commentary on Ṛk Veda Saṁhitā *(Apaurusheya Bhāshya)*," that the first syllable of Ṛk Veda, अक (Ak), is elaborated in the first *Pāda* (phrase of eight syllables with *Ṛishi* quality).

Figure 3-10 (on page 58) relates Quantum Network Architecture with the structure of Ṛk Veda from the quantum network perspective of dynamism, *Prakṛiti*. Network ingress/input is associated with *Ṛishi* (observer), network processing is associated with *Devatā* (process of observation), and network egress/output is associated with *Chhandas* (object of observation). Each of the network computational steps of ingress/input, processing, and egress/output contains a standard group of eight quantum bits (qubits), for a total of 24 qubits (3 steps × 8 qubits = 24 qubits). The first ingress/input qubit corresponds to

Figure 3-10: Holistic Functioning of the Cosmic Computer and Cosmic Switchboard—First Three *Richās* of Ṛk Veda—Quantum Computer Network Case

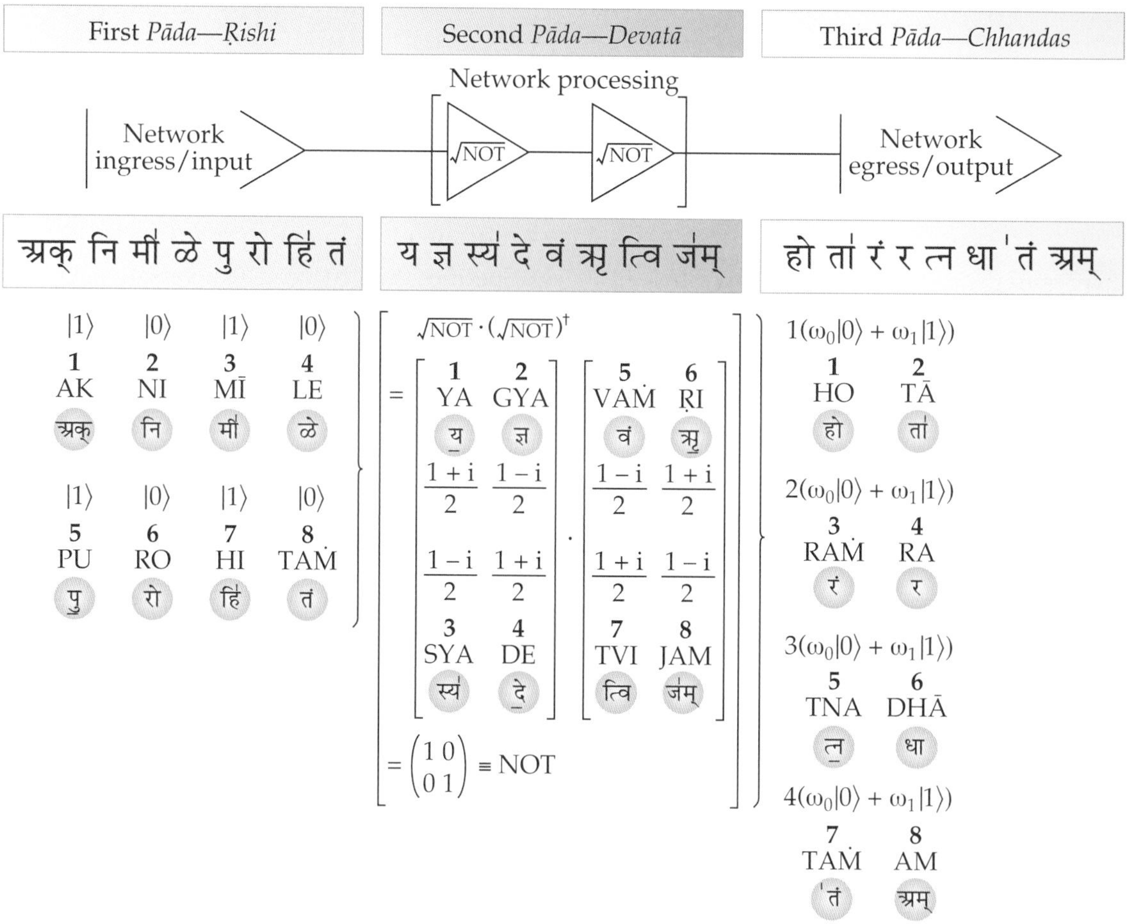

the first syllable of Ṛk Veda, अक (Ak), and the 24 qubits correspond to the first three *Richās* of Ṛk Veda.

There are eight standard classical and quantum computer network architectural interfaces and functional layers corresponding to the qualities of the eight Gap *Prakṛiti* factors introduced earlier. These eight Gap *Prakṛitis,* with their variations and interactions, determine the nature and precision of computer network ingress/input *(Ṛishi),* processing *(Devatā),* and egress/output *(Chhandas).* Figure 3-11 (beginning on page 59) presents the one-to-one correspondence of the eight Gap *Prakṛiti* factors and the eight computer network interfaces/layers.

The eight standard computer network architectural interfaces and functional layers (as specified by International Organization for Standardization–Open Systems Interconnection [ISO-OSI]) also directly correspond to *Ṛichās* two through nine of the first *Maṇḍala* of Ṛk Veda, as shown in Figure 3-12 (on page 61).

Figure 3-11: Direct Correspondence of the Eight Gap *Prakṛitis* to Eight Computer Network Architectural Interfaces and Layers

Gap *Prakṛiti* Qualities	Computer Network Interface/Layer Functions (OSI)
***Ahaṁkār*—Cosmic Ego** • Expresses the status of the Gap as a whole in terms of its general structure, feedback loops integral to its activation, deactivation, and readiness to respond. • Embodies the Self of the Gap—the ego quality. • Corresponds to network computational self-awareness and logical peer-level relationships between communicating application processes.	**Application Programming Interface (API)** • Specifies the structured (conversational, transaction, and dialog) programming interface between end-user application processes (i.e., application program, relational database, file system, storage system, Web client, Web server, device, and operator) and the Application Layer. • Presents end-user application processes with logical, peer-level exchange views.
***Buddhi*—Intellect** • Orchestrates Gap discrimination and differentiation between all possible software instruction and hardware primitive inputs. • Sorts and discriminates between software instruction set and hardware primitive qualities. • Embodies the Gap intellect. • Corresponds to network computational decision logic.	**Application Layer** • Contains service elements to provide application processes (i.e., application program, relational database, file system, storage system, Web client, Web server, device, or operator) interface into network information services (i.e., distributed transaction processing, data exchange, electronic mail, file transfer, directory services, system management, network clock synchronization, metadirectory, virtual file, virtual terminal, and job management). • Concerned with data semantics.
***Manas*—Mind** • Facilitates Gap passage of software instructions and hardware primitives while maintaining their integrity through Virtual Operands™ present in the Gap junction. • Embodies the mind of the Gap. • Corresponds to network computational processing logic.	**Presentation Layer** • Presents and describes data structures to end users in machine-independent formats. • Codes/formats data from sender internal formats into a common transfer format and decodes to the required receiver representation. • Identifies and negotiates communications transfer syntax.
Ākāsh—Space • Provides the precise Gap space required for intra-Gap *(Pradhwaṁsā-Abhāva, Atyanta-Abhāva, Anyonya-Abhāva, Prāg-Abhāva)* Virtual Operand processing. • Corresponds to network computational logical topology and associations.	**Session Layer** • Enables application process dialogs. • Binds/unbinds communications. • Exchanges normal and expedited data flows between end users (i.e., unicast, multicast, simulcast, alternate transmission, checkpoint procedures, and data flow resynchronization).

Figure 3-11 (continued): Direct Correspondence of the Eight Gap *Prakṛitis* to Eight Computer Network Architectural Interfaces and Layers

Gap *Prakṛiti* Qualities	Computer Network Interface/Layer Functions (OSI)
***Vāyu*—Air** • Embodies the Gap transmission medium within the Gap *Ākāsh* (space). • Corresponds to network protocol and logic exchange.	**Transport Layer** • Specifies the logical interface between remote (non-link-attached) Data Terminal Equipment (DTE). • Provides end-to-end information interchange and control. • Orchestrates establishment, data transfer, and termination of connections between Session Layer entities. • Isolates end-user application processes from physical and functional network components.
***Agni*—Fire** • Provides the Gap feedback logic necessary to maintain the excitability of the Gap junction and its ability to properly transmit and integrate electronic and optical impulses. • Corresponds to optical and electronic network components, as well as to AgniWall™ (firewall) rules, logic, and processes.	**Network Layer** • Selects network switching, routing, and Internetworking services. • Defines datagram-based security access control. • Segments and blocks network messages. • Provides error detection, recovery, and notification. • Specifies the DTE network interface.
***Jal*—Water** • Permeates the Gap Virtual Operand instruction set and constitutes intra-Gap linkage. • Corresponds to network component direct connection and interoperability.	**Data Link Layer** • Initializes data links between adjacent network nodes. • Transfers data across wide-area, metropolitan-area, and campus links. • Delimits the flow of bits from the Physical Layer, provides DTE flow control, and detects/corrects link transmission errors. • Disconnects data links between adjacent network nodes.
***Pṛithivī*—Earth** • Structures the physical Gap junction components: their number, position, and interrelationships. These in turn, depend on a variety of factors related to previous Gap activation sequences. • Corresponds to chip substrate and network physical topology.	**Physical Layer** • Activates, maintains, and deactivates physical interfaces (optical, opto-electronic, and electronic) and circuits (terrestrial and celestial) between DTE and Data Circuit-terminating Equipment (DCE). • Provides local and remote network clock signaling.

Figure 3-12: Eight Computer Network Architectural Interfaces and Layers Correspond to *Ṛichās* Two Through Nine of the First *Maṇḍala* of Ṛk Veda

In *Ṛichās* two through nine of the first *Maṇḍala* of Ṛk Veda, the 24 syllables of each *Ṛichā* are represented by a default 24 qubits (quantum)/bits (classical) for each of eight quantum or classical computer network architectural layers and interfaces (calculated as 8 qubits/bits for network ingress/input *[Ṛishi]* + 8 qubits/bits for network processing *[Devatā]* + 8 qubits/bits for network egress/output *[Chhandas]* = 24 qubits/bits for each layer).

Network Ingress/Input *Ṛishi*	Network Processing *Devatā*	Network Egress/Output* *Chhandas*	
2nd *Ṛichā* — **Local/remote program invocation**	**API**	**Data request/reply**	= 24 qubits/bits
3rd *Ṛichā* — **Data**	**Application**	**Application Header (AH) + data**	= 24 qubits/bits
4th *Ṛichā* — **Data**	**Presentation**	**Presentation Header (PH) + data**	= 24 qubits/bits
5th *Ṛichā* — **Data**	**Session**	**Session Header (SH) + data**	= 24 qubits/bits
6th *Ṛichā* — **Data**	**Transport**	**Transport Header (TH) + data**	= 24 qubits/bits
7th *Ṛichā* — **Data**	**Network**	**Network Header (NH) + data**	= 24 qubits/bits
8th *Ṛichā* — **Data**	**Data Link**	**Data Link Header (DLH) + data + Data Link Trailer (DLT)**	= 24 qubits/bits
9th *Ṛichā* — **Data**	**Physical**	**Bit stream**	= 24 qubits/bits
			= 192 qubits/bits

2nd *Ṛichā*: **Application Program Interface (API)** (*Ṛishi* is local/remote program invocation; *Devatā* is processing; *Chhandas* is local/ remote data request/reply)

3rd *Ṛichā*: **Application Layer** (*Ṛishi* is the local/remote data request/reply output from the API *Chhandas* as data; *Devatā* is Application Layer Interface processing; *Chhandas* is a resultant AH appended to data)

4th *Ṛichā*: **Presentation Layer** (*Ṛishi* is the AH appended to data output from the Application Layer *Chhandas* as data; *Devatā* is Presentation Layer Interface processing; *Chhandas* is a resultant PH appended to data)

5th *Ṛichā*: **Session Layer** (*Ṛishi* is the PH appended to data output from the Presentation Layer *Chhandas* as data; *Devatā* is Session Layer Interface processing; *Chhandas* is a resultant SH appended to data)

6th *Ṛichā*: **Transport Layer** (*Ṛishi* is the SH appended to data output from the Session Layer *Chhandas* as data; *Devatā* is Transport Layer Interface processing; *Chhandas* is a resultant TH appended to data)

7th *Ṛichā*: **Network Layer** (*Ṛishi* is the TH appended to data output from the Transport Layer *Chhandas* as data; *Devatā* is Network Layer Interface processing; *Chhandas* is a resultant NH appended to data)

8th *Ṛichā*: **Data Link Layer** (*Ṛishi* is the NH appended to data output from the Network Layer *Chhandas* as data; *Devatā* is Data Link Layer Interface processing; *Chhandas* is data encapsulated within a resultant DLH and DLT)

9th *Ṛichā*: **Physical Layer** (*Ṛishi* is the data encapsulated within the DLH and DLT output from the Data Link Layer *Chhandas* as data; *Devatā* is Physical Layer Interface processing; *Chhandas* is a qubit/bit stream that propagates over local or wide area terrestrial or celestial media)

*Represented in qubit/bit-reversed order

MAHARISHI'S *APAURUSHEYA BHĀSHYA* REFL[...]

	First *Pāda*—*Ṛishi*									
	Network Ingress/Input									

24 syllables of the 1st *Ṛichā* of the 1st *Maṇḍala* of Ṛk Veda	क्र	नि	मीं	ले	पु	रो	हिं	तं	य	ज्ञ
24 qubits/bits (3 qubytes/bytes) corresponding to the 24 syllables of the 1st *Ṛichā* of Ṛk Veda	$|1\rangle$	$|0\rangle$	$|1\rangle$	$|0\rangle$	$|1\rangle$	$|0\rangle$	$|1\rangle$	$|0\rangle$	$\frac{1+i}{2}$	$\frac{1-i}{2}$
Sanskrit transliteration of the 1st *Ṛichā* of Ṛk Veda	A	NI	MĪ	LE	PU	RO	HI	TAṀ	YA	GYA

The 8 factors (*Prakṛiti*) in the 24 Gaps between the 24 qubits/bits present 8 × 24 = 192 factors of classical and Quantum Network Architecture, corresponding to the 192 syllables of *Ṛichās* 2–9 of the 1st *Sūkta* of Ṛk Veda

K̄ — Gap 2 — Gap 3 — Gap 4 — Gap 5 — Gap 6 — Gap 7 — Gap 8 — Gap 9 — Gap 10 — Gap 11

The 8 *Prakṛiti* are transparently encoded as:

	Ahaṁkār	Buddhi	Manas	Ākāsh	Vāyu	Agni	Jal	Pṛithivi	Ahaṁkār	Buddhi

In *Ṛichās* 2–9 of the 1st *Maṇḍala* of Ṛk Veda the 24 syllables of each *Ṛichā* are represented by a default 24 qubits/bits for each of 8 computer network architectural layers and interfaces (See also Figures 3-11 and 3-12):

2nd *Ṛichā* ▷	**API** ▷	API II_0	API II_1	API II_2	API II_3	API II_4	API II_5	API II_6	API II_7	API P_0	API P_1
3rd *Ṛichā* ▷	**Application** ▷	ALI II_0	ALI II_1	ALI II_2	ALI II_3	ALI II_4	ALI II_5	ALI II_6	ALI II_7	ALI P_0	ALI P_1
4th *Ṛichā* ▷	**Presentation** ▷	PLI II_0	PLI II_1	PLI II_2	PLI II_3	PLI II_4	PLI II_5	PLI II_6	PLI II_7	PLI P_0	PLI P_1
5th *Ṛichā* ▷	**Session** ▷	SLI II_0	SLI II_1	SLI II_2	SLI II_3	SLI II_4	SLI II_5	SLI II_6	SLI II_7	SLI P_0	SLI P_1
6th *Ṛichā* ▷	**Transport** ▷	TLI II_0	TLI II_1	TLI II_2	TLI II_3	TLI II_4	TLI II_5	TLI II_6	TLI II_7	TLI P_0	TLI P_1
7th *Ṛichā* ▷	**Network** ▷	NLI II_0	NLI II_1	NLI II_2	NLI II_3	NLI II_4	NLI II_5	NLI II_6	NLI II_7	NLI P_0	NLI P_1
8th *Ṛichā* ▷	**Data Link** ▷	DLLI II_0	DLLI II_1	DLLI II_2	DLLI II_3	DLLI II_4	DLLI II_5	DLLI II_6	DLLI II_7	DLLI P_0	DLLI P_1
9th *Ṛichā* ▷	**Physical** ▷	PhLI II_0	PhLI II_1	PhLI II_2	PhLI II_3	PhLI II_4	PhLI II_5	PhLI II_6	PhLI II_7	PhLI P_0	PhLI P_1

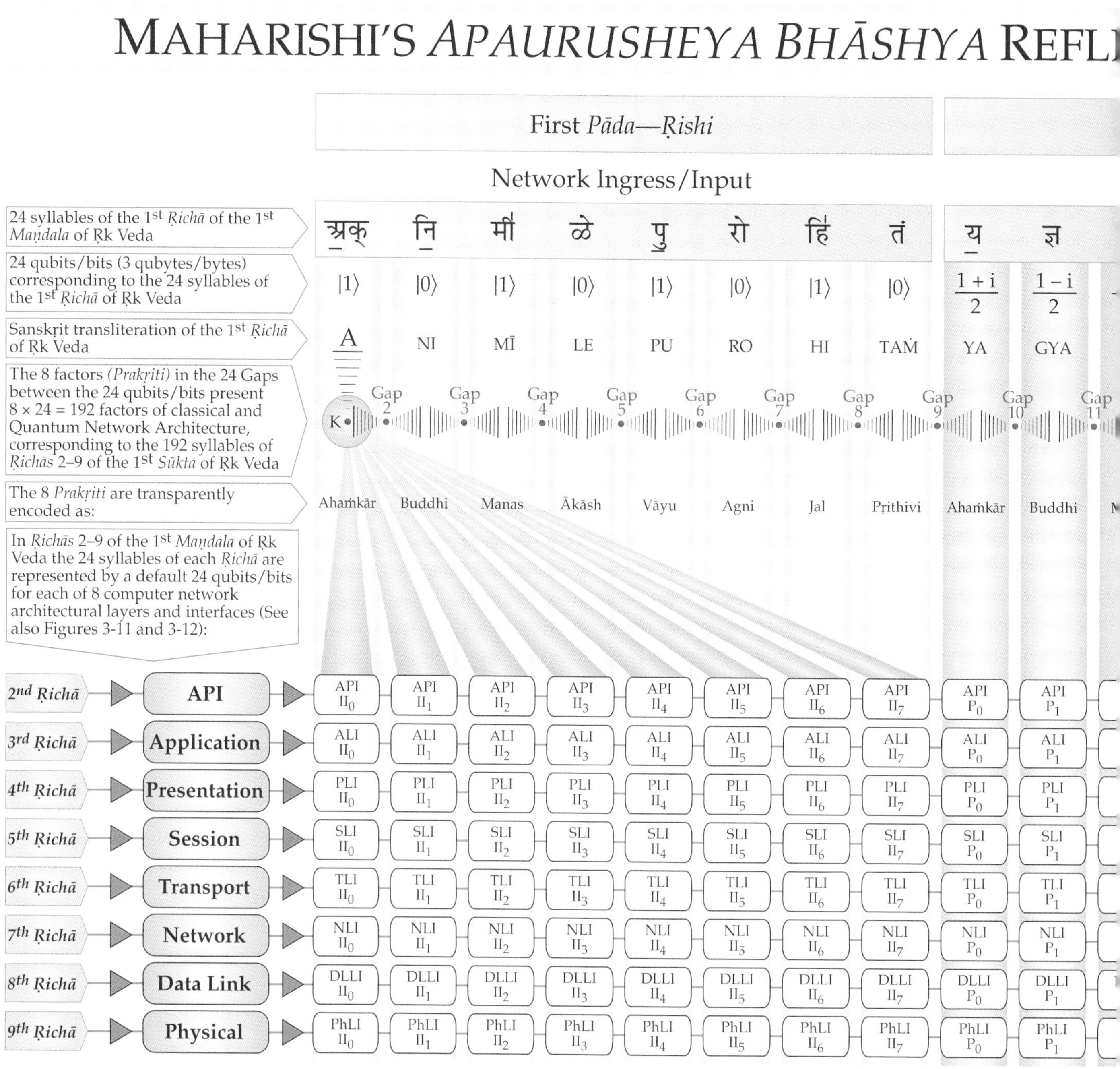

Figure 3-13: Maharishi's *Apaurusheya Bhāshya* Reflected in Quantum Network Architecture

This figure provides an overall picture of the structure and sequential unfoldment of Ṛk Veda within classical and Quantum Network Architecture. The Sanskrit letters in the boxes on the top line of the chart are the 24 syllables *(Akshara)* of the first *Ṛichā* of Ṛk Veda. In the first step, the 24 qubits/ bits of the ingress/processing/egress *(Ṛishi/Devatā/Chhandas)* components of a network node (i.e., server, host, client, switch, router) and/or the 24 qubits/bits of the input/processing/output *(Ṛishi/Devatā/Chhandas)* of a source or destination end system, correspond to these 24 syllables of the first *Ṛichā* of the first *Maṇḍala* of Ṛk Veda.

In the second step, at each of the individual Gaps between the 24-qubit/ bit default sequential elaboration of network node and/or end system *Ṛishi/Devatā/Chhandas,* eight factors *(Prakṛiti)* determine the accuracy and completeness of transmission. For computer network information, or a signal, to proceed in a precise and orderly way, the integrity of the eight factors of the Gap is crucial. Otherwise, the message could be distorted and result in an inappropriate and partial experience of the data. The eight

factors *(Prakṛiti)* in the 24 Gaps between the default 24 qubits/bits (3 qubytes/ bytes) sequentially elaborate networked application input/processing/ output at each of the eight interfaces/layers of the reference classical and Quantum Network Architecture present 8 × 24 = 192 factors of network functioning, and correspond to the 192 syllables of *Ṛichās* 2–9 of the first *Sūkta* of Ṛk Veda. The 8 *Prakṛiti* follow:

- **Pṛithivī** (Earth)—physical topology, chip substrate
- **Jal** (Water)—system and component interoperability
- **Agni** (Fire)—optical network components, logic, processes
- **Vāyu** (Air)—protocol and logic exchange
- **Akāsh** (Space)—logical topology and associations
- **Manas** (Mind)—processing logic
- **Buddhi** (Intellect)—decision logic
- **Ahaṁkār** (Ego)—network self-awareness

Headers plus data associated with the 8 interfaces/layers of classical and Quantum Network Architecture emerge (on the *Chhandas* or egress/output component) as a result of processing at the Hardware-Software Gap™, just as the *Akshara, Shabdas, Ṛichās, Pādas, Sūktas,* and *Maṇḍals* of Ṛk Veda sequentially emerge from the Gaps.

...ED IN QUANTUM NETWORK ARCHITECTURE

...nd *Pāda*—*Devatā*					Third *Pāda*—*Chhandas*							
...work Processing					Network Egress/Output							
दे	वं	ऋ	त्वि	जम्	हो	तां	रं	र	त्	धा	'तं	ञम्
$\frac{1+i}{2}$	$\frac{1-i}{2}$	$\frac{1+i}{2}$	$\frac{1+i}{2}$	$\frac{1-i}{2}$	$\omega_0|0\rangle$	$\omega_1|1\rangle$	$\omega_0|0\rangle$	$\omega_1|1\rangle$	$\omega_0|0\rangle$	$\omega_1|1\rangle$	$\omega_0|0\rangle$	$\omega_1|1\rangle$
DE	VAṀ	ṚI	TVI	JAM	HO	TĀ	RAṀ	RA	TNA	DHĀ	TAṀ	AM

EMERGING *MAṆDALS*

Gap 13, Gap 14, Gap 15, Gap 16, Gap 17, Gap 18, Gap 19, Gap 20, Gap 21, Gap 22, Gap 23, Gap 24 — 2ND

Ākāsh	Vāyu	Agni	Jal	Pṛithivi	Ahaṁkār	Buddhi	Manas	Ākāsh	Vāyu	Agni	Jal	Pṛithivi

API P$_3$	API P$_4$	API P$_5$	API P$_6$	API P$_7$	API EO$_0$	API EO$_1$	API EO$_2$	API EO$_3$	API EO$_4$	API EO$_5$	API EO$_6$	API EO$_7$	3RD
ALI P$_3$	ALI P$_4$	ALI P$_5$	ALI P$_6$	ALI P$_7$	AH EO$_0$	AH EO$_1$	AH EO$_2$	AH EO$_3$	AH EO$_4$	AH EO$_5$	AH EO$_6$	AH EO$_7$	4TH
PLI P$_3$	PLI P$_4$	PLI P$_5$	PLI P$_6$	PLI P$_7$	PH EO$_0$	PH EO$_1$	PH EO$_2$	PH EO$_3$	PH EO$_4$	PH EO$_5$	PH EO$_6$	PH EO$_7$	5TH
SLI P$_3$	SLI P$_4$	SLI P$_5$	SLI P$_6$	SLI P$_7$	SH EO$_0$	SH EO$_1$	SH EO$_2$	SH EO$_3$	SH EO$_4$	SH EO$_5$	SH EO$_6$	SH EO$_7$	6TH
TLI P$_3$	TLI P$_4$	TLI P$_5$	TLI P$_6$	TLI P$_7$	TH EO$_0$	TH EO$_1$	TH EO$_2$	TH EO$_3$	TH EO$_4$	TH EO$_5$	TH EO$_6$	TH EO$_7$	7TH
NLI P$_3$	NLI P$_4$	NLI P$_5$	NLI P$_6$	NLI P$_7$	NH EO$_0$	NH EO$_1$	NH EO$_2$	NH EO$_3$	NH EO$_4$	NH EO$_5$	NH EO$_6$	NH EO$_7$	8TH
DLLI P$_3$	DLLI P$_4$	DLLI P$_5$	DLLI P$_6$	DLLI P$_7$	DLH-T EO$_0$	DLH-T EO$_1$	DLH-T EO$_2$	DLH-T EO$_3$	DLH-T EO$_4$	DLH-T EO$_5$	DLH-T EO$_6$	DLH-T EO$_7$	9TH
PhLI P$_3$	PhLI P$_4$	PhLI P$_5$	PhLI P$_6$	PhLI P$_7$	BIT/QUBIT EO$_0$	BIT/QUBIT EO$_1$	BIT/QUBIT EO$_2$	BIT/QUBIT EO$_3$	BIT/QUBIT EO$_4$	BIT/QUBIT EO$_5$	BIT/QUBIT EO$_6$	BIT/QUBIT EO$_7$	

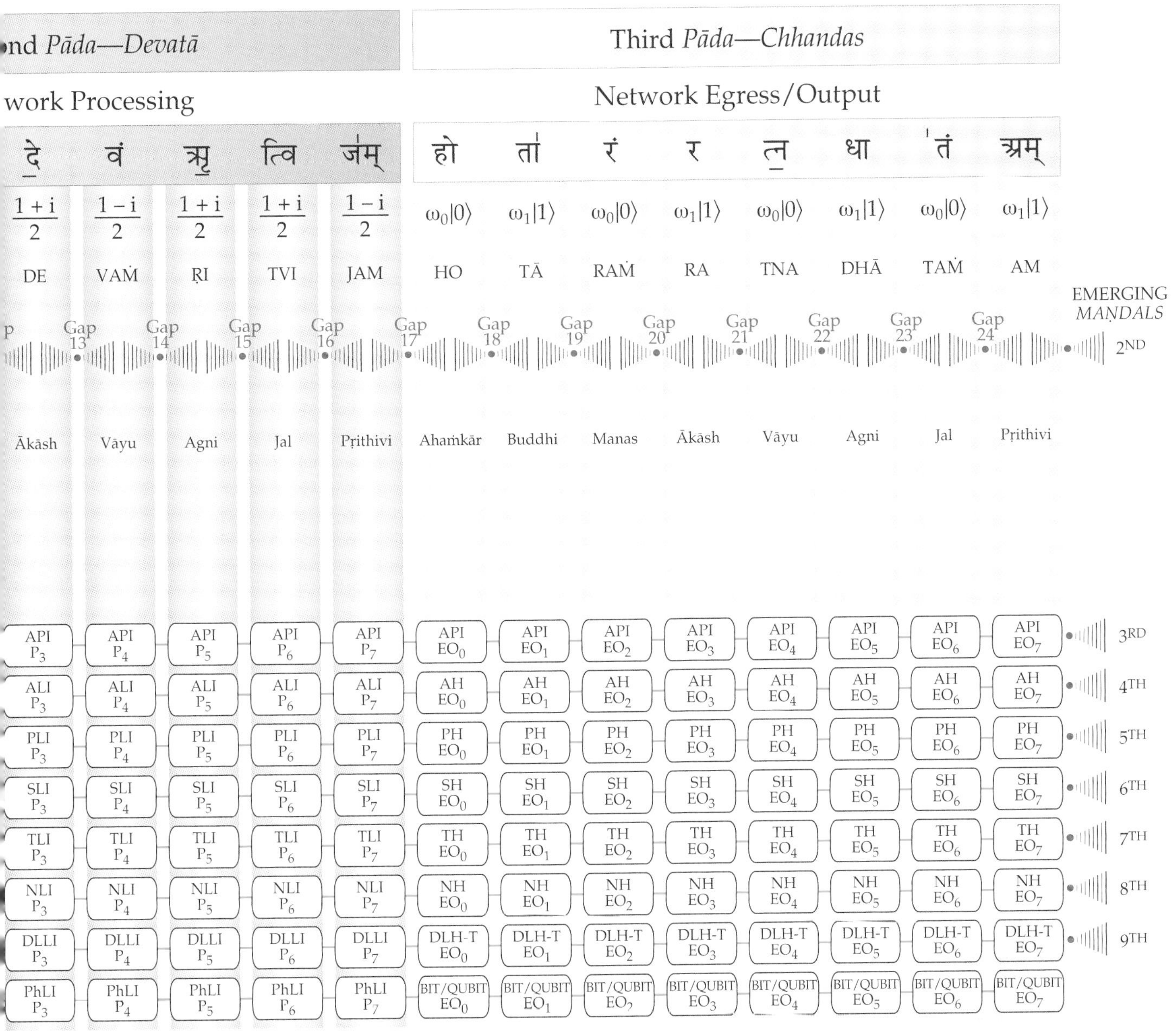

The 2nd *Maṇdala* emerges from the Gap between the end of the 1st *Richā* and the beginning of the 2nd *Richā* of the 1st *Maṇdala* of Ṛk Veda.

The 3rd *Maṇdala* emerges from the Gap between the 2nd and 3rd *Richās* of the 1st *Maṇdala* of Ṛk Veda.

The 4th *Maṇdala* emerges from the Gap between the 3rd and 4th *Richās* of the 1st *Maṇdala* of Ṛk Veda.

The 5th *Maṇdala* emerges from the Gap between the 4th and 5th *Richās* of the 1st *Maṇdala* of Ṛk Veda.

The 6th *Maṇdala* emerges from the Gap between the 5th and 6th *Richās* of the 1st *Maṇdala* of Ṛk Veda.

The 7th *Maṇdala* emerges from the Gap between the 6th and 7th *Richās* of the 1st *Maṇdala* of Ṛk Veda.

The 8th *Maṇdala* emerges from the Gap between the 7th and 8th *Richās* of the 1st *Maṇdala* of Ṛk Veda.

The 9th *Maṇdala* emerges from the Gap between the 8th and 9th *Richās* of the 1st *Maṇdala* of Ṛk Veda.

The 1st *Maṇdala* arises as the 2nd level of self-elaboration from the 192 Gaps between the 192 *Akshara* (syllables) of the 1st *Maṇdala* of Ṛk Veda.

The 10th *Maṇdala* emerges as the 3rd level of self-elaboration of the 192 *Sandhi* between the 192 *Sūktas* (including the AVYAKTA SUKTA, 97th *Sūkta*) of the 1st *Maṇdala* of Ṛk Veda.

• The balance of the complete Ṛk Veda (*Maṇdals* 2–9) emerges as the 4th level of self-elaboration of the Gaps between all the 9 *Richās* of the 1st *Sūkta*.

Legend

qubit	Quantum bit
qubyte	Quantum byte
API	Application Programming Interface
II	Ingress/Input
P	Processing
EO	Egress/Output
ALI	Application Layer Interface
AH	Application Header
PLI	Presentation Layer Interface
PH	Presentation Header
SLI	Session Layer Interface
SH	Session Header
TLI	Transport Layer Interface
TH	Transport Header
NLI	Network Layer Interface
NH	Network Header
DLLI	Data Link Layer Interface
DLH	Data Link Header
DLT	Data Link Trailer
PhLI	Physical Layer Interface

$|0\rangle$ or $|1\rangle$ The notation '$|\ \rangle$' is called the Dirac notation and is the standard state notation in quantum mechanics. One major difference between classical bits and qubits is that a qubit can be in a state other than $|0\rangle$ or $|1\rangle$. It is also possible to form linear combinations of qubit states called superpositions.

ω_0 or ω_1 ($|\omega\rangle$) State vector

On the basis of the foregoing analysis, Figure 3-13 (on pages 62–63) provides an overall picture of the structure and sequential unfoldment of Ṛk Veda within Quantum Network Architecture:

- Twenty-four qubits or 24 classical bits correspond to the 24 syllables of the first *Ṛichā* of Ṛk Veda.
- From the 24 *Sandhi* (Gaps) between the 24 qubits/bits in the reference Quantum Network Architecture, eight interfaces and functional layers emerge, corresponding to the 192 syllables (8 × 24 = 192) of *Ṛichās* two through nine of the first *Sūkta* of Ṛk Veda.
- The eight basic Gap *Prakṛitis* correspond to *Maṇḍals* two through nine of Ṛk Veda.
- The first *Maṇḍala* of Ṛk Veda arises as the second level of self-elaboration from the Gaps between the 192 syllables of the first *Sūkta* of Ṛk Veda.
- The tenth *Maṇḍala* of Ṛk Veda emerges as the third level of self-elaboration of the 192 Gaps between the 192 *Sūktas* of the first *Maṇḍala* of Ṛk Veda.
- Gaps between all the nine *Ṛichās* of the first *Sūkta* emerge as the fourth level of self-elaboration within *Maṇḍals* two through nine of Ṛk Veda. Now the total Ṛk Veda with all 10 of its *Maṇḍals* has unfolded.

We now see from three distinct angles how the study of Information Science and Technology is the study of Maharishi's Vedic Science and Technology:

1 Theoretical and applied aspects of Information Science and Technology have been presented as direct expressions of the Unified Field. The Unified Field contains within itself the whole field of Veda and the Vedic Literature (refer to Figure 1-1 on pages 4–6).

2 All the major theories of Information Science and Technology—ranging from Classical to Quantum Information Theory—are directly related (without reference to the Unified Field) to the dynamics of consciousness, as displayed in one key verse of Ṛk Veda *(Ṛk Veda, 1.164.39)* (refer to Figure 3-1 on pages 41–43).

3 Computer network architecture (quantum and classical)—the major structural and functional subset of Information Science and Technology—expresses a one-to-one correspondence with Ṛk Veda, the unified *Saṁhitā* of all 40 branches of Veda and the Vedic Literature (refer to Figures 3-10 through 3-13, beginning on page 58).

Specific Computer Network Architecture Expressions of Ṛk Veda

Figure 3-14 (below), Figure 3-15 (on page 68), Figure 3-16 (on pages 70 and 71), Figure 3-20 (on pages 78 and 79), and Figure 3-21 (on pages 80 and 81) present applied cases of

Figure 3-14: OSI, TCP/IP and SNA/APPN/HPR
Layered Network Architecture Models

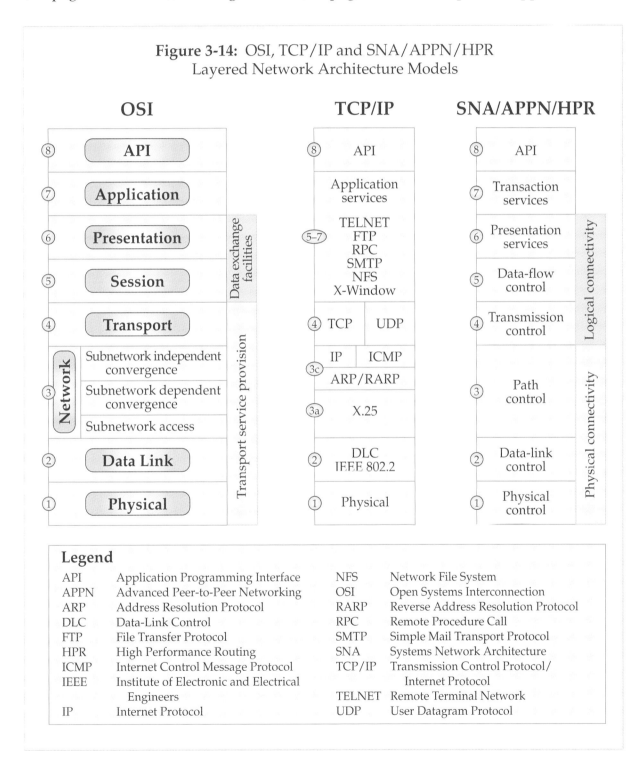

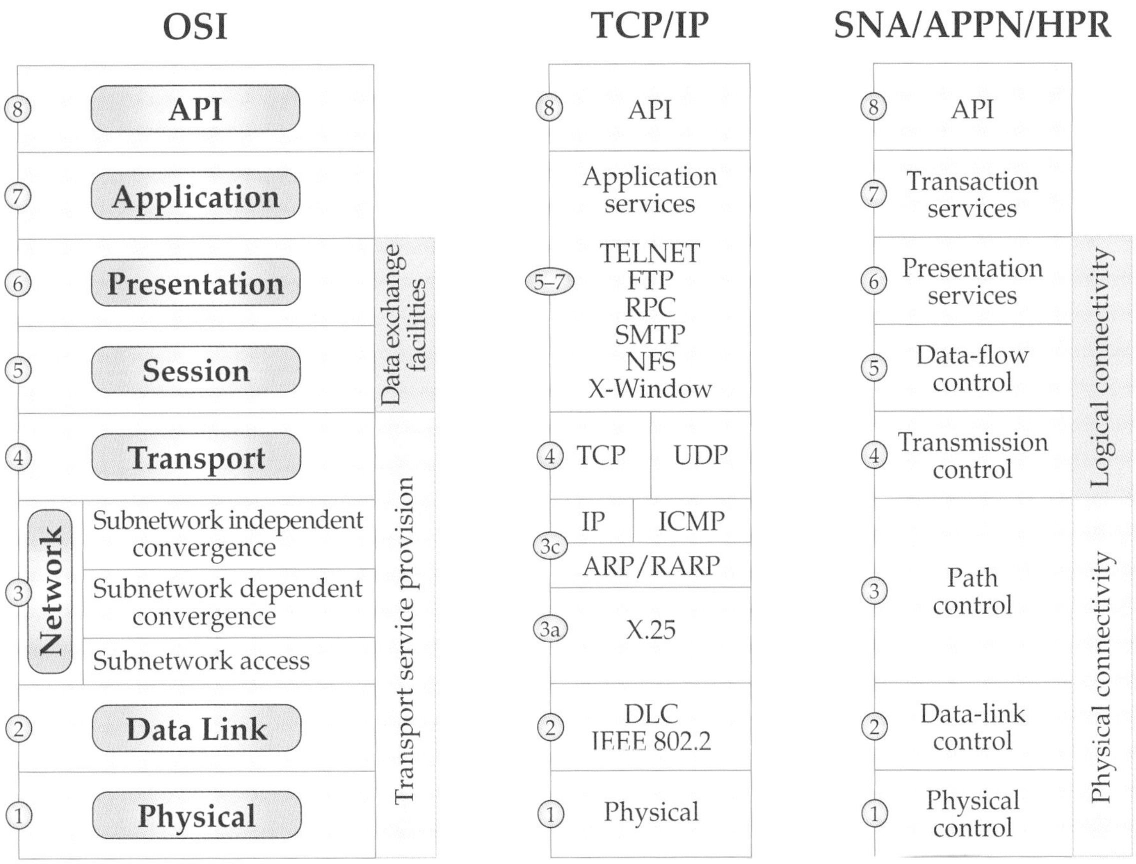

Legend

API	Application Programming Interface
APPN	Advanced Peer-to-Peer Networking
ARP	Address Resolution Protocol
DLC	Data-Link Control
FTP	File Transfer Protocol
HPR	High Performance Routing
ICMP	Internet Control Message Protocol
IEEE	Institute of Electronic and Electrical Engineers
IP	Internet Protocol
NFS	Network File System
OSI	Open Systems Interconnection
RARP	Reverse Address Resolution Protocol
RPC	Remote Procedure Call
SMTP	Simple Mail Transport Protocol
SNA	Systems Network Architecture
TCP/IP	Transmission Control Protocol/ Internet Protocol
TELNET	Remote Terminal Network
UDP	User Datagram Protocol

computer network architectural layered protocol expressions of Ṛk Veda. Figure 3-14 compares the ISO-OSI network architecture reference model standard to the Transmission Control Protocol/Internet Protocol (TCP/IP) and IBM's Systems Network Architecture (SNA) protocol suites. The OSI Computer Network interface/layer functions are described in Figure 3-11 (beginning on page 59). In general, the upper layers (Layers 4 and above) of the three layered-architecture protocol suites provide end-to-end, logical connection facilities, and the lower layers (Layers 3 and below) provide transport facilities consisting of a variety of transmission subnetworks and multihop wide-area networks.

Both the TCP/IP and SNA network architecture and protocol suites refer internally to functions described and defined in the OSI computer network architecture reference model, services, and protocols. Each of the three network architectures summarized in Figure 3-14 elaborates a complete set of specifications and protocols that define, incorporate, and orchestrate the following characteristics:

- Nodes and links
- Resource identification—resource names and addresses, and their interrelationships
- Routing and topology
- Transport
- Upper-layer definitions and APIs

Both TCP/IP and SNA—including Advanced Peer-to-Peer Networking (APPN) and High Performance Routing (HPR)—are complete architectural and protocol stacks that have been implemented across the entire spectrum of mission-critical enterprise- and carrier-class platforms and runtime environments in response to business, technical, and scientific network computing drivers.

TCP/IP was originally designed in the late 1960s for networks of medium-sized end systems to transfer files between researchers at different sites working on related projects. These early file transfers did not yet require fast response times because they were not designed for interactive applications. Remote, interactive host access was a later development that led to rapid improvements in throughput. TCP/IP is a collection of applications as well as network protocols interconnected by routers and switches within single and multiple virtual networks.

SNA was introduced by IBM in September 1974 as their strategic network architecture from which to define, design, and implement networked applications and devices. SNA, from its inception, has been implemented as a set of architectural specifications of logical structures, procedures, formats, and protocols within a wide range of hardware, software, and firmware products. SNA superimposes a logical network interface between end users (application programs and devices) and the underlying physical network. SNA networks, traditionally host-centric and hierarchical in nature, provide devices access into host-resident applications. Host-based SNA networks (subarea networks) have evolved into peer-to-peer networks through APPN and HPR.

Both TCP/IP and SNA provide end users transparency from physical, link, and network interconnection and switching/routing details. They each define a set of layered logical networks, where the outermost network provides the end-user interface, and each successive inner network provides a distinct set of functions to the next higher layer in a clearly-defined fashion. TCP/IP has been classically connectionless at the Network Layer; SNA has traditionally been connection-oriented at the Network Layer. (HPR, however, enables both connection-oriented and connectionless functionality at the Network Layer.)

OSI Reference Model

Figure 3-15 (on page 68) indicates (using standard OSI designations) that computer networks incorporate logical peer protocols. In general, any Layer n entity generates a Layer-n-specific message unit. This Layer n message unit is presented to the next lower layer (Layer n–1) as data, and Layer n–1 appends its unique header (or header plus trailer in the Layer 2 case). Layer 1 in all cases does not construct message units, but is concerned with placing bits/qubits over terrestrial or celestial transmission media (i.e., twisted pair wire, optical fiber waveguide, coaxial cable, microwave, wireless cellular, wireless optical, and satellite).

Figure 3-16 (on pages 70 and 71), Figure 3-20 (on pages 78 and 79), and Figure 3-21 (on pages 80 and 81) summarize the following specific cases of layered computer network architectures and protocol suites, each mapped to the OSI computer network architecture reference model:

- TCP/IP
- IP-based video/audio/data
- Wireless networking based on Global System for Mobile Telecommunications (GSM) and Code Division Multiple Access (CDMA)

Figure 3-15: Computer Network Peer Protocols

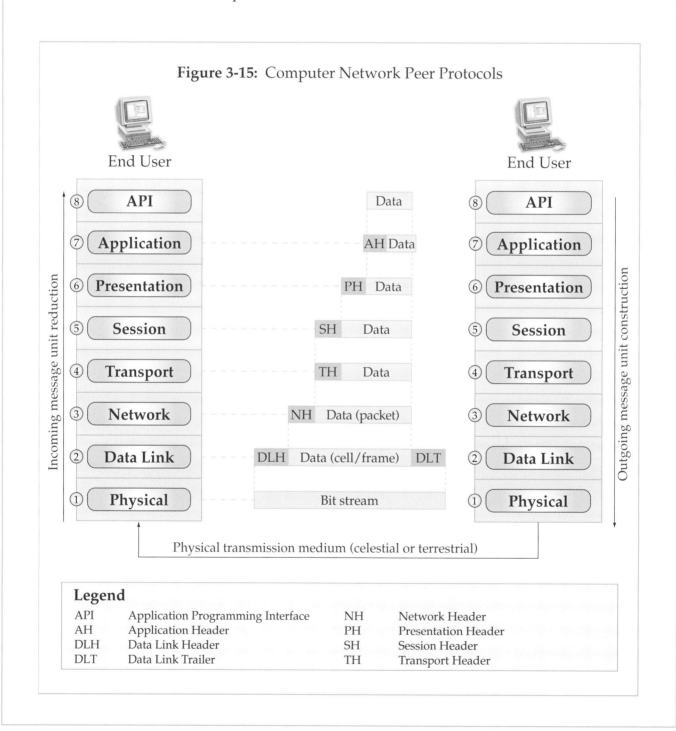

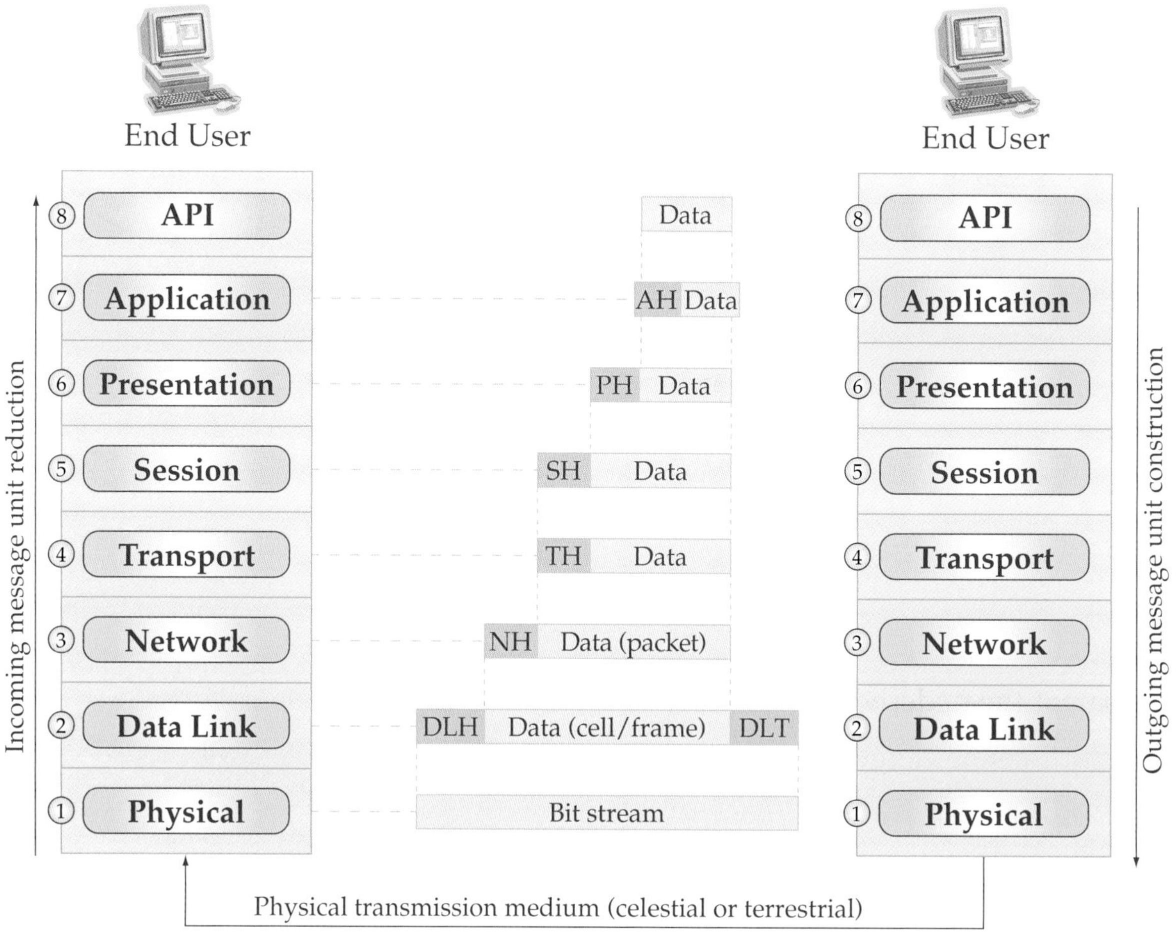

Legend

API	Application Programming Interface	NH	Network Header
AH	Application Header	PH	Presentation Header
DLH	Data Link Header	SH	Session Header
DLT	Data Link Trailer	TH	Transport Header

TCP/IP Protocol Suite

Figure 3-16 (on pages 70 and 71) maps the TCP/IP protocol suite to the OSI computer network architecture reference model. The TCP/IP protocol suite lies at the heart of the Internet. The Internet, in turn, consists of large national backbone networks (i.e., National Science Foundation Network [NSFnet]), and several regional and campus networks throughout the world, including 13 Internet root server technical entities located in the US, Japan, UK, Sweden and elsewhere. TCP, IP, and related Internet protocols have traditionally been developed and enhanced in the public domain.

The original TCP/IP design goal was to build an interconnection of networks that provides universal communications services. The design point was to allow each physical network to maintain its own technology-unique set of communications interfaces.

TCP/IP standards are developed through a Request for Comments (RFC) process managed by the Internet Engineering Task Force (IETF). Figure 3-16 shows that TCP is a Layer 4 protocol and provides a reliable, connection-oriented transport service. User Datagram Protocol (UDP), also a Layer 4 protocol, provides a connectionless transport service with no provision for flow control. TCP connections are defined and identified by a pair of sockets, each of which combines four parameters: originating port and IP_address, and destination port and IP_address.

IP is a Layer 3c protocol and provides connectionless services over End System–Intermediate System (ES-IS), and IS-IS links; however, TCP/IP application services and their underlying network infrastructure are collectively referred to as TCP/IP. IP renders transparent the underlying physical network by creating a virtual network view. IP is a best-effort, connectionless packet delivery protocol. IP version 4 (IPv4) addresses are 32-bit fields with optional 32-bit masks that specify source and destination hosts (end systems in the form NetID and hostID) that may be interconnected through one or several intermediate gateways (routers and/or switches) and networks.

IP datagrams are finite-length packets of bits containing a header and payload (data). Hosts and routers/switches are all involved in the processing of IP headers. End systems create IP headers and datagrams on sending, and process on receipt. Routers/switches examine IP headers as routing-decision input and modify them as IP packets propagating from source to destination hosts.

Figure 3-16: TCP/IP Protocol Suite Mapped to the OSI Computer Network Architecture Reference Model

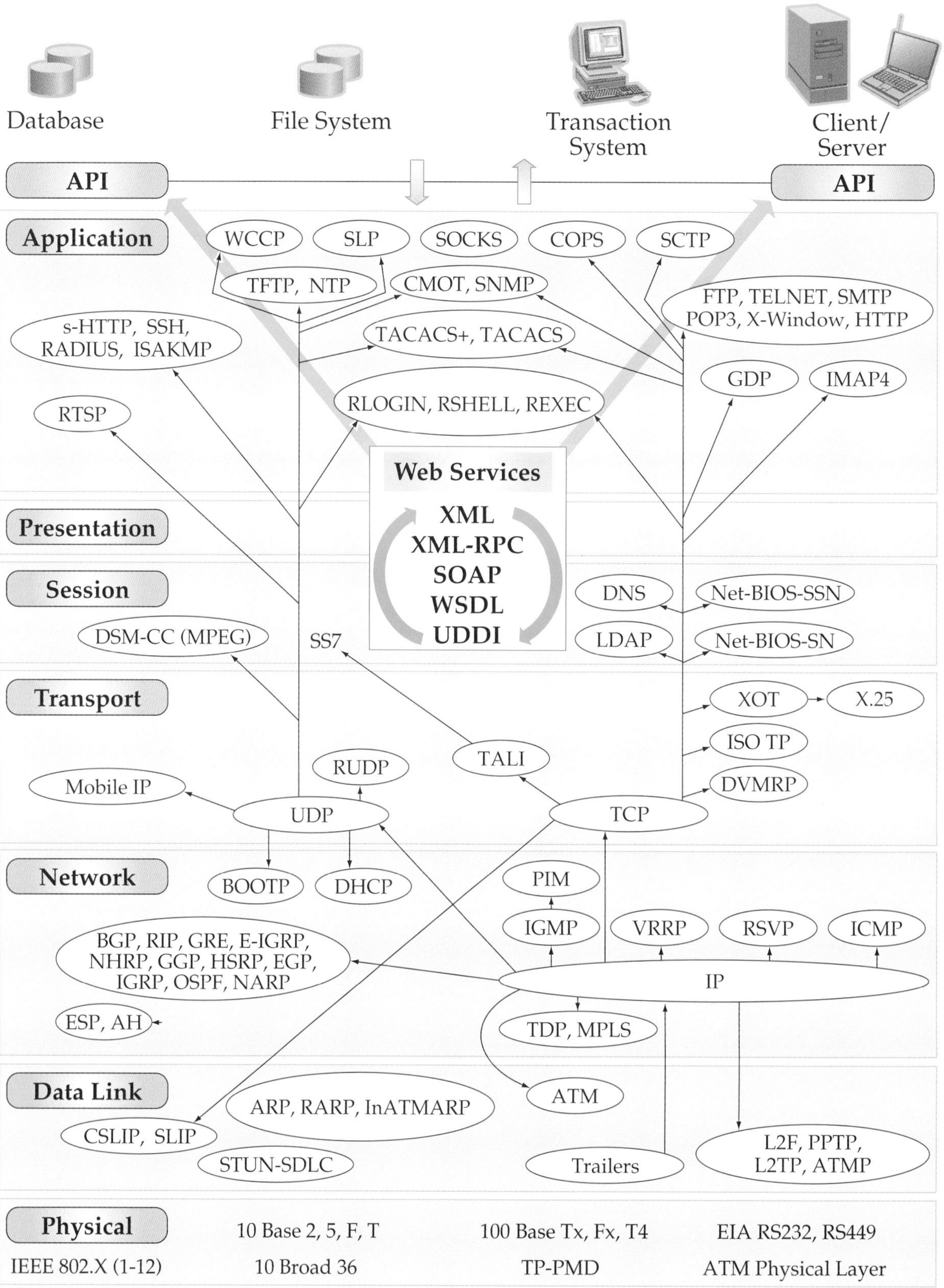

Figure 3-16 (continued): TCP/IP Protocol Suite Mapped to the OSI Computer Network Architecture Reference Model

API

API	Application Programming Interface

Application

CMOT	Common Management Open Transport
COPS	Common Open Policy Service
FTP	File Transfer Protocol
GDP	Gateway Discovery Protocol
HTTP	Hypertext Transfer Protocol
IMAP-4	Internet Message Access Protocol rev 4
IPDC	IP Device Control
ISAKMP	Internet Key Exchange
NTP	Network Time Protocol
POP3	Post Office Protocol ver 3
RADIUS	Remote Authentication Dial-In User Service
REXEC	Remote Executive
RLOGIN	Remote Login
RSHELL	Remote Shell
RTSP	Real-Time Streaming Protocol
SCTP	Stream Control Transmission Protocol
S-HTTP	Secure Hypertext Transfer Protocol
SLP	Service Location Protocol
SMTP	Simple Mail Transfer Protocol
SNMP	Simple Network Management Protocol
SOCKS	Sockets Interface
SSH	Secure Shell
TACACS+	Terminal Access Controller Access Control System
TELNET	Remote Terminal Network
TFTP	Trivial File Transfer Protocol
WCCP	Web Cache Coordination Protocol
X-Window	Remote Windowing Interface

Web Services

SOAP	Simple Object Access Protocol
UDDI	Universal Description, Discovery, and Integration
WSDL	Web Service Description Language
XML	Extensible Markup Language
XML-RPC	Extensible Markup Language-Remote Procedure Call

Session

DNS	Domain Name System
DSM-CC	Digital Storage Medium Command and Control
LDAP	Lightweight Directory Access Protocol
MPEG	Motion Pictures Experts Group
Net-BIOS	Network Basic Input/Output System
Net-BIOS-SN	NetBIOS Subnetwork
Net-BIOS-SSN	NetBIOS Subsystem Network
SS7	Signaling System No. 7

Transport

DVMRP	Distance Vector Multicast Routing Protocol
ISO TP	International Organization for Standardization Transport Protocol
RUDP	Reliable UDP
TALI	Transport Adapter Layer Interface
TCP	Transmission Control Protocol
UDP	User Datagram Protocol
XOT	X.25 Over TCP

Network

BOOTP	Bootstrap Protocol
DHCP	Dynamic Host Configuration Protocol
ICMP	Internet Control Message Protocol
IGMP	Internet Group Management Protocol
PIM	Protocol Independent Multicast
RSVP	Resource ReSerVation setup Protocol
VRRP	Virtual Router Redundancy Protocol

Security

AH	Authentication Header
ESP	Encapsulating Security Payload

Routing

BGP	Border Gateway Protocol
EGP	Exterior Gateway Protocol
E-IGRP	Enhanced Interior Gateway Routing Protcol
GGP	Gateway-Gateway Protocol
GRE	Generic Routing Encapsulation
HSRP	(Cisco) Hot Standby Router Protocol
IGRP	Interior Gateway Routing Protocol
IP	Internet Protocol
MPLS	Multiprotocol Label Switching
NARP	Non-Broadcast Multiple Access (NBMA) Address Resolution Protocol
NHRP	Next Hop Resolution Protocol
OSPF	Open Shortest Path First
RIP	Routing Information Protocol
TDP	Tag Distribution Protocol

Data Link

ARP	Address Resolution Protocol
ATM	Asynchronous Transfer Mode
InATMARP	Inverse ATM ARP
RARP	Reverse Address Resolution Protocol
SLIP	Serial Line Internet Protocol
STUN-SDLC	(Cisco) Serial Tunneling Protocol–Synchronous Data Link Control

Tunneling

ATMP	Ascend Tunnel Management Protocol
L2F	Layer 2 Forwarding Protocol
L2TP	Layer 2 Tunneling Protocol
PPTP	Point-to-Point Tunneling Protocol

Physical

ATM	Asynchronous Transfer Mode
Base	Baseband
Broad	Broadband
EIA	Electronic Industries Association
F	Fiber
IEEE	Institute of Electrical and Electronic Engineers
RS	Recommended Standard
T	Twisted pair
TP-PMD	Twisted Pair–Physical Layer Medium

Each IP address actually identifies a network interface rather than an entire end system. Devices with more than one network interface—such as routers/switches and multi-homed hosts—have more than one IP address. Various address classes have been developed to enable the 32-bit IPv4 address to accommodate diverse organizational host and device addressability requirements.

IPv6 addresses, used increasingly, are 128 bits in length (to resolve IPv4 addressing constraints) and support unicast, anycast, and multicast operations. Unicast IPv6 addresses identify a single interface; anycast addresses enable packet delivery to one set member; and multicast addresses provide delivery to all interfaces within a group. The IPv6 address, at 128 bits, is four times the length of the 32-bit IPv4 address, and it generates an address space that is four billion (2^{96}) times the extent of an IPv4 (2^{32}) address space. The IPv6 address can theoretically support greater than 665×10^{21} addresses per square meter on earth; however, assignment hierarchies reduce the actual value to the range 8×10^{17} to 2×10^{33} nodes.

Figure 3-16 (on pages 70 and 71) also summarizes a wealth of TCP/IP services and protocols:

- Mapping of Internet addresses to physical addresses—Address Resolution Protocol (ARP)
- Determining an Internet address at startup—Reverse Address Resolution Protocol (RARP)
- IP error and control messages—Internet Control Message Protocol (ICMP)
- Wide range of Internet core and peer routing algorithms and protocols
- Exterior gateway protocols and autonomous systems—Border Gateway Protocol (BGP)
- Routing within autonomous systems—Routing Information Protocol (RIP) and Open Shortest Path First (OSPF)
- Bootstrap Protocol (BOOTP) and autoconfiguration—Dynamic Host Configuration Protocol (DHCP)

- Domain Name System (DNS)
- A wide range of applications (remote login, file transfer and access, electronic mail, World Wide Web, and Internet management)

We have not summarized several additional Internet services, notably Internet Security and Firewall Design (Internet Protocol Security [IPSec]), voice and video over IP (Real-time Transport Protocol [RTP]), and private network interconnection (Network Address Translation [NAT] and Virtual Private Network [VPN]).

Web Services

Web services are any services that are available over the Internet by using a standardized XML messaging system that is independent of any single operating system or programming language. For example, XML-based Web services enable Linux-based Java scripts to interact with Windows XP-based Perl scripts.

The original and still predominant World Wide Web interactivity paradigm is a human-centric Web in which end-user individuals initiate Web-based requests. Figure 3-17 illustrates the human-centric Web model predicated on initial-generation electronic-commerce (e-commerce) or mobile-commerce (m-commerce) logic, in which a client logs onto a target Web site via a Web browser, which issues a Hypertext Transfer Protocol (HTTP)-based request, and the targeted Web server responds with an HTTP-based Hypertext Markup Language (HTML) page containing the requested data.

Figure 3-17: Human-Centric Web Model

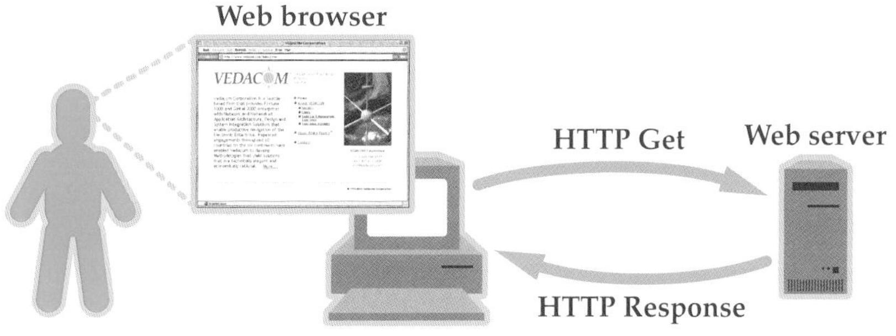

In the user-centric Web paradigm, users access Web servers through browsers. Web services evolve these interactions to an application-centric Web, where networked applications interact directly rather than through Web browsers and servers. The Web services-based application-centric Web model is presented in Figure 3-18, where, in this example, a banking application issues an XML-based request to a Web server, which returns an XML-based response that updates the banking application. Banking application updates automatically trigger updates to end users and other affected applications (i.e., general ledger, funds transfer, cost accounting database, Just-in-Time ordering application, etc.). Application-centric Web services are becoming indispensable in networked applications including credit checking, financial transactions, credit card verification, package tracking, shopping bots, portfolio tracking, currency conversion, virtual team calendar management, e-mail, and language translation.

The concept of an application-centric Web is not new, as network software developers have for some time created Common Gateway Interface (CGI) program- and Java servlet-based applications. These, however, have been ad hoc to a great extent; XML-based Web services are far more standardized and hardware/software platform-independent.

Figure 3-18: Application-Centric Web Model

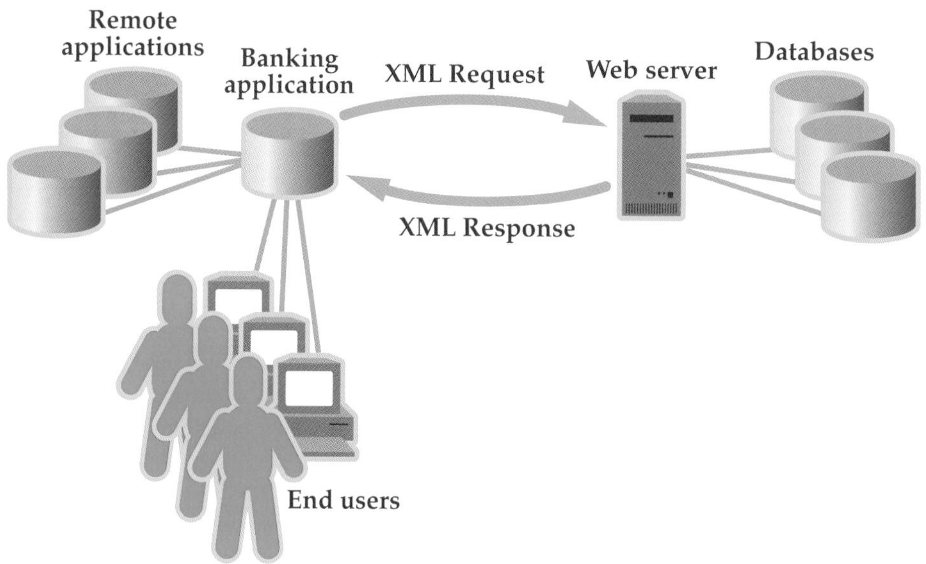

Web services are evolving to an Automated Web, where Web services promise to become self-describing, discoverable, and standards-based, giving rise to automated application integration or Just-in-Time application integration. As Figure 3-19 indicates, networked applications, upon activation, could self-issue discovery requests to network directories or meta-directories, which return updated pointers to globally networked services and service descriptions. In this example, a recently activated banking application automatically retrieves a Web server-resident target database service description that would contain all pertinent details on connecting to the service. The banking application could then automatically invoke the service.

Figure 3-16 ("TCP/IP Protocol Suite Mapped to the OSI Computer Network Architecture Reference Model," on pages 70 and 71), depicts the following technologies as central to Web services:

- Extensible Markup Language (XML)
- XML-Remote Procedure Call (XML-RPC)
- Simple Object Access Protocol (SOAP)
- Web Services Description Language (WSDL)
- Universal Description, Discovery, and Integration (UDDI)

Web services technologies are shared by the predominant, competing Web services frameworks: Microsoft .NET, IBM Web Services, and Sun Open Net Environment (ONE).

Figure 3-19: Web-Based Automation in Administration

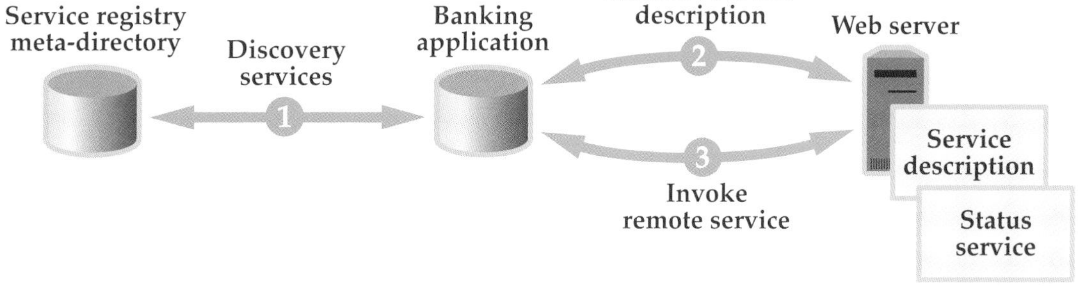

Web services incorporate the entire spectrum of networked applications and services, including electronic and mobile commerce chains, financial transactions, stock market reporting, news syndication, weather reporting, package-tracking systems, transportation reservations, accommodation reservations, and collaborative computing. The Web service protocol stack currently consists of four layers:

1 **Service Transport**—Service Transport Layer transports messages between applications and uses HTTP, Simple Mail Transfer Protocol (SMTP), File Transfer Protocol (FTP), and Blocks Extensible Exchange Protocol (BEEP).

2 **XML Messaging**—XML Messaging Layer encodes messages in a common XML format to ensure message understandability at both ends and uses XML-RPC, SOAP, and XML.

3 **Service Description**—Service Description Layer describes the public interface to a specific Web service through the use of WSDL.

4 **Service Discovery**—Service Discovery Layer centralizes services into a common registry and provides straightforward publish/find functionality via UDDI.

The Web services protocol stack also incorporates SOAP-DSIG (SOAP Security Extensions: Digital Signature), and USML (UDDI Search Markup Language).

During the early period of the Internet, FTP data transfers accounted for approximately one-third of traffic. By 1995, Web traffic overtook FTP to become the most significant consumer of Internet backbone bandwidth, and, by 2000, Web traffic completely eclipsed all other Internet application traffic volume.

IP-Based Audio and Video

Figure 3-20 (on pages 78 and 79) maps IP-based audio, video, and data (H.323) protocols to the OSI computer network architecture reference model. In essence, audio and video data is transferred across the Internet by digitizing analog audio and video signals (through the use of PCM, ADPCM, CELP, and related signaling technologies introduced earlier in this chapter) to generate data files, which are subsequently decoded at the receiving end to reproduce the original analog signal. This general technique is not optimized for interactive exchanges because placing encoded audio or video into files and transferring the files introduces delays.

The classical issue associated with IP-based interactive audio and video has been that IP networks are not isochronous. Isochronous designs, introduced by traditional telephony, are engineered to deliver output with precisely the same timing as was used to generate input. IP datagrams, on the other hand, can be duplicated, delayed, and/or arrive out of order. Delay variance (jitter) is especially persistent within IP networks and is the main contributor to their non-isochronous behaviors. IP-based transmissions accommodate jitter through use of timestamps that notify the receiver at what time the data in the packet should be played back. Receivers are able to recreate an audio or video signal accurately in the face of jitter by implementing playback buffers.

Real-time Transport Protocol (RTP) is designed to transport a wide variety of real-time audio and video data and provides two key facilities: a sequence number in each packet that allows a receiver to detect out-of-sequence delivery or loss, and a timestamp that enables the receiver to control playback. RTP provides translation (changing the encoding of a stream at an intermediate station) and mixing (stations receiving streams of data from multiple sources, such as during video teleconferences, combine them into a single stream and send the result). RTP Control Protocol (RTCP) is a companion protocol to RTP that allows senders and receivers to transmit a series of reports to one another that contains additional information about the data being transferred and network performance.

Wireless Internet and Wireless Web

Figure 3-21 (on pages 80 and 81) maps wireless networking to the OSI computer network architecture reference model with emphasis placed on GSM and CDMA. From its inception in 1982 as part of the Conference Europeenne des Postes et Telecommunications (CEPT) Groupe Special Mobile, GSM interfaces, protocols, and protocol stacks have been aligned with OSI principles. As a result, the open GSM architecture enables maximum independence between key wireless network elements including the Base Station Controller (BSC), Mobile Switching Center (MSC), and Home Location Register (HLR), greatly simplifying design, testing, and system implementation.

Figure 3-20: IP-Based Audio/Video/Data H.323 Protocols Mapped to the OSI Computer Network Architecture Reference Model

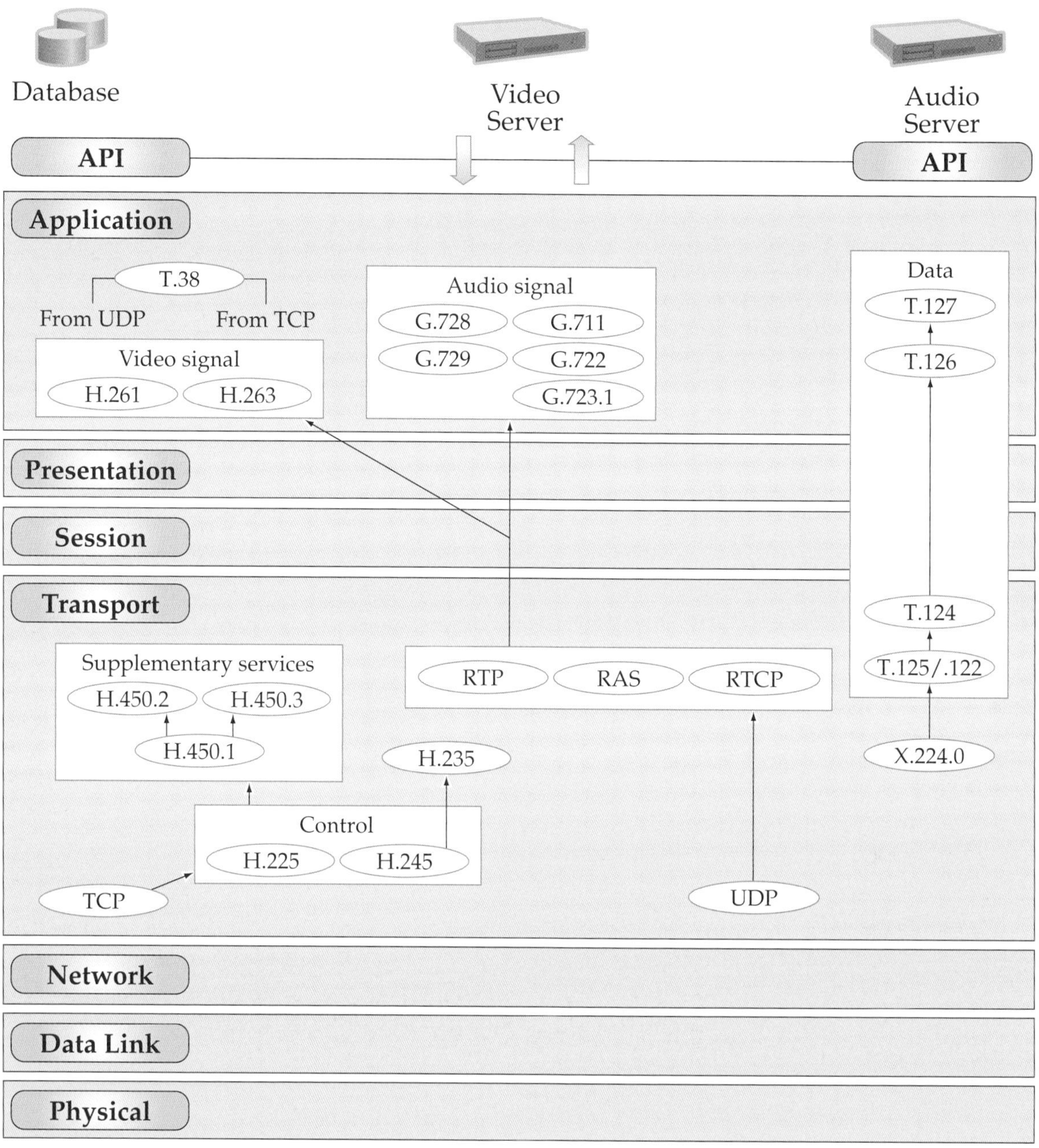

Figure 3-20 (continued): IP-Based Audio/Video/Data H.323 Protocols Mapped to the OSI Computer Network Architecture Reference Model

Legend

API

API	Application Programming Interface

Application

Audio Signal

G.711	Audio encoder/decoder (codec)
G.722	Audio codec
G.723.1	Audio codec
G.728	Audio codec
G.729	Audio codec

Video Signal

H.261	Describes video stream for transport using RTP
H.263	Specifies payload format for encapsulating in RTP
T.38	IP-based fax service
TCP	Transmission Control Protocol
UDP	User Datagram Protocol

Application/Presentation/Session/Transport

Data

T.12X	Defines Multipoint Communication Service Protocol (MCS)

Transport

Supplementary Services

H.450.1	Procedures and signaling protocol between H.323 entities
H.450.2	Call Transfer supplementary service for H.323
H.450.3	Call diversion supplementary service for H.323

Control

H.225	H.200/AV.120-Series Recommendations Narrow-band visual telephone services

H.245	Line transmission of non-telephone signals; H.245 messages are in Abstract Syntax Notation.1 (ASN.1)
H.235	Enhancements to incorporate security services such as Authentication and Privacy (data encryption)
RAS	Registration, Admission and Status channel
RTCP	RTP Control Protocol
RTP	Real-Time Transport
TCP	Transmission Control Protocol
UDP	User Datagram Protocol

Figure 3-21: Wireless Networking (GSM/CDMA) Protocol Suite Mapped to the OSI Computer Network Architecture Reference Model

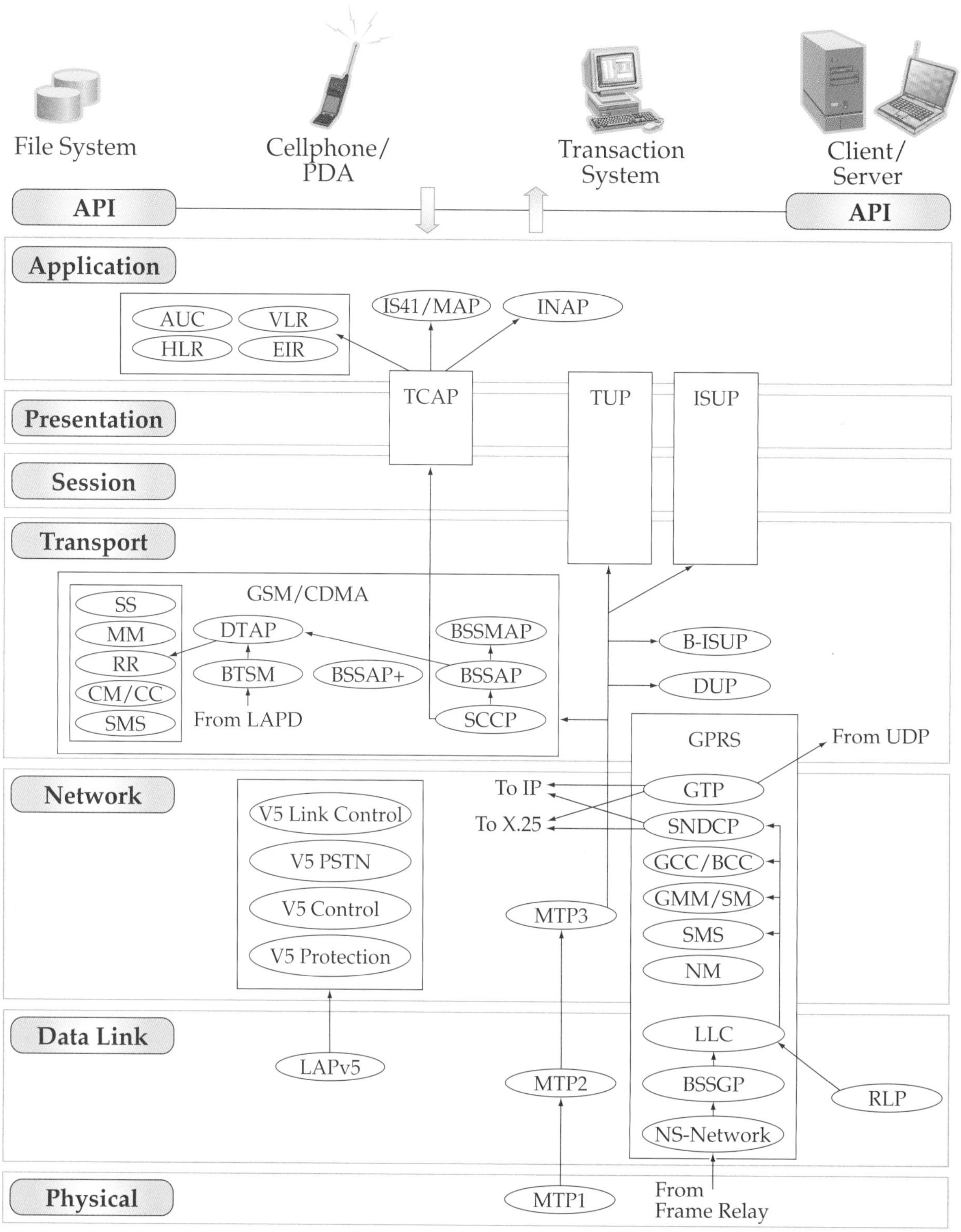

Figure 3-21 (continued): Wireless Networking (GSM/CDMA) ProtocolSuite Mapped to the OSI Computer Network Architecture Reference Model

Legend

API

API — Application Programming Interface

Application

AUC	Authentication Center
EIR	Equipment Identity Register
HLR	Home Location Register
INAP	Intelligent Network Application Part
IS41/MAP	Interim Standard 41/Mobile Application Part
VLR	Visitor Location Register

Presentation/Session

ISUP	ISDN User Part (of Signalling System 7)
TCAP	Transaction Capabilities Application Part
TUP	Telephone User Part (SS7)
SS7	Signaling System No. 7

Transport

B-ISUP	Broadband-ISUP
BSS	Base Station Subsystem
BSSAP	BSS Application Part
BSSAP+	BSS Application Part+
BSSMAP	BSS Management Application Part
BTSM	Base Station Controller to Base Transceiver Station (BSC-BTS) interface protocol (A-bis interface)
CM/CC	Connection Management/Call Control
DUP	Data User Part
DTAP	Direct Transfer Application sub-Part
GPRS	General Packet Radio Service
GSM/CDMA	Global System for Mobile Telecommunications/ Code Division Multiple Access
LAPD	Link Access Protocol (D-channel)
MM	Mobility Management
RR	Radio Resource
SCCP	Signaling Connection Control Point
SS	Spread Spectrum
SMS	Short Message Service
UDP	User Datagram Protocol

Transport/Network

GCC/BCC	GCC/Base Transceiver Color Code
GMM/SM	Global System for Mobile Telecommunications (GSM) Mobility Management (MM)/Session Management (SM)
GTP	GPRS Tunneling Protocol
NM	Network Management
SNDCP	Subnetwork Dependent Convergence Protocol
MTP3	Message Transfer Part 3
PSTN	Packet Switched Data Network

Data Link

BSSGP	Base Station Subsystem GPRS Protocol
LAPv5	Link Access Protocol version 5
LLC	Low Layer Compatibility
RLP	Radio Link Protocol

Physical

MTP1 — Message Transfer Part 1

CEPT has allocated GSM frequency bands at 900 MHz for use in Europe, North Africa, the Middle East, several East Asian countries, and Australia. GSM has also been adapted at 1800 MHz (1.8 GHz, Personal Communications Services [PCS] 1800) in South America, and 1.9 GHz (PCS 1900) in North America.

GSM was introduced as part of second-generation (2G) digital cellular systems (the first generation systems were analog cellular). In 2G, GSM uses eight channels per carrier with a gross data rate of 22.8 Kbps (a net rate of 13 Kbps) in the full-rate channel and a frame of 4.6 milliseconds (ms). Each GSM user transmits in every eighth time slot (duration 0.575 ms) and receives in a corresponding time slot. 2G GSM introduced data services over wireless—for example, General Packet Radio Service (GPRS) over GSM. 3G GSM introduces hierarchical cell structures and increases data rates to 144 Kbps, with 2 Mbps and higher now emerging at the hand set.

Freedom of Mobile Multimedia Access (FOMA) is another 3G mobile communications platform that is built on the Wireless CDMA (WCDMA) system and is compliant with IMT-2000, an international standard for 3G mobile networking. FOMA is evolving voice transmission clarity consistent with fixed-lined devices and supports diverse wireless multimedia services based on videophone and music-video content. 4G and 5G wireless Internet and Web standards are currently in final form as well.

Exponential Evolution of the Global Internetwork

Figures 3-22 through 3-25, as a group, indicate that network computing, expressed at the macroscopic scale within the Global Internetwork, continues to scale exponentially in information processing and carrying capacities as well as in price-performance and bandwidth efficiencies.

Figure 3-22, "Broadband Network Trends," summarizes the major enterprise drivers and technology enablers to the rapid increase in broadband utility over time. By 1999, for example, approximately 350 Gbps of raw network capacity were available in the US alone, with a 50 percent household penetration rate for personal computers and a 26 percent Internet penetration rate. During 2005, global traffic over the Internet is expected to

Figure 3-22: Broadband Network Trends

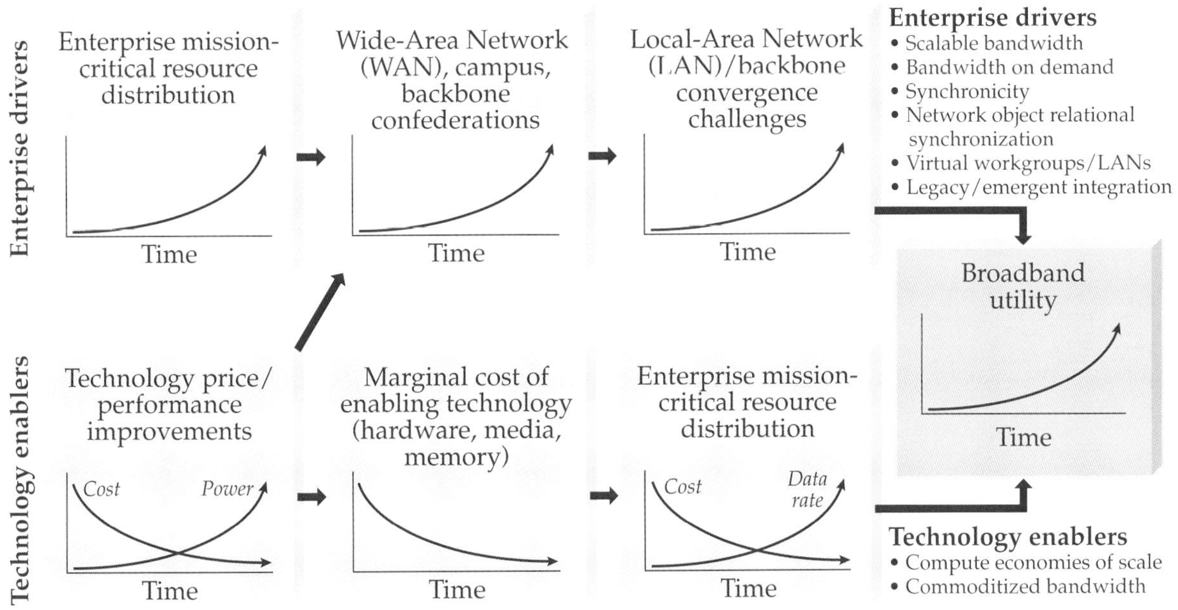

exceed multi-petabit-per-second aggregate throughput. (Refer to Appendix B, "Units of Measurement and Orders of Magnitude—Powers of Ten and Two," for scientific notation-based equivalencies to *n*-bits per second.) One petabit per second corresponds to 660 million simultaneously active television channels, or would enable each person on earth to download the full Encyclopedia Britannica from the Web every day.

Figure 3-23 (on page 84), "Price-Performance Trends," shows the results of Moore's Law in the inexorable Flowing Wakefulness of the Global Internetwork. Every 18 months on average over the past four decades, the number of components on chip substrates doubles at a halving of the cost. One of the significant outcomes of this exponential evolution is in the area of wireless technologies. There are an estimated one billion fixed telephones and 500 million cellular phones worldwide. By 2010, the total number of phones worldwide is projected to be 2.5 billion, half of which will be wireless. Wired telephony infrastructure and services are anticipated to diminish in several developed countries throughout the world during the next few years.

Figure 3-24 (on page 85), "Bandwidth Efficiencies," translates the price-performance trends introduced in Figure 3-23 into significantly increasing bandwidth at markedly

Figure 3-23: Price-Performance Trends

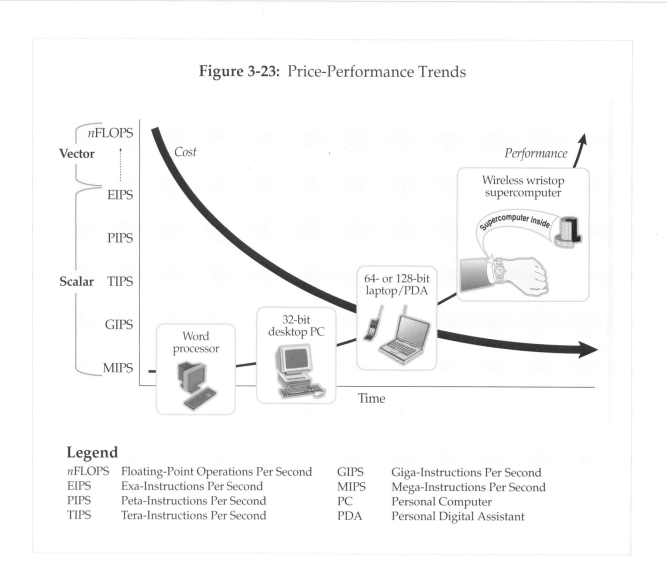

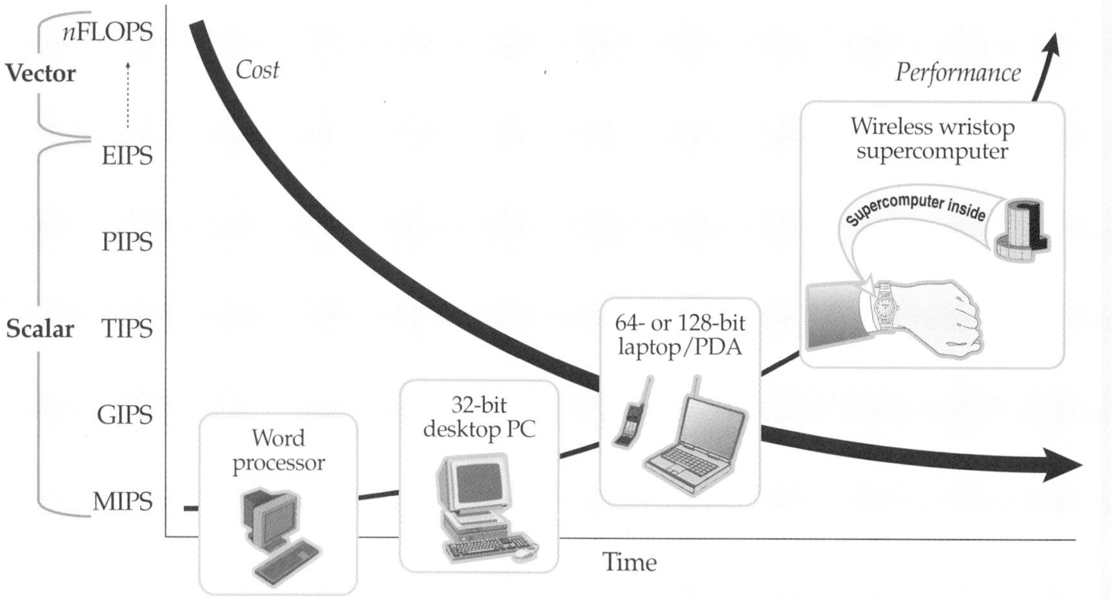

Legend

*n*FLOPS	Floating-Point Operations Per Second	GIPS	Giga-Instructions Per Second
EIPS	Exa-Instructions Per Second	MIPS	Mega-Instructions Per Second
PIPS	Peta-Instructions Per Second	PC	Personal Computer
TIPS	Tera-Instructions Per Second	PDA	Personal Digital Assistant

diminishing marginal costs. Ever-increasing degrees of broadband services are wireless in nature to support dramatic tendencies for enterprises and individuals alike to transcend previous boundaries of space and time.

Wireless technologies have also quickly evolved during the course of the past several decades to accommodate increasing requirements for any-to-any connectivity, pervasive computing, and resource sharing on a bandwidth-intensive basis. As Figure 3-25 (on page 86) shows, wireless technologies have supported increasingly higher frequencies, and therefore they operate at increasingly shorter wavelengths—from 30 MHz High Frequency (HF) during the 1960s, to the Extremely High Frequency (EHF) ranges of the electromagnetic frequency spectrum at greater than 30 GHz—during the past two decades. Usable spectra are projected to be in the multi-terahertz and higher ranges in

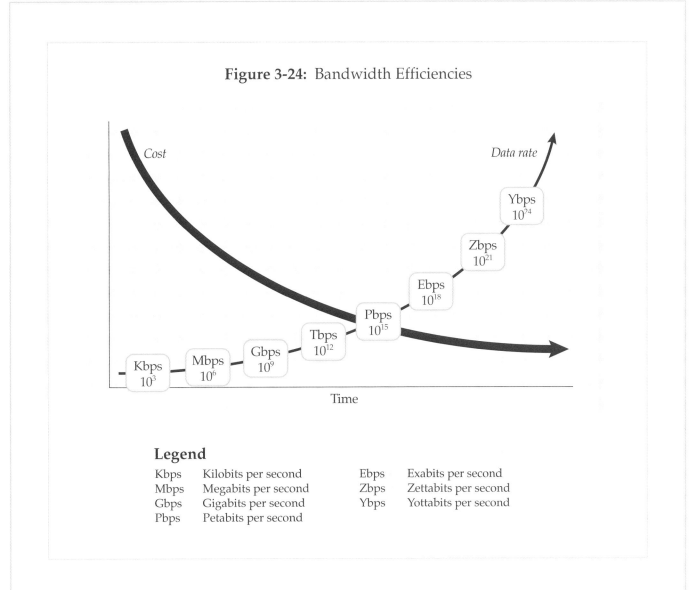

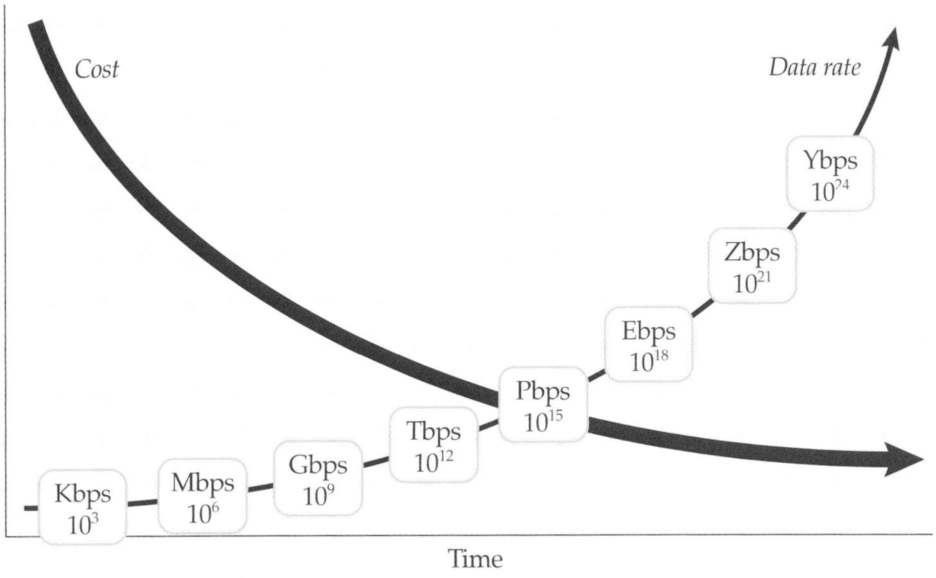

Figure 3-24: Bandwidth Efficiencies

Legend

Kbps	Kilobits per second	Ebps	Exabits per second
Mbps	Megabits per second	Zbps	Zettabits per second
Gbps	Gigabits per second	Ybps	Yottabits per second
Pbps	Petabits per second		

the foreseeable future. These higher frequencies are associated with significantly lower wavelengths and higher information-carrying capabilities than their predecessors, and they are supported celestially by Low Earth Orbit (LEO), Medium Earth Orbit (MEO), and Geosynchronous Orbit (GEO) satellite technologies, as well as by terrestrial wireless (electronic and optical) systems.

Figure 3-25: Wireless Technologies Evolution

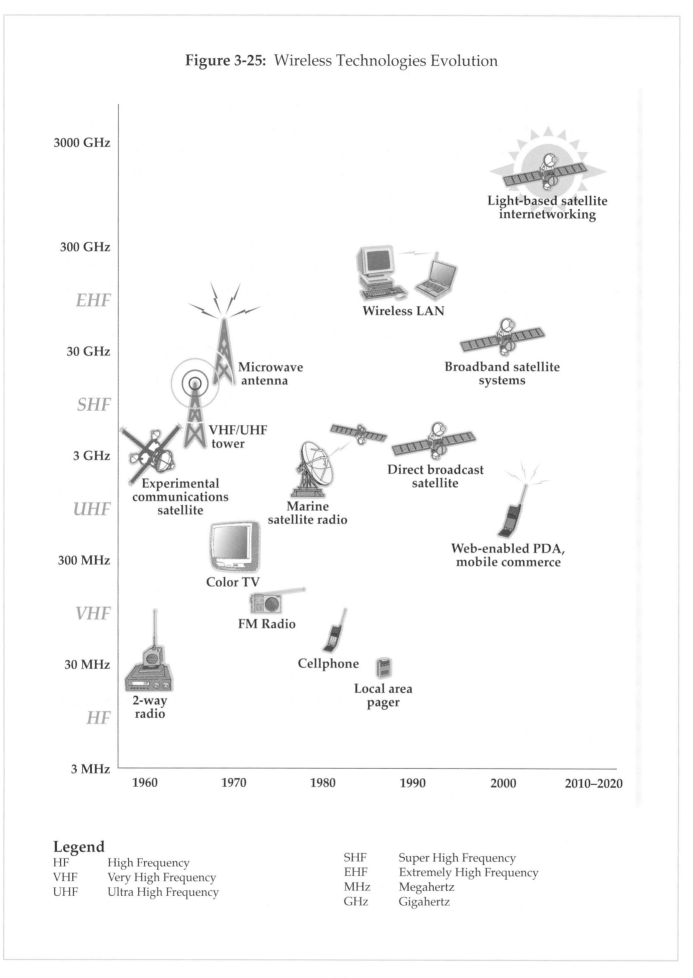

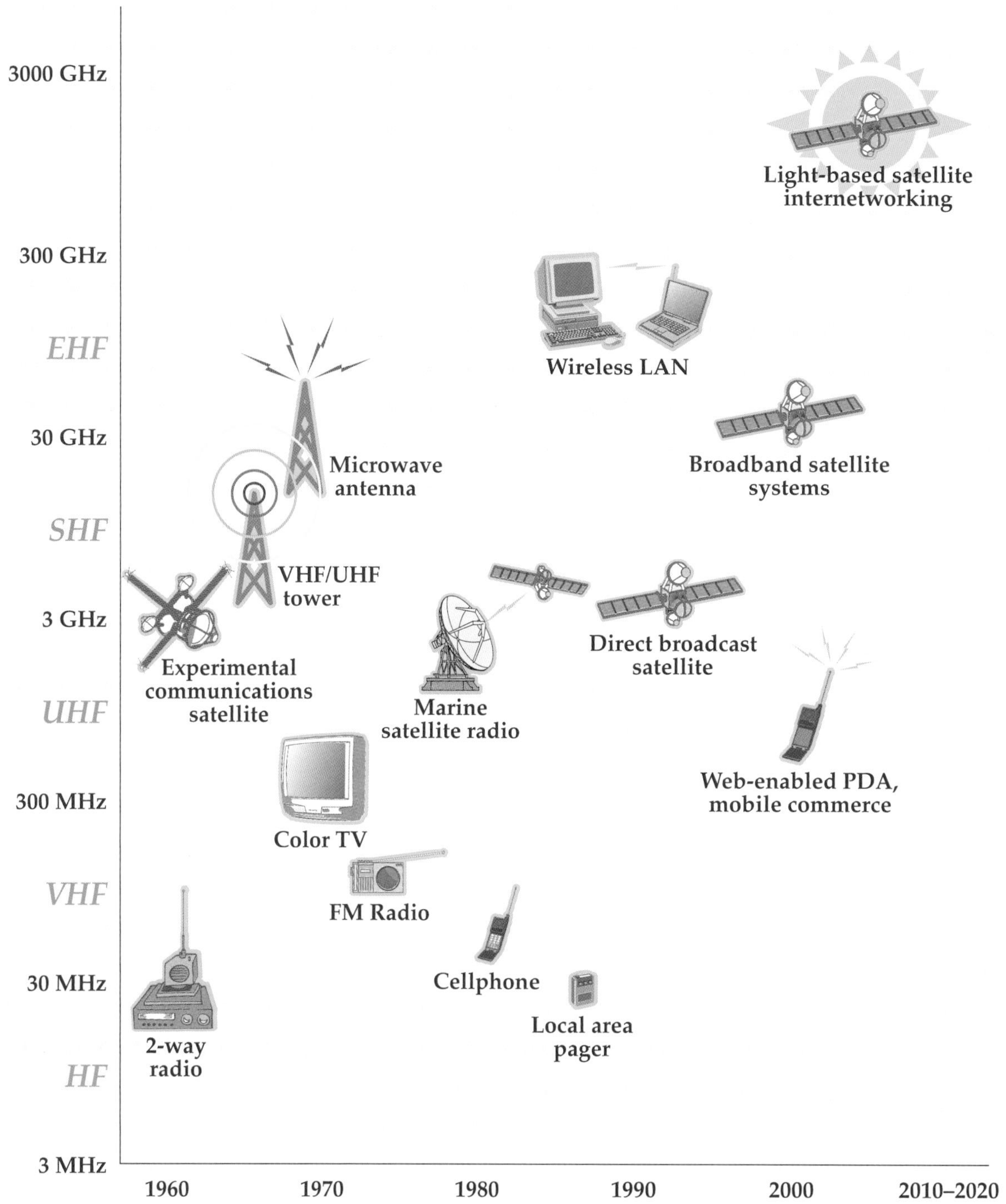

Legend

HF	High Frequency
VHF	Very High Frequency
UHF	Ultra High Frequency
SHF	Super High Frequency
EHF	Extremely High Frequency
MHz	Megahertz
GHz	Gigahertz

Summary of the Four Veda in Quantum Nework Architecture

The four major aspects of Veda are Ṛk Veda, Sāma Veda, Yajur-Veda, and Atharva Veda, with predominantly *Saṁhitā, Ṛishi, Devatā,* and *Chhandas* values, respectively. Figure 3-26 (beginning on page 88) summarizes the four major holistic aspects of Veda and illustrates the one-to-one expression of the four Veda into the structure and function of Quantum Network Architecture. This chapter has focused up to now on Ṛk Veda and its expression in Quantum Network Architecture. Brief elaborations of the one-to-one relationships of Sāma Veda, Yajur-Veda, and Atharva Veda follow:

- **SĀMA VEDA—*Flowing Wakefulness*—Network Self-Referral and Feedback Systems**
  Sāma Veda is the sum total of all that pertains to *Saṁhitā* with a predominance of *Ṛishi,* the observer value. Sāma Veda represents the totality of network information units (refer to Figure 2-8 on pages 32 and 33, "Quantum Network Architecture According to Veda and the Vedic Literature") as *Network Self-Referral and Feedback Systems.* Sāma Veda incorporates the billions of edge and core computing and networking devices and nodes extant within the Global Internetwork, with their individual and logically organized input/ingress, processing, and output/egress channels of continuous and self-aware communication.

- **YAJUR VEDA—*Offering and Creating*—Network Processing Systems**
  Yajur-Veda is the sum total of all that pertains to *Saṁhitā* with a predominance of *Devatā*—the process of observation value. Yajur-Veda represents the totality of network processing units as the totality of the transforming, processing, and interpreting components, subsystems, and systems of the Global Internetwork. Yajur Veda is expressed in Quantum Network Architecture as *Network Processing Systems.*

- **ATHARVA VEDA—*Reverberating Wholeness*—Nodal Input/Output Systems**
  Atharva Veda is the sum total of all that pertains to *Saṁhitā* with a predominance of *Chhandas*—the observed, or object of observation value. Atharva Veda represents the totality of network architecture topology units as the totality of the *Reverberating Wholeness* quality of intelligence, available in the components, subsystems, and systems of the Global Internetwork. Atharva Veda is expressed in Quantum Network Architecture as *Nodal Input/Output Systems.*

Figure 3-26: Vision of the Four Veda in Quantum Network Architecture™

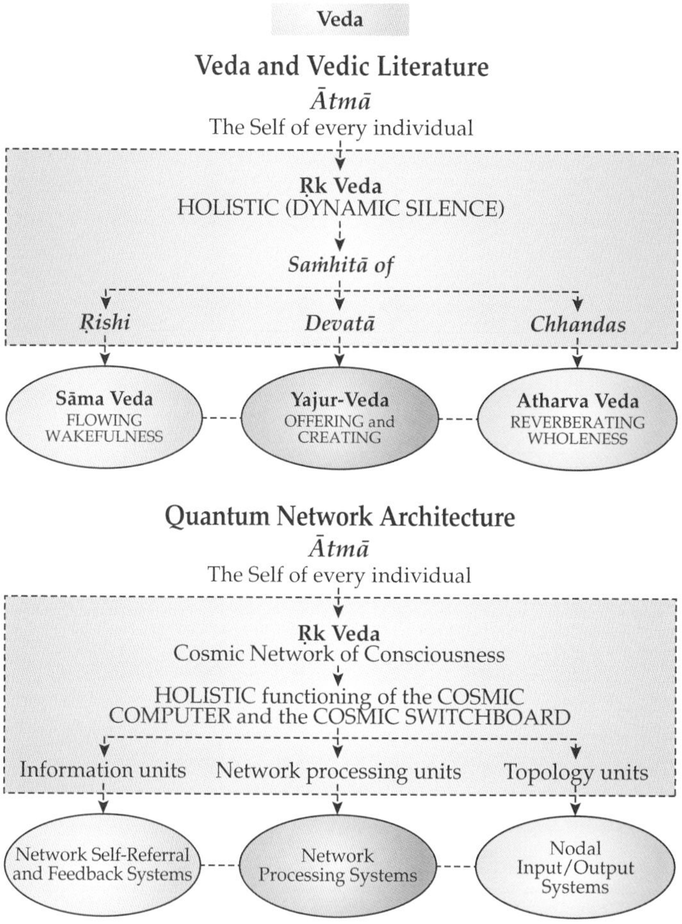

Vedic Term *Quality of Intelligence* Vedic *Shākhās* (Divisions)	**Quantum Network Architecture Term** *Quality of Intelligence* Quantum Network Architecture Divisions
Ṛk Veda *Saṁhitā of Ṛishi, Devatā, Chhandas: Holistic (Dynamic Silence)* 192 *Sūkta* in the first *Maṇdala*, 10 *Maṇdals* in the Ṛk Veda	**Cosmic Network of Consciousness: Holistic functioning of the Cosmic Computer and Cosmic Switchboard** *Saṁhitā of Ṛishi, Devatā, Chhandas: Holistic (Dynamic Silence)* Holistic, classical, and quantum computer network architectures consisting of: • Eight functional layers and interfaces • Each of the eight functional layers and interfaces incorporates three qualities of input/ingress *(Ṛishi)*, processing *(Devatā)*, and output/egress *(Chhandas)*

Figure 3-26 (continued): Vision of the Four Veda in Quantum Network Architecture™

Vedic Term *Quality of Intelligence* Vedic *Shākhās* (Divisions)	**Quantum Network Architecture Term** *Quality of Intelligence* Quantum Network Architecture Divisions
Ṛk Veda (continued)	**Cosmic Network of Consciousness: Holistic functioning of the Cosmic Computer and Cosmic Switchboard (continued)** • The elaborated computational unit of each layer and/or interface and quality is an eight-bit byte (used in classical, space-time symmetry-bound network computing) or eight-qubit qubyte (used in quantum network computing): **8** functional layers/interfaces × **3** qualities of input/ingress *(Ṛishi)*, processing *(Devatā)*, and output/egress *(Chhandas)* × **8** qubit-qubyte or **8** bit-byte = **192** *Sūkta* network computing basis to the first *Maṇdala* of Ṛk Veda, and to the elaboration basis of the entire 10 *Maṇdals* of the Ṛk Veda within the Cosmic Network of Consciousness. The Cosmic Computer and Cosmic Switchboard are an infinitely aware and computational celestial or absolute nervous system and are simultaneously located within the Gap of the Routt Addressable Absolute Memory Gate™ (RAAM Gate™) (unfolded in Chapter 8) and the massively recursive, parallel Gap of the analog and digital infinite and self-referral Cosmic Network of Consciousness.
Sāma Veda *Ṛishi—Flowing Wakefulness* 1000 *Shākhās*, or branches	**Network Self-Referral and Feedback Systems** *Ṛishi—Flowing Wakefulness* Exponentiation of 1000-fold improvements The Global Internetwork—functioning as the logical, physical, and ubiquitous confluence of the Internet, the World Wide Web, and several million private computer networks—is a global, self-referral, conscious superfabric that collects, interprets, processes, interconnects, and integrates, at any given moment, billions of people with hundreds of millions of applications, through a trillion intelligent devices.

Figure 3-26 (continued): Vision of the Four Veda in Quantum Network Architecture™

Vedic Term *Quality of Intelligence* Vedic *Shākhās* (Divisions)	**Quantum Network Architecture Term** *Quality of Intelligence* Quantum Network Architecture Divisions
Sāma Veda (continued)	**Network Self-Referral and Feedback Systems (continued)**
	Magnitudes (powers of 10) of hardware, software, and firmware price-performance improvements continue to be experienced in computer network input/ ingress *(Rishi)*, processing *(Devatā)*, and output/ egress *(Chhandas)* components, subsystems and systems, each from its own perspective as observer *(Ṛishi)*, generating a minimum of 1000-fold improvements every 1000 days.
The *Pūrvāchika* part of Sāma Veda has seven divisions with 64 *Kāṇdas*	Eight architectural layers and interfaces with: **8** functional layers/interfaces × **8** qubits/qubyte (or 8 bits/byte) = **64** functional component network computing basis to Sāma Veda from the perspective of observer *(Ṛishi)*
Uttarārchika part of Sāma Veda	Logical associative and physical topologic components, subsystems, and systems of the Global Internetwork, each from its perspective as observer *(Ṛishi)*
Yajur Veda	**Network Processing Systems**
Devatā—Offering and Creating	*Devatā—Offering and Creating*
Two categories of Yajur-Veda: Shukl (white) and Kṛishṇ (black)	
Shukl-Yajur-Veda has 15 *Shākhās* (divisions) grouped into two categories: Mādhyandina and Kāṇwa.	Shukl (white) Quantum Network Architecture divisions are the *open, seen, conscious* set of 15 external Application Program Interfaces (APIs) grouped into two categories.
Kṛishṇ-Yajur-Veda has 86 *Shākhās*.	Kṛishṇ (black) computer network architecture divisions are the *closed, hidden, subconscious:* **1** Internal APIs **2** Interface definitions **3** Local APIs **4** Interprocess Communications (IPC) **5** Distributed Object RMI (Remote Method Invocation)

Figure 3-26 (continued): Vision of the Four Veda in Quantum Network Architecture™

Vedic Term *Quality of Intelligence* Vedic *Shākhās* (Divisions)	Quantum Network Architecture Term *Quality of Intelligence* Quantum Network Architecture Divisions
Yajur Veda (continued)	**Network Processing Systems (continued)** **6–86** Nine remote interface and invocation semantics × nine functional properties (communication modules, remote reference modules, proxies, dispatchers, server threads, server programs, client binders, client programs, and authentication)
Atharva Veda *Chhandas—Reverberating Wholeness* Nine *Shākhās*, or branches	**Nodal Input/Output Systems** *Chhandas—Reverberating Wholeness* <u>Nine groups:</u> 1 Bus systems (processor-memory, Input/Output [I/O], and backplane) 2 Memory I/O 3 Direct Memory Access (DMA) 4 Processor I/O 5 Operating system I/O 6 Supercomputer I/O benchmarks 7 Transaction processing I/O benchmarks 8 File system I/O benchmarks 9 Network I/O benchmarks

4: VEDĀNGA in Quantum Network Architecture

Vedānga is the limb—or body—of Veda. Figure 4-1 presents the six aspects of Vedānga and their corresponding six aspects in Quantum Network Architecture™.

Shikshā, the first aspect of Vedānga, is the quality that accounts for the mechanics of *Expressing* Veda, has a predominantly *Ṛishi* value, and is expressed in Quantum Network Architecture as *Dynamic Computer Network Architecture.*

From that level of expression, *Ātmā* gets transformed from unmanifest to manifest. This *Transforming* quality is Kalp. Kalp is the fundamental value that transforms the being level into the becoming level. It describes how singularity of consciousness diversifies by means of its self-referral nature, and has a predominantly Devatā value. Kalp is expressed in Quantum Network Architecture as the *Network Architecture Design and Implementation Process.*

From this transformation emerges the quality of *Expanding,* which is Vyākaraṇ. Vyākaraṇ has a predominantly *Chhandas* value, and is expressed in Quantum Network Architecture as *Redundant Network Systems.*

To maintain connectedness with the source, Vedānga operates in a feedback loop fashion. Therefore, the three values of Shikshā, Kalp, and Vyākaraṇ are upheld by a reverse process, which keeps any step of expression, transformation, and expansion connected with the source. Feedback looping maintains connectedness with *Ātmā*—self-referral consciousness. This connection of the three qualities to their source, *Ātmā,* is upheld by Nirukt (*Self-Referral* quality, *Chhandas* predominance), Chhand (*Measuring and Quantifying* quality, *Devatā* predominance), and Jyotish (*All-Knowing* quality, *Ṛishi* predominance), which are expressed, respectively, in Quantum Network Architecture as *Feedback Loops; Dynamic Bandwidth, Load Balancing, and Content Management;* and *Self-Aware, Massively Parallel Network Architecture.*

Figure 4-1: Vision of Vedānga in Quantum Network Architecture™

Vedānga

Veda and Vedic Literature

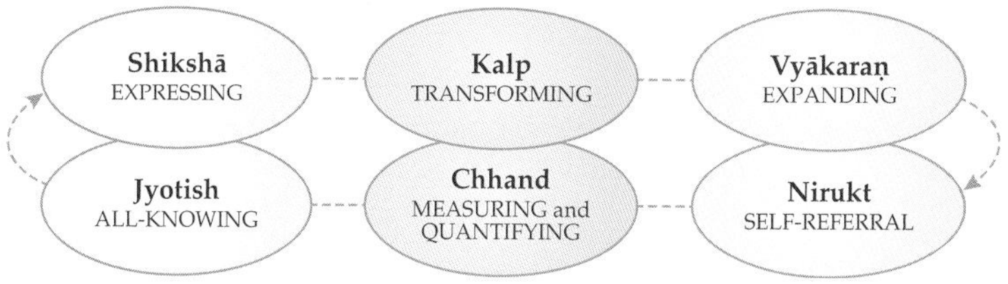

Quantum Network Architecture

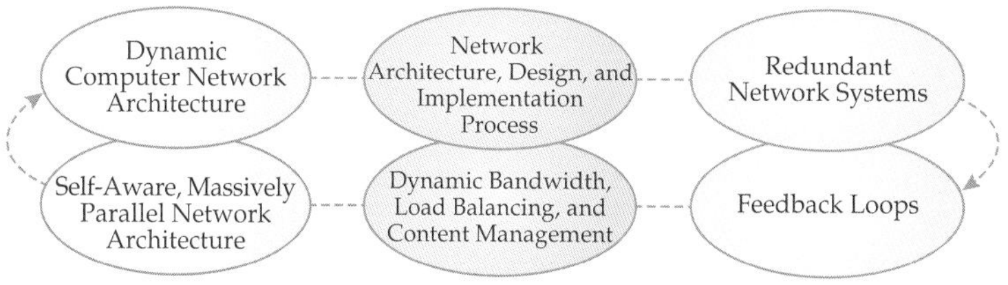

Vedic Term *Quality of Intelligence* Vedic *Shākhās* (Divisions)	**Quantum Network Architecture** *Quality of Intelligence* Quantum Network Architecture Divisions
Shikshā	**Dynamic Computer Network Architecture**
Ṛishi—Expressing	*Ṛishi—Expressing*
Thirty-six main books:	Thirty-six main divisions:
1 Shamāna शमना	1 Business model
2 Vyāli व्यालि	2 Service model
3 Swaravyanjana स्वरव्यञ्जन	3 Network system development life cycle
4 Shaishirīya शैशिरीय	4 Design model
5 Vyāsa व्यास	5 Performance model
6 Chārāyaṇīya छारायणीय	6 Availability model
7 Ātreya आत्रेय	7 Data architecture
8 Vāsishtha वासिष्ठ	8 Applications architecture
9 Pāṇinīya पाणिनीय	9 Technology architecture

Figure 4-1 (continued): Vision of Vedānga in Quantum Network Architecture™

Vedic Term *Quality of Intelligence* Vedic *Shākhās* (Divisions)	**Quantum Network Architecture** *Quality of Intelligence* Quantum Network Architecture Divisions
Shikshā (continued)	**Dynamic Computer Network Architecture (continued)**
10 Lakshmīkānta लक्ष्मीकान्त	**10** Layered computer network architecture
11 Pārāsharī पाराशरी	**11** Network model
12 Padyātmikā keshavī पद्यात्मिका केशवी	**12** Neural network architecture
13 Svarabhaktilakshaṇa parishishta स्वरभक्तिलक्षणपरिशिष्ट	**13** Quantum Network Architecture
14 Kātyāyanī कात्यायनी	**14** Pervasive computing architecture
15 Varṇaratnapradīpikā (Āmaresha) वर्णरत्नप्रदीपिका आमरेश	**15** Application Programming Interface (API) model
16 Mādhyandinīya माध्यन्दिनीय	**16** Internetwork architecture
17 Māṇḍavya माण्डव्य	**17** Grid metacomputer network architecture
18 Vāsishthī वासिष्ठी	**18** Internet architecture
19 Yāgyavalkya याज्ञवल्क्य	**19** Web model
20 Mallasharmakṛitā मल्लशर्मकृता	**20** Intranet architecture
21 Amoghānandinī अमोघानन्दिनी	**21** Extranet architecture
22 Avasānanirṇaya अवसाननिर्णय	**22** Network memory architecture
23 Siddhanta सिद्धान्त	**23** Network database architecture
24 Āpishali आपिशलि	**24** Transaction processing model
25 Sarvasammata सर्वसम्मत	**25** Network file system architecture
26 Āraṇya आरण्य	**26** Connection-oriented network architecture

Figure 4-1 (continued): Vision of Vedānga in Quantum Network Architecture™

Vedic Term *Quality of Intelligence* Vedic *Shākhās* (Divisions)	**Quantum Network Architecture** *Quality of Intelligence* Quantum Network Architecture Divisions
Shikshā (continued)	**Dynamic Computer Network Architecture (continued)**
27 Shambhu शम्भु	**27** Connectionless network architecture
28 Kālanirṇaya कालनिर्णय	**28** Resource naming and allocation convention
29 Bhāradvāja भारद्वाज	**29** Address architecture
30 Kauhalīya कौहलीय	**30** Congestion control model
31 Pāriḥ पारिः	**31** Security architecture
32 Shodashashlokī षोडशश्लोकी	**32** Server and client processor architecture (Multiple Instruction–Multiple Data [MIMD], Single Instruction–Multiple Data [SIMD], Multiple Instruction–Single Data [MISD], and Single Instruction–Single Data [SISD])
33 Māṇdūkī माण्डूकी	**33** Gateway model
34 Nāradīyā नारदीया	**34** Switch router architecture
35 Gautamī गौतमी	**35** Bridge model
36 Lomashī लोमशी	**36** Link topology
Kalp	**Network Architecture, Design, and Implementation Process**
Devatā—Transforming	*Devatā—Transforming*
Four main divisions with 54 components:	Four main divisions; 54 components:
Grihya Sūtra (19 books):	*User and application requirements and elaboration (19 components):*
1 Āshwalāyana आश्वलायन	**1** Business mission
2 Khadira (Drāhyāyaṇa) खदिर (द्राह्यायण)	**2** Market analysis
3 Kāthaka (Laugākshi) काठक (लौगाक्षि)	**3** Technology strategy

Figure 4-1 (continued): Vision of Vedānga in Quantum Network Architecture™

Vedic Term *Quality of Intelligence* Vedic *Shākhās* (Divisions)	**Quantum Network Architecture** *Quality of Intelligence* Quantum Network Architecture Divisions
Kalp (continued)	**Network Architecture, Design, and Implementation Process (continued)**
4 Kaushītaka कौषीतक	4 Internal environment
5 Mānava मानव	5 External environment
6 Pāraskara पारस्कर	6 Enterprise distributed processing requirements
7 Baudhāyana बौधायन	7 Networked application requirements
8 Kaushika कौशिक	8 Computer network strategy
9 Hiranyakeshīya हिरण्यकेशीय	9 Engineering network requirements
10 Vārāha वाराह	10 Alternatives analysis
11 Gobhila गोभिल्ल	11 Constraint analysis
12 Agniveshya अग्निवेश्य	12 Network Net Present Value (NPV) model
13 Shānkhāyana शाङ्खायन	13 Network Internal Rate of Return (IRR) model
14 Vādhūla वाधूल	14 Network Net Future Worth (NFW) model
15 Jaiminī जैमिनी	15 Alternatives weighting and recommendations
16 Bhāradvāja भारद्वाज	16 Alternatives selection
17 Āpastamba आपस्तम्ब	17 Project selection criteria
18 Vaikhānasa वैखानस	18 Risk analysis
19 Kauthuma कौथुम	19 Project selection
Shrauta Sūtra (20 books):	*Architecture (20 components):*
20 Shānkhāyana शाङ्खायन	20 Network services definition

Figure 4-1 (continued): Vision of Vedānga in Quantum Network Architecture™

Vedic Term *Quality of Intelligence* Vedic *Shākhās* (Divisions)	**Quantum Network Architecture** *Quality of Intelligence* Quantum Network Architecture Divisions
Kalp (continued)	**Network Architecture, Design, and Implementation Process (continued)**
21 Āpastamba आपस्तम्ब	**21** Network services interface mapping
22 Mashaka मशक	**22** Distributed object model
23 Kaushika कौशिक	**23** Remote invocation definitions
24 Vaitana वैतन	**24** Application resource naming convention
25 Hiranyakeshīya हिरण्यकेशीय	**25** Network resource naming convention
26 Vādhūla वाधूल	**26** Address convention
27 Mānava मानव	**27** Name-address mapping convention
28 Bhāradvāja भारद्वाज	**28** Network timing and synchronization model
29 Drāhyāyaṇa द्राह्यायण	**29** Global states mapping
30 Lātyāyana लात्यायन	**30** Transaction and concurrency definitions
31 Vārāha वाराह	**31** Network database conventions
32 Kātyāyana कात्यायन	**32** Replication conventions
33 Kāthaka (Laugākshi) काठक (लौगाक्षि)	**33** Network file system conventions
34 Āshwalāyana आश्वलायन	**34** Network multimedia system conventions
35 Jaiminīya जैमिनीय	**35** Networked application security policies
36 Nidāna निदान	**36** Shared memory conventions
37 Baudhāyana बौधायन	**37** Availability conventions
38 Vaikhānasa वैखानस	**38** Load balancing and content management conventions

Figure 4-1 (continued): Vision of Vedānga in Quantum Network Architecture™

Vedic Term *Quality of Intelligence* Vedic *Shākhās* (Divisions)	**Quantum Network Architecture** *Quality of Intelligence* Quantum Network Architecture Divisions
Kalp (continued)	**Network Architecture, Design, and Implementation Process (continued)**
39 Anupāda अनुपाद	**39** Broadband network architecture
Shulba Sūtra (eight books):	*Design (eight components):*
40 Kāthaka (Laugākshi) काठक (लौगाक्षि)	**40** Predictive modeling
41 Hiraṇyakeshīya हिरण्यकेशीय	**41** Global design parameters
42 Baudhāyana बौधायन	**42** Hierarchical and network design models
43 Vārāha वाराह	**43** Wide Area Network (WAN), Metropolitan Area Network (MAN), Local Area Network (LAN), campus, and access designs
44 Vādhūla वाधूल	**44** Availability and Service Level Agreement (SLA) designs
45 Mānava मानव	**45** Security design
46 Āpastamba आपस्तम्ब	**46** Logical topology design
47 Kātyāyana कात्यातन	**47** Physical topology design
Dharma Sūtra (seven books):	*Implementation (seven components):*
48 Vishṇu विष्णु	**48** Software coding
49 Vasishtha वसिष्ठ	**49** Software testing
50 Āpastamba आपस्तम्ब	**50** Configuration coding
51 Hiraṇyakeshiya हिरण्यकेशीय	**51** Configuration testing
52 Gautama गौतम	**52** Hardware interface definitions and testing
53 Vaikhānasa वैखानस	**53** Subsystem and global system testing
54 Baudhāyana बौधायन	**54** Network certification

Figure 4-1 (continued): Vision of Vedānga in Quantum Network Architecture™

Vedic Term *Quality of Intelligence* Vedic *Shākhās* (Divisions)	**Quantum Network Architecture** *Quality of Intelligence* Quantum Network Architecture Divisions
Vyākaraṇ	**Redundant Network Systems**
Chhandas—Expanding	*Chhandas—Expanding*
One book with eight chapters of four divisions each, totaling 32 divisions:	Eight groups of four divisions each, totaling 32 divisions:
First chapter: प्रथमोऽध्याय:	*Highly available data management:*
1 १ वृद्धिरादैच्	1 Redundant Array of Independent (or Inexpensive) Disks (RAID)
2 २ गङ्कुटादिभ्योऽञ्णिन् ङित्	2 Small Computer Systems Interface (SCSI)
3 ३ भूवादयो धातव:	3 FibreChannel
4 ४ आ कडारादेका संज्ञा	4 Disk space and FileSystems
Second chapter: द्वितीयोऽध्याय:	*Reliable data service:*
5 ५ समर्थ: पदविधि:	5 Web servers
6 ६ पूर्वापराधरोत्तरमेकदेशिनैकाधिकरणे	6 Dynamic load balancing
7 ७ अनभिहिते	7 Network FileSystem services
8 ८ द्विगुरेकवचनम्	8 Database servers
Third chapter: तृतीयोऽध्याय:	*Replication techniques (Grammar aspect of Vyākaraṇ):*
9 ९ प्रत्यय:	9 Replication applications
10 १० कर्मण्यण्	10 Database replication
11 ११ उणादयो बहुलम्	11 FileSystem replication
12 १२ धातुसम्बन्धे प्रत्यया:	12 Process replication
Fourth chapter: चतुर्थोऽध्याय:	*Redundant server design:*
13 १३ ङ्याप्प्रातिपदिकात्	13 Failover requirements
14 १४ तेन रक्तं रागात्	14 Application-centric approach
15 १५ युष्मदस्मदोरन्यतरस्यां खञ् च	15 Network failover (heartbeat, production, and administrative)
16 १६ प्राग्वहतेष्ठक्	16 Disk failover
Fifth chapter: पञ्चमोऽध्याय:	*Redundant network services:*
17 १७ प्राक् क्रीताच्छ:	17 Network failure taxonomy
18 १८ धान्यानां भवने क्षेत्रे खञ्	18 Network service reliability
19 १९ प्राग् दिशो विभक्ति:	19 Physical network redundancy
20 २० पादशतस्य सङ्ख्यादेर्वीप्सायां वुन्लोपश्च	20 Logical network redundancy

Figure 4-1 (continued): Vision of Vedānga in Quantum Network Architecture™

Vedic Term *Quality of Intelligence* Vedic *Shākhās* (Divisions)	**Quantum Network Architecture** *Quality of Intelligence* Quantum Network Architecture Divisions
Vyākaraṇ (continued)	**Redundant Network Systems (continued)**
Sixth chapter: षष्ठोऽध्यायः	*Backups and restores:*
21 २१ एकाचो द्वे प्रथमस्य	**21** Backup rule set
22 २२ बहुव्रीहौ प्रकृत्या पूर्वपदम्	**22** Restore rule set
23 २३ अलुगुत्तरपदे	**23** Backup software
24 २४ अङ्गस्य	**24** Backup windows
Seventh chapter: सप्तमोऽध्यायः	*Application recovery:*
25 २५ युवोरनाकौ	**25** Application failure modes and recovery techniques
26 २६ सिचि वृद्धिः परस्मैपदेषु	**26** Internal application failures and recovery
27 २७ देविकाशिशपादित्यवाड्दीर्घसत्रश्रेयसामात्	**27** Application recovery from system failures
28 २८ णौ चङ्युपधाया ह्रस्वः	**28** Data service failures and recovery
Eighth chapter: अष्टमोऽध्यायः	*Disaster recovery:*
29 २९ सर्वस्य द्वे	**29** Disaster recovery vs. high availability calculations
30 ३० पूर्वत्रासिद्धम्	**30** Prioritized applications
31 ३१ मतुवसो रु सम्बुद्धौ छन्दसि	**31** Local failover
32 ३२ रषाभ्यां नो णः समानपदे	**32** Disaster recovery site hardware, software, and procedures
Nirukt	**Feedback Loops**
Chhandas—Self-Referral	*Chhandas—Self-Referral*
One book with 13 chapters:	Thirteen divisions:
1 अध्याय १	**1** Error detecting codes
2 अध्याय २	**2** Error correcting codes
3 अध्याय ३	**3** Self-checking combinational logic design
4 अध्याय ४	**4** Self-checking checkers
5 अध्याय ५	**5** Self-checking sequential circuit design
6 अध्याय ६	**6** Information redundancy
7 अध्याय ७	**7** Hardware redundancy
8 अध्याय ८	**8** Software redundancy
9 अध्याय ९	**9** Data redundancy
10 अध्याय १०	**10** Network system-level fault tolerance

Figure 4-1 (continued): Vision of Vedānga in Quantum Network Architecture™

Vedic Term *Quality of Intelligence* Vedic *Shākhās* (Divisions)	**Quantum Network Architecture** *Quality of Intelligence* Quantum Network Architecture Divisions
Nirukt (continued)	**Feedback Loops (continued)**
11 अध्याय ११	**11** If-Then-Else conditional branch
12 अध्याय १२	**12** Variable array index loop
13 अध्याय १३	**13** While loop
Chhand	**Dynamic Bandwidth, Load Balancing, and Content Management**
Devatā—Measuring and Quantifying	*Devatā—Measuring and Quantifying*
<u>One book with eight chapters:</u>	<u>Eight divisions:</u>
1 First *Sūtra* of the first chapter धीश्रीस्त्री म् ।१.१।	**1** Policy architecture
2 First *Sūtra* of the second chapter छन्दः ।२.१।	**2** Network traffic classification
3 First *Sūtra* of the third chapter पादः ।३.१।	**3** User and application identification, classification
4 First *Sūtra* of the fourth chapter चतुःशतमुत्कृतिः ।४.१।	**4** Differentiated Services (DiffServ)
5 First *Sūtra* of the fifth chapter वृत्तम् ।५.१।	**5** Device traffic handling
6 First *Sūtra* of the sixth chapter यतिर्विच्छेदः ।६.१।	**6** Path selection traffic handling
7 First *Sūtra* of the seventh chapter प्रहर्षिणी म्नौ जरौ ग् त्रिकदशकौ ।७.१।	**7** Load balancing
8 First *Sūtra* of the eighth chapter अत्रानुक्तं गाथा ।८.१।	**8** Content management
"Chhand is the point of return where expansion is in tune with returning back to the source. In the point there is a whorling of the Reality. It has a multiple directional dynamism." *His Holiness Maharishi Mahesh Yogi, MERU, 2 July 2002*	

Figure 4-1 (continued): Vision of Vedānga in Quantum Network Architecture™

Vedic Term *Quality of Intelligence* Vedic *Shākhās* (Divisions)	**Quantum Network Architecture** *Quality of Intelligence* Quantum Network Architecture Divisions
Jyotish	**Self-Aware, Massively Parallel Network Architecture**
Ṛishi—All-Knowing	*Ṛishi—All-Knowing*
Nine *Grahas* (Planets):	Nine computer network components:
1 Sūrya सूर्य Sun	1 Network node, Central Processing Unit (CPU)/ Network Processing Unit (NPU), and Network-on-a-Chip™
2 Chandra चन्द्र Moon	2 Redundant network, clocking, and synchronization systems. Motherboard.
3 Maṇgala मङ्गल Mars	3 Network security architecture and Arithmetic Logic Unit (ALU)
4 Budha बुध Mercury	4 Hot standby systems, shared network memory, e-commerce, e-business, and m-commerce
5 Guru गुरु Jupiter	5 Scaleable network architecture, broadband network architecture, and distance learning
6 Shukra शुक्र Venus	6 High-end, state-of-the-art computer network architecture
7 Shani शनि Saturn	7 Murphy's Law and disaster recovery plan
8 Rāhu राहु Ascending Node	8 Unanticipated network tangible and intangible benefits, and unscheduled system outages and downtime
9 Ketu केतु Descending Node	9 Quantum metacomputer
Twelve *Rāshis* (Signs):	Twelve aspects of computer network intelligence:
1 Mesha (Movable—Fire)	1 Remote viewing system and vision system
2 Vṛishabh (Fixed—Earth)	2 Signal and image identification system
3 Mithuna (Dual—Air)	3 Robotic networked manipulator controller, and radar and image signal processing system
4 Karka (Movable—Water)	4 Voice network, and text-to-speech synthesis system
5 Siṁha (Fixed—Fire)	5 Video broadband network, Web cam, machine vision, and visual quality inspection system
6 Kanyā (Dual—Earth)	6 Network telemetry
7 Tulā (Movable—Air)	7 Trajectory control network
8 Vṛishchik (Fixed—Water)	8 Web-centric Global Positioning System (GPS), directional mapping system, and image signal processing with data compression

Figure 4-1 (continued): Vision of Vedānga in Quantum Network Architecture™

Vedic Term *Quality of Intelligence* Vedic *Shākhās* (Divisions)	**Quantum Network Architecture** *Quality of Intelligence* Quantum Network Architecture Divisions
9 Dhanu (Dual—Fire)	9 Operational analysis system
10 Makara (Movable—Earth)	10 Aircraft, ship, or spaceship autopilot system, automobile automatic guidance system, and transportation routing optimization system
11 Kumbha (Fixed—Air)	11 Speech recognition system, speech data compression, vowel classification, and real-time translation of spoken language
12 Mīna (Dual—Water)	12 Process analysis system
Twenty-seven *Nakshatras* (Constellations):	Twenty-seven computer network processes and components:
1 Ashvinī	1 Network initialization and activation
2 Bharaṇī	2 Interoperable network architecture
3 Kṛittikā	3 Firewall (AgniWall™)
4 Rọhiṇī	4 Knowledge-based, expert systems
5 Mṛigashirā	5 Search engine
6 Ārdrā	6 Daughterboard and spawned network processes
7 Punarvasu	7 Dense Wave Division Multiplexer (DWDM)
8 Pushya	8 Feedback loops
9 Āshleshā	9 Intrusion detection and reconciliation
10 Maghā	10 User and end-system interactions
11 Pūrvāphālgunī	11 Preliminary design review
12 Uttarāphālgunī	12 Detail design review
13 Hasta	13 Handheld Personal Digital Assistant (PDA) and palmtop
14 Chitrā	14 Optical network
15 Swāti	15 Self-referral, recursive network
16 Vishākhā	16 Gateway, portal
17 Anurādhā	17 Nanotechnologies
18 Jyeshthā	18 Motherboard
19 Mūla	19 Root directory, base$_n$ number systems (binary, octal, decimal, and hexadecimal), and conversion from base$_b$ to base$_{bn}$
20 Pūrvāshādhā	20 Internet data center
21 Uttarāshādhā	21 Virtual Private Network (VPN)

Figure 4-1 (continued): Vision of Vedānga in Quantum Network Architecture™

Vedic Term *Quality of Intelligence* Vedic *Shākhās* (Divisions)	**Quantum Network Architecture** *Quality of Intelligence* Quantum Network Architecture Divisions
Jyotish (continued)	**Self-aware, Massively Parallel Network Architecture (continued)**
22 Shravaṇ	**22** Voice-Over-Packet-Over-Silence™
23 Dhanishthā	**23** Signal-to-noise ratio, Signal-to-Silence Ratio™
24 Shatabhishā	**24** Network and system management and security architecture
25 Pūrvābhādrapada	**25** Dynamic Internetwork security architecture inclusive of protection, intrusion detection, and compromise reconciliation
26 Uttarābhādrapada	**26** Trojan horse
27 Revatī	**27** Technically elegant, high Net Present Value (NPV)/Internal Rate of Return (IRR) computer network
"Jyotish [Maharishi Vedic Astrology] is the expression of the quality of all-directional dynamism expressed in a point, contained within the point, and that is total knowingness, total intelligence, Ritam Bhara Pragya—established consciousness, intelligence—Ritam Satyam, the eternal reality of Self-referral Ātmā, the quality of Self-referral knowingness, all knowingness. This is why in the mathematics of Jyotish, everything is predictable—all past, present, future—on the basis of a point. The birth point is the point from where the entire dynamism of life is calculated. And this is the precision of Vedic Science." *His Holiness Maharishi Mahesh Yogi, MERU, 2 July 2002*	

5: UPĀNGA in Quantum Network Architecture

Upānga are the six aspects of Vedic Literature corresponding to the subordinate *(upa)* limbs *(anga),* or body, of the Veda. They have been classically known as the six Darshana, or six systems of Indian philosophy. Upānga deal with higher cognitive function and balance between specific and holistic aspects of Natural Law.

Figure 5-1 presents the six aspects of Upānga and their corresponding six aspects in Quantum Network Architecture™. Upānga operates in the same way as Vedānga, by means of a loop—going and coming back to the source—and consists of Nyāya, Vaisheshik, Sāṁkhya, Yoga, Karma Mīmāṁsā, and Vedānt.

Nyāya, the first value of Upānga, represents that value which allows one to see going and coming back at the same time. Nyāya has a *Distinguishing and Deciding* quality, maintains coexistence of opposite values, is predominantly of *Ṛishi* value, and is expressed in Quantum Network Architecture as *Central Processing Unit/Network Processing Unit.*

> Having finished the six Vedāngas, Nyāya is expansion of Jyotish. The first Nyāya Sūtra says: *Pramā-ṇa prameya*—That is *Pramā,* consciousness, intelligence. Intelligence, not physical. And it has another meaning to it: *Pramā ṇa-prameya—Pramā* is authenticity. What is the authenticity of all-knowingness? It is *Pramā,* consciousness, not physical. It is unphysical, unmanifest, transcendental. In Nyāya, the whole knowledge is in a balanced state, balancing state, of silence and dynamism. Silence and dynamism, perfectly balanced, is justice (balance). Now this balance is the balance of two opposite qualities of Self-referral intelligence. And that is termed as *Lamp at the Door* which lights inside and outside at the same time. So Nyāya features the reality of the quality of all-knowingness,

> that is, the quality of that intelligence which becomes the silence value and the dynamic value of consciousness.
>
> His Holiness Maharishi Mahesh Yogi
> MERU, 2 July 2002.

Vaisheshik deals with specific aspects, points, or values of infinity (*Specifying* quality), and their specific sequence, has a predominantly *Devatā* value, and is expressed in Quantum Network Architecture as *System Configuration/Connection.*

The points of Vaisheshik are counted in terms of 25 values described in Sāṁkhya, which represents the *Enumerating* quality of intelligence, has a predominantly *Chhandas* value, and is expressed in Quantum Network Architecture as *Arithmetic Logic Unit.*

It is important to note that these points are in the state of Unity and therefore, as a complete contrast to the consideration from the value of these points, we have that Unity, oneness, singularity. This *Unifying* quality is handled by Yoga (*Chhandas* predominant), expressed in Quantum Network Architecture as *Logical Network Topology and Associations.* Yoga is the Unified quality of holistic knowledge and diversified total knowledge as counted in the theme of Number System (Sāmkhya). In Yoga, in the unity value, the goal of "know thyself" is reached. Immediately, through the process of knowing oneself, the concept of knower *(Ṛishi),* process of knowing *(Devatā),* and known *(Chhandas)* emerges.

As a result, dynamic activity (Karma) emerges. Karma Mīmāṁsā is the field of analysis of action (*Analyzing* quality; Karma Mīmāṁsā is analysis of action within the silence of Yoga), is *Devatā*-predominant, and is expressed in Quantum Network Architecture as the *Backbone Network System.*

Yoga and Karma Mīmāṁsā together find themselves as totally opposite qualities within Vedānt. Vedānt is Wholeness left to itself, but fully awake—*Living Wholeness—I-ness or Being,* Lively Absolute. Vedānt is Living Wholeness, the integrated value of silence (Yoga) and action (Karma Mīmāṁsā), is *Ṛishi* predominant, and is expressed in Quantum Network Architecture as *Integrated Functioning of the Backbone Network System.*

Figure 5-1: Vision of Upānga in Quantum Network Architecture™

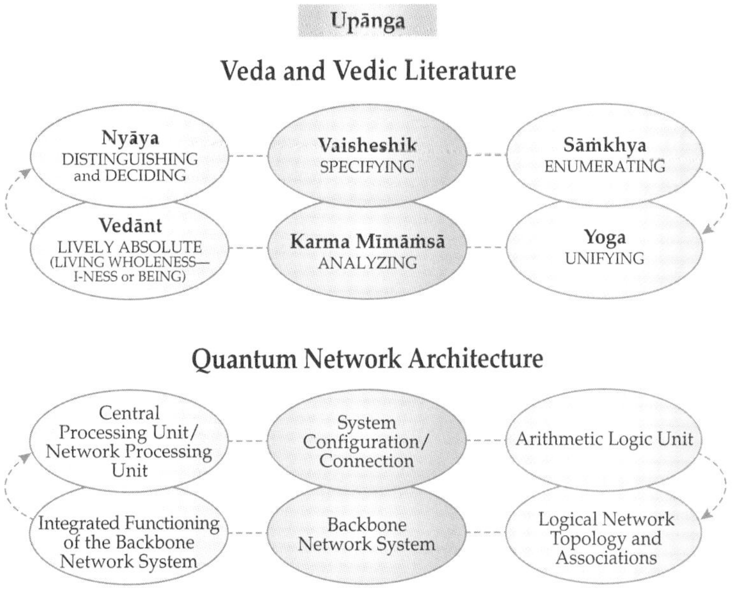

Vedic Term *Quality of Intelligence* Vedic *Shākhās* (Divisions)	**Quantum Network Architecture** *Quality of Intelligence* Quantum Network Architecture Divisions
Nyāya	**Central Processing Unit/Network Processing Unit**
Ṛishi—Distinguishing and Deciding	*Ṛishi—Distinguishing and Deciding*
<u>Five chapters with two divisions each, totalling 10 divisions:</u>	<u>Five classic components found in Central Processing Unit (CPU) and Network Processing Unit (NPU) each, totaling 10 components:</u> 1 Datapath 2 Control 3 Memory 4 Input 5 Output
<u>Sixteen categories:</u>	<u>Sixteen component categories:</u>
1 *Pramāṇa* प्रमाण Means of Valid Knowledge	1 Hardware primitives
2 *Prameya* प्रमेय Object of Valid Knowledge	2 Hardware operands
3 *Saṁshaya* संशय Doubt	3 Registers
4 *Prayojana* प्रयोजन Purpose	4 Hardware-Software Gap™
5 *Dṛishṭānta* दृष्टान्त Example	5 $Base_n$ numbers

Figure 5-1 (continued): Vision of Upānga in Quantum Network Architecture™

Vedic Term *Quality of Intelligence* Vedic *Shākhās* (Divisions)	**Quantum Network Architecture** *Quality of Intelligence* Quantum Network Architecture Divisions
Nyāya (continued)	**CPU/NPU (continued)**
6 *Siddhānta* सिद्धान्त Established Principle	6 Codes and encoding
7 *Avayava* अवयव Parts of a Logical Argument	7 Algorithms
8 *Tarka* तर्क Process of Reasoning	8 Truth tables
9 *Nirṇaya* निर्णय Art of Drawing Conclusion	9 Boolean algebra
10 *Vāda* वाद Discussion	10 Gates
11 *Jalpa* जल्प Polemics	11 Programmable circuits for combinational design
12 *Vitaṇḍā* वितण्डा Cavil	12 Read-Only Memory (ROM)
13 *Hetvābhāsa* हेत्वाभास Fallacies	13 Random Access Memory (RAM)
14 *Chhala* छल Equivocation	14 Flip-flops
15 *Jāti* जाति Futile Argument	15 Synchronous counters
16 *Nigrahasthāna* निग्रहस्थान Disagreement on First Principles	16 Synchronous finite state machines
Vaisheshik	**System Configuration/Connection**
Devatā—Specifying	*Devatā—Specifying*
One book with 10 chapters of two divisions each, totaling 20 divisions with 370 *Sūtras:*	Ten groups with two divisons each, totaling 20 divisions:
1 *Prathamo'dhyāyaḥ* प्रथमोऽध्याय:	1 Resource naming convention: Naming standards Naming administration
2 *Dvitīyo'dhyāyaḥ* द्वितीयोऽध्याय:	2 Addressing convention: Address assignment Address translation
3 *Tritīyo'dhyāyaḥ* तृतीयोऽध्याय:	3 Routing and switching tables: Table maintenance Table debugging

Figure 5-1 (continued): Vision of Upānga in Quantum Network Architecture™

Vedic Term *Quality of Intelligence* Vedic *Shākhās* (Divisions)	Quantum Network Architecture *Quality of Intelligence* Quantum Network Architecture Divisions
Vaisheshik (continued)	**System Configuration/Connection (continued)**
4 *Chaturtho'dhyāyaḥ* चतुर्थोऽध्याय:	4 Static routes: Default Configured
5 *Panchamo'dhyāyaḥ* पञ्चमोऽध्याय:	5 Dynamic routes: Default Configured
6 *Shashtho'dhyāyaḥ* षष्ठोऽध्याय:	6 Topology and directory convention: Topology and directory databases Topology and directory configurations
7 *Saptamo'dhyāyaḥ* सप्तमोऽध्याय:	7 End-system connection process: Connection setup Signaling
8 *Ashtamo'dhyāyaḥ* अष्टमोऽध्याय:	8 Route calculation: Routing decision processes Physical topology and hop costs calculations
9 *Navamo'dhyāyaḥ* नवमोऽध्याय:	9 Traffic management and congestion control: Connection setup phase Data transfer phase
10 *Dashamo'dhyāyaḥ* दशमोऽध्याय:	10 Virtual Circuit connectivity: Permanent circuits Switched circuits
Sāṁkhya *Chhandas—Enumerating* Six chapters with 25 basic values (listed by first and last *Sūtra* of the chapter): 1 *Atha trividhaduḥkhātyan-tanivṛittiratyantapurushārthaḥ* अथ त्रिविधदु: खात्यन्तनिवृत्तिरत्यन्तपुरुषार्थ: ॥१॥ *Uparāgāt karttṛitvaṁ chitsān-nidhyāch chitsānnidhyāt* उपरागात्कर्तृत्वं चित्सान्निध्याच्चित्सान्निध्यात् ॥१६४॥	**Arithmetic Logic Unit** *Chhandas—Enumerating* Six Arithmetic Logic Unit (ALU) hardware building blocks and functions: *Four ALU hardware building blocks:* 1 AND Gate

Figure 5-1 (continued): Vision of Upānga in Quantum Network Architecture™

Vedic Term *Quality of Intelligence* Vedic *Shākhās* (Divisions)	**Quantum Network Architecture** *Quality of Intelligence* Quantum Network Architecture Divisions
Sāṁkhya (continued)	**Arithmetic Logic Unit (continued)**
2 *Vimuktamokshārthaṁ swārthaṁ vā pradhānasya* विमुक्तमोत्त्वार्थं स्वार्थं वा प्रधानस्य ॥१॥ *Samānakarmayoge buddheḥ prādhānyaṁ lokaval lokavat* समानकर्मयोगे बुद्धेः प्राधान्यं लोकवल्लोकवत् ॥४७॥	**2** OR Gate
3 *Avisheshād visheshārambhaḥ* अविशेषाद् विशेषारम्भः ॥१॥ *Vivekānniḥsheshaduḥkhani-vṛittau kṛitakṛityatā netarānnetarāt* विवेकान्निःशेषदुःखनिवृत्तौ कृतकृत्यता नेतरान्नेतरात् ॥८४॥	**3** Inverter
4 *Rājaputravat tattvopadeshāt* राजपुत्रवत् तत्त्वोपदेशात् ॥१॥ *Na bhūtiyoge'pi kṛitakṛityatopāsyasiddhivad upāsyasiddhivat* न भूतियोगेऽपि कृतकृत्यतोपास्यसिद्धिवदुपास्यसिद्धिवत् ॥३२॥	**4** Multiplexer
5 *Mangalācharaṇam shishtāchārāt phaladarshanāch chhrutitashcheti* मङ्गलाचरणं शिष्टाचारात् फलदर्शनाच्छ्रुतितश्चेति ॥१॥ *Na bhūtachaitanyaṁ pratyekādṛishteḥ sāṁhatye'pi cha sāṁhatye'pi cha* न भूतचैतन्यं प्रत्येकादृष्टेः सांहत्येऽपि च सांहत्येऽपि च ॥१२९॥	*Two major ALU functions:* **5** Operation

Figure 5-1 (continued): Vision of Upānga in Quantum Network Architecture™

Vedic Term *Quality of Intelligence* Vedic *Shākhās* (Divisions)	**Quantum Network Architecture** *Quality of Intelligence* Quantum Network Architecture Divisions
Sāṁkhya (continued)	**Arithmetic Logic Unit (continued)**
6 *Astyātmā nāstitvasādhanābhāvāt* ग्रस्त्यात्मा नास्तित्वसाधनाभावात् ॥१॥ *Yadvā tadvā tad uchchhittiḥ purushārthas tad uchchhittiḥ purushārthaḥ* यद्वा तद्वा तदुच्छित्तिः पुरुषार्थस्तदुच्छित्तिः पुरुषार्थः ॥७०॥	**6** Result
	<u>Twenty-five basic ALU values:</u> **1** "Infinite" hardware **2** Integer addition hardware **3** Ripple adder **4** Carry skip adder **5** Carry-select and conditional-sum adder **6** Carry lookahead adder **7** Canonic adder **8** Ling adder **9** Emitter-Coupled Logic (ECL) adder **10** Floating-Point Unit (FPU) architecture **11** High-speed floating point addition algorithms and topologies **12** Variable-latency floating point addition topologies **13** Floating-point Unit cost Performance Analysis (FUPA) metric **14** Regular multiplier topologies **15** Irregular multiplier topologies **16** Division topologies **17** Very high radix division algorithms and hardware **18** Shift Register Transfer (SRT) division topologies **19** Reciprocal algorithms and hardware **20** Square root algorithms and hardware **21** Pipelining circuitry

Figure 5-1 (continued): Vision of Upānga in Quantum Network Architecture™

Vedic Term *Quality of Intelligence* Vedic *Shākhās* (Divisions)	**Quantum Network Architecture** *Quality of Intelligence* Quantum Network Architecture Divisions
Sāṁkhya (continued)	**Arithmetic Logic Unit (continued)** **22** Wave-pipeline circuitry **23** Scalar unit architecture **24** Vector unit architecture **25** Metacomputer and grid computer virtual ALU
Yoga *Chhandas—Unifying* One book with four chapters with 195 *Sūtras:* **1** *Samādhi-Pādaḥ* (*Sūtras* 1–51) समाधिपादः On Concentration **2** *Sādhana-Pādaḥ* (*Sūtras* 52–106) साधनपादः On Practice **3** *Vibhūti-Pādaḥ* (*Sūtras* 107–161) विभुतपादः Supernormal Powers **4** *Kaivalya–Pādaḥ* (*Sūtras* 162–195) कैवल्यपादः On the Self-In-ItSelf or Liberation	**Logical Network Topology and Associations** *Chhandas—Unifying* Four major associative divisions: **1** ES-to-ES logical associations and logical connectivity (End System [ES]: end-users, applications, databases, file systems, transaction systems, clients, servers, supercomputers, mainframes, midrange systems, PCs, laptops, subnotebooks, palmtops, PDAs, and cell phones) **2** ES-to-IS logical associations and logical connectivity (Intermediate System [IS]: routers, switches, firewalls, load balancers, and content balancers) **3** IS-to-IS logical associations and logical connectivity **4** Internetwork system logical associations and logical connectivity
Karma Mīmāṁsā *Devatā—Analyzing* One book with twelve chapters and 60 *Pādas*, or divisions	**Backbone Network System** *Devatā—Analyzing* Internetwork and Internet processing of ingress/input and egress/output flows of each to or from the following six backbone network system levels: 6 levels ingress + 6 levels egress = 12 levels • Level 0—The Global Internetwork • Level 1—Interconnect level—Network Access Points (NAPs) • Level 2—National backbone level

Figure 5-1 (continued): Vision of Upānga in Quantum Network Architecture™

Vedic Term *Quality of Intelligence* Vedic *Shākhās* (Divisions)	**Quantum Network Architecture** *Quality of Intelligence* Quantum Network Architecture Divisions
Karma Mīmāṁsā (continued)	**Backbone Network System (continued)** • Level 3—Regional networks • Level 4—Internet Service Providers (ISPs) • Level 5—Consumer and business market
Vedānt	**Integrated Functioning of the Backbone Network System**
Ṛishi—Lively Absolute (Living Wholeness —I-ness or Being)	*Ṛishi—Lively Absolute (Living Wholeness —I-ness or Being)*
	Quantum computer (summarized in this *Quantum Network Architecture Term* column associated with Ṛk Veda Prātishākhya) corresponds to the holistic quality of Vedānt.
<u>One book with four *Adhyayas* (chapters), 16 divisions and 192 subdivisions:</u> 1 The Book of Reconciliation 2 No Conflict Between Vedānt and Other *Shāstras* 3 The *Sadhanas* or Means of Reaching Brāhmaṇ 4 *Mukti* and Its Nature and Kinds of *Muktas*	The four expressions of logical network topology (summarized in this column associated with Yoga) in their integrated functioning correspond to the four *Adhyayas* (chapters) of Vedānt.
Sixteen divisions	The 16 categories of the CPU/NPU (summarized in this column associated with Nyāya) in their integrated functioning correspond to the 16 divisions of Vedānt.
192 *Adhikaraṇas* (subdivisions)	The 192 components of Quantum Network Architecture (summarized in this column associated with Ṛk Veda) correspond to the 192 *Adhikaraṇas* (subdivisions) of Vedānt.

6: UPA-VEDA in Quantum Network Architecture

The 12 Upa-Veda are the aspects of Vedic Literature corresponding to subordinate *(upa)* Veda. Upa-Veda means *subordinate Veda.*

Gandharva Veda is the Upa-Veda of Sāma Veda, Dhanur Veda is the Upa-Veda of Yajur-Veda, and Sthapātya Veda is the Upa-Veda of Atharva Veda. The remaining nine Upa-Veda are generally considered as a group to be the Upa-Veda of Ṛk Veda. Maharishi has brought to light that these 12 Upa-Veda are the Upa-Veda of the four main Veda (Ṛk Veda, Sāma Veda, Yajur Veda, Atharva Veda).

Figure 6-1 presents the 12 aspects of Upa-Veda and their corresponding 12 aspects in Quantum Network Architecture.™ Gandharva Veda is the *Integrating and Harmonizing* quality of intelligence, has *Ṛishi* predominance, and is expressed in Quantum Network Architecture as *Network/Computer Clocking and Synchronization.*

Dhanur-Veda is the *Invincible and Progressive* quality of intelligence, has Devatā predominance, and is expressed in Quantum Network Architecture as *Security Architecture.*

Sthapātya Veda is the quality of *Establishing Everything in the Light of Natural Law,* has *Chhandas* predominance, and is expressed in Quantum Network Architecture as *Physical Network Topology.*

Hārīta Saṁhitā represents the *Nourishing* quality of Natural Law, has *Chhandas* predominance, and is expressed in Quantum Network Architecture as *Bandwidth Management, Quality of Service.*

Bhel Saṁhitā is the *Differentiating* quality of intelligence, has *Devatā* predominance, and is expressed in Quantum Network Architecture as *Prioritized Queueing Systems.*

Kāshyap Saṁhitā is the quality of *Equivalency* in Natural Law, has *Ṛishi* predominance, and is expressed in Quantum Network Architecture as *Availability Logic*.

The second loop of Upa-Veda emerges as a *Balancing* quality of intelligence, which is a self-sufficient loop formed by the following six *Saṁhitā*: Charak, Sushrut, Vāgbhatt, Mādhav Nidān, Shārngadhar, and Bhāva-Prakāsh. This second Upa-Veda loop eliminates the mistake of the intellect, which sees the parts of life as separate from the holistic value of life. It is the perfect science of health and total integration.

Charak Saṁhitā is the quality of *Balancing—Holding Together and Supporting* in Natural Law, has *Ṛishi* predominance, and is expressed in Quantum Network Architecture as *Network-on-a-Chip*™.

Sushrut Saṁhitā is the *Separating* quality of Natural Law, has *Devatā* predominance, and is expressed in Quantum Network Architecture as *Field and Gate Logic*.

Vāgbhatt Saṁhitā is the *Communication and Eloquence* quality of Natural Law, has *Chhandas* predominance, and is expressed in Quantum Network Architecture as *Dynamic Network Modeling*.

Mādhav Nidān Saṁhitā is the *Diagnosing* quality of Natural Law, has *Chhandas* predominance, and is expressed in Quantum Network Architecture as *Network/Systems Management*.

Shārngadhar Saṁhitā is the *Synthesizing* quality of Natural Law, has Devatā predominance, and is expressed in Quantum Network Architecture as *Database and Transaction Processing*.

Bhāva-Prakāsh Saṁhitā is the *Enlightening* quality of Natural Law, has *Ṛishi* predominance, and is expressed in Quantum Network Architecture as *Optical Networks*.

Figure 6-1: Vision of Upa-Veda in Quantum Network Architecture™

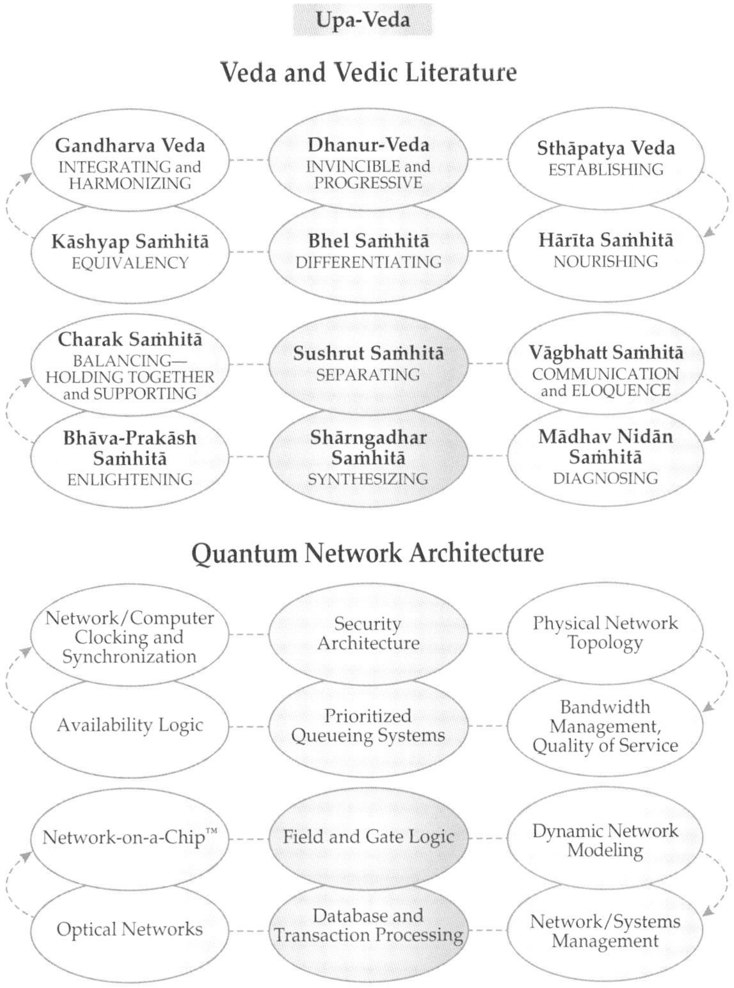

Vedic Term *Quality of Intelligence* Vedic *Shākhās* (Divisions)	**Quantum Network Architecture** *Quality of Intelligence* Quantum Network Architecture Divisions
Gandharva Veda *Ṛishi—Integrating and Harmonizing*	**Network/Computer Clocking and Synchronization** *Ṛishi—Integrating and Harmonizing*
Seven *Swaras* (musical notes):	Seven computer and network clocking structures and functions:
1 NI नी	1 Global state
2 DHA धा	2 Coordinated Universal Time (UTC)
3 PA पा	3 Network Time Protocol (NTP)
4 MA मा	4 Logical/vector clock
5 GA गा	5 Central Processing Unit (CPU) execution time for a program
6 RE रे	6 Clock cycles Per Instruction (CPI)
7 SĀ सा	7 Clock cycle time, clocked flip-flops

Figure 6-1 (continued): Vision of Upa-Veda in Quantum Network Architecture™

<table>
<tr><th>Vedic Term
Quality of Intelligence
Vedic Shākhās (Divisions)</th><th>Quantum Network Architecture
Quality of Intelligence
Quantum Network Architecture Divisions</th></tr>
<tr><td>Dhanur Veda
Devatā—Invincible and Progressive
Four chapters; Chapter 1 has 100 Sūtras (The first Sūtra is considered a holistic introduction to the entire book.); Chapters 2, 3, and 4 each contain a multiple of 33 Sūtras.</td><td>Security Architecture
Devatā—Invincible and Progressive
<u>Four major divisions:</u>
1 Security-specific taxonomies, models and methods
2 Perimeter security and pervasive computing authentication
3 External or internal network access control
4 Intrusion detection and resolution</td></tr>
<tr><td>Sthāpatya Veda
Chhandas—Establishing
Mānasāra Vāstu Shāstra contains 70 chapters, Māyāmata contains 36 chapters, and Asumad Bheda Vāstu Shāstra has 86 chapters.</td><td>Physical Network Topology
Chhandas—Establishing
<u>Seven major physical network topology cases, each with an average of ten components:</u>
1 End users (user, application, database, file system, printer, storage device/system)
2 End user-to-ES physical link or channel (multiple terrestrial and celestial)
3 End systems (servers, supercomputers, mainframes, midrange systems, PCs, laptops, subnotebooks, palmtops, PDAs, cell phones)
4 ES-to-ES physical link or channel (multiple terrestrial and celestial)
5 ES-to-IS physical link or channel (multiple terrestrial and celestial)
6 IS (routers, switches, firewalls, load balancers, content balancers)
7 IS-to-IS physical link or channel (multiple terrestrial and celestial)</td></tr>
<tr><td>Hārīta Saṁhitāc
Chhandas—Nourishing
Seven divisions</td><td>Bandwidth Management, Quality of Service
Chhandas—Nourishing
<u>Seven components:</u>
1 Network Application Quality of Service (QoS) model
2 Congestion management
3 Transport-level flow control
4 Network prioritization</td></tr>
</table>

Figure 6-1 (continued): Vision of Upa-Veda in Quantum Network Architecture™

Vedic Term *Quality of Intelligence* Vedic *Shākhās* (Divisions)	**Quantum Network Architecture** *Quality of Intelligence* Quantum Network Architecture Divisions
Hārīta Saṁhitā (continued)	**Bandwidth Management, Quality of Service (continued)** 5 Link prioritization 6 Bandwidth-managed network 7 Broadband on demand
Bhel Saṁhitā *Devatā—Differentiating* Eight divisions	**Prioritized Queueing Systems** *Devatā—Differentiating* Eight principal divisions: 1 Markovian/exponential (M)/M/n Queueing Systems (M/M/1, M/M/∞, M/M/m, M/M/1/K, M/M/m/m, M/M/1//M, M/M/∞//M, M/M/m/K/M) 2 M/General (G)/1 queueing system (Single-server, Poisson arrivals, arbitrary service time distribution) 3 G/M/m queueing system (m-server system, embedded Markov chain) 4 G/G/1 queueing system (independent arrival times, single server, embedded Markov process at arrival times) 5 First Come, First Served (FCFS) queueing 6 Priority queueing 7 Weighted Fair Queueing (WFQ), flow-based and class-based 8 Modified Weighted Round Robin (MWRR) and Modified Deficit Round Robin (MDRR) queueing
Kāshyap Saṁhitā *Ṛishi—Equivalency* Nine divisions	**Availability Logic** *Ṛishi—Equivalency* Nine divisions: 1 Synchronous network algorithms 2 Asynchronous network algorithms 3 Asynchronous shared memory algorithms 4 Partially synchronous network algorithms 5 Hypercube

Figure 6-1 (continued): Vision of Upa-Veda in Quantum Network Architecture™

Vedic Term *Quality of Intelligence* Vedic *Shākhās* (Divisions)	**Quantum Network Architecture** *Quality of Intelligence* Quantum Network Architecture Divisions
Kāshyap Saṁhitā (continued)	**Availability Logic (continued)** 6 Cube-connected-cycles 7 Packet routing algorithms 8 Minimum-weight spanning trees 9 Fast Fourier Transform (FFT) or Quantum Fast Fourier Transform (QFFT)
Charak Saṁhitā *Ṛishi—Balancing—Holding Together and Supporting*	**Network-on-a-Chip™** *Ṛishi—Balancing—Holding Together and Supporting* • CPU of CPUs • Network-on-a-Chip™ fabric with network switch fabric adapters • Chip-level expansions include single-stage port, multi-stage port, performance, speed, link paralleling, network paralleling • Datapath logic cells • Integral network and gate logic
Sushrut Saṁhitā *Devatā—Separating* Six divisions with 186 chapters	**Field and Gate Logic** *Devatā—Separating* Six divisions: 1 Programmable Logic Device (PLD) 2 Programmable Logic Controller (PLC) 3 Field Programmable Gate Array (FPGA) 4 Gate-isolated and oxide-isolated gate arrays 5 Programming technologies (One-Time Programmable [OTP], In-System Programming [ISP], Static Random Access Memory [SRAM], Electrically Programmable Read-Only Memory [EPROM], and Electronically Erasable Programmable Read-Only Memory [EEPROM]) 6 Computer-Aided Engineering (CAE)

Figure 6-1 (continued): Vision of Upa-Veda in Quantum Network Architecture™

Vedic Term *Quality of Intelligence* Vedic *Shākhās* (Divisions)	Quantum Network Architecture *Quality of Intelligence* Quantum Network Architecture Divisions
Vāgbhatt Saṁhitā *Chhandas—Communication and Eloquence* Six divisions, 120 chapters	**Dynamic Network Modeling** *Chhandas—Communication and Eloquence* Six major approaches: 1 Rules of thumb 2 Analytic queueing 3 Simulation 4 Linear programming 5 Mathematical programming 6 Benchmarking/benchtesting
Mādhav Nidān Saṁhitā *Chhandas—Diagnosing* Seventy chapters	**Network/Systems Management** *Chhandas—Diagnosing* Ten categories: 1 Framework models 2 Model-based, dependency-graphed system 3 Inventory management 4 Asset management 5 Configuration management 6 Change management 7 Problem management 8 Service Level Agreement (SLA) 9 Enterprise License Agreement (ELA) 10 Real-time systems and network views *Each of the 10 categories above with the following seven capabilities (10 x 7 = 70):* 1 Dynamic networked application modeling; dynamic adjustment to adds, changes, and/or deletes of network and application resources 2 Comprehensive service-level management solution 3 Automated remedial action invocation 4 Dynamic escalation procedures 5 Interoperability

Figure 6-1 (continued): Vision of Upa-Veda in Quantum Network Architecture™

Vedic Term *Quality of Intelligence* Vedic *Shākhās* (Divisions)	**Quantum Network Architecture** *Quality of Intelligence* Quantum Network Architecture Divisions
Mādhav Nidān Saṁhitā (continued)	**Network/Systems Management, (continued)** 6 What-If scenario and contingency analysis 7 Root cause and business impact analysis
Shārngadhar Saṁhitā *Devatā—Synthesizing* Three divisions Thirty-two chapters	**Database and Transaction Processing** *Devatā—Synthesizing* Three divisions: 1 Database system 2 Transaction processing system 3 Client-server and server-server models *Thirty-two components:* 1 Database internal schema 2 Database conceptual schema 3 Database external schema 4 Dimensional schema 5 Database mappings 6 Server-requester model 7 Remote unit of work 8 Distributed unit of work 9 Distributed request 10 Distributed query processing 11 Relational algebra 12 Set operators (Union, Intersection, Difference, and Cartesian product) 13 Special relational operators (Restrict, Project, Join, and Divide) 14 Nested relational expressions 15 Relational calculus 16 Tuple calculus 17 Domain calculus 18 Relation Variable (RelVar) 19 Object-relational database

Figure 6-1 (continued): Vision of Upa-Veda in Quantum Network Architecture™

Vedic Term *Quality of Intelligence* Vedic *Shākhās* (Divisions)	**Quantum Network Architecture** *Quality of Intelligence* Quantum Network Architecture Divisions
Shārngadhar Saṁhitā (continued)	**Database and Transaction Processing (continued)** **20** View retrieval **21** Semantic modeling **22** Optimization **23** Entity-Relationship (ER) modeling **24** Association matrix **25** Properties matrix **26** Data Flow Diagram (DFD) **27** State Transition Diagram (STD) **28** Transaction state transformation ACID properties (Atomic, Consistent, Isolated, Durable) **29** Transaction BEGIN, COMMIT, ROLLBACK, and recovery **30** Distributed two-phase commit, concurrency **31** Discretionary access control **32** Distributed transaction management
Bhāva-Prakāsh Saṁhitā *Ṛishi—Enlightening* Five divisions, 109 chapters	**Optical Networks** *Ṛishi—Enlightening* Five principal divisions: 1 Optical transmitter 2 Optical link (terrestrial or celestial) 3 Optical networking node 4 Optical receiver 5 Optical network

7: BRĀHMAṆA in Quantum Network Architecture

Brāhmaṇa are the six aspects of Vedic Literature that represent the mechanics of transformation. In Chapter 2 we find that Veda is *Mantra* and *Brāhmaṇa* together. *Mantra* refers to the sounds of Veda and the Vedic Literature, and is expressed in Quantum Network Architecture™ as chip substrates and network physical topologies. *Brāhmaṇa*—in its overall role in the mechanics of transformation—is correlated with the Hardware-Software Gap.™

Figure 7-1 presents the six aspects of Brāhmaṇa and their corresponding six aspects in Quantum Network Architecture. The values of Brāhmaṇa in Quantum Network Architecture present the Laws of Nature that promote the structure and function of network computation from one aspect, or expression, to another. They process the evolution of function and structure from abstract to concrete and from concrete to abstract. Brāhmaṇa are the knowledge of transformation—*Kalp-Vidya*—the knowledge of how the unmanifest aspects materialize and how the material creation submerges back into consciousness.

Brāhmaṇa form the fifth loop of the Vedic Literature, consisting of Upanishad, Āraṇyak, Brāhmaṇa, Itihās, Purāṇ, and Smṛiti.

Upanishad is the first of the Brāhmaṇa and has the quality of *Transcending*. Transcending is the process of moving from the gross, to the subtle, and beyond the subtlest, to unmanifest pure consciousness. Upanishad has *Ṛishi* predominance, and is expressed in Quantum Network Architecture as *Wireless Networks, Pervasive Computing*.

Āraṇyak is the *Stirring* quality of Natural Law, has *Devatā* predominance, and is expressed in Quantum Network Architecture as *Application Programming Interface*.

Brāhmaṇa is the *Structuring* quality of Natural Law, has *Chhandas* predominance, and is expressed in Quantum Network Architecture as *Network/Systems Standards and Protocols.*

Itihas is the *Blossoming of Totality* quality of Natural Law, has *Chhandas* predominance, and is expressed in Quantum Network Architecture as *End-User Application Interactions.*

Purāṇ is the *Ancient and Eternal* quality of Natural Law, has *Devatā* predominance, and is expressed in Quantum Network Architecture as *End-User and Application Interfaces.*

Smṛiti is the *Memory* quality of Natural Law, has *Ṛishi* predominance, and is expressed in Quantum Network Architecture as *Random Access Memory (RAM)/Routt Addressable Absolute Memory Gate™ (RAAM Gate™)/Storage Area Network (SAN)/Network-Attached Storage (NAS)/Hologram.*

Figure 7-1: Vision of Brāhmaṇa in Quantum Network Architecture™

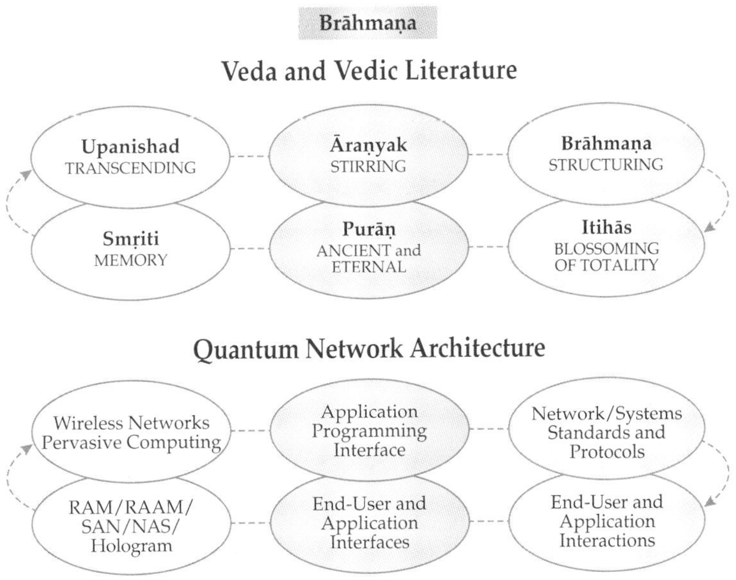

Vedic Term *Quality of Intelligence* Vedic *Shākhās* (Divisions)	**Quantum Network Architecture** *Quality of Intelligence* Quantum Network Architecture Divisions
Upanishad *Ṛishi—Transcending* Ten principal Upanishads (over 200 known): 1 Īshā ईशा 2 Kena केन 3 Katha कठ 4 Prashna प्रश्न 5 Muṇḍaka मुण्डक 6 Māṇḍūkya माण्डूक्य 7 Aitareya ऐतरेय 8 Taittirīya तैत्तिरीय 9 Bṛihad-Āraṇyak बृहदारण्यक 10 Chhāndogya छान्दोग्य	**Wireless Networks, Pervasive Computing** *Ṛishi—Transcending* Ten principal divisions: 1 Domains—time and frequency 2 Radio Frequency (RF) cells and satellite footprints 3 Power 4 Passive components at RF 5 Semiconductors 6 Signaling and propagation 7 Modulation and spread spectrum 8 Vocoding and shift keying 9 Generations and air interfaces 10 Link budget

Figure 7-1 (continued): Vision of Brāhmaṇa in Quantum Network Architecture™

Vedic Term *Quality of Intelligence* Vedic *Shākhās* (Divisions)	**Quantum Network Architecture** *Quality of Intelligence* Quantum Network Architecture Divisions
Āraṇyak *Devatā—Stirring* Six main books	**Application Programming Interface** *Devatā—Stirring* Six main divisions: 1 Distributed object model 2 Human-Computer Interface (HCI) 3 Object-oriented graphical interface 4 Interface Definition Languages (IDLs) 5 Remote Method Invocation (RMI) 6 Binding and authentication
Brāhmaṇa *Chhandas—Structuring* Fifteen main Brāhmaṇa:	**Network/Systems Standards and Protocols** *Chhandas—Structuring* Fifteen main groups:
1 Gopatha गोपथ	1 End-System (ES) interfaces
2 Vaṁsha वंश	2 Application Layer specifications and interfaces
3 Shatapatha शतपथ	3 Application Layer protocols
4 Tāṇdya Panchaviṁsha ताण्ड्य पञ्चविंश	4 Presentation Layer specifications and interfaces
5 Chhāndogya छान्दोग्य	5 Presentation Layer protocols
6 Ārsheya आर्षेय	6 Session Layer specifications and interfaces
7 Shānkhāyana शाङ्खायन	7 Session Layer protocols
8 Sāmavidhāna सामविधान	8 Transport Layer specifications and interfaces
9 Aitareya ऐतरेय	9 Transport Layer protocols
10 Taittirīya तैत्तिरीय	10 Network Layer specifications and interfaces
11 Jaiminīya जैमिनीय	11 Network Layer protocols

Figure 7-1 (continued): Vision of Brahmaṇa in Quantum Network Architecture™

Vedic Term *Quality of Intelligence* Vedic *Shākhās* (Divisions)	**Quantum Network Architecture** *Quality of Intelligence* Quantum Network Architecture Divisions
Brāhmaṇa (continued)	**Network/Systems Standards and Protocols (continued)**
12 Tāṇdya Shadviṁsha ताण्ड्य षड्विंश	**12** Data Link Layer specifications and interfaces
13 Saṁhitopanishad संहितोपनिषद्	**13** Data Link Layer protocols
14 Kauthuma Ārsheya कौथुन आर्षेय	**14** Physical Layer specifications and interfaces
15 Daivatādhyāya दैवताध्याय	**15** Physical Layer protocols
Itihās	**End-User and Application Interactions**
Chhandas—Blossoming of Totality	*Chhandas—Blossoming of Totality*
Rāmāyaṇ (seven books):	Seven components:
1 Bala Kanda	1 Middleware layers
2 Ayodhya Kanda	2 Remote object invocation model
3 Aranya Kanda	3 Interprogram invocation model
4 Kishkindha Kanda	4 Remote Method Invocation (RMI) model
5 Sundara Kanda	5 Remote Procedure Call (RPC) model
6 Yuddha Kanda	6 Request reply protocol
7 Uttara Kanda	7 External data representation
Mahābhārat (18 books):	Eighteen components of the distributed object model:
1 Ādi Parva १. आदि पर्व	1 Invocation semantics
2 Sabhā Parva २. सभा पर्व	2 Remote interfaces
3 Vana Parva ३. वन पर्व	3 Remote reference modules
4 Virāta Parva ४. विराट पर्व	4 Remote object references
5 Udyoga Parva ५. उद्योग पर्व	5 Distributed object actions
6 Bhīshma Parva ६. भीष्म पर्व	6 Client-server interactions

Figure 7-1 (continued): Vision of Brāhmaṇa in Quantum Network Architecture™

Vedic Term *Quality of Intelligence* Vedic *Shākhās* (Divisions)	**Quantum Network Architecture** *Quality of Intelligence* Quantum Network Architecture Divisions
Itihās (continued)	**End-User and Application Interactions (continued)**
7 Droṇa Parva ७. द्रोण पर्व	7 Server processes
8 Karṇa Parva ८. कर्ण पर्व	8 Server threads
9 Shalya Parva ९. शल्य पर्व	9 Server-server interactions
10 Sauptika Parva १०. सौप्तिक पर्व	10 Remote object activation
11 Strī Parva ११. स्त्री पर्व	11 Persistent object stores
12 Shānti Parva १२. शान्ति पर्व	12 Binding
13 Anūshāsanika Parva १३. अनुशासनिक पर्व	13 Authentication
14 Āshwamedhika Parva १४. आश्वमेधिक पर्व	14 Events
15 Āshramavāsika Parva १५. आश्रमवासिक पर्व	15 Notifications
16 Mausala Parva १६. मौसल पर्व	16 Delivery semantics
17 Mahāprasthānika Parva १७. महाप्रस्थानिक पर्व	17 Third-party agents
18 Swargārohaṇa Parva १८. स्वर्गारोहण पर्व	18 Parameter and result passing
Purāṇ	**End-User and Application Interfaces**
Devatā—Ancient and Eternal	*Devatā—Ancient and Eternal*
Eighteen Maha Purāṇ (with approximately 400,000 verses):	Eighteen principal interface groups:
Loop of Rishi:	*Loop of Rishi:*
1 Bhāgavat भागवत	1 Local application interface
2 Padma पद्म	2 Local service interface
3 Brahma ब्रह्म	3 Local procedure interface

Figure 7-1 (continued): Vision of Brāhmaṇa in Quantum Network Architecture™

Vedic Term *Quality of Intelligence* Vedic *Shākhās* (Divisions)	**Quantum Network Architecture** *Quality of Intelligence* Quantum Network Architecture Divisions
Purāṇ (continued)	**End-User and Application Interfaces (continued)**
4 Vishṇu विष्णु	4 Intersystem interface
5 Shiva शिव	5 Local object interface
6 Nārada नारद	6 Interprocess interface
Loop of Devatā:	*Loop of Devatā:*
7 Agni अग्नि	7 Request-reply interface
8 Mārkaṇdeya मार्कण्डेय	8 Communications interface
9 Vārāha वाराह	9 Dialog interface
10 Linga लिङ्ग	10 Proxy interface
11 Brahma Vaivarta ब्रह्मवैवर्त	11 Repository interface
12 Bhavishya भविष्य	12 Interprogram interface
Loop of Chhandas:	*Loop of Chhandas:*
13 Vāmana वामन	13 Remote object interface
14 Brahmāṇda ब्रह्माण्ड	14 Remote service interface
15 Skanda स्कन्द	15 Remote procedure interface
16 Garuda गरुड	16 Query interface
17 Kūrma कूर्म	17 File system interface
18 Matsya मत्स्य	18 Database interface

Figure 7-1 (continued): Vision of Brāhmaṇa in Quantum Network Architecture™

Vedic Term *Quality of Intelligence* Vedic *Shākhās* (Divisions)	**Quantum Network Architecture** *Quality of Intelligence* Quantum Network Architecture Divisions
Smṛiti	**RAM/RAAM/SAN/NAS/Hologram**
Ṛishi—Memory	*Ṛishi—Memory*
Eighteen Smṛiti:	Eighteen main divisions:
1 Angiras अङ्गिरस्	1 Memory hierarchies
2 Vyāsa व्यास	2 First-level cache
3 Āpastamba आपस्तम्ब	3 Second-level cache
4 Daksha दक्ष	4 Main memory
5 Vishṇu विष्णु	5 Read-Only Memory (ROM)
6 Yāgyavalkya याज्ञवल्क्य	6 Random Access Memory (RAM)
7 Likhita लिखित	7 Dynamic RAM (DRAM) and Solid State Disk (SSD)
8 Samvarta सम्वर्त	8 Magnetic RAM (MRAM)
9 Shankha शङ्ख	9 Static RAM (SRAM)
10 Bṛihaspati बृहस्पति	10 Routt Addressable Absolute Memory Gate™ (RAAM Gate™), defined in the Shukl-Yajur-Veda Prātishākhya section of Chapter 8
11 Atri अत्रि	11 Translation-Lookaside Buffer (TLB)
12 Kātyāyan कात्यायन	12 Virtual memory and Direct Memory Access (DMA)
13 Parāshara पराशर	13 Hologram/holographic memory
14 Manu मनु	14 Network RAM (NRAM)
15 Aushanas औशनस	15 Distributed Shared Memory (DSM) systems
16 Hārita हारीत	16 Storage Area Network (SAN)

Figure 7-1 (continued): Vision of Brāhmaṇa in Quantum Network Architecture™

Vedic Term *Quality of Intelligence* Vedic *Shākhās* (Divisions)	**Quantum Network Architecture** *Quality of Intelligence* Quantum Network Architecture Divisions
Smṛiti (continued)	**RAM/RAAM/SAN/NAS/Hologram (continued)**
17 Gautam गौतम	**17** Network-Attached Storage (NAS)
18 Yama य	**18** Content Addressable Memory (CAM)

8: PRĀTISHĀKHYA in Quantum Network Architecture

Prātishākhya represents that aspect of consciousness that integrates all the parts and creates a whole that is more than the collection of its parts through which *Ātmā* emerges as Unity and diversity. Wholeness and all the point values are integrated together within the self-sufficient, self-referral, omnipresent, holistic value of Totality—*Brahm*. अयम् आत्मा ब्रह्म *Ayam Ātmā Brahm*. "This *Ātmā* is *Brahm*."

There are six Prātishākhyas, forming the final six aspects of the Vedic Literature. These do not form a loop because each brings reality in terms of the source—looping is on the basis of emergence and submergence. Prātishākhya brings to the awareness the reality of the "sap" at the basis of all aspects of the tree—the whole tree is fundamentally nothing but sap. Whatever has *Ṛishi* value is actually *Saṁhitā;* whatever is *Devatā* or *Chhandas,* is actually *Saṁhitā*. Prātishākhya verifies all diversity, so there is actually no returning, no two values—manifest and unmanifest.

Prātishākhya is expressed in Quantum Network Architecture™ by the structure and function of the quantum computer and quantum network, ultimately revealed through the RAAM Gate™ as the Cosmic Computer and Cosmic Switchboard. The full potential of the quantum computer network emerges when its holistic functioning sustains itself as a global, celestial, nervous system, or self-referral, conscious superfabric, that collects, interprets, processes, interconnects, and integrates enterprise and personal data and information throughout the world.

Different branches of Veda and the Vedic Literature have been shown to have different values; now all have to be made significant in the reality of the whole. Prātishākhya brings to light all aspects of the Vedic Literature, demonstrating the structuring dynamics of Veda with reference to Wholeness of the *Saṁhitā* value while maintaining their specific character within the structuring dynamics of Natural Law.

All the preceding aspects of the Vedic Literature have brought to light the different structuring dynamics of Ṛk Veda. Prātishākhya integrates them all in the context of *Saṁhitā* and brings out the holistic value of Natural Law, indicating that all the structuring dynamics maintain their self-referral nature. In the ultimate sense, all the aspects of Veda and the Vedic Literature—all laws of administration, functional within their specific mode, awake within their sphere of influence—are fully alert in terms of their holistic bases as well.

Following are excerpts regarding the significance of the Prātishākhyas from Maharishi Mahesh Yogi's, *Maharishi's Absolute Theory of Government: Automation in Administration*:

- The Prātishākhyas connect the farthest ends of infinity and maintain one homogeneous Wholeness of intelligence:

  अन्वयव्यतिरेकाभ्यां निष्प्रपञ्चं प्रपञ्चते
  Anvaya vyati rekābhyāṁ .nishprapanchaṁ prapanchate

  By virtue of synthesis of analysis, the indivisible Unity is realized in the world of multiplicity.

- The Prātishākhyas bring to light that non-material material field of intelligence, or consciousness, which is motivated by the structuring dynamics (Vyākaraṇ) in the direction of expansion, and is simultaneously motivated by the structuring dynamics (Nirukt) in the direction of the source.

  This means that the Prātishākhyas bring to light the potential of *Saṁhitā,* the Unified Field, the source of the laws that uphold the opposite direction of the laws of Vyākaraṇ and Nirukt.

  Vyākaraṇ expresses the laws that give the direction of expansion to the structuring dynamics of the Veda, and Nirukt expresses the laws that give the direction of the source to the structuring dynamics of the Veda, but that non-material material structure of intelligence which assumes directionality by virtue of Vyākaraṇ and Nirukt is the subject matter of the Prātishākhyas.

  Like the cotton that gets woven into the thread, or the earth that gets molded by the potter, consciousness is given one direction by Vyākaraṇ and an opposite direction by Nirukt, but that reality (intelligence) which is itself motivated in two opposite directions is brought to light by the Prātishākhyas.

- The Prātishākhyas are that body of knowledge which locates the directionless potential of all directionality—the transcendental field of *Saṁhitā* level of consciousness.
- The Prātishākhyas explore the junction point between any and every two expressions of the Vedic structure.

In the ultimate analysis, the knowledge of the Prātishākhyas actually unfolds the one Ultimate Reality, the Unified Field of all the Laws of Nature, the field of the unity of all the Laws of Nature—all the structuring dynamics, all the laws that are engaged in formulating the structure of Veda and its expression in creation.

- The Prātishākhyas, digging deeper into the process of expansion of the sequential progression of the structure of the Veda, ultimately locate that essential field of intelligence, *Saṁhitā,* which is expressed by Shikshā, transformed by Kalp, given direction by Vyākaraṇ and Nirukt, hidden by Chhand, and fully awake in terms of Jyotish—*Jyotish-matī pragyā*—that fully awake field of intelligence which knows everything.

Similarly, the Prātishākhyas explore the nature of the basic reality which blossoms into the different values of the Upānga: Nyāya, Vaisheshik, Sāṁkhya, Yoga, Karma Mīmāṁsa, Vedānt; and likewise the Prātishākhyas explore the nature of the basic reality which blossoms into the different values of the Upa-Veda: Sāma Veda, Yajur-Veda, Atharva Veda, Sthāpatya Veda, Dhanur-Veda, Gandharva Veda, and all other aspects of the Vedic Literature—Upanishad, Āraṇyak, Brāhmaṇa, Itihās, Purāṇ, Smṛiti, and the six aspects of Āyur-Veda.

- The Prātishākhyas, recognizing the separate values of the structuring dynamics of the Veda as available in different aspects of the Vedic Literature, make every value transparent so that the ultimate *Atyantābhāva* shines through everything: Vedānt shines through Veda—Vedānt shines through all the structuring dynamics of Veda—connectedness characterizes the entire Veda and Vedic Literature; *Brahm,* Totality—the Unified Field of all the Laws of Nature—shines through all the differentiated laws; Wholeness shines through all the parts; the holistic value of the Constitution of the Universe is available in every aspect of the Veda and Vedic Literature.

The Prātishākhyas stand as a powerful referee for all aspects of the Veda and Vedic Literature. The Prātishākhyas are that one powerful unifying force which locates the whole Veda and Vedic Literature within the self-referral state of *Ātmā*:

स्वरूपेऽवस्थानम्
Swarūpe avasthānam
(*Yog-Sūtra, 1.3*)

वृत्तिसारूप्यमितरत्र
Vṛitti sārūpyam itaḥ atra
(*Yog-Sūtra, 1.4*)

- The Prātishākhyas examine the gaps between any two and every two values of the structuring dynamics of consciousness and locate the one most basic element of absolute abstraction—*Atyantābhāva*.
- The Prātishākhyas locate different kinds of *Atyantābhāva* and the corresponding quality of *Anyonyābhāva* within the structure of *Atyantābhāva* in different gaps that contain the mechanics of transformation, the mechanics of evolution of Natural Law, responsible for the sequential development of the entire structure of the Veda—the Constitution of the Universe.

  The Prātishākhyas bring to light the potential absolute abstraction—*Atyantābhāva*—and clearly visualize the existence of the Veda and Vedic Literature within the Ultimate Reality, the absolute silence of *Atyantābhāva*—absolute abstraction, pure intelligence, self-referral level of absolute Unity—eternally unified state of all the laws that structure the Veda and Vedic Literature.
- The Prātishākhyas, in conjunction with all other aspects of the Veda and Vedic Literature, unfold the whole field of the total Science and Technology of Consciousness, the complete science and technology of "Being and becoming" within the Self of everyone, within Transcendental Consciousness, the simplest state of everyone's awareness.
- The Prātishākhyas establish the Wholeness of the Constitution of the Universe in every part of it—the total Constitution of the Universe in the intelligence of every grain of creation.
- The Prātishākhyas reveal the source of every point of the whole course of the Veda and Vedic Literature, substantiating Vasishtha's cognition that unfolds the whole range of the Prātishākhyas:

दूरेदृशं गृहपतिमथर्युम्
Dūre dṛishaṁ gṛihapatim atharyum
(*Ṛk Veda, 7.1.1*)
Far in the distance is seen the owner of the house, reverberating.

- The conclusion is *Anyonyābhāva* is *Atyantābhāva*:

  जीवो ब्रह्मैव नापरः
  Jīvo Brahmaiv nāparaḥ
  Jīva is Brahm, none other.

  योगस्थः कुरु कर्माणि
  Yogasthaḥ kuru karmāṇi
  (Bhagavad-Gītā, 2.48)
  Established in Yoga (Unity), perform action.

  यतीनां ब्रह्मा भवति सारथिः
  Yatīnāṁ Brahmā bhavati sārathiḥ
  (Ṛk Veda, 1.158.6)

  Action—administration from the field of self-referral intelligence—is executed by the infinite organizing power of Natural Law, which is the display of the process of government from the holistic level of governing, or the display of the process of administration from the holistic level of Creative Intelligence.

- The Prātishākhyas awaken that intelligence which makes every aspect of the Vedic Literature a mirror on which the student of Vedic Science sees himself: no matter what aspect of the Vedic Literature the student reads, in it he reads himself; no matter what he sees, in it he sees himself; he is able to pick up any *Sūtra* (verse) or phrase and in it he finds himself.

- The Prātishākhyas promote the study of any word *(Mantra)* or phrase *(Sūtra)* in a way that one sees the form of the written text but simultaneously appreciates the transcendental value of each *Sūtra,* and the Wholeness (of *Saṁhitā*), the common basis of all *Sūtras.*

  The influence of the Prātishākhyas on the intelligence of the student of Vedic Science is so enriching and nourishing and is so supremely enlightening that the student of Vedic Science feels to have entered into a shop that has all kinds of small and big mirrors; whichever piece he picks up, in it he sees himself.

- The student of the Prātishākhyas appreciates the transcendental element beyond the expressed words *(Mantra)* and, visualizing the mechanics of transformation or the structuring dynamics of the words of the Vedic Literature, spontaneously familiarizes his awareness with the organizing power of Creative Intelligence inherent within the word. He also appreciates the reality of the sequence of the gaps (between the *Mantra* and *Sūtra*) and locates, within each gap, the Creative Intelligence that presents the mechanics of transformation of one syllable into the other, one *Mantra* into the other, one *Sūtra* into the other. (Refer to Figure 2-2 on page 24, "Maharishi's Commentary on Ṛk Veda—*Apaurusheya Bhāshya*").

- This is how the Prātishākhyas enliven the infinite organizing power of the Veda and the structuring dynamics of the Veda, the Vedic Literature, in the awareness of the student. Vedānt unfolds in Veda; Veda unfolds in Vedānga; Vedānga unfolds in Upānga; Upānga unfolds in the Brāhmaṇa and the Upa-Veda, and every aspect of the Vedic Literature blossoms into the Veda and Vedānt; every aspect of the Veda and Vedic Literature unfolds Totality—*Brahm*—which is the potentiality of the Self of the student of my Vedic Science.

  Whatever aspect of the Vedic Literature the student studies in the light of the Prātishākhyas he finds that everything is so transparent that he sees behind the structure and behind the meaning of the sound the all-meaningful Wholeness, *Saṁhitā,* the Veda, percolated with Vedānt; and finally the reality of himself.

- The gift of the Prātishākhyas to the student of Vedic Science is that awakening which brings the student back to himself, so that he finds in himself all fields of study and all types of experiences—past, present, and future. He is awake in the totality of himself. He wakes up to the reality of:

  अयम् आत्मा ब्रह्म
  Ayam Ātmā Brahm
  (Māṇḍūkya Upanishad, 2)

  अहं ब्रह्मास्मि
  Ahaṁ Brahmāsmi
  (Bṛihadāraṇyak Upanishad, 1.4.10)

  प्रज्ञानं ब्रह्म
  Pragyānaṁ Brahm
  (Aitareya Upanishad, 3.1.3)

  सर्वं खल्विदं ब्रह्म
  Sarvaṁ khalwidaṁ Brahm
  (Chhāndogya Upanishad, 3.14.1)

Evolution of the manifest levels from the unmanifest, and the maintenance of the unmanifest level of intelligence within every level of manifestation, is the function of Prātishākhya. The expanding outward quality of Vyākaraṇ and the self-referral inward quality of Nirukt remain awake through the Prātishākhya level of Natural Law. They remain fully awake in terms of *Brahm*—Totality. The general character of the unmanifest remains lively with the self-interacting dynamics of intelligence evolving in the sequentially developing structures of Veda and the Vedic Literature.

The continuing process of evolution gives rise to different structures of network computational intelligence such as the quantum computer, the quantum network, and the Global Internetwork. The ultimate cosmic foundation and expressions of network computational intelligence are the Cosmic Computer and Cosmic Switchboard, as revealed by the RAAM Gate unfolded in this chapter.

Figure 8-1 (beginning on page 144) illustrates the one-to-one correspondence of Prātishākhya in Vedic Literature with all the aspects of Quantum Network Architecture.

Figure 8-1: Vision of Prātishākhya in Quantum Network Architecture™

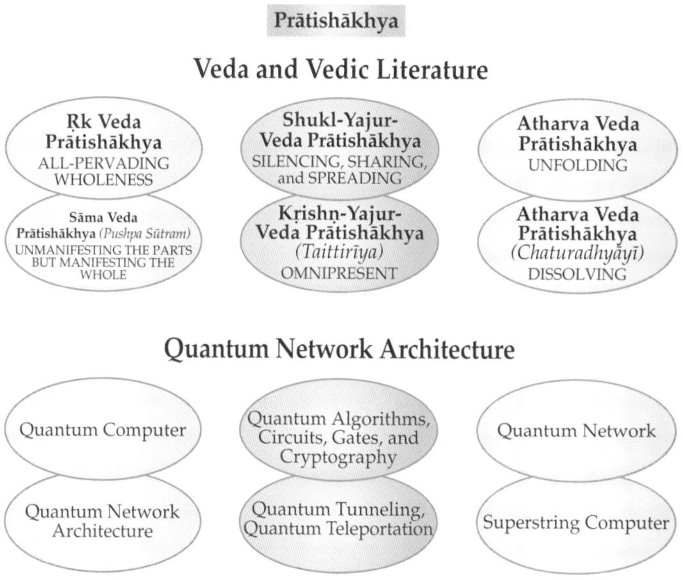

Vedic Term *Quality of Intelligence* Vedic *Shākhās* (Divisions)	**Quantum Network Architecture Term** *Quality of Intelligence* Quantum Network Architecture Divisions
Ṛk Veda Prātishākhya *Ṛishi—All-Pervading Wholeness* Holistic transcendental aspect of Wholeness itself—totally integrated, with every point in infinity and infinity in every point	**Quantum Computer** *Ṛishi—All-Pervading Wholeness* <u>Quantum computer characteristics:</u> • Superpositionality • Quantum bit (qubit) representation • Unitarity • Preparation of initial qubit states • Measurement of final qubit states <u>Quantum logic gates</u> <u>Quantum memory registers</u> <u>Quantum information theory:</u> • Quantum Fano inequality • Coherent information • Holevo's Bound • von Neumann entropy • No-cloning • Schumacher's Quantum Noiseless Channel Coding Theorem

Figure 8-1 (continued): Vision of Prātishākhya in Quantum Network Architecture™

Vedic Term *Quality of Intelligence* Vedic *Shākhās* (Divisions)	**Quantum Network Architecture Term** *Quality of Intelligence* Quantum Network Architecture Divisions
Ṛk Veda Prātishākhya (continued)	**Quantum Computer (continued)** Quantum information theory (continued): • Holevo-Schumacher-Westmoreland Theorem • Majorization condition for entanglement transformation • Pure-state entanglement distillation and dilution • Quantum cryptography Quantum computer realization: • Harmonic oscillator quantum computer • Square-well-based quantum computer • Optical photon quantum computer • Optical cavity quantum electrodynamics • Ion trap-based quantum computer • Nuclear magnetic resonance-based quantum computer • Spintronics and the spin transistor • Nanotube computer • Evolving quantum computer realizations
Shukl-Yajur-Veda Prātishākhya *Devatā—Silencing, Sharing, and Spreading* Wholeness with reference to *Devatā* value	**Quantum Algorithms, Circuits, Gates, and Cryptography** *Devatā—Silencing, Sharing, and Spreading* Quantum algorithms: • Classical computations on a quantum computer • Quantum parallelism • Deutsch's Algorithm • Quantum simulation algorithm • Quantum Fast Fourier Transform (QFFT) • Quantum factoring • Quantum search algorithm (a.k.a. Grover's Algorithm) • Quantum counting

Figure 8-1 (continued): Vision of Prātishākhya in Quantum Network Architecture™

Vedic Term *Quality of Intelligence* Vedic *Shākhās* (Divisions)	**Quantum Network Architecture Term** *Quality of Intelligence* Quantum Network Architecture Divisions
Shukl-Yajur-Veda Prātishākhya (continued)	**Quantum Algorithms, Circuits, Gates, and Cryptography (continued)** Quantum algorithms (continued): • Quantum cryptography • Quantum error-correcting codes Quantum circuits and gates: • Universally unitary • Logically reversible • Qubit representation • Single-qubit gates (Hadamard, Pauli-X, Pauli-Y, Pauli-Z, Phase, π/8) • Controlled-NOT (CNOT) gate • Universal single-qubit and CNOT gates • Universal *n*-qubit Routt Addressable Absolute Memory Gate™ (RAAM Gate™, refer to Appendix D, pages 327–328) Quantum cryptography: • Quantum Key Distribution (QKD) (i.e., BB84, B92, and modified Lo-Chau protocols)
Atharva Veda Prātishākhya *Chhandas—Unfolding* Wholeness with reference to *Chhandas* value	**Quantum Network** *Chhandas—Unfolding* • Quantum client processors • Quantum tunneling links • Quantum teleportation links • Quantum nodal processors • Quantum switch/routers • Quantum servers • Quantum distributed databases

Figure 8-1 (continued): Vision of Prātishākhya in Quantum Network Architecture™

Vedic Term *Quality of Intelligence* Vedic *Shākhās* (Divisions)	**Quantum Network Architecture Term** *Quality of Intelligence* Quantum Network Architecture Divisions
Atharva Veda Prātishākhya *(Chaturadhyāyī)* *Chhandas—Dissolving*	**Superstring Computer** *Chhandas—Dissolving* • Sub-Planck time (< 10^{-43} sec) and sub-Planck space (< 10^{-33} cm), massively parallel analog and/or digital processors
Krishṇ-Yajur-Veda Prātishākhya *(Taittirīya)* *Devatā—Omnipresent*	**Quantum Tunneling, Quantum Teleportation** *Devatā—Omnipresent* • Quantum tunneling transistor • Einstein, Podolsky, and Rosen (EPR) entangled pair of particles • Quantum teleportation
Sāma Veda Prātishākhya *(Pushpa Sūtram)* *Ṛishi—Unmanifesting the Parts but Manifesting the Whole*	**Quantum Network Architecture** *Ṛishi—Unmanifesting the Parts but Manifesting the Whole* • Cosmic memory *(Smṛiti)* • Infinite security • Hidden and eternally flawless operation • Automation of administration • Quantum specifications and protocols • Quantum Application Programming Interface™ (QAPI™) • Quantum extensions to Transmission Control Protocol (TCP) and Internet Protocol (IP)

ṚK VEDA PRĀTISHĀKHYA—
All-Pervading Wholeness—Quantum Computer

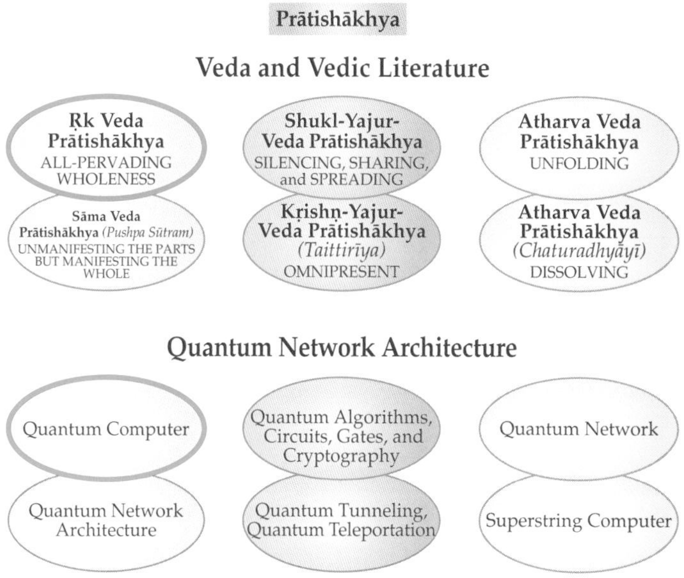

Ṛk Veda Prātishākhya is the holistic, transcendental aspect of Wholeness itself—totally integrated, with every point in infinity and infinity in every point, with reference to *Ṛishi* value. Ṛk Veda Prātishākhya represents *All-Pervading Wholeness*, the field of consciousness, and is available within Quantum Network Architecture as the *Quantum Computer*. The Quantum Computer functions and interacts within itself, yet remains apart from and independent of the external environment. It is a self-referral Wholeness, corresponding to Ṛk Veda Prātishākhya.

This *All-Pervading Wholeness* quality of intelligence, available in the Vedic Literature in Ṛk Veda Prātishākhya, is also available within the *Atyanta-Abhāva* and *Anyonya-Abhāva* of the Cosmic Computer and Cosmic Switchboard, and in every computational and network component, subsystem, and system of the Global Internetwork.

Classical Space-Time Symmetry-Bound Computation

During the past four decades we have witnessed a dramatic acceleration of miniaturization in computer technology. This was remarkably projected by Dr. Gordon E. Moore, who, while an engineer and research director at Fairchild Semiconductor Co. (and future co-founder and Chairman Emeritus of Intel Corporation), noted in 1965 (published in the

35th anniversary edition of *Electronics* magazine) that the number of transistors per square inch on integrated circuits had doubled each year since the invention of the integrated circuit. He projected that trend to continue for at least 10 years. In 1975, Dr. Moore presented a paper updating his original 1965 projection and predicted that the number of devices on a microchip would continue to double every two years. Thirty years hence, that geometric growth, now canonized as "Moore's Law," remains the fundamental economic force driving the computer industry and shows no signs of abating. For example, Intel's Andy Grove has predicted a 1 billion transistor chip by 2010 that will be able to execute 100 billion instructions per second, or 100,000 Million Instructions Per Second (MIPS).

Network evolution has paralleled that of computer chip breakthroughs. During the 1960s, T1 transmission technology allowed transmissions at 1.544 Megabits per second (Mbps), enabling 24 calls per wire pair. During the 1980s, optical fiber began to replace copper wire at an increasing rate. Today it is commonplace to transmit 40–100 Gigabits per second (Gbps) over single-mode step-index optical fiber; however, that transmission rate does not even approach the multi-terabit and petabit theoretical limits of optical fiber as a broadband transmission medium.

Wavelength Division Multiplexing (WDM), Dense WDM (DWDM), and Selective DWDM techniques have been increasingly employed to expand optical fiber information-carrying capacities. WDM and its derivatives separate transmitted light into a rainbow of colors and send, for example, 10 Gbps streams each over green, yellow, blue, and multiple other colors of light. At the receiving end, the individual colors are reintegrated by wavelength. For example, In early 1998, MCI began using an eight-channel WDM fiber to transmit at 80 Gbps.

During 2000, MCI integrated 128 colors of light and successfully transmitted over optical fiber at 10 Gbps each, yielding 1280 Gbps (1.28 Terabits per second [Tbps]) of data. Nortel integrated 160 channels of 10 Gbps data each over a single fiber, yielding 1600 Gbps (1.6 Tbps). Nippon Telephone and Telegraph (NTT) tested an optical fiber system that boosts each "color's" data rate from 10 Gbps to 160 Gbps and integrates 19 of these streams into a single fiber, yielding three Tbps of data through one hair-thin glass strand during 2002. During 2004, Hitachi generated 40 Gbps using 16 levels per symbol. DWDM techniques are expected to successfully integrate thousands of wavelengths within single-fiber strands during the next year, yielding greater than one terabyte (TB) per second per optical fiber strand.

Given the dramatic ramp-up in the number of Internet and World Wide Web users, the other critical component of the throughput equation, the ability to efficiently switch and route these data and information to and from the correct locations on a timely basis, is undergoing dramatic evolution as well.

One outgrowth of the exponential evolution of computing and network technologies is the diminishing distinction between transmission channels (terrestrial and celestial) and constituent switching/routing intelligence. Optical transmission and optical switch/routers evolved from the requirement to optimize the use of scarce network computing resources, while increasing numbers of highly efficient switching nodes within the Global Internetwork used terrestrial and celestial channel capacity more efficiently. Conversely, as transmission capacity has increased exponentially, fewer switching/routing nodes are required.

Taken to a natural evolutionary conclusion, and given "infinite" transmission capacity, it would be possible to architect a purely transmission-based Global Internetwork without switches or routers, either electronic, optical, or optoelectronic. That is, given theoretically unlimited transmission capacity, all possible database repositories (exceeding 100 Yottabytes, or $> 100 \times 10^{24}$ bytes in storage capacity) could be integrated and served from a virtual multi-Yottabit-per-second (Ybps) (a single, virtual multi-10^{24} bps) planetary-scale logical ring and could "circulate" continuously. Users requiring access to targeted data would connect to this virtual core ring, and access time could be engineered on the order of less than 10^{-9} second for all possible users throughout the Global Internetwork. This would be tantamount to the creation of a switchless planetary-scale meta-network.

More than 150 million hosts are currently connected to the Internet, and their number is growing exponentially. Current Web evolution (introduced in Chapter 3 under "Web

Services") is moving toward an Automated Web, with Internet-scale applications and an Internet-Scale Operating System (ISOS). Existing Internet-scale networked computing systems include the following:

- GIMPS (Great Internet Mersenne Prime Search): http://www.mersenne.org/
  GIMPS searches for large prime numbers. The 42nd Mersenne Prime—$M_{25,964,951}$—was first calculated during February 2005 and contains 7,816,230 digits.

- Gnutella: http://www.gnutella.com/
  Gnutella is an Internet-wide shared file system.

- Distributed.net: http://www.distributed.net/
  Distributed.net is an Internet-wide, distributed decryption engine employing brute-force searches through the space of possible encryption keys. Greater than 100 billion keys are tried each second. It also searches for sets of numbers called *Optimal Golomb Rulers*, with applications in coding and networking.

In order to continue to accelerate computer and network capacity, throughput, and availability to these levels and beyond, the following conditions must be met:

- Computer and network components, subsystems and systems must be driven at increasingly higher clock frequencies within shrinking chip geometries and diminishing memory latencies.

- Computer and network components, subsystems, and systems must be increasingly integrated due to the speed of light limitation while remaining within classical space-time symmetries.

- Increasingly miniaturized componenets and systems need to be continually more energy-efficient, while avoiding serial architecture (Von Neumann) bottlenecks and resistance-capacitance delays. These issues are only temporarily delayed within parallel processing platforms.

The inexorable evolution of computing and networking to the molecular, atomic, and electronic/photonic scales promises hyperexponential price-performance improvements and expansion in the *Flowing Wakefulness* quality of intelligence throughout the structure and function of the Global Internetwork.

Evolution of the Quantum Computer

As introduced in Chapter 1, exponential trends of miniaturization indicate the attainment of a limit of single-atom bits and Single Electron Transistors (SETs) between the years 2010–2020. Prior to efficient attainment of the single-atom bit and SET scales, it will be necessary to use quantum effects to read bits from and write bits to the memory registers of nano- and pico- (and soon thereafter, femto-, atto-, zepto-, and yocto-) scale computers and network nodes.

Of all the candidate technologies to continue scaling beyond the Very Large Scale Integration (VLSI) era, quantum logic has one unique feature: It is not contained by classical space-time physics. Moore's Law is exponential; any classical approach demands exponential increases in space or time. Even Avogadro's number of elements in a molecular computer is quickly limited by the size of the exponential problem. Quantum computing accesses Hilbert space, the one exponential resource that has been untapped for computation.

There are two essential bases to quantum computer and network systems:

- *Fermions,* which have 1/2-integer spin and cannot be in the same state due to the Pauli exclusion principle, and
- *Bosons,* which have integer spin and can share the same state.

Electrons are fermions; photons are bosons. Electronic computing and networking is ultimately fermion-based, where N_8 must be either 0 or 1 because there cannot be more than one fermion in a single state. Optical computing and networking is ultimately boson-based, where the sum over N_8 runs from 0 to ∞.

Bosons—named after the Indian physicist Satyendra Bose—are the ultimate basis of optical computing and networking and are particles whose spin is a whole number. Fermions—named after the Italian physicist Enrico Fermi—are the ultimate basis of electronic computing and networking and are particles whose spin is half of a whole (odd) number and tend to give cancelling quantum-mechanical contributions.

Like opposite ends of a seesaw, when the quantum jitters of a boson are positive, those of a fermion tend to be negative, and vice versa. Since supersymmetry ensures that bosons and fermions occur in pairs, substantial cancellations occur from the outset—cancellations that ultimately calm the apparently frenzied quantum effects.

Continuing trends in miniaturization have brought us to the point where quantum physics must be used to describe elementary and complex operations of computers and networks. Classical models of computation, based on a mathematical idealization known as the Universal Turing Machine, are rendered invalid at the atomic (10^{-10} meter) and electronic/photonic (10^{-12} meter) quantum computational scales. At that juncture or earlier, the entire spectrum of computing and computer networking—including designing algorithms, loading programs, loading network configurations, running programs and configurations, and reading results—is increasingly dominated by quantum effects.

Deterministic, Probabilistic, and Quantum Turing Machines

Although the Turing Machine model is essentially flawed outside of classical physics-based computations, it is as applicable today as it was at its inception by Alan Turing in 1936. (It is noteworthy that Alonso Church, Kurt Godel, and Emil Post each independently created mathematical models of the computing process around the same period.) The Deterministic Turing Machine (DTM) model consists of an infinitely long tape that is marked off into a sequence of cells on which can be written a 0, 1, or a blank, and a read/write head that is able to move back and forth along the tape scanning the contents of each tape cell. The head can exist in one of a finite number of internal states and contains a set of instructions (that constitute the program) specifying how the state must change given the bit currently being read under the head, whether the bit should be subsequently changed, and in which direction the head should then be advanced. Unfortunately, the Turing model proves that, given sufficient time and memory capacity, there is no computation that a supercomputer could perform that a personal computer could not also perform.

The Probabilistic Turing Machine (PTM) model imbues a DTM with the ability to make a random choice. The PTM has multiple possible successor states available to any given state; whereas a DTM, in a given state and reading a certain symbol, has precisely one successor state available to itself. The probabilistic computation model introduces tradeoffs between the time required to return an answer to a computation and the probability that the returned answer is correct. Therefore, if a correct answer is required (almost always the case), uncertainty is encountered in the length of time a probabilistic algorithm must run. The Turing Machine model has been known to contain fundamental flaws since the early 1980s, when it first became evident that DTM and PTM models were bounded by classical space-time symmetry physics. As computers, network nodes, and their components increasingly miniaturize, their behavior must be properly described through the branch of physics appropriate for small scales—quantum physics.

The first truly Quantum Turing Machine (QTM) was outlined in 1985 by David Deutsch of Oxford University following initial descriptions of quantum mechanical computation by Richard Feynman of Caltech in 1982. Whereas a classical Turing machine could only encode a 0, 1, or blank in each cell of its tape, a QTM could encode a blend, or *superposition,* of 0 and 1 simultaneously. Quantum computing superposition encoding enables performance of calculations on all of the inputs in the time required to perform just one calculation classically, a phenomenon known as quantum parallelism.

The determination that each quantum bit (qubit) in a QTM can be a blend of 0 and 1 can be illustrated by representing each qubit as a vector contained within a sphere. A "straight up" position within the sphere represents the (classical) binary value of 0, and a "straight down" position represents the binary value of 1. When the vector is at any other position, the angle the vector makes with the vertical axis is a measure of the ratio of "0-ness" to "1-ness" within the qubit. The angle made by this vector with the vertical axis is related to the relative contributions of the $|\psi_0\rangle$ and $|\psi_1\rangle$ eigenstates to the whole state. Therefore, a given qubit state can have equal proportions of 0-ness and 1-ness but actually can display multiple amplitudes due to varying phase factors.

A QTM is a quantum mechanical generalization of a PTM with the significant difference that in a classical PTM only one particular computational trajectory is followed, and in a QTM all possible computational trajectories are followed simultaneously. The resulting superposition in a QTM results from the summation over all possible trajectories achievable in time *t*. Figure 8-2 represents a qubit both in terms of electronic states within an atom and as points on a three-dimensional sphere called a Bloch sphere.

Figure 8-2: Electronic and Bloch Sphere Qubit Representations

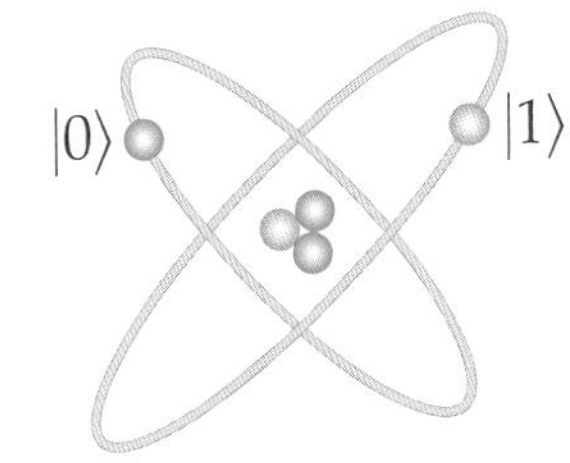

Qubit shown as two electronic states

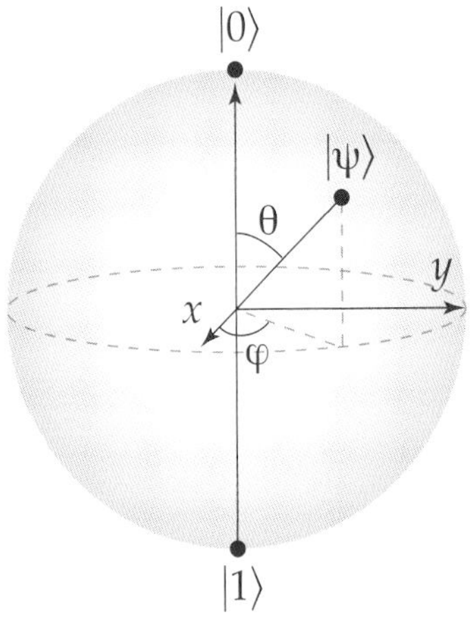

Bloch sphere qubit representation

Qubits and the Principle of Superposition

The atomic qubit model of Figure 8-2 indicates that an electron (qubit) can exist in either *ground* ($|0\rangle$) or *excited* ($|1\rangle$) states. The "$|\ \rangle$" notation is called the *Dirac notation* and is the standard state notation in quantum mechanics. (Refer to Appendix C for more information about Dirac notation as well as the mathematical notation used throughout this chapter.) Qubit superpositionality may occur as the two different polarizations of a photon, as the alignment of a nuclear spin in a uniform magnetic field, or as two states of an electron orbiting a single atom. Bloch sphere qubit representation indicates that a qubit can be in a state other than $|0\rangle$ or $|1\rangle$: It is possible to encounter linear combinations of states called superpositions.

Each qubit in a quantum computer can be represented by a simple two-state quantum system such as the spin state of a 1/2-spin particle. Its spin, when measured, is always found to exist in one of two possible states, represented as *spin-up* ($|+1/2\rangle$) or *spin-down* ($|-1/2\rangle$). Particle spins are quantized, and we can use one spin state to represent the binary value 0 and the other spin state to represent the binary value 1.

The Principle of Superposition, however, enables quantum systems to exist in all possible allowed states simultaneously, a phenomenon that is not possible classically. Just as a classical bit exhibits a *state*—either 0 or 1—a qubit can exist in the states $|0\rangle$ or $|1\rangle$, or can be in a state other than $|0\rangle$ or $|1\rangle$. Linear combinations of qubit states (superpositions) are represented as

$$|\psi\rangle = \alpha|0\rangle + \beta|1\rangle, \qquad (8.1)$$

where the values α and β are complex numbers. The special states $|0\rangle$ and $|1\rangle$ are called *computation basis states* and form an orthonormal basis for this vector space.

Classical Versus Quantum Computation

Figures 8-3 and 8-4 (on pages 157 and 159) present examples of classical and quantum computing complexity, respectively. These complexity classifications are based on the growth rates of algorithm run-times and memory requirements, rather than on absolute run times and memory requirements, in order to factor out variations in performance encountered by different makes of computers.

Figures 8-3 and 8-4 also present growth-rate-based complexity classes for classical and quantum computing, respectively, where a particular algorithm becomes an intrinsic measure of the difficulty of the problem the algorithm addresses. The resulting most important quantitative distinction is between polynomially growing costs (deemed tractable) and exponentially growing costs (deemed intractable). Exponential growth eventually exceeds polynomial growth, regardless of the degree of the polynomials.

As shown in Figure 8-3, problems that can be solved in polynomial time are deemed tractable and placed into class P. Class NP is nondeterministic polynomial time. Class NP-Complete is the "complete" set of problems mappable into one another in polynomial time (currently, approximately 1000 distinct NP-complete problems are known and include route planning, scheduling, and matching).

Figure 8-3: Classical Computing Complexity Classes

Classical Computing Complexity Class Significance	Computational Examples
P (Includes PTIME, PSPACE) Polynomial time (PTIME) is the class of problems that can be solved in polynomial time and are deemed tractable on a classical computer. The worst-case run-time of the algorithm is a polynomial in the size of the input. PSPACE consists of those problems that can be solved using resources that are few in spatial size ("small" computer) but not necessarily long in time.	Multiplication
NP Non-deterministic polynomial time is the class of problems which have solutions that can be quickly checked on a classical computer.	Factoring of composite integers
NP-Complete Since P is a subset of NP, and P does not equal NP, NP-Complete problems are a subclass of NP problems that can be mapped into one another in polynomial time. That is, if just one of the problems in the NP-Complete class is shown to be tractable, then they must all be tractable.	Clique (Graph Theory): In an undirected graph *G*, is a subset of vertices, each pair of which is connected by an edge. The size of the clique is the number of vertices it contains. Given an integer *m* and a graph *G*, does *G* have a clique of size *m*? Vertex Cover (Graph Theory): A vertex cover for an undirected graph *G* is a set of vertices *V'* such that every edge within the graph has one or both vertices contained in *V'*. Given an integer *m* and a graph *G*, does *G* have a vertex cover *V'* containing *m* vertices? Zero to One Integer Programming (Linear Programming): Given an integer $m \times n$ matrix *A* and an *m*-dimensional vector y with integer values, does there exist an *n*-dimensional vector x with entries in the set {0, 1} such that $Ax \leq y$? Subset-Sum (arithmetic): Given a finite collection *S* of positive integers and a target *t*, is there any subset of *S* which sums to *t*? Traveling salesman problem, scheduling, satisfiability
ZPP ZPP problems are tractable with certainty by Probabilistic Turing Machines (PTMs) in average case polynomial time.	
BPP BPP problems are tractable by PTMs in polynomial time with probability greater than .67, with a 1.0 success probability by iterating the algorithm a prescribed number of times.	Problems that can be solved using randomized algorithms in polynomial time (becomes the quantum class BQP)

In Figure 8-4, the classical classes P, ZPP, and BPP become the quantum classes QP, ZQP, and BQP. This means that a problem can be solved with certainty in worst-case polynomial time and in average-case polynomial time, and with a probability of greater than .67 in worst-case polynomial time using a QTM.

Because quantum computation and information are quantum mechanical in nature, the most succinct notational form in which to express their states and processes is a combination of linear algebra and Dirac notation adopted by quantum physicists for quantum mechanics. Figure 8-5 and Appendix C provide an overview of some of the notational forms associated with quantum computation and quantum information.

n Qubits and a Glance into the Cosmic Computer and Cosmic Switchboard

Two classical bits generate four possible states: 00, 01, 10, and 11. A two-qubit quantum computer has four computational basis states: $|00\rangle$, $|01\rangle$, $|10\rangle$, and $|11\rangle$. However, these qubit pairs can also exist in superpositions of the four states. Therefore, the quantum state of two qubits requires association of a complex coefficient—referred to as an *amplitude*—with each computational basis state. The resulting state vector describing the two qubits becomes

$$|\omega\rangle = \alpha_{00}|00\rangle + \alpha_{01}|01\rangle + \alpha_{10}|10\rangle + \alpha_{11}|11\rangle. \quad (8.2)$$

A significant two-qubit state is the Bell state, or Einstein, Podolsky, Rosen (EPR) pair,

$$|00\rangle + |11\rangle / \sqrt{2}. \quad (8.3)$$

This very important two-qubit state is the key component in quantum teleportation and superdense coding, which we will elaborate in the Krishṇ-Yajur-Veda Prātishākhya *(Taittirīya)* portion of this chapter.

In general, a two-state quantum computer has two eigenstates, which we refer to as $|\psi_0\rangle$ and $|\psi_1\rangle$. The general state of a two-state quantum computer system (the basic building

Figure 8-4: Quantum Computing Complexity Classes

Quantum Computing Complexity Class Significance	**Relationships to Classical Computing Complexity Classes**
QP The class of computational problems that can be solved with certainty in worst-case polynomial time by a quantum computer	$P \subset QP$ A quantum computer can solve more problems in worst-case polynomial time than a classical computer.
BQP The class of computational problems that can be solved with probability greater than .67 in worst-case polynomial time by a quantum computer (where the error probability is bounded)	$BPP \subseteq BQP \subseteq PSPACE$ It is not known whether Quantum Turing Machines (QTMs) are more powerful than Probabilistic Turing Machines (PTMs). Factoring is in BQP.
ZQP The class of computational problems that can be solved with zero error probability in expected polynomial time by a quantum computer	$ZPP \subset ZQP$

Figure 8-5: Dirac Notation in Quantum Computation

Quantum Computation Notation	**Description**
$\vert\psi\rangle$	Vector, also known as a *ket*
$\langle\psi\vert$	Vector dual to $\vert\psi\rangle$, also known as a *bra*
$\langle\varphi\vert\psi\rangle$	Inner product between the vectors $\vert\varphi\rangle$ and $\vert\psi\rangle$
$\vert\varphi\rangle \otimes \vert\psi\rangle$	Tensor product of $\vert\varphi\rangle$ and $\vert\psi\rangle$
$\vert\varphi\rangle\,\vert\psi\rangle$	Abbreviated notation for tensor product of $\vert\varphi\rangle$ and $\vert\psi\rangle$
$\mathbf{A}^*$	Complex conjugate of the **A** matrix
$\mathbf{A}^T$	Transpose of the **A** matrix
$\mathbf{A}$	Hermitian conjugate or adjoint of the **A** matrix, $\mathbf{A}^T = (\mathbf{A}^T)^*$
$\langle\varphi\vert\mathbf{A}\vert\psi\rangle$	Inner product between $\vert\varphi\rangle$ and $\mathbf{A}\vert\psi\rangle$. Equivalently, inner product between $\mathbf{A}^T\vert\varphi\rangle$ and $\vert\psi\rangle$
$\mathbf{Z}^*$	Complex conjugate of the complex number z. $(1 + i)^* = 1 - i$

block of a quantum memory register) can be expressed as a superposition of these eigenstates in the form

$$|\psi\rangle = |\psi_0\rangle + \omega_1|\psi_1\rangle \equiv \begin{pmatrix}\omega_0\\ \omega_1\end{pmatrix}, \qquad (8.4)$$

where the weights, ω_i, are complex numbers and the eigenstates, $|\psi_i\rangle$, generate a complete orthogonal basis for the state vector, $|\psi\rangle$.

The quantum superposition principle can be generalized beyond a two-state system. If a quantum computing system can exist in any one of n eigenstates, $|\psi_0\rangle, |\psi_1\rangle, |\psi_2\rangle, \ldots, |\psi_{n-1}\rangle$, it can also exist in the superposed state

$$|\psi\rangle = \sum_{i=0}^{n-1} |\psi_i\rangle\omega_i. \qquad (8.5)$$

It would appear that the larger ω_1 is relative to other weighting coefficients, the more the eigenstate, $|\psi_i\rangle$, contributes to the state vector, $|\psi\rangle$. However, the weighting coefficients are all complex numbers, and therefore the probabilities must be real numbers between 0 and 1. For any complex number $z = x + iy$, the product of z with a complex conjugate is always a positive real number, meaning specifically that $\omega_i\omega_i = |\omega_i|^2$ is guaranteed to be a positive real number.

This would suggest that $|\omega_i|^2$ is the probability of the system in state $|\psi_1\rangle$. However, there is no guarantee that $|\omega_i|^2$ currently exists between 0 and 1. Furthermore, since this quantum computer system can exist in n possible states, $|\psi_0\rangle, |\psi_1\rangle, \ldots, |\psi_n\rangle$, the sum of the probabilities of its being in each state must be additive to 1. Therefore, an n-state quantum computer dictates that the probability (Pr) of the system being in state $|\psi_i\rangle$ be given by

$$\Pr(|\psi_i\rangle) = \frac{|\omega_i|^2}{\sum_{i=0}^{n-1} |\omega_i|^2}, \qquad (8.6)$$

where the weighting coefficients, ω_i, are known as *probability amplitudes*.

When we consider a quantum computational system of n qubits we find that the computational basis states of this system are of the form $|\chi_1, \chi_2, \ldots, \chi_n\rangle$. Therefore, a quantum state of such a system is specified by 2^n amplitudes. For $n \geq 300$, this number is larger than the estimated number of atoms in the known physical universe (10^{80}). Yet the Cosmic Computer and Cosmic Switchboard are perpetually processing far greater quantities of data even for systems that contain only a few hundred atoms, to say nothing of the massively parallel infinity–point calculations that are forever proceeding behind the scenes to evolve and maintain all the Laws of Nature on every level of creation.

The scale of Natural Law calculations by the Cosmic Computer and Cosmic Switchboard is further estimated to extend by an exponentiation of factors beyond the atomic level when we shift our attention to the scales of the fundamental force particles (photons for the Electromagnetic Force, weak-gauge bosons for the Weak Force, gluons for the Strong Force, and gravitons for the Gravitational Force). The fundamental force computation density of the Cosmic Computer is again eclipsed hyperexponentially at the superstring dimensions that pervade sub-Planck scales of less than 10^{-33} centimeter (cm) ($< 10^{-35}$ m [meter]).

Quantum computing researchers initially attempted to understand how the basic operation of a conventional computer (a computer constrained to operation within classical space-time symmetries) could be accomplished while using quantum mechanical interactions. It is now clear, however, that by exploiting quantum phenomena with no classical analogs, it is possible to perform certain computational tasks far more efficiently than can be done by any classical space-time symmetry-based computer.

Quantum phenomena associated with quantum computing enable the rapid accomplishment of previously unprecedented results:

- Quantum information teleportation
- Generation of true random numbers
- Breaking heretofore classically unbreakable cryptosystems
- Communicating with messages that reveal the presence of eavesdropping
- Factoring of complex polynomials

- Quantum searching to extract statistics, such as the minimal element from an unordered data set, far more quickly and efficiently than on a classical computer
- Quantum searching of an unstructured database
- Quantum counting, where the number of solutions, M, to an N-item search problem can be found if M is not known in advance, far more quickly and efficiently than on a classical computer
- Quantum Fast Fourier Transform (QFFT), which can be used to solve discrete logarithm and factoring problems and to find a hidden subgroup (a generalization of finding the period of a periodic function)

While full quantum computational realization is completely outside the realm of classical computation, Figure 8-6 provides comparative examples of Classical and Quantum Information Theory.

Quantum Computer Realization

Quantum computation is based on transformation of quantum information states where quantum bits, as two-level quantum systems, are the fundamental building blocks of a quantum computer. Four essential requirements exist for any quantum computational implementation:

1 Qubit representation

2 Controllable unitary evolution

3 Preparation of initial qubit states

4 Measurement of final qubit states

Harmonic Oscillator Quantum Computer

A harmonic oscillator is a particle in a parabolic potential well, such as $V(x) = mw^2x^2/2$. Quantum computation is enabled by taking a finite subset of discrete energy eigenstates of a simple harmonic oscillator, $|n\rangle$; where $n = 0, 1, \ldots, \infty$; the qubits have lifetimes determined by physical parameters such as the cavity factor, Q; and where unitary transforms can be applied by allowing the quantum system to evolve over time. In this system,

Figure 8-6: Classical vs. Quantum Information Theory

Classical Information Theory	Quantum Information Theory
Entropy	
Shannon Entropy of an Information Source $$H = -k \sum_{i=1}^{n} p_i \log p_i$$ Where k is a positive constant that measures the uncertainty associated with a classical probability distribution	von Neumann Entropy of a Quantum State $S(\rho) \equiv -\mathrm{tr}(\rho \log \rho)$ Where the logarithms are Base 2, entropy is non-negative (0 if and only if the state is pure), and entropy is at most $\log d$ in a d-dimensional Hilbert space
Noiseless channel	
Shannon's Fundamental Theorem for a Noiseless Channel $$n_{\text{bits}} = H(x), \text{ not} > \frac{C}{H}$$ Quantifies the extent to which information from a classical source can be compressed	Schumacher's Quantum Noiseless Channel Coding Theorem $$n_{\text{qubits}} = S\left(\sum_x p_x \rho_x\right)$$ Treats quantum states as information. Describes a reliable quantum compression scheme.
Noisy Channel	
Shannon's Fundamental Theorem for a Discrete Channel with Noise $C = \max(H(x) - H_y(x))$ Where x is the input and y is the output. Generalizes symmetric channel capacity to the case of a discrete memoryless channel	Holevo-Schumacher-Westmoreland Theorem $$x^{(\varepsilon)} \equiv \max_{\{p_j, \rho_j\}} \left[S\left(\varepsilon\left(\sum_j p_j \rho_j\right)\right) - \sum_j p_j^{S(\varepsilon(\rho_j))} \right]$$ Where $x^{(\varepsilon)}$ is the product state channel capacity
Information	
Mutual $H(X{:}Y) = H(Y) - H(Y\|X)$	Coherent $I(\rho, \varepsilon) \equiv S(\varepsilon(\rho)) - S(\rho, \varepsilon)$
Fano Inequality	
$H(p_e) + p_e \log(\|X\| - 1) \geq H(X\|Y)$	$H(F(\rho, \varepsilon)) + (1 - F(\rho, \varepsilon))\log(d^2 - 1) \geq S(\rho, \varepsilon)$
Data Processing Inequality	
$X \to Y \to Z$ $H(X) \geq H(X{:}Y) \geq H(X{:}Z)$	$\rho \to \varepsilon_1(\rho) \to (\varepsilon_2 \bullet \varepsilon_1)(\rho)$ $S(\rho) \geq I(\rho, \varepsilon_1) \geq I(\rho, \varepsilon_2 \bullet \varepsilon_1)$

Legend

- H entropy in bits/qubits per symbol
- H(x|y) Conditioned entropy (uncertainty) in Classical Information Theory
- log logarithm base 2
- F Fano
- ρ quantum state, or, density matrix on a Hilbert space
- ε quantum channel, quantum operation
- ε_n trace-preserving quantum operations
- I quantum coherent information
- S entropy exchange
- C channel capacity
- x random variables associated with an information source
- y random variables associated with an information receiver

n qubits are provided via energy levels $|0\rangle$, $|1\rangle$,..., $|2^n\rangle$. Unfortunately, a single harmonic oscillator does not enable digital information representation.

Square Well-Based Quantum Computer

A square well—a particle within a one-dimensional box—is a prototypical quantum system and behaves according to Schrödinger's equation,

$$i\hbar\frac{d|\psi\rangle}{dt} = H|\psi\rangle, \tag{8.7}$$

where $\hbar$ is a physical constant (Planck's constant) whose value must be experimentally determined. By absorbing $\hbar$ into H, we effectively set $\hbar = 1$, where H is a fixed Hermitian operator known as the Hamiltonian of the closed system. Knowledge of the Hamiltonian of a system and knowledge of $\hbar$ provides a complete understanding of the dynamics of the system. Single qubits can be represented by the two lowest levels in a square well potential. However, finite square wells are just sufficiently deep to contain two bound states; transitions from any given set of bound states to a continuum of bound states is possible, leading to decoherence that can obviate qubit superpositionality.

Optical Photon Quantum Computer

Optical photons are chargeless particles and do not interact very strongly with each other or with other particles; therefore, they are strong candidates for representing qubits. For example, single photons can be generated by attenuating the output of a laser where the coherent state $|\alpha\rangle$ is defined as

$$|\alpha\rangle = e^{-|\alpha|^2/2}\sum_{n=0}^{\infty}\frac{\alpha^n}{\sqrt{n!}}|n\rangle \tag{8.8}$$

and where $|n\rangle$ is an n-photon energy eigenstate. Devices that can predictably generate, detect, and manipulate single photons with high quantum efficiency include *mirrors* (high reflectivity mirrors with less than or equal to 0.01% loss that can reflect photons and change their direction in space), *phase shifters* (units of transparent media with refractive index n different from that of free space), and *beam splitters* (partially silvered pieces of glass that reflect a fraction R of incident light and transmit $1 - R$). In these quantum computer realizations, quantum information is encoded both in the photon number and phase, with interferometers used to convert between the two state representations, $|0\rangle$ and $|1\rangle$. Realization of optical photon quantum computers is also encouraged by increasing reliance on purely optical networks. One major advantage of optical over electronic networks is that significantly less energy is required to transmit a bit or qubit using a photon over an optical fiber than is required to charge a typical 50 Ω electronic transmission link over the same distance. The major drawback to realization of an optical photon quantum computer is the difficulty of realizing nonlinear Kerr media (cross-phase modulation) with a large ratio of cross-phase modulation strength-to-absorption loss.

Optical Cavity Quantum Electrodynamics

Cavity quantum electrodynamics (QED), especially the single-atom cavity, provides a potential solution to the drawback in an optical photon quantum computer. This is because well-isolated single atoms do not experience the same degree of decoherence effects and could also provide cross-phase modulation between photons. However, the coupling of a photon pair is mediated by an atom, and coupling a photon into and out of the cavity becomes difficult, limiting cascadability and scalability.

Ion Trap-Based Quantum Computer

The main components of an ion trap quantum computer are an electromagnetic trap with lasers, photodetectors, and ions. Ion traps are used to tune incident monochromatic light to selectively cause transitions that change certain atomic and nuclear spin states depending upon other spin states. A particle has spin when it possesses a magnetic moment as if it were a composite particle with current running in a loop. *Bosons*—including photons—are integer spin particles, are massless, and have ±1 spin (corresponding to orthogonal polarization states) with no 0-spin components.

Fermions—including electrons, protons, and neutrons—are 1/2-spin particles, meaning that their spin component is either spin-up (+1/2 spin) or spin-down (–1/2 spin). Generally, "spin" refers to a 1/2-spin particle. In general, spin states provide good representations for quantum computation and information because they live in an inherently finite state space where quantum computation with trapped ions is predicated on the ability to construct arbitrary unitary transforms on the internal states of the atoms. The greatest drawback to the realization of an ion trap quantum computer is the weakness of the phonon-mediated spin-spin coupling technique and its decoherence susceptibility. (A phonon is a quantum of spin-based or vibrational energy, just as a photon is a quantum of electromagnetic radiation. Particle spin is always integer or 1/2-integer in nature.)

Nuclear Magnetic Resonance-Based Quantum Computer

Nuclear magnetic resonance (NMR) directly manipulates and detects nuclear spin states using radio frequency (RF) waves. There are two major issues inherent in using NMR to realize a quantum computer: (1) Approximately 10^8 molecules must be present in order to produce a measurable induction signal, and (2) NMR is generally applied to systems in equilibrium at ambient room temperature, meaning that the initial state of the spins is nearly completely random. However, one of the greatest strengths of realizing a quantum computer through NMR is that NMR realizes arbitrary unitary transforms on a spin system to small granularity using RF pulses.

Spintronics and the Spin Transistor

Spintronics (spin electronics) takes advantage of spin over charge in that electronic spin can be easily manipulated by externally applied magnetic fields, a property already invoked in magnetic storage technology. Spin properties also include a relatively long coherence, or relaxation time. Once created, spin tends to remain in a given state for a long time relative to charge states, due to spin state immunity to the long-range electrostatic Coulomb interactions between charges. Motorola, Inc., and IBM Corp., for example, have introduced Spin Field-Effect Transistors (Spin FETs, or SFETs) to exploit spin in Magnetic Random Access Memory (MRAM).

Spin-based quantum computing technologies are now emerging with the following advantages:

- Spin long coherence times
- Immunity to power disruption and outages
- Memory elements that can be in two different states simultaneously
- Quantum logic gates whose functions—AND, OR, NOR, etc.—can be changed greater than one billion times per second

Figure 8-7 illustrates the magnetic tunnel junction, a spintronic device consisting of two layers of ferromagnetic material (light green) separated by a nonmagnetic barrier (blue). The top part of the figure indicates that when the spin orientation (pink arrows) of the electrons in the two ferromagnetic layers is equal, a voltage is quite likely to pressure the electrons to tunnel through the barrier, resulting in high current flow. Flow of current is restricted by flipping the spins in one of the two layers (yellow arrows, bottom part of the figure), resulting in the two layers having oppositely aligned spins.

Figure 8-7: Magnetic Tunnel Junction

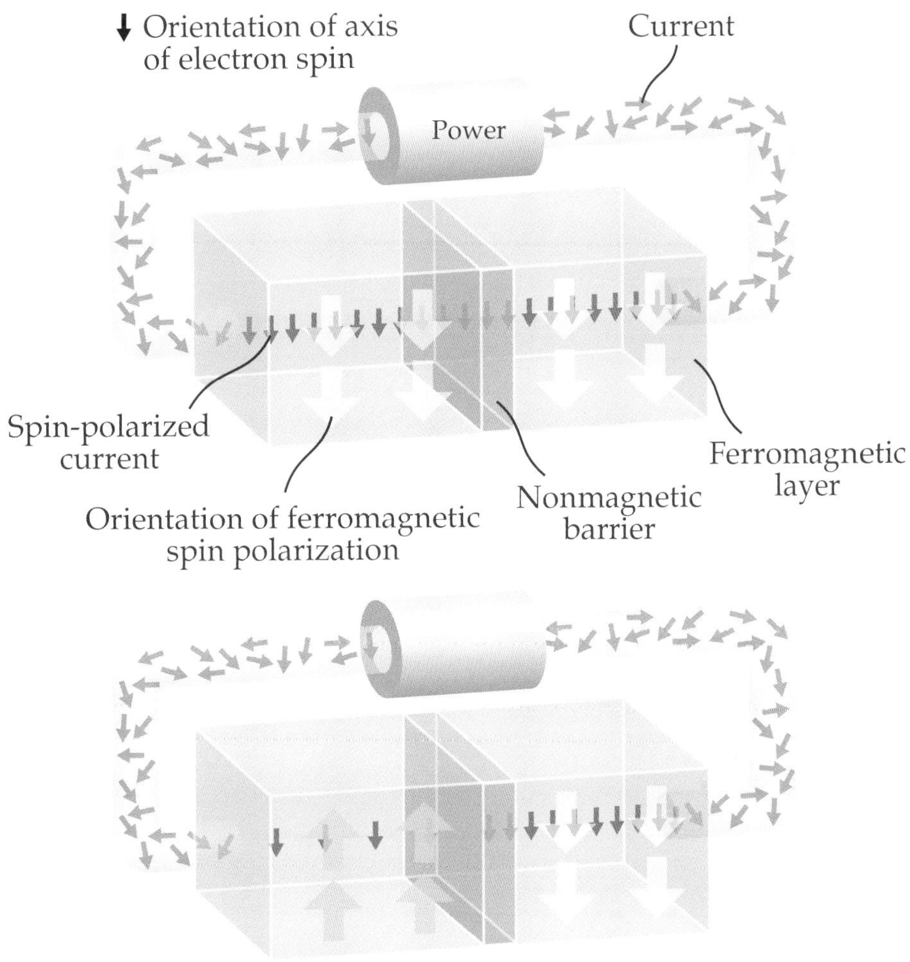

Nanotube Computer

Single-molecule diodes were first predicted in 1974, and the first molecular electronic components appeared in 1997 in the form of an electromechanical amplifier using a single C-60 (carbon buckyball) molecule. The first nanotube Field-Effect Transistor (FET) was also demonstrated during 1997. Switches and memory elements made of organic molecules caught between gold electrodes were first demonstrated during 1999.

Nanotube computers are emerging, based upon carbon nanotubes draped over gold electrodes. IBM Research has developed a logic gate from a single carbon nanotube on the scale of a few billionths of a meter in diameter, over 100 times smaller than transistors currently used in computer chips. This device is an early example of electronic circuitry constructed out of individual molecules, and it ushers in the era of nanoelectronics.

The microelectronics state-of-the-art during 2005 includes, for example, Intel's Centrino® mobile technology, produced on 90 nm (0.09 μ) process technology.

Further Quantum Computer Realizations

Atomic, molecular, and optical quantum computing realizations for quantum computers are under increasing development focus. It is also quite likely that we will see quarks, mesons, and gluons investigated as implementation platforms. However, greater than US $1 trillion is estimated to have been invested in silicon technology since the invention of the transistor in the late 1940s; therefore, the impetus to perfect a solid state quantum computer is also quite significant.

As projected earlier, we are witnessing the inexorable evolution of computing to the requirement to use quantum effects to read qubits from and write qubits to the memory registers of nano-, pico-, and increasingly smaller-scale computers and network nodes.

SHUKL-YAJUR-VEDA PRĀTISHĀKHYA—
Silencing, Sharing, and Spreading—
Quantum Algorithms, Circuits, Gates, and Cryptography

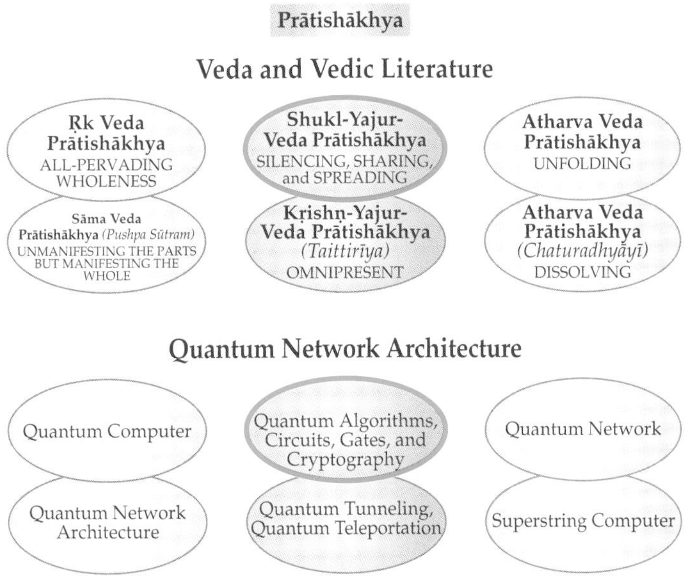

Elaboration of the RAAM Gate™ (Routt Addressable Absolute Memory Gate™)—Discovery of the Cosmic Computer and Cosmic Switchboard

Shukl-Yajur-Veda Prātishākhya represents the *Silencing, Sharing, and Spreading* values of consciousness. Yajur-Veda represents Wholeness with reference to *Devatā* value. *Devatā* is the link between *Ṛishi* and *Chhandas*—between the knower and the known. Yajur-Veda corresponds in Quantum Network Architecture to *Network Processing Systems*. The highest-order level of this *Silencing, Sharing, and Spreading* aspect of Quantum Network Architecture resides in *Quantum Algorithms, Quantum Circuits, Quantum Gates, and Quantum Cryptography*. They have the ability to silence, share, and spread both required and unwanted information, and correspond to Shukl-Yajur-Veda Prātishākhya.

The *Silencing, Sharing, and Spreading* quality of intelligence, available in the Vedic Literature in Shukl-Yajur-Veda Prātishākhya is also available within the *Atyanta-Abhāva* and *Anyonya-Abhāva* of the Cosmic Computer and Cosmic Switchboard, and in every network computing component of the Global Internetwork. This section elaborates the

RAAM Gate as the processing fabric basis to the discovery of the Cosmic Computer and Cosmic Switchboard.

Classical Computation and Gates

Classical computers are constructed from sets of electrical circuits containing wires and logic gates, where the wires convey information around the circuit, and logic gates manipulate the information. The only non-trivial example of a classical single-bit logic gate is the NOT gate, whose operation is defined by its truth table, in which $0 \rightarrow 1$ and $1 \rightarrow 0$, meaning that the 0 and 1 states are interchanged.

Figure 8-8 summarizes elementary classical (non-quantum) computing single- and multiple-bit logic gates and their truth tables. Classical AND, NAND, OR, XOR, and NOR gates receive two bits as input and generate a single bit as output; the NOT gate receives and generates a single bit as input and output, respectively. The AND gate outputs 1 if and only if both of its inputs are 1. The NAND and NOR gates take the AND and OR, respectively, of their inputs, and apply a NOT function to the output. The XOR gate outputs the sum modulo 2 of its inputs.

Two classical gates not shown in Figure 8-8 are the FANOUT and CROSSOVER gates. The FANOUT circuit gate enables bits to replicate; that is, FANOUT replaces a bit with two copies of itself. The CROSSOVER gate interchanges the value of two bits. Figure 8-8 also does not illustrate the preparation of additional *ancilla* or *work* bits, which create additional working space during classical computation.

Circuit elements ranging from simple to highly complex are routinely assembled from combinations of classical gates to compute all possible classical functions. Five major elements utilized in universal circuit construction include:

1 Wires, which preserve the states of bits

2 Ancilla bits prepared in standard states and used in the $n = 1$ case of a given proof

3 CROSSOVER operation

4 FANOUT operation

5 AND, XOR, and NOT gates

Figure 8-8: Classical Single- and Multiple-Bit Gates with Truth Tables

AND

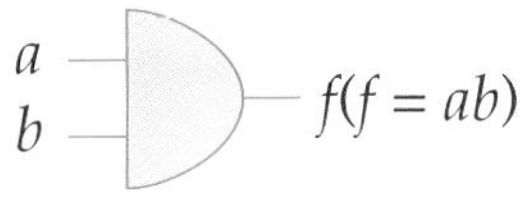

a	b	f
0	0	0
0	1	0
1	0	0
1	1	1

NAND

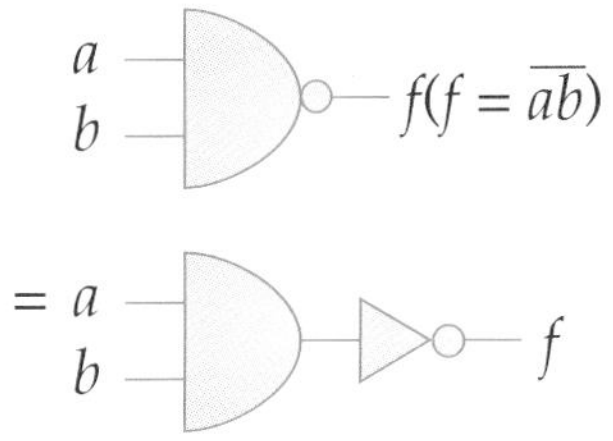

a	b	ab	f
0	0	0	1
0	1	0	1
1	0	0	1
1	1	1	0

OR

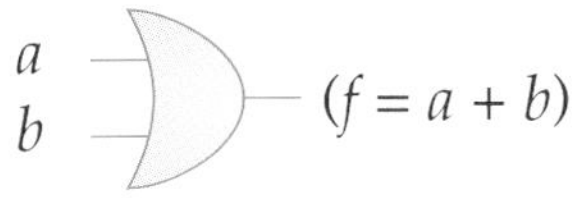

a	b	f
0	0	0
0	1	1
1	0	1
1	1	1

XOR

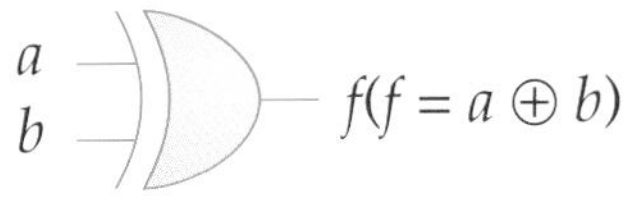

a	b	f
0	0	0
0	1	1
1	0	1
1	1	0

NOT

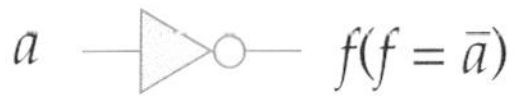

a	f
0	1
1	0

NOR

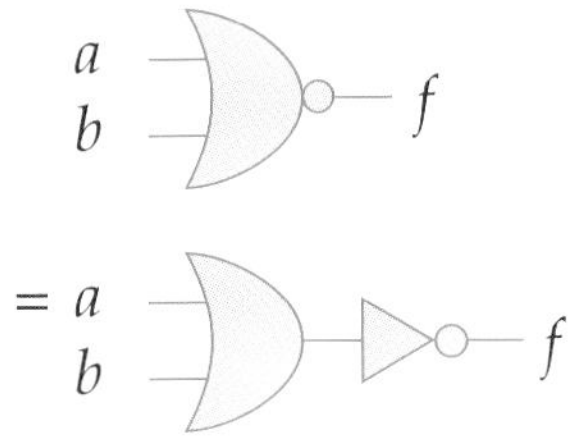

a	b	a + b	f
0	0	0	1
0	1	1	0
1	0	1	0
1	1	1	0

Quantum Computation and Gates

Quantum computers can be built from quantum circuits containing wires and elementary quantum gates that propagate and manipulate quantum information. As we have seen, changes that occur to a quantum state can be described using the language of quantum computation. If we could create a process that transforms the quantum state $|0\rangle$ to $|1\rangle$, this would suggest that perhaps we have developed the quantum logic analog to the classical NOT operation. However, specifying the action of the gate on the states $|0\rangle$ and $|1\rangle$ does not necessarily reveal what happens to superpositions of the states $|0\rangle$ and $|1\rangle$. In fact, the quantum NOT gate behaves linearly; that is, it transforms the state

$$\alpha|0\rangle + \beta|1\rangle \tag{8.9}$$

to the corresponding state in which the roles of $|0\rangle$ and $|1\rangle$ are interchanged:

$$\alpha|1\rangle + \beta|0\rangle . \tag{8.10}$$

Linear behavior is a general property of quantum computational systems. Therefore, we can define a matrix X to represent the quantum NOT gate as

$$X \equiv \begin{bmatrix} 0 & 1 \\ 1 & 0 \end{bmatrix} . \tag{8.11}$$

The quantum state $\alpha|0\rangle + \beta|1\rangle$ is written in vector notation as

$$\begin{bmatrix} \alpha \\ \beta \end{bmatrix} , \tag{8.12}$$

where the top entry represents the amplitude for $|0\rangle$, and the bottom entry represents the amplitude for $|1\rangle$, resulting in the following output from the quantum NOT gate:

$$X \begin{bmatrix} \alpha \\ \beta \end{bmatrix} = \begin{bmatrix} \beta \\ \alpha \end{bmatrix} . \tag{8.13}$$

Single-qubit quantum gates can be described by 2×2 matrices where the only constraint is the matrix U describing the single qubit gate to be unitary; that is, $U^\dagger, U = I$, where U is the adjoint of ***U*** (obtained by transposing and then complex-conjugating ***U***), and where *I* is the 2×2 identity matrix.

Two significant single-qubit gates are the Z gate and the Hadamard gate. The Z gate leaves $|0\rangle$ unchanged and flips the sign of $|1\rangle$ to $-|1\rangle$:

$$Z \equiv \begin{bmatrix} 1 & 0 \\ 0 & -1 \end{bmatrix}. \tag{8.14}$$

The Hadamard gate (also known as the "square-root of NOT" gate) transforms a $|0\rangle$ into a $(|0\rangle + |1\rangle)/\sqrt{2}$ (first column of the H matrix, midpoint between $|0\rangle$ and $|1\rangle$), and transforms a $|1\rangle$ into a $(|0\rangle - |1\rangle)/\sqrt{2}$ (second column of the H matrix, also at the midpoint between $|0\rangle$ and $|1\rangle$):

$$H \equiv \frac{1}{\sqrt{2}}\begin{bmatrix} 1 & 1 \\ 1 & -1 \end{bmatrix}. \tag{8.15}$$

Hadamard gate properties for quantum computation can be understood fundamentally as an arbitrary qubit unitary gate that can be decomposed as a product of rotations and reflections of a Bloch sphere, where the Hadamard operation is a rotation of the sphere about the y axis by 90°, followed by a reflection through the $x - y$ plane. In general, an arbitrary single qubit unitary gate can be decomposed as a product of rotations as

$$\begin{bmatrix} \cos\frac{\Upsilon}{2} & -\sin\frac{\Upsilon}{2} \\ \sin\frac{\Upsilon}{2} & \cos\frac{\Upsilon}{2} \end{bmatrix}, \tag{8.16}$$

and a gate can be represented as being a rotation about the z axis with a global phase shift expressed as a constant multiplier of the form $e^{i\alpha}$:

$$\begin{bmatrix} e^{-i\beta/2} & 0 \\ 0 & e^{i\beta/2} \end{bmatrix}. \tag{8.17}$$

Quantum computation (the quantum circuit model of computation) generally requires the following key elements:

- Suitable state space—quantum computational circuits operate on some number, n, of qubits; therefore, the quantum computational state space is a 2^n-dimensional Hilbert space, with product state of the form $|\chi_1,\ldots, \chi_n\rangle$, where $\chi_i = 0, 1$ are called computational basis states.
- Any computational basis state $|\chi_1,\ldots, \chi_n\rangle$ that can be prepared in less than or equal to n steps
- Quantum gates, which can be applied to any subset of qubits and a universal family of gates that can be implemented
- Ability to perform measurements in the computational basis of greater than or equal to 1 qubit(s)
- Inherent ability to perform classical (non-quantum) computations if quantum computations are not required

Figure 8-9 summarizes single-qubit quantum computing gates and their corresponding Unitary matrices. The overall purpose of all computational logic gates is to enable the processing of algorithms—classical and quantum. From a single-qubit gate perspective, a qubit is a vector $|\psi\rangle = a|0\rangle + b|0\rangle$ that is parameterized by two complex numbers that satisfy $|a|^2 + |b|^2 = 1$. A single qubit in the state $a|0\rangle + b|0\rangle$ can be visualized as a point (θ, φ) on the Bloch unit sphere (the vector [$\cos\varphi \sin\theta$, $\sin\varphi \sin\theta \cos\theta$] is the Bloch vector), where $a = \cos(\theta/2)$, $b = e^{i\varphi}\sin(\theta/2)$, and a is assumed to be real because the overall phase of the state is unobservable.

Figure 8-10 depicts the prototypical controlled-NOT (CNOT) quantum logic gate and its matrix representation. CNOT is a quantum gate with two input qubits—the control qubit and target qubit, respectively. CNOT gate action is given by $|c\rangle|t\rangle \rightarrow |c\rangle|t \oplus c\rangle$, where, if the control qubit is set to $|1\rangle$, then the target qubit is flipped, otherwise, the target qubit is not changed.

The Toffoli gate and its corresponding truth table is shown in Figure 8-11 (on page 176) and is interesting because it can be implemented both as a classical and as a quantum logic

Figure 8-9: Single Qubit Gates with Unitary Matrices

Hadamard	H	$\frac{1}{\sqrt{2}}\begin{bmatrix} 1 & 1 \\ 1 & -1 \end{bmatrix}$
Pauli-X	X	$\begin{bmatrix} 0 & 1 \\ 1 & 0 \end{bmatrix}$
Pauli-Y	Y	$\begin{bmatrix} 0 & -i \\ i & 0 \end{bmatrix}$
Pauli-Z	Z	$\begin{bmatrix} 1 & 0 \\ 0 & -1 \end{bmatrix}$
Phase	S	$\begin{bmatrix} 1 & 0 \\ 0 & i \end{bmatrix}$
π/8	T	$\begin{bmatrix} 1 & 0 \\ 0 & e^{i\pi/4} \end{bmatrix}$

Figure 8-10: CNOT Multiple-Qubit Gate with Unitary Matrix

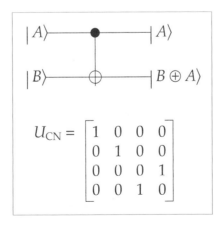

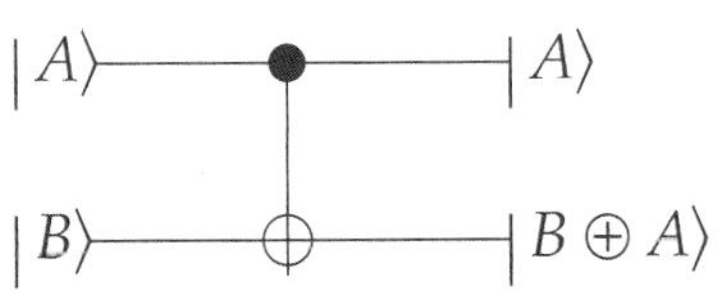

$$U_{CN} = \begin{bmatrix} 1 & 0 & 0 & 0 \\ 0 & 1 & 0 & 0 \\ 0 & 0 & 0 & 1 \\ 0 & 0 & 1 & 0 \end{bmatrix}$$

- Generalization of the classical XOR gate
- Gate action is $|A, B\rangle \rightarrow |A, B \oplus A\rangle$, where $\oplus$ is addition modulo 2
- Control qubit and target qubit are XORed and stored in the target qubit

Figure 8-11: Toffoli Multiple-Bit/Qubit Gate with Truth Table

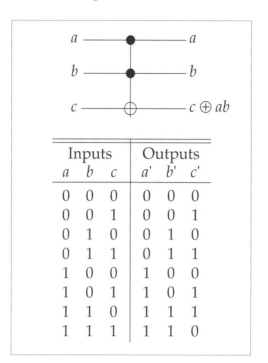

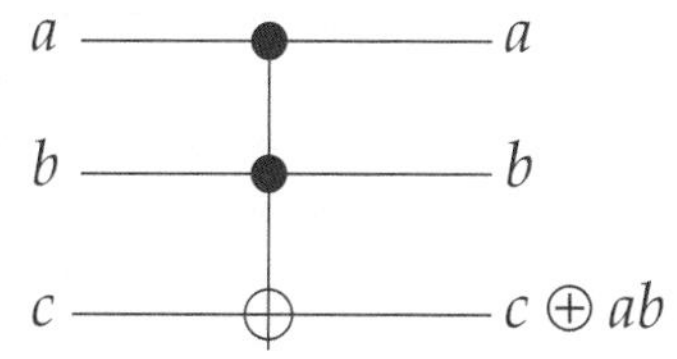

Inputs			Outputs		
a	b	c	a'	b'	c'
0	0	0	0	0	0
0	0	1	0	0	1
0	1	0	0	1	0
0	1	1	0	1	1
1	0	0	1	0	0
1	0	1	1	0	1
1	1	0	1	1	1
1	1	1	1	1	0

- Can be implemented as both a classical and a quantum logic gate
- Can be used to simulate NAND gates
- Can be used to perform FANOUT

gate. One of its main roles as a quantum gate is to enable simulation of classical logic circuitry. Whereas several classical logic gates such as the NAND gate are inherently irreversible, any classical circuit can be replaced by an equivalent quantum circuit containing only reversible elements through use of the reversible Toffoli quantum gate. Toffoli gates have three input bits and three output bits, and two of the bits are control bits that are unaffected by the action of the gate. The third bit is a target bit that is flipped if both control bits are set to 1; otherwise, the target bit is not changed. Toffoli gate reversability is demonstrated by applying the gate twice to a set of bits as $(a, b, c) \rightarrow (a, b, c \oplus ab) \rightarrow (a, b, c)$.

Quantum Algorithms

Quantum logic gates are the basic units of quantum computational algorithms, just as classical logic gates are the basic units of classical computational algorithms. The major distinction between the quantum and classical computational contexts is that quantum gates must be implemented unitarily and, in particular, must incorporate reversible operations. The OR statement on two classical bits, for example, is not invertible because the four possible inputs, {00, 01, 10, 11}, map onto only two possible outputs, {0, 1}.

Following are ten major classes of quantum algorithms:

1 **Classical Computations on a Quantum Computer**

These are enabled, for example, by the Toffoli gate.

2 **Quantum Parallelism**

Quantum parallelism is a feature of several quantum algorithms that enables quantum computers to evaluate a function $f(x)$ for multiple values of x simultaneously. If, for example, $f(x):\{0, 1\} \rightarrow \{1, 0\}$ is a function with a one-qubit domain and range, and a two-qubit quantum operation initializes in the state $|x, y\rangle$, an appropriate sequence of quantum logic gates can transform this state $\rightarrow |x, y \oplus f(x)\rangle$, where $\oplus$ is addition modulo 2, the first register is the data register, and the second register is the target register. The transformation map $|x, y\rangle \rightarrow |x, y \oplus f(x)\rangle$ is unitary (U_f). Quantum circuits can be constructed that apply U_f to inputs not in the computational basis and where the data register is prepared in the superposition $(|0\rangle + |1\rangle)/\sqrt{2}$. Hadamard gates, for example, act on $|0\rangle$; then U_f is applied and results in the state $(|0, f(0)\rangle + |1, f(1)\rangle)/\sqrt{2}$. This result contains information about both $f(0)$ and $f(1)$ where a single quantum $f(x)$ circuit is therefore used to evaluate the function for multiple values of x simultaneously.

3 **Deutsch's Algorithm**

Deutsch's quantum algorithm combines quantum parallelism with the interference property of quantum mechanics, resulting in the ability to determine a global property of $f(x)$, that is, $f(0) \oplus f(1)$, through a single evaluation of $f(x)$. The Deutsch-Jozsa Algorithm is related.

4 **Quantum Simulation Algorithm**

Quantum simulation seeks to solve differential equations that capture laws governing the dynamic behavior of a system. Classical computation cannot effectively simulate quantum system behavior, because even simple quantum systems are governed by Schrödinger's equation

$$i\hbar\frac{d}{dt}|\psi\rangle = H|\psi\rangle, \tag{8.18}$$

where a significant issue is the exponential number (2^n) of differential equations that must be solved. The quantum simulation algorithm is concerned with the solution of

$$id|\psi\rangle/dt = H|\psi\rangle, \tag{8.19}$$

which, for a time-dependent H, is

$$|\psi(t)\rangle = e^{-iHt}|\psi(0)\rangle. \tag{8.20}$$

5 **Quantum Fast Fourier Transform (QFFT)**

QFFT is the key component of quantum factoring, order-finding, period-finding, order of a permutation, hidden linear function, and Abelian stabilizer algorithms. The discrete (non-quantum) Fast Fourier Transform (FFT) receives as input a vector of complex numbers, $x_0,\ldots, x_{N-1}$, where the length of the vector, N, is fixed. Transformed data is output as a vector of complex numbers, $y_0,\ldots, y_{N-1}$, where

$$y_k \equiv \frac{1}{\sqrt{N}}\sum_{j=0}^{N-1} x_j e^{2\pi ijk/N}. \tag{8.21}$$

QFFT performs the same transformation as the classical FFT, with the notable exception that the quantum transform is computed on an orthonormal basis, $|0\rangle,\ldots, |N-1\rangle$, and a linear operator performs the following on the basis states:

$$|j\rangle \rightarrow \frac{1}{\sqrt{N}}\sum_{k=0}^{N-1} e^{2\pi ijk/N}|k\rangle. \tag{8.22}$$

QFFT action on an arbitrary state is

$$\sum_{j=0}^{N-1} x_j|j\rangle \rightarrow \sum_{k=0}^{N-1} y_k|k\rangle, \tag{8.23}$$

where the amplitudes y_k are the discrete Fourier transform of the amplitudes x_j.

6 Quantum Factoring

Finding the prime factorization of an n-bit integer requires approximately $\exp[\Xi(n^{1/3} \log^{2/3} n)]$ operations using the classical number field sieve and is exponential in the size of the number being factored. Classical (non-quantum) prime factorization therefore quickly becomes an intractable problem with increasing values of n. By contrast, quantum computers, using $O(n^2 \log n \log \log n)$ operations, can factor any number exponentially faster than the most efficient classical factoring algorithms.

Shor's quantum factoring algorithm was an early demonstration of the unique use of quantum computing, since the difficulty of factoring numbers, N, which are the products of two large primes, was well known as crucial to the security of certain public key encryption schemes.

Euclid's algorithm can be used to efficiently find a classical factor of $N(y, N)$, provided N is not very large. As N increases, it quickly becomes impractical to compute r (unknown period) classically, as it requires evaluating $O(N)$ powers of y. Quantum computation, however, enables evaluation of all the powers of y simultaneously, where the remaining challenge becomes one of adjusting the probability amplitudes to obtain the value of r with a reasonably high probability.

Shor's quantum factoring algorithm recognizes that the powers of $y \bmod (N)$ define a periodic function. Second, Shor's algorithm (as is true of Simon's algorithm) invokes the finite Fourier transform to transform the cyclic behavior of a periodic function into enhanced probability amplitudes of certain quantum states. An example of Shor's quantum factoring algorithm follows for $N = 15$, based on *An Introduction to Quantum Computing Algorithms* by Arthur O. Pittenger:

Step 1: Initialize $n = 4$ so that $15 \leq S \equiv 2^4 = 16$. Choose y so that $(y, 15) = 1$. Therefore, for example, if $y = 13$, then $(13, 15) = 1$.

Step 2: Initialize two four-qubit registers to state 0: $|\psi_0\rangle = |0\rangle|0\rangle$.

Step 3: Randomize the first register,

$$|\psi_0\rangle \rightarrow |\psi_1\rangle = \sum_{k=0}^{15} a_k|k\rangle|0\rangle, \tag{8.24}$$

where $a_k = 1/\sqrt{16}$.

Step 4: Unitarily compute the function $f(k) = 13^k \bmod (15)$:

$$|\psi_1\rangle \rightarrow |\psi_2\rangle = \sum_{k=0}^{15} a_k|k\rangle|f(k)\rangle. \tag{8.25}$$

Step 5: Operate on the first four qubits by the finite Fourier transform $F = F_{16}$. The result is

$$|k\rangle \rightarrow \frac{1}{\sqrt{16}}\sum_{u=0}^{15} \exp(2\pi iuk/16)|u\rangle \tag{8.26}$$

and is unitarily implementable; therefore,

$$|\psi_2\rangle \rightarrow |\psi_3\rangle = \frac{1}{16}\sum_{u=0}^{15} |u\rangle \sum_{u=0}^{15} \exp(2\pi iuk/16)|f(k)\rangle. \tag{8.27}$$

Step 6: Since 13 has (unknown) period r, the function f is periodic. In this case, the period is divisible by 16. We can therefore write $k = m + jr$, where $0 \le m < r$ and $0 \le j < 16/r$, and $f(k)$ can be written as $f(m)$, resulting in the new state:

$$|\psi_3\rangle = \frac{1}{16}\sum_{u=0}^{15} |u\rangle \sum_{m=0}^{r-1} |f(m)\rangle \exp(2\pi iukm/16) \sum_{j=0}^{(16/r)-1} \exp(2\pi iurj/16). \tag{8.28}$$

Calculation of the summation over j, inclusive of the lead factor of $1/16$, generates

$$|\psi_3\rangle = \sum_{u=0}^{15} |u\rangle b_u \sum_{m=0}^{r=1} |f(m)\rangle \exp(2\pi ium/16), \tag{8.29}$$

where $bu = 1/r$ if 16 divides ur, or $16|ur$, and is zero otherwise.

Step 7: We then measure the state of the first register. If *Pu* denotes the projection mapping onto the quantum state denoting the value *u*, then, as defined in the Chinese Remainder Theorem, the probability of observing *u* is

$$\langle \psi_3 | P_u | \psi_3 \rangle = r|b_u|^2 = \begin{cases} \frac{1}{r} \text{ if } 16/ur, 0 \text{ otherwise} . \end{cases} \tag{8.30}$$

Step 8: We then use the known values of *u* and 16 to deduce a putative value of *r*. If no inference is obtainable or if *r* is odd, go to Step 2 and repeat. If $r = 2s$ is even, and $y^s = -1 \bmod (15)$, return to Step 2 and repeat. If $(15, y^s \pm 1) > 1$, quit; otherwise, return to Step 2 and repeat.

Shor's algorithm also works for odd *N* that are not powers of primes.

Seven-Qubit Realization of Shor's Quantum Factoring Algorithm

On December 20, 2001, scientists at IBM's Almaden Research Center announced successful performance of the most complicated quantum computer calculation reported to that date. They caused approximately 10^{18} molecules in a vial to become a seven-qubit molecule that successfully executed Shor's algorithm and correctly identified 3 and 5 as the factors of 15. While this is only a beginning, it opens the doorway to performing quantum calculations on massively parallel and distributed scales. In general, the complexity of factoring large numbers while constrained to classical computers doubles the time to discover the factors. By contrast, quantum factoring time increases by only a constant increment with each additional digit.

Figure 8-12 (on page 182) illustrates the seven-qubit molecule that IBM used to successfully perform Shor's quantum factoring algorithm. The molecule has seven nuclear spins—the nuclei of five fluorine and two carbon atoms—which interact as qubits, are programmable by radio frequency pulses, can be detected by Nuclear Magnetic Resonance (NMR) instruments, and, while at ambient room temperature, behave as if they were in a very cold system. The result is that all measured nuclear spins appear to be oriented in the same direction. This result is especially interesting because it demonstrates a simple quantum version of the mathematical problem that lies at the heart of a wide range of data-security cryptographic systems.

Figure 8-12: IBM Seven-Qubit Molecule That Performed Shor's Quantum Factoring Algorithm

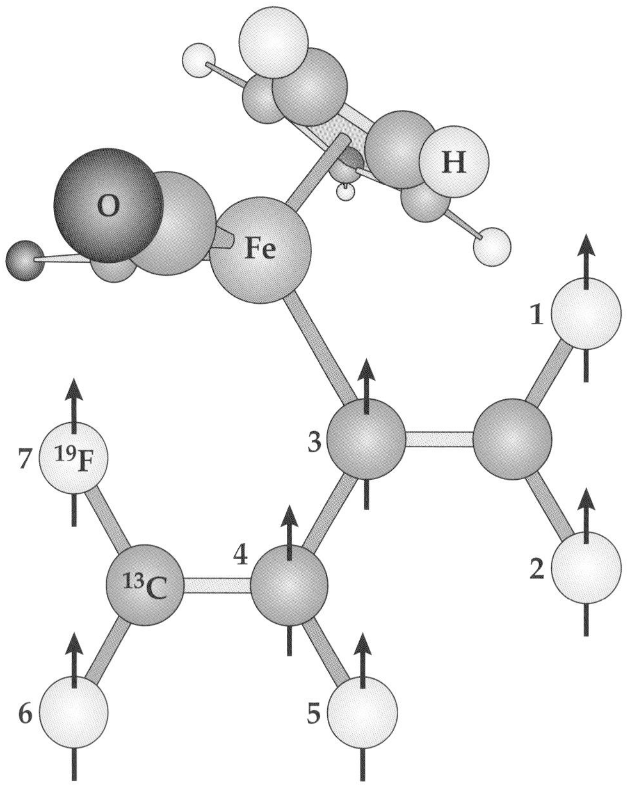

IBM's work builds on earlier breakthroughs by the same researchers (Dr. Isaac L. Chuang, et al.) who previously successfully implemented the quantum database search algorithm invented by Lov Grover of Bell Labs. The team demonstrated that, whereas a classical computer requires approximately $n/2$ iterations to locate an item in a list of n entries, Grover's Algorithm running on a quantum computer reduces the numbers of tries to the square root of n.

7 **Quantum Search Algorithm (a.k.a. Grover's Algorithm)**

Rather than search through a space of N elements directly, a quantum oracle can be invoked, for example, to focus on the index to those elements, which is a number $0 \le$ element index $\le N - 1$. If $N = 2^n$, the index can be stored in n qubits, and the quantum search problem will have M solutions, with $1 \le M \le N$. The quantum search oracle obtains a search solution within $O(\sqrt{N/M})$ iterations. Figure 8-13 provides a

Figure 8-13: Circuit Overview for the Quantum Search Algorithm

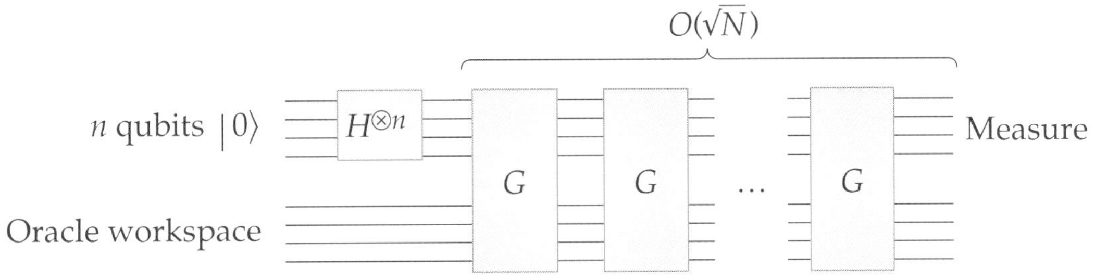

circuit overview for the quantum search algorithm with the algorithm utilizing a single n-qubit register.

In general, quantum search problems can be formulated in terms of an oracle, $f(x)$, that equals 1 for arguments, x, that solve the problem of interest, where x may be, for example, a pair of integers and $f(x)$ a check for prime factors. Alternatively, x may be database entries and $f(x)$ a test for answers to a query. Lov Grover has shown that a quantum computer can solve the quantum search problem in $\sqrt{N}$ steps.

The quantum search algorithm is also referred to as the database search algorithm, where a quantum database is structured in quantum memory containing $N = 2^n$ cells of l qubits each. The contents d_x of the xth memory cell are added to the data register as $|d\rangle \rightarrow |d \oplus d_x\rangle$, and the addition is performed bitwise, modulo 2.

8 Quantum Counting

Classical computation requires $\Xi(N)$ iterations with an oracle to determine the number of solutions, M, to an N-item search problem if M is not known in advance. Quantum counting estimates the number of solutions significantly more rapidly by combining the Grover iteration with the phase estimation technique based upon the QFFT.

9 Quantum Cryptography

Classical cryptography incorporates both private key and public key systems. The major challenge within private key cryptosystems is secure distribution of key bits. Quantum cryptography, or Quantum Key Distribution (QKD), uses the principles of quantum mechanics to enable provably secure distribution of private information and utilizes quantum corollaries of classical private cryptography, information reconciliation (error-correction conducted over a public channel), and privacy amplification. QKD is provably secure in that private key bits can be created between two parties over a public channel, and the key bits can be used to implement a classical private key cryptosystem, enabling parties to communicate securely.

The QKD protocol transmits non-orthogonal qubits over a public channel. The sender and receiver establish an upper bound on any noise or eavesdropping occurring within their communication channel through the use of "check" qubits that are randomly interspersed among data qubits. Information reconciliation and privacy amplification are then performed to distill a shared secret key string, with security of the resulting key ensured by the properties of quantum information.

Three QKD protocol cases include BB84, B92, and EPR. In the BB84 QKD protocol, for example, one user, Alice, initializes with a and b two strings each of $(4 + \delta)n$ random classical bits. (By convention, cooperating quantum cryptographic users are referred to as Bob and Alice, and someone attempting to eavesdrop into a quantum communication channel is referred to as Eve.) These bits are next encoded as strings of a block of $(4 + \delta)n$ qubits,

$$|\psi\rangle = \bigotimes_{k=1}^{(4+\delta)n} |\psi a_k b_k\rangle, \tag{8.31}$$

where a_k is the kth bit of a, b_k is the kth bit of b, and each qubit is one of the four states

$$\begin{aligned} |\psi_{00}\rangle &= |0\rangle \\ |\psi_{10}\rangle &= |1\rangle \\ |\psi_{01}\rangle &= |+\rangle = (|0\rangle + |1\rangle)\sqrt{2} \\ |\psi_{11}\rangle &= |-\rangle = (|0\rangle - |1\rangle)\sqrt{2}. \end{aligned} \tag{8.32}$$

These four states are not all mutually orthogonal; therefore, no measurement can distinguish among all of them with certainty. At this point, Alice sends $|\psi\rangle$ to Bob over a public quantum communication channel. Bob receives $\varepsilon(|\psi\rangle\langle\psi|)$, where ε describes the quantum operation that results from the combined effect of the channel between Bob and Alice and any possible eavesdropping actions by Eve. Bob then publicly announces this quantum operation state set, and each of the three has their unique quantum state set described by separate density matrices. It is also true that Alice has not revealed b; it is also possible that ε may be a poor channel artifact in addition to possible eavesdropping by Eve.

Bob next measures each qubit in basis X or Z, as determined by a random $(4 + \delta)n$-bit string that he creates, b', with his measurement result equaling a'. Next, Alice publicly announces b. Then, by public channel communication, Bob and Alice discard all bits in $\{a', a\}$ except those for which corresponding bits b' and b are equal. The remaining bits satisfy $a' = a$. Alice then randomly selects n bits (of a mutual 2^n bits) and announces the selection to Bob over a public channel. They both then publish and compare the value of these check bits, and, if more than t bits disagree, they re-initialize the protocol. If t is mutually selected, then they can apply information reconciliation and privacy amplification algorithms to obtain m acceptably secret shared key bits from the remaining n bits.

Figure 8-14 (on page 186) summarizes a working topology at IBM over a 10 kilometer (km) distance in which Bob initiates coherent states, $|\alpha\rangle$, using a Laser Emitting Diode (LED) operating at a wavelength (λ) equalling 1.3 micrometers (μm) and transmits to Alice. Alice then attenuates them to approximately generate a single photon. Alice polarizes the photon in one of the four states of the BB84 protocol (equation 8.32), using as $|0\rangle$ and $|1\rangle$ states horizontal and vertical polarization, respectively. Alice then returns the photon to Bob, who measures it using a polarization analyzer operating randomly. The photon traverses the same path twice; then Alice and Bob select the subset of results in which they have used the same basis. They perform information reconciliation and privacy amplification and communicate over a public channel with photons of 1.55 μm λ. QKD protocols have been successfully executed over distances greater than 40 km.

10 Quantum Error-Correcting Codes

Classical network error detection and correction is well known and in prevalent use at multiple architectural layers. There are two basic approaches generally taken in classical (non-quantum) network designs for handling transmission errors: (1) Include

Figure 8-14: Quantum Key Distribution Topology

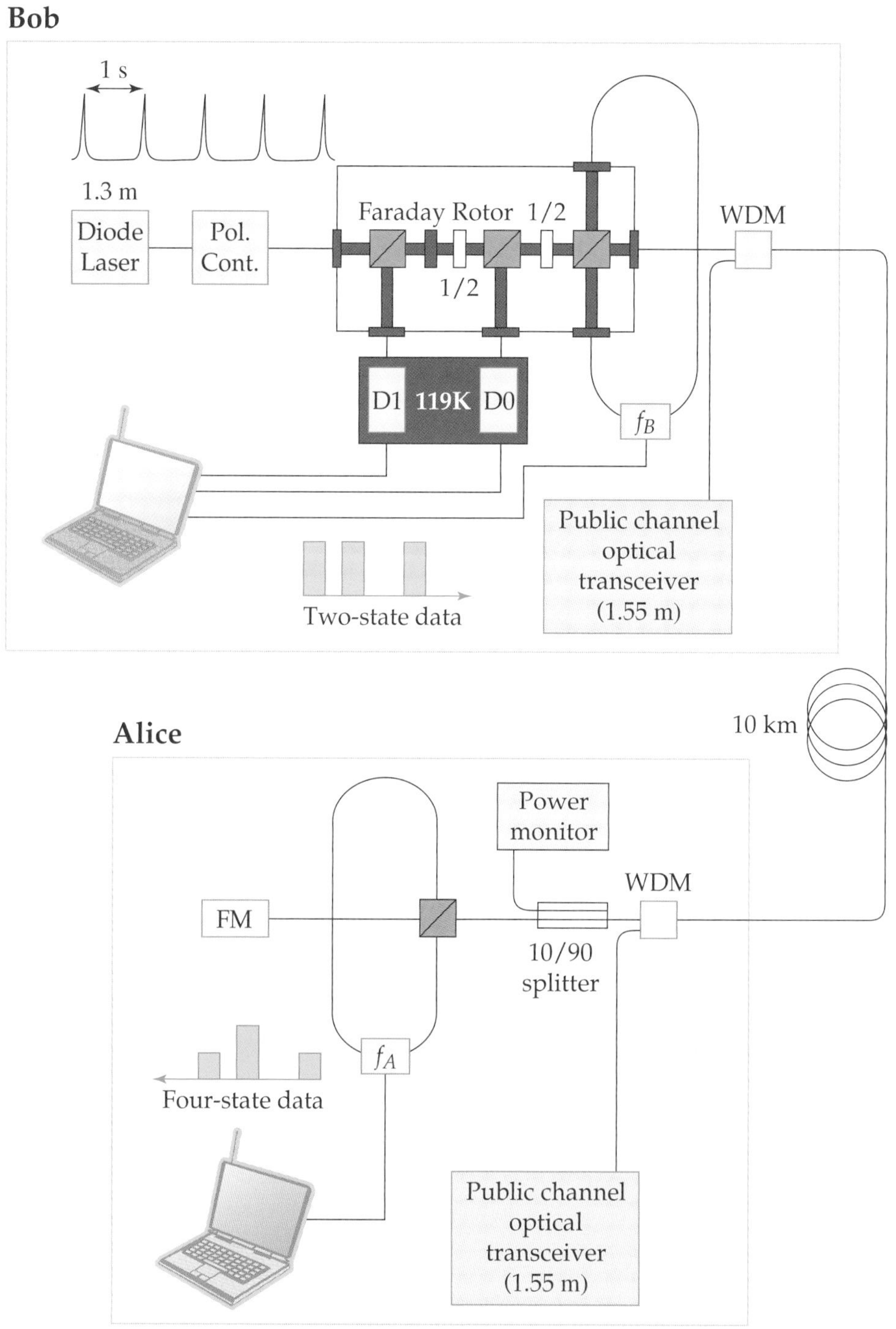

Legend

s	microsecond	FM	Frequency Modulator
m	micron (1 = 1000 nanometers)	km	kilometer
f	frequency	WDM	Wavelength Division Multiplexer

sufficient redundant information with each block of data sent to enable the receiver to deduce the transmitted character correctly (error-correcting codes), or (2) Incorporate only sufficient redundancy to allow the receiver to determine that a transmission error has occurred (error-detecting codes).

Very generally, transmitted classical frames consist of m data bits and r redundant bits, or checkbits, where the total length equals $n(n = m + r)$. An n-bit classical network transmission unit that contains data and checkbits is referred to as an n-bit codeword. Given two possible codewords, for example 10001001 and 10110001, an EXCLUSIVE OR (XOR) logic operation using modulo-2 arithmetic and yielding a remainder can determine that they differ by three bits. The number of bit positions in which a pair of codewords differs is the Hamming distance. This is significant because two codewords that are a Hamming distance d apart will require d single-bit errors to convert one into the other.

It was originally thought that analogous error-correction techniques would not apply to the quantum network transmission of qubits, due to the assumption that qubit measurement would force the collapse of the qubit into a specific state, therein losing superpositionality. It was also noted that an inherent problem exists with copying or cloning an arbitrary quantum state. However, Shor and others have developed nine-, seven-, and five-qubit error-correcting codes (algorithms). Shor's nine-qubit error-correcting code, for example, presumes that one qubit is encoded into nine qubits via the following scheme:

$$\begin{aligned} \alpha|0\rangle + \beta|1\rangle \rightarrow\ & \alpha(|000\rangle + |111\rangle) \otimes (|000\rangle + |111\rangle) \otimes (|000\rangle + |111\rangle) \\ & \beta(|000\rangle + |111\rangle) \otimes (|000\rangle + |111\rangle) \otimes (|000\rangle + |111\rangle), \end{aligned} \tag{8.33}$$

where constant factors that can be recovered from the normalization are ignored. Once the nine qubits are received, the goal of the algorithm is to recover the original superposition, assuming that no greater than one Pauli-type error has occurred within the quantum network. Shor's code invokes specific quantum entanglements with additional, or ancillary, qubits and measures the ancillary qubits to correct any error. The process of error correction must be accomplished while retaining the original quantum information superposition.

Shor's code is a combination of the three-qubit phase-flip and bit-flip codes. In this algorithm, the qubit is first encoded using the phase-flip code:

$$|0\rangle \to |{+}{+}{+}\rangle,\ |1\rangle \to |{-}{-}{-}\rangle. \tag{8.34}$$

The second step is to encode each of the qubits using the three-qubit phase-flip code. $|+\rangle$ is encoded as $(|000\rangle + |111\rangle)\sqrt{2}$, and $|-\rangle$ is encoded as $(|000\rangle - |111\rangle)\sqrt{2}$. This results in a nine-qubit code with codewords given by

$$\begin{aligned} |0\rangle \to |0_L\rangle &\equiv \frac{(|000\rangle + |111\rangle)(|000\rangle + |111\rangle)(|000\rangle + |111\rangle)}{2\sqrt{2}} \\ |1\rangle \to |1_L\rangle &\equiv \frac{(|000\rangle + |111\rangle)(|000\rangle + |111\rangle)(|000\rangle + |111\rangle)}{2\sqrt{2}}. \end{aligned} \tag{8.35}$$

Figure 8-15 illustrates the quantum circuit encoding the Shor algorithm. The first part of the circuit encodes the qubit using the three-qubit phase-flip code as described above. The second part of the circuit encodes each of these three qubits using the bit-flip code through use of three copies of the bit-flip encoding circuit. The result is that the Shor code can protect against phase-flip and qubit-flip errors on any qubit.

Figure 8-15: Shor's Nine-Qubit Quantum Error Correction Encoding Circuit

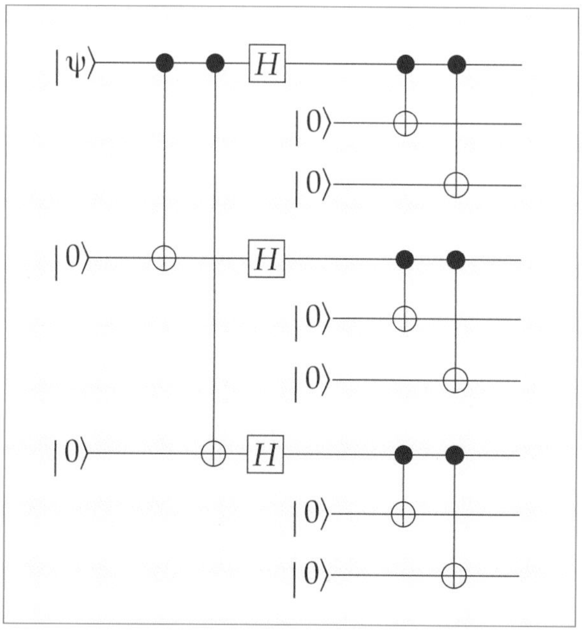

Quantum error-detection and error-correction can also be performed in the absence of measurement, using only unitary operations and ancilla systems prepared in standard quantum states. This technique is essentially the same as those used for modeling arbitrary quantum computing and networking operations. The major advantage of quantum error-detection and error-correction in the absence of measurement is that it becomes increasingly difficult for real-world quantum information systems to render a reliable procedure to perform quantum measurements. In essence, the solution is to introduce an ancilla system with basis states, $|i\rangle$, corresponding to possible error syndromes, where that system initializes in a standard pure state, $|0\rangle$, prior to error-correction. A unitary operator, $\boldsymbol{U}$, is then defined on the principal system plus ancilla and operates on the whole state space. The result is that $\boldsymbol{U}$ preserves inner products and can also be extended to a unitary operator on the entire (Hilbert) state space.

Discovery of the Cosmic Computer and Cosmic Switchboard through Derivation of the RAAM Gate

As we introduce in Chapter 1, Maharishi Mahesh Yogi has identified the Cosmic Computer and Cosmic Switchboard as integral to his Vedic Science and Technology as the cosmic computational foundation for perfection of evolution within the human physiology and for the universal automation of administration within our Cosmic Counterparts. The RAAM Gate provides the quantum network computational discovery basis from which we can model and compute the source, course, and goal of the Cosmic Computer and Cosmic Switchboard.

Cosmic Computer and Cosmic Switchboard Requirement Statements

When we apply computer network architectural disciplines to the architecture, design, and operation of the Cosmic Computer and Cosmic Switchboard, we can characterize the following requirement statements for the Cosmic Network of Consciousness:

- Massively parallel network computation, wherein any intention or action contemplated or executed at any point within the infinite spectrum of creation—ranging, at a minimum, from the cosmological extent of the observable universe to that of the Planck scale—is instantly known

- The computational basis for each succeeding step in the cosmic evolutionary process is contained within, and obtainable from, the results of the previous cosmic network computation
- Cosmic memory *(Smṛiti)*
- Instantaneous and refreshed quantum and superstring network computation of Cosmic Counterparts throughout the spectrum of creation
- Infinite and eternal fault-tolerance
- Perpetual availability
- Mean Time Between Failures (MTBF) is infinite
- Mean Time Between Outages (MTBO) is infinite
- Mean Time To Repair (MTTR) is zero
- Zero access and processing latencies within the entire cosmic spectrum of creation
- Absolute reliability
- Infinite security
- Hidden and eternally flawless operation
- Automation of administration throughout the cosmic spectrum of creation, ranging from the quantum to the cosmological scales

RAAM Gate Basis to Addressable Absolute Memory†

The general state of a two-qubit quantum memory register can be shown as

$$|\psi^{(1,2)}\rangle = \omega_{00}|00\rangle + \omega_{01}|01\rangle + \omega_{10}|10\rangle + \omega_{11}|11\rangle, \tag{8.36}$$

† RAAM Gate derivations, spatial and functional scales, clocking mechanisms, and methods to achieve quantum memory, memory associations, quantum computation, and quantum networking (as described in brief on pages 190–199, 227, 231, and 241–242) are a partial reflection of United States Patent Application Number US2004/0078421, "Methods for Transmitting Data Across Quantum Interfaces and Quantum Gates Using Same," Thomas J. Routt. Refer to Appendix D.

and the general state of a three-qubit quantum memory register can be shown as

$$|\psi^{(1)}\rangle \otimes |\psi^{(2)}\rangle \otimes |\psi^{(3)}\rangle, \tag{8.37}$$

where each $|\psi^{(i)}\rangle$ has the form,

$$|\psi^{(i)}\rangle = \omega_0^{(i)}|0\rangle + \omega_1^{(i)}|1\rangle. \tag{8.38}$$

Therefore, an n-qubit quantum memory register in the RAAM Gate can assume the form,

$$|\psi^{(1)}\rangle \otimes |\psi^{(2)}\rangle \otimes |\psi^{(3)}\rangle \otimes \ldots \otimes |\psi^{(n)}\rangle, \tag{8.39}$$

where the RAAM Gate can store an exponential number of inputs using only a polynomial number of qubits.

RAAM Gate Atomic Network Computing Quantum Scale

The currently observable universe has a scale of approximately 10^{27} meters ($\cong 10^{27}$ m; exponent-based scalar expressions that follow will not necessarily display the "$\cong$" symbol), the atomic scale is 10^{-10} m; and there are thought to be 10^{80} atoms in the observable universe. Quantum computing and networking begins at the nanoscale (10^{-9} m) and the atomic (10^{-10} m) scales. The scalar range from the spectrum of the observable universe (10^{27} m) to the atomic scale (10^{-10} m) is 10^{37}, suggesting an order of 10^{43} atoms (calculated as 10^{80} atoms/10^{37} cosmological-to-atomic scalar range = 10^{43} atoms) on average per magnitude of distance scale (interestingly, a magnitude density-based reciprocal of the Planck time scale of 10^{-43} second).

If all the atoms in the universe were to write a cosmic-scale binary number using one atom per bit, that number (converted to base 10) would be

$$2^{10^{80}} = 2^{10\times10^{79}} = 2^{(10)^{10^{79}}} \approx (10^3)^{10^{79}} = 10^{3\times10^{79}} \tag{8.40}$$

RAAM Gate Pico (Electronic and Photonic) Network Computing Quantum Scale

While quantum computing and networking is inexorably ushered in at the atomic scale (10^{-10} m), the picoscale (10^{-12} m) is completely intrinsic to quantum network computation due to the quantum properties of superposition and to quantum entanglement (the latter, where the spins of particles polarized together remain correlated, even if spatially separated). The Single Electron Transistor (SET, at a scale of 10^{-12} m), for example, enables an electron to tunnel across an insulator onto a conducting island if states are available to it on both sides. This creates a periodic modulation, called the *Coulomb blockade,* in the charging current due to the integer number of electrons allowed on the island. SET technology could also be applied to create a single-electron memory cell.

We can approximate the number of electrons and photons within the observable universe on the basis of the previous atomic scale calculations. There are approximately 10^{80} atoms in the observable universe, and the atomic scale is 10^{-10} m. The electronic and photonic scale is 10^{-12} m, an order of 10^2 smaller than the atomic scale. Therefore, the estimated number of electrons and photons within the observable universe is 10^{82}, calculated as follows: 10^{80} atoms within the observable universe × 10^2 magnitudes between the atomic and electronic and photonic scales = 10^{82}. The spectral range of the observable universe (10^{27} m) to the electronic and photonic scale (10^{-12} m) is 10^{39}, suggesting an order of 10^{43} electrons and photons on average per magnitude of distance scale (calculated as follows: 10^{82} electrons and photons/10^{39} cosmologic to electronic scalar range = 10^{43} electrons and photons). Again, interestingly, we see here a magnitude density-based reciprocal of the Planck time scale of 10^{-43} second.

RAAM Gate Superstring Network Computing Scale

An even more comprehensive cosmic accounting of the network computational spectrum of creation must necessarily incorporate the superstring dimensions found at the Planck and sub-Planck scales. Therefore, we need first to estimate the number of superstrings to exist within the known universe. We show in the preceding sections that the atomic scale is 10^{-10} m, and there are thought to be approximately 10^{80} atoms within the observable universe. The Planck scale is resolvable at 10^{-35} m, an order of 10^{25} smaller than the atomic scale. Therefore, the estimated number of superstrings within the observable universe is 10^{105}, and could be calculated as follows: 10^{80} atoms within the observable universe × 10^{25} magnitudes between the atomic and Planck scales = 10^{105} superstrings. The spectral range of the observable universe (10^{27} m) to the Planck scale (10^{-35} m) is 10^{62}, suggesting an order of 10^{105} superstrings divided by 10^{62} cosmologic-to-Planck scalar range, equaling 10^{43} superstrings on average per magnitude of distance scale (once again, interestingly, a magnitude density-based reciprocal of the Planck time scale of 10^{-43} second).

RAAM Gate Accommodations for Cosmological and Sub-Planck Extensions

In order to allow for possible continuing breakthroughs in both cosmological and superstring scale physics, we could extend, for discussion purposes, the spectrum of the universe to be on the cosmological order of 10^{32} m (an order of 10^{5} greater than the scale of the currently observable universe) and further extend the superstring sub-Planck scale to be on the order of 10^{-40} m (an order of 10^{5} smaller than the Planck scale of 10^{-33} cm or 10^{-35} m). On this basis, the calculated spectral range from extended cosmological to sub-Planck scales would be 10^{72}, or 10^{10} greater than the 10^{62} scalar range of the currently observable universe. This additional 10^{10} scale has not been integrated into the RAAM Gate computational and connection basis states calculations for the Cosmic Computer and Cosmic Switchboard that follow; however, they could be integrated in the future as needed.

Derivation of RAAM Gate Quantum and Superstring Connectivity and Cosmic Counterparts Correlation

A one-to-one Cosmic Counterpart correlation exists between the number of estimated stars within our galaxy and the estimated number of neurons in the human brain ($1–2 \times 10^{11}$ for each, galactically and neurally). There is an estimated baseline default of 10^{4} (quantum tunnelling- and quantum teleportation-based) connections per network node (star or neuron, respectively), yielding a baseline default of approximately 10^{15} (calculated as $10^{11} \times 10^{4} = 10^{15}$) interconnections per quantum computing node group for the quantum metacomputer.

While 10^{4} connections per stellar or neural node would appear substantial, at least at the scales of stars or neurons, the Cosmic Computer and Cosmic Switchboard scalability density would need to be substantially greater in order to support cosmic requirements for massively parallel, instantaneous, and refreshed network computation of the one-to-one interrelationships of Cosmic Counterparts throughout the spectrum of creation while maintaining perpetual availability of the Laws of Nature at every point in creation. Increasingly dense and scalable interconnections could be achieved at $n(f + 1)/2$, where, for any combination of node count, n, and fault tolerance, f, $(n - 1) > f > 0$. We now approach a K-cube-connected cycle where, to ensure a truly scalable network, we let the minimum node degree, $f + 1$, grow in proportion, p_{wc}, to the total number of nodes, n. We could also assume irregular, partial mesh, and/or multi-tier topologies.

It is evident, however, that in order to support their cosmic requirements, the Cosmic Computer and Cosmic Switchboard are inextricably interlinked within a multi-tier full-mesh fashion, where the full-mesh cosmic nodal (n) topology is defined as $n(n - 1)/2$ on each of at least three quantum network computational tiers of the universe—atomic, electronic/photonic, and superstring. Furthermore, because we assume meshed virtual associations among these three network computational tiers, the following RAAM Gate calculations presume connectivity at $[n(n - 1)/2] \rightarrow (n^2/2) \rightarrow n^2$.

Derivation of the RAAM Gate Cosmic Clock™ at **Atomic, Electronic, Photonic, and Superstring Scales**

The RAAM Gate, in its highest-order *Devatā* role expressing Shukl-Yajur-Veda Prātishākhya in the quantum network computation of the Cosmic Computer and Cosmic Switchboard, requires a Cosmic Clock™ to ensure eternally flawless operation in sub-Planck time. At the atomic (10^{-10} m) and electronic and photonic (10^{-12} m) quantum network computing scales, there is no way to quantum-mechanically distinguish between two atoms; therefore, clocks based upon atomic resonators keep the same time.

Terrestrial and celestial (i.e., Global Positioning System [GPS]) computer network clocks have switched from quartz to cesium (^{133}Cs) beams, with the latter generating a frequency of transition of $v = 9{,}192{,}631{,}770$ Hz ($\cong 9.19 \times 10^9$ Hz, or 9.19 Ghz) that has become the standard definition of a second. The ^{133}Cs stable isotope of Cesium has a nuclear spin of $I = 7/2$ and a single outer electron that in its ground state is in an s orbital with angular momentum of $L = 0$. Since the electron spin is $S = 1/2$, the total angular momentum $J = L + S$ can be $\pm 1/2$. When the electron is parallel to the nucleus, the angular momentum of both together is $F = I + J = 4$, and when they are anti-parallel, $F = 3$.

The switch in networks from quartz to a cesium beam reduced the relative time uncertainty to approximately 10^{-12}. Relative time uncertainties are further diminished to approximately 10^{-15} when lasers are used to perform state selection and to cool the atoms, enabling them to be dropped into a gravitational fountain.

While these triple-magnitude relative time uncertainty reductions are significant, they are nonetheless insufficient to provide the clock precision required at the scale of the Cosmic Network of Consciousness. This suggests a requirement for a Cosmic Clock to govern the eternal and cosmic-scale operation of the Cosmic Computer and Cosmic Switchboard.

The three-way, n^2-meshed virtual associations among the atomic, electronic/photonic, and superstring network computational tiers for the Cosmic Computer and Cosmic Switchboard account for the necessary spatial spectral resolutions within the RAAM Gate. They do not, however, account for the temporal granularities required at Planck (10^{-43} second) and sub-Planck time scales. Nevertheless, there exists an average magnitude density-based reciprocal of the Planck time scale of 10^{-43} second from the perspectives of each of the atomic, electronic, photonic, and superstring spatial scales (i.e., 10^{43} atoms, electrons, photons, and superstrings on average per magnitude of distance scale). This reciprocity indicates a massive and mutually-predictive interrelationship between space and time at each of these scales—this is not surprising, since the seeds of quantum mechanics were apparent in the invariance of the speed of light in Einstein's special relativity. The apparent passage of time was found to depend upon motion and gravity, at least as long as gravity itself defied quantum explanation.

Maharishi Mahesh Yogi has indicated that time is subtler than space, underscored in the central role of *Kalapurusha* in Maharishi Jyotish. These realizations from Maharishi's Vedic Science and Technology, taken together with the foregoing analysis, further suggest the need to derive a Cosmic Clock for the Cosmic Computer and Cosmic Switchboard. Therefore, the RAAM Gate in the quantum network computation of the Cosmic Network of Consciousness introduces an n^2-based temporal factor to the three-way, n^2-meshed virtual associations among the atomic, electronic/photonic, and superstring network computational tiers in the Cosmic Computer and Cosmic Switchboard. This Cosmic Clock integration within the RAAM Gate expresses its highest-order *Devatā* role within the context of Shukl-Yajur-Veda Prātishākhya.

RAAM Gate Computational and Connection Basis States for the Cosmic Computer and Cosmic Switchboard

We can now derive the RAAM Gate computational and connection basis states of the Cosmic Computer and Cosmic Switchboard to exist as a quantum computational network system of the form, $|\chi_1, \chi_2, \ldots, \chi_n\rangle$. Therefore, a quantum state of this system is specified by 2^n amplitudes (converted from 10^n amplitudes) as follows:

RAAM Gate Derivation of Cosmic Computer and Cosmic SWITHCBOARD Three-tier Quantum Computational Network Density (8.41)

= (n^2 atoms × n^2 electrons and photons × n^2 superstrings)^2 connections

= [Tier_1 Atoms ($10^{80} \times 10^{80}$) × Tier_2 Electrons and Photons ($10^{82} \times 10^{82}$) × Tier_3 Superstrings ($10^{105} \times 10^{105}$)]^2 connections

= 10^{534^2} connections

= 10^{1068} Cosmic Computer memory cells

= 2^{3548} Cosmic Switchboard switch cells

<u>Where:</u>

- Tier_1 = atomic full-mesh connections = (10^{80} atoms)^2
- Tier_2 = electronic and photonic full-mesh connections = (10^{82} electrons and photons)^2
- Tier_3 = superstring full-mesh connections = (10^{105} susperstrings)^2
- Cosmic Clock integration squares the three-tier space based quantum matrix

RAAM Gate quantum network computational density for the Cosmic Computer is therefore calculated to be on the order of 10^{1068} memory cells, and the Cosmic Switchboard is calculated to be on the order of 2^{3548} switch cells. These quantum computations and interconnections occur at every cosmic moment and point within the *Atyanta-Abhāva* and *Anyonya-Abhāva* of the *Sandhi* (the self-referral, massively parallel nexuses of infinity-within-all-points, all-points-within-infinity) throughout the universe. The radix-10-component Cosmic Computer memory cell density base corresponds to the 10 *Maṇdals* of Ṛk Veda, which in turn constitute the dynamics of *Anyonya-Abhāva* in the silent nature or *Atyanta-Abhāva* (refer to Figure 2-7 on page 30, "Self-Referral, Self-Looping, Invincible Nature of Ṛk Veda").

We associate each of the 10 *Maṇḍals* of Ṛk Veda with a successive calculation radix from which to fully apprehend and incorporate the cosmic computational and network scale of Natural Law. That is, the 10 *Maṇḍals* of Ṛk Veda generate a radix-10 exponentiation basis to the infinity-within-all-points and all-points-within-infinity eternal calculations of the Cosmic Computer and Cosmic Switchboard.

The 1068-power exponent calculated above as the RAAM Gate quantum network computational amplitude basis corresponds to the approximately 1000 *Sūktas*, (including the 97th *Sūkta—Avyakta Sūkta*—within the first and 10th *Maṇḍals*) of the 10 *Maṇḍals* of Ṛk Veda.

We have now identified the Cosmic Computer and Cosmic Switchboard as the Computational Constitution of the Universe, as discovered through the RAAM Gate. The RAAM Gate 2^{3548}-qubit switch address relationships (Cosmic Switchboard) and 10^{1068} memory cells (Cosmic Computer) are elaborated in Figure 8-16 (on pages 198 and 199).

Maharishi's Space-Time-Goal Continuum—Context for the RAAM Gate

Maharishi Mahesh Yogi has brought to light that Veda is total Natural Law. Veda is unmanifest in the transcendental field of pure intelligence—the Unified Field of Natural Law—and is manifest in the sounds of Veda and the Vedic Literature. In the discovery of Veda and the Vedic Literature within Quantum Network Architecture, it is shown that Veda and the Vedic Literature are the blueprint of creation—the blueprint that expresses itself completely within both classical and quantum Computer Network Architecture.

The interrelationships among Veda, the Vedic Literature, and the multifarious expressions of their manifestations can be compared to the interrelationships between quantum computation and networking (Quantum Network Architecture, the basis of quantum physics-based network computing), and classical computation and networking (classical computer network architecture, the basis of classical physics-based network computing). Each presents a particular point of view—a distinct instrumentation through which to observe, compute, and interconnect Natural Law in a massively parallel fashion.

Figure 8-16: RAAM Gate™ Calculation Density of the Cosmic Computer and Cosmic Switchboard

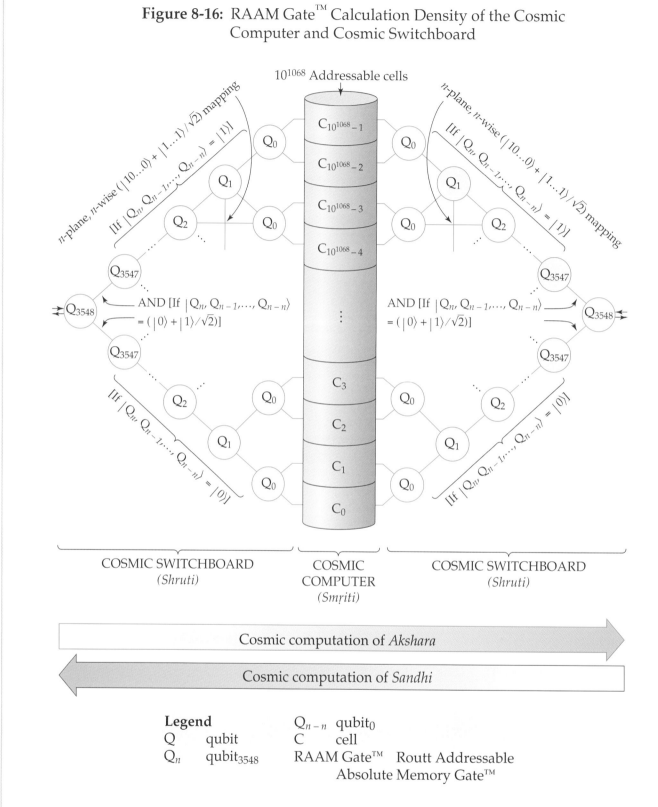

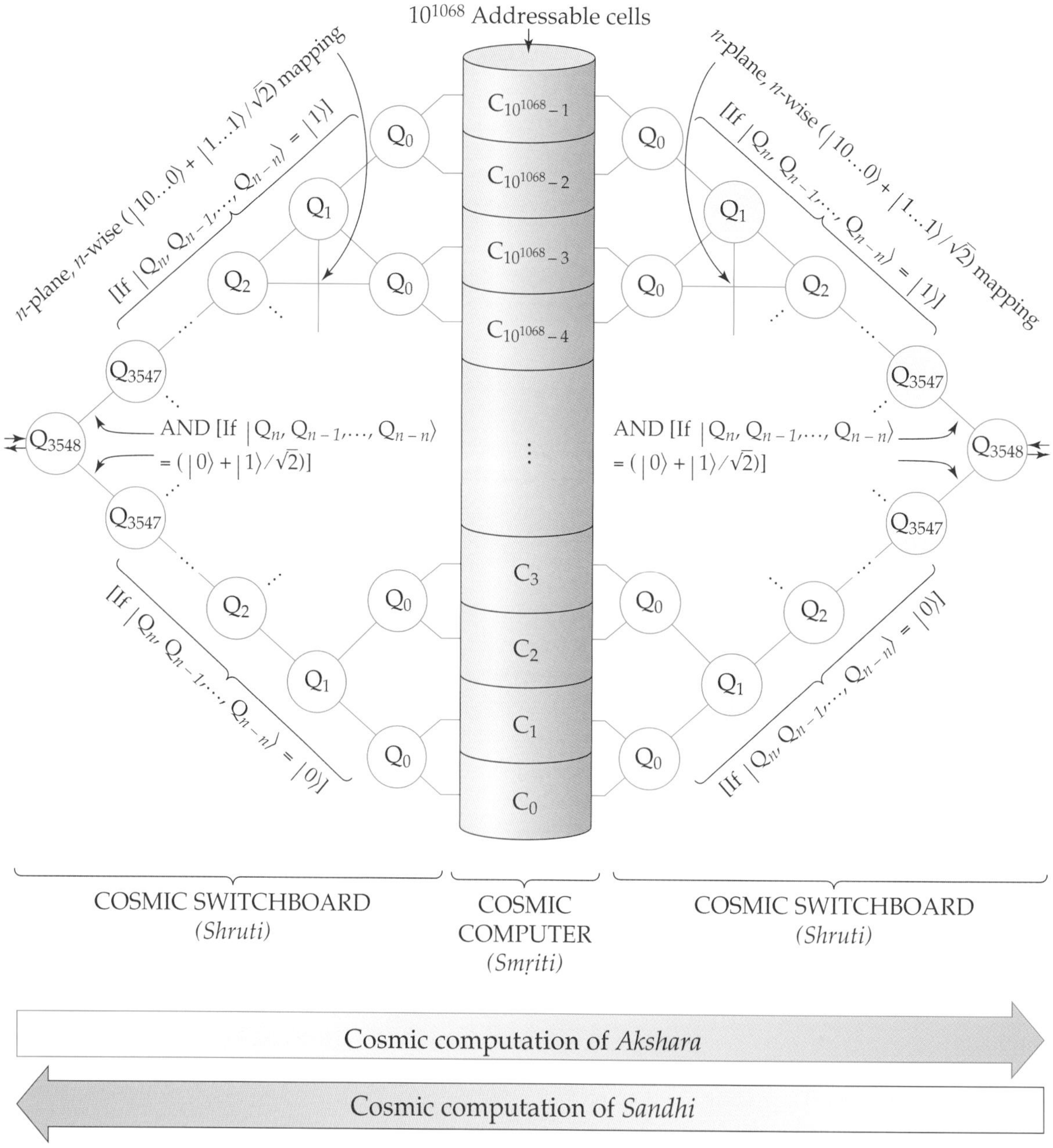

Legend

Q	qubit	Q_{n-n}	qubit_0
Q_n	qubit_{3548}	C	cell
		RAAM Gate™	Routt Addressable Absolute Memory Gate™

Reference: T.J. Routt, "Methods for Transmitting Data Across Quantum Interfaces and Quantum Gates Using Same," United States Patent Application Number US2004/0078421. Refer to Appendix D.

Figure 8-16 (continued): RAAM Gate™ Calculation Density of the Cosmic Computer and Cosmic Switchboard

- The Routt Addressable Absolute Memory Gate™ (RAAM Gate™) quantum computational network system is an n-quantum bit (n-qubit) quantum computational gate that is extensible to $[(n^2$ atoms $\times n^2$ electrons and photons $\times n^2$ superstrings$)^2 = [(10^{80} \times 10^{80}) \times (10^{82} \times 10^{82}) \times (10^{105} \times 10^{105})]^2 = (10^{534})^2 = 10^{1068}$ Cosmic Computer memory cells $= 2^{3548}$ switching cells].
- The 10^{1068} memory cells of the Cosmic Computer are addressable through a 3548-qubit quantum (2^{3548}-qubit) switching address structure.
- The RAAM Gate operates in a 2^n–10^n dimensional complex Hilbert space.
- The 10 *Maṇdals* of Ṛk Veda generate a radix-10 exponentiation basis to the infinity-within-all-points and all-points-within-infinity eternal calculations of the Cosmic Computer.
- The 1068-exponent RAAM Gate quantum network computational amplitude basis corresponds to the approximately 1000 *Sūktas* (including the 97th *Sūkta—Avyakta Sūkta*—within the first and 10th *Maṇdals*) of the 10 *Maṇdals* of Ṛk Veda.
- Each Natural Law-based network computation is based on two passes through the RAAM Gate. The forward pass through the RAAM Gate calculates the massively parallel *Mantra* or *Akshara* value throughout the cosmos.
- The reverse pass through the RAAM Gate calculates the massively parallel *Sandhi, Brāhmaṇa,* or Gap that contains the Natural Law-based silent computation (Cosmic Computer) and connection (Cosmic Switchboard) for the next *Mantra* or *Akshara* at all points in creation. All computations and connections maintain sequentiality and simultaneity on a Cosmic scale. A dual pass through the RAAM Gate, therefore, encounters and enlivens 2×10^{1068} addressable cells.
- Each circle within Figure 8-16 represents a switch in the Cosmic Switchboard, addressable by the qubit inscribed within.
- If a given qubit $|Q_n\rangle = |0\rangle$, the corresponding switch within the Cosmic Switchboard routes the input qubit toward a lower numbered cell within the Cosmic Computer. If $|Q_n\rangle = |1\rangle$, it is routed toward a higher numbered cell within the Cosmic Computer.
- If a given qubit $|Q_n\rangle = (|0\rangle + |1\rangle)/\sqrt{2}$, then an equal superposition of both routes is taken within the Cosmic Switchboard.
- Dual-qubit superpositionalities are logically associated in pairwise fashion "vertically" within any given n-plane ($Q_n \rightarrow Q_{n-n}$) of the Cosmic Switchboard as Einstein, Podolsky, Rosen (EPR) pairs ($|00\rangle + |11\rangle$ / $\sqrt{2}$). Multiple (n)-qubit superpositionalities are logically associated in n-wise fashion "vertically" throughout any given n-plane, and/or in full or partial combination and permutation, of n-planes of the Cosmic Switchboard as ($|0\ldots0\rangle + |1\ldots1\rangle$ / $\sqrt{2}$), providing the unitary and universal basis for massively parallel, massively distributed, superdense quantum database computing.
- Input qubits are routed to the Cosmic Computer database defined within the RAAM Gate by the Cosmic Switchboard at the sub-Planck time scale, where their states are changed or not, according to the contents of memory. The qubits are then routed into a definite position containing the retrieved information (the *Mantra*, or *Akshara*).
- Qubits are then routed back via the Cosmic Switchboard defined within the RAAM Gate through the Cosmic Computer database at the sub-Planck time scale, into a precise (non-superposed) position, containing retrieved information (the memory-basis of the *Sandhi*, the Gap, from which the succeeding *Akshara* is projected).
- The RAAM Gate enables any unitary operation to be approximated to arbitrary accuracy by a quantum circuit (including quantum teleportation circuit) and is therefore a universal quantum network computational gate; that is, it is universally unitary, measurable, and logically reversible.
- The RAAM Gate employs massive quantum parallelism intrinsic to processing quantum algorithms, enabling, for example, simultaneous evaluation of a function, $f(x)$, for n different values of x.
- Each calculation step within the Cosmic Switchboard contains complete knowledge of all previous steps and its computational relationship to the Cosmic Computer.

Figure 8-17 (beginning on page 204) unfolds the Cosmic range of existence introduced above—from the cosmological scale of the observable universe (10^{27} m), to the Planck- and sub-Planck scale realm of the Unified Field of Natural Law ($\leq 10^{-33}$ cm, $\leq 10^{-35}$ m). Quantum physics describes everything in terms of waves or fields and has identified four fundamental force fields (refer to the "Force Fields" portion of Figure 1-1 on pages 4–6, "Unified Field Chart for Quantum Network Architecture"):

1 Electromagnetism

2 Weak interaction

3 Strong interaction

4 Gravitation

Modern scientific discoveries and theories have demonstrated that these four fields are unified at the most fundamental level of Nature's functioning. All fields are based on the Unified Field of Natural Law.

It is the Unified Field that takes on different levels of expression and appears as electronic computing and networking, optical computing and networking, and quantum computing and networking (refer again to Figure 1-1) or as any other material expression or phenomenon. From this perspective, we can see that everything is wave-like—a "vibrational" expression of the Unified Field. This includes every particle, every atom, every molecule, every object, and every structure or aspect of the universe.

Indeed, every thought, every action, the movements of every planet, every star, and every galaxy or cluster of galaxies are only vibrational expressions of the Unified Field. When we move our hand, we are creating a ripple—a wave or vibration—in the universe. We also create waves, ripples, and vibrations every time we think a thought or undertake any activity. Some vibrations are subtle, such as a thought or a faint sound; some are more expressed, such as a loud noise or the movement of a solid object. Matter is the most expressed aspect of vibration or wave.

The senses not only perceive a narrow band of the vibrational spectrum of the universe (i.e., human eyes detect wavelength on the order of 400 nm $\leq \lambda \leq$ 700 nm within the infinite range of λ in the universe; human ears detect sound frequencies of approximately 20 Hz to 20,000 Hz), but also perceive objects as being confined to a narrow band of space that they occupy for a specific period of time. From a classical computational and network perspective, objects are separated by space and time. This partial and fragmented view of the universe leads inexorably to segregation of objects and events.

Einstein's theories of special and general relativity introduced the notions of the space-time continuum and the curvature of space-time—particles and all objects and events exist, move, are transformed, and behave within the space-time continuum. The fundamental pillars of these relativity principles are the conservation and symmetry laws. These laws state that there are continuous symmetries of space-time translations and rotation—that is, all points in space, in time, and in all directions are equivalent as far as physical laws are concerned. This indicates that every point in creation is equivalent as far as Natural Law is concerned.

The advent of the Lagrangian formulation of physics has established that the existence of conservation laws is related to the existence of underlying symmetries. For example, the conservation of linear momentum is a direct consequence of invariance of the Lagrangian under space translation, or homogeneity, of space. Similarly, conservation of energy follows from invariance under time translation. The conservation of angular momentum is a result of rotational invariance. And yet, there is a dynamic "shape" to the universe that is defined by space-time curvature, which results from the spacio-temporal relationship of its constituent matter (i.e., it is also an energy continuum where matter and energy are equivalent).

From a Unified Field perspective, let us imagine what would happen if our eyes were able to see gravitational fields, rather than the narrow band of wave energy in the electromagnetic field that we call visible light. The universe would appear quite different from the way it appears to our eyes now. The Earth would no longer be apparently limited in its dimension by the physical surface on which we live. We would see the Earth extend far beyond its apparent dimensions and fade gradually into infinity; we would also see that the Sun and the planets physically touch us, even though extremely lightly.

This simplified example indicates how the perception of fullness or void can be a phenomenon that depends on the perceptual or computational instrumentation being used. The statement that between the Earth and Sun space is essentially empty is true only in a relative sense. Since the force of gravity is operating, there must be a field-energy exchange of particles (gravitons). Space is not, therefore, empty even from that relative perspective. It is nevertheless true that as we move away from the Sun, its gravitational force diminishes until it becomes practically zero.

In intergalactic space, therefore, there is greater silence than within inter-planetary space. These values of greater and smaller silence—greater and smaller dynamism—define structure within the observable universe. The reality, however, is that at every point of the universe there exists both infinite silence and infinite dynamism (see Figure 2-1 on page 19, "Ṛk Veda—Infinity to a Point"). Manifestation in the relative sense incorporates points of greater silence (less manifest) and other points of greater dynamism (more manifest). This is what gives structure to the structureless Absolute.

If we were able to cognize the entire set of all fluctuations and fields, including their sequence (the time element among them), we would be gazing at the space-time continuum of the universe. If we were able to see, superimposed on the space-time continuum, the logic—the purpose, the force that guides every particle and all collections or particles in the perfectly sequential scheme of evolution—we would be directly cognizing and beholding the structure of pure consciousness, Veda and the Vedic Literature.

Maharishi has foreseen a new continuum, which at once integrates a new dimension to space-time and is yet beyond the limitations of space and time. This new curvature has been referred to as the "space-time-goal continuum" and describes the principle that every particle in the universe does not just develop in space and time but also in goal. Each particle's history includes the extent to which it has achieved its goal in the whole scheme of the ever-expanding universe. Achieving the goal means that time and space vanish—the particle dissolves back into the Unified Field.

The sequential unfoldment of the Vedic Literature and all its *Akshara* (syllables), *Sandhi* (Gaps), *Shabdas* (words), *Ṛichās* (verses), *Pādas* (phrases), *Sūktas* (hymns), and *Maṇḍals* (self-referral, circular, cyclical, and eternal structures that comment upon the mechanics of transformation inherent within their constituent *Sandhi;* see Figure 2-2 on pages 22–23, "Maharishi's Commentary on Ṛk Veda Saṁhitā—*Apaurusheya Bhāshya*") occurs in perfect order and in conformity with the space-time-goal continuum. Every *Akshara* emerges and submerges; every *Shabda* manifests and then unmanifests after fulfilling its goal. If the goal is not achieved, then repetition and re-emergence take place. Rebirth takes place. This process continues until wholeness of purpose is achieved and the goal is attained. The driving force that provides impetus for motion toward the goal vanishes spontaneously.

This driving force, when experienced in the human mind, is called desire. It is interesting to mention here as a side note—and as is beautifully brought to light by Maharishi in his Science of Creative Intelligence—that it is not by suppressing the desire that one gains unity with the absolute Unified Field of life—enlightenment—but rather, by fulfilling the goal of evolution through the ability to achieve all purposes and all goals and to fulfil one's desires. This is made practically possible through Maharishi's Vedic Science and Technology.

This same evolutionary impulse, when experienced and played out as quantum algorithms and circuits within the quantum computational and network RAAM Gate, is expressed in terms of *n*-qubit superpositionality, addressability, unitarity, measurability, and network computational reversibility at the Hardware-Software Gap™ omnipresent within the Cosmic Computer and Cosmic Switchboard, locatable as infinity-within-all-points and all points-within-infinity in *Ātmā* and *Brahm*.

Mathematics of Invincibility

Mathematical exploration of the Hardware-Software Gap reveals a dynamic quality of Veda, embedded in eternal silence, Vedic Mathematics, the mathematics of the Absolute Number, as described by Maharishi. The expression of the Absolute Number is ⑩, the expression that presents one zeroed—Unity zeroed—Unity made manifest—State of Unity devoid of expression (*Purusha*). Vedic Mathematics is Quantum Mathematics—the mathematics of the quantum field, expressed in the syllables of speech rather than in numerical symbols. Modern Mathematics is the field of steps, whereas Vedic Mathematics is the field of pure intelligence, the field of infinite correlation, the field of simultaneity of all steps, because it functions in the field of self-referral intelligence.

Figure 8-17: RAAM Gate™ Calculation Basis to the Cosmic Computer and the Cosmic Switchboard

<table>
<tr><th>Name
Scale
Form</th><th>Description
Calculation Density</th></tr>
<tr><td>Observable Universe
10^{27} meters
</td><td>Description
The universe and everything that is in it—Anoraniyan Mahato-mahiyan—(the Self is) finer than the finest, bigger than the biggest—is contained within the Unified Field of Natural Law.

As Maharishi Mahesh Yogi has revealed in his commentary on Ṛk Veda Saṁhitā—Apaurusheya Bhāshya (see Figure 2-2 on page 22–23), the Sandhi (Gaps) are the Saṁhitā, the self-referral basis of infinity in a point, the Veda and Vedic Literature. The cognition of this value of the Gap is the cognition of the total potential of Veda—total knowledge of Natural Law lively in its full potential.

Our calculations indicate that the Central Sun and self-referral center (Brahmasthan) of the observable universe lies in the direction of Kṛittikā Nakshatra and is the most luminous, energetic, and lively Sandhi locatable.

We extrapolate a lively, massively parallel, and non-localized quantum teleportation, channel-based entanglement among the Central Sun (Brahmasthan, Sandhi) of the observable universe, the Central Sun of our galaxy (Sagittarius A, located in Mūla Nakshatra; see "Radius of the Milky Way Galaxy," below in this figure), the Sun of our solar system (see "Sun" below in this figure), and the Brahmasthan of the human brain. This quantum entanglement constitutes the inner and outer Cosmic Counterparts of the Sandhi of the Cosmic Computer and Cosmic Switchboard, which are eternally engaged in the massively parallel calculations and interconnections required to create and maintain all the Laws of Nature from point to infinity.

There are approximately 10^{11} galaxies in the observable universe.

Calculation Density
The currently observable universe has a scale of approximately 10^{27} meters ($\cong 10^{27}$ m; exponent-based scalar expressions that follow will not necessarily incorporate the "≅" symbol), the atomic scale is 10^{-10} m, and there are thought to be 10^{80} atoms in the observable universe.</td></tr>
</table>

Figure 8-17 (continued): RAAM Gate™ Calculation Basis to the Cosmic Computer and the Cosmic Switchboard

Name **Scale** **Form**	**Description** **Calculation Density**
Observable Universe (continued)	The electronic and photonic scale is 10^{-12} m, an order of 10^2 smaller than the atomic scale. Therefore, the estimated number of electrons and photons within the observable universe is 10^{82} (calculated as follows: 10^{80} atoms within the observable universe × 10^2 magnitudes between the atomic and electronic and photonic scales = 10^{82} electrons and photons). Planck scale—the superstring domain—is resolvable at 10^{-35} m, an order of 10^{25} smaller than the atomic scale. Therefore, the estimated number of superstrings within the observable universe is 10^{105} (calculated as follows: 10^{80} atoms × 10^{25} magnitudes = 10^{105} superstrings). The Cosmic Computer and Cosmic Switchboard are inextricably interlinked within a multi-tier full-mesh fashion, where the full-mesh cosmic nodal *(n)* topology is defined as $n(n-1)/2$ on each of at least three quantum network computational tiers of the universe—atomic, electronic, photonic, and superstring. Routt Addressable Absolute Memory Gate™ (RAAM Gate™) calculations presume $[n(n-1)/2] \rightarrow (n^2/2) \rightarrow n^2$. The RAAM Gate requires a Cosmic Clock™ to ensure eternally flawless operation in sub-Planck time and introduces an n^2 temporal factor to the three-way, n^2-meshed virtual associations among the atomic, electronic/photonic, and superstring network computational tiers in the Cosmic Computer and Cosmic Switchboard. The resulting computational and connection basis states of the Cosmic Computer and Cosmic Switchboard exist as a quantum computational network system of the form $\lvert \chi_1, \chi_2, \ldots, \chi_n \rangle$. Therefore, a quantum state of this system is specified by 2^n amplitudes (converted from 10^n amplitudes): **RAAM Gate Derivation of Cosmic Computer and Cosmic Switchboard Three-Tier Quantum Computational Network Density** = (n^2 atoms × n^2 electrons and photons × n^2 superstrings)^2 connections = $[(10^{80} \times 10^{80}) \times (10^{82} \times 10^{82}) \times (10^{105} \times 10^{105})]^2$ connections = 10^{534^2} connections

Figure 8-17 (continued): RAAM Gate™ Calculation Basis to the Cosmic Computer and the Cosmic Switchboard

Name **Scale** **Form**	**Description** **Calculation Density**
Observable Universe (continued)	= 10^{1068} Cosmic Computer memory cells = 2^{3548} Cosmic Switchboard switch cells Where: • $Tier_1$ = atomic full-mesh connections = (10^{80} atoms)^2 • $Tier_2$ = electronic and photonic full-mesh connections = (10^{82} electrons and photons)^2 • $Tier_3$ = superstring full-mesh connections = (10^{105} susperstrings)^2 • Cosmic Clock integration squares the three-tier space-based quantum matrix The RAAM Gate radix-10 basis to the infinity-within-all-points and all-points-within-infinity eternal calculations of the Cosmic Computer and Cosmic Switchboard express the 10 *Maṇdals* of Ṛk Veda, and the 1068-power exponent quantum network computational amplitude basis corresponds to the approximately 1000 *Sūktas* (including the 97th *Sūkta—Avyakta Sūkta*—within the first and 10th *Maṇdals*) of the 10 *Maṇdals* of Ṛk Veda. The RAAM Gate quantum network computational scale proceeds at every cosmic moment and point within the *Atyanta-Abhāva* and *Anyonya-Abhāva* of the *Sandhi* centered within the intimately connected *Brahmasthans* of the human brain, the Sun of our solar system, the central Sun of our galaxy, and the central Sun of the observable universe. Light requires approximately 10^{10} years to traverse the observable universe.
Cluster of Galaxies 10^{26} meters 	Clusters of galaxies are orderly groups of galaxies. Our "local group" of galaxies consists of two large and several minor galaxies and is part of the virgo supercluster, containing several tens of thousands of galaxies.

Figure 8-17 (continued): RAAM Gate™ Calculation Basis to the Cosmic Computer and the Cosmic Switchboard

Name **Scale** **Form**	**Description** **Calculation Density**
Galaxy 10^{21} meters 	Galaxies are orderly groups of stars and solar systems. There are between 10^6 to 10^{13} stars within a galaxy. Light takes approximately 10^5 years to traverse a galaxy.
Radius of the Milky Way Galaxy 10^{20} meters 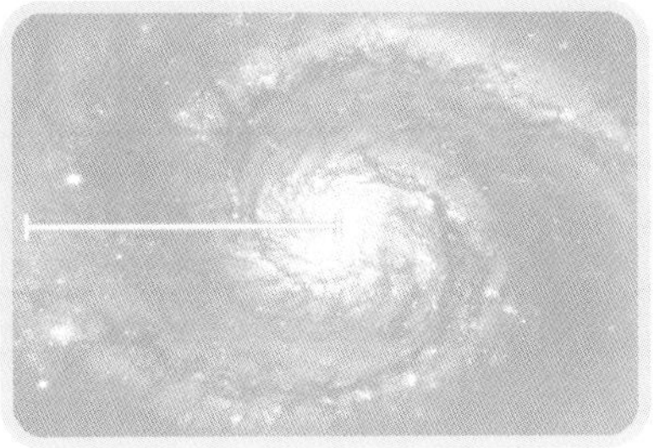	**Description** Based upon radio and infrared telescope observations and calculations, Sagittarius A is the self-referral center *(Brahmasthan, Sandhi)* of the Milky Way Galaxy—located within *Mūla Nakshatra*—and is the most luminous and energetic object in the galaxy. Three hundred forty stars have been detected within 1.3 light-years of Sagittarius A, all of which orbit the Galactic Central Sun at very high velocities. **Calculation Density** The Milky Way Galaxy contains 100–200 × 10^9 (or 1–2 × 10^{11}) stars, and the human brain contains 100–200 × 10^9 neurons, a clear indication of galactic Cosmic Counterparts to the human neural network. Both the human brain and its galactic Cosmic Counterparts can be considered as a nonlinear, massively parallel, recursive, self-referral quantum metacomputer, each with 1–2 × 10^{11} switched computing nodes and a baseline default of 10^4 connections per node (per neuron or star, respectively), yielding a baseline default of 10^{15} interconnections for each.
Solar System 10^{13} meters 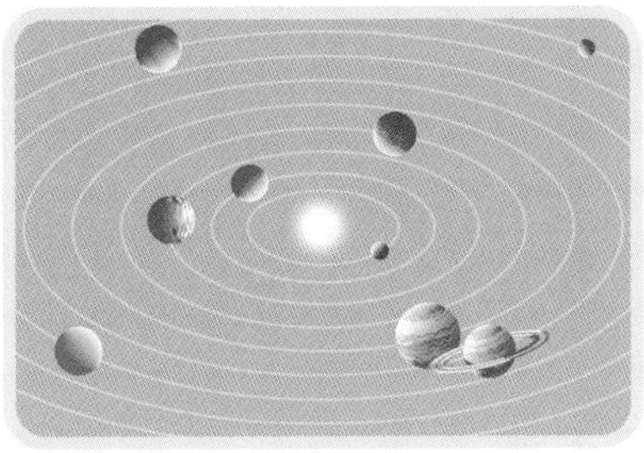	A solar system is an orderly group of one or more stars and several planets. Light takes approximately 5 hours to traverse our solar system.

Figure 8-17 (continued): RAAM Gate™ Calculation Basis to the Cosmic Computer and the Cosmic Switchboard

Name **Scale** **Form**	**Description** **Calculation Density**
Distance from the Earth to the Sun 10^{11} meters 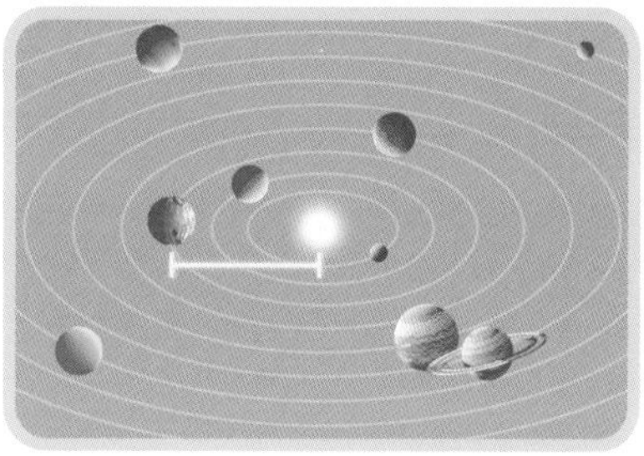	One Astronomical Unit (AU).
Sun 10^{9} meters 	The sun, Sūrya, is the self-referral center *(Brahmasthan, Sandhi)* and source of evolution of this solar system.
Global Internetwork/World Wide Web/Earth 10^{8} meters 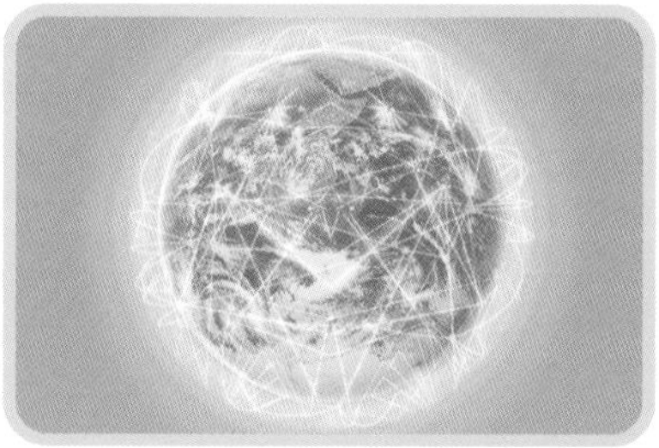	**Description** The Global Internet is the physical, logical, and ubiquitous confluence of the Internet, World Wide Web, intranets, extranets, and private computer networks, acting as a global, celestial nervous system, or self-referral superfabric that collects, interprets, processes, interconnects, and integrates enterprise and personal data throughout the world. **Calculation Density** Estimated Internet core backbone traffic density during 2005 is 10^{17-18} bytes.
Multinational Backbone Network 10^{7} meters 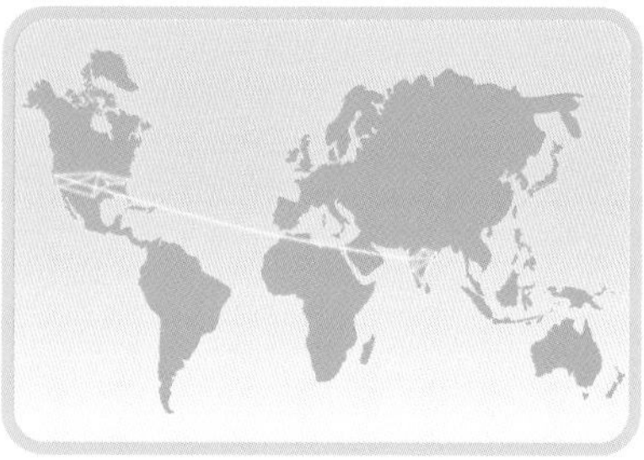	**Description** Multinational backbone networks are single or logical groups of Wide Area Networks (WANs) that enable global Internet ingress/egress. **Calculation Density** 4×10^{7} m is the altitude of a Geosynchronous Orbit (GEO) satellite above the Earth's equatorial plane.

Figure 8-17 (continued): RAAM Gate™ Calculation Basis to the Cosmic Computer and the Cosmic Switchboard

Name **Scale** **Form**	**Description** **Calculation Density**
National Backbone Network 10^6 meters 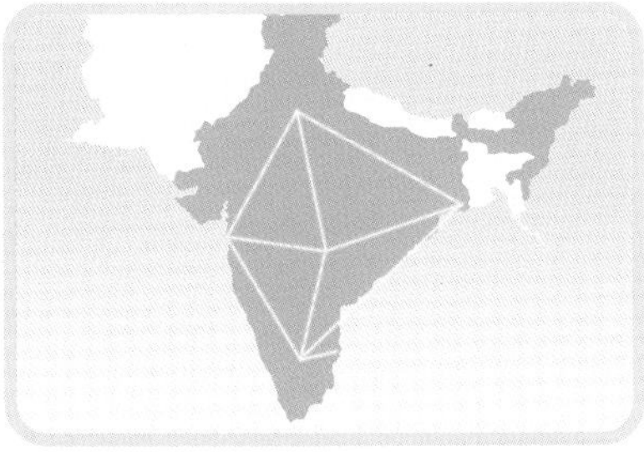	National backbone networks provide global Internetwork ingress/egress at the national level.
Regional Internet Service Provider (ISP) 10^5 meters 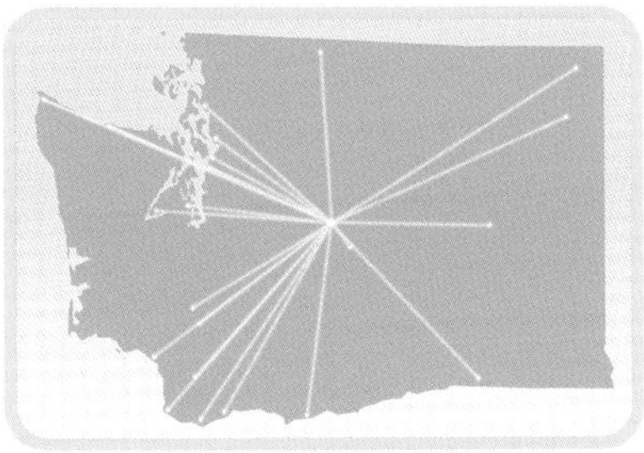	**Description** Regional ISPs enable global Internet ingress/egress at a country regional level. **Calculation Density** The average altitude of a Low Earth Orbit (LEO) satellite above the Earth is 4×10^5 m.
Metropolitan Area Network (MAN) 10^4 meters 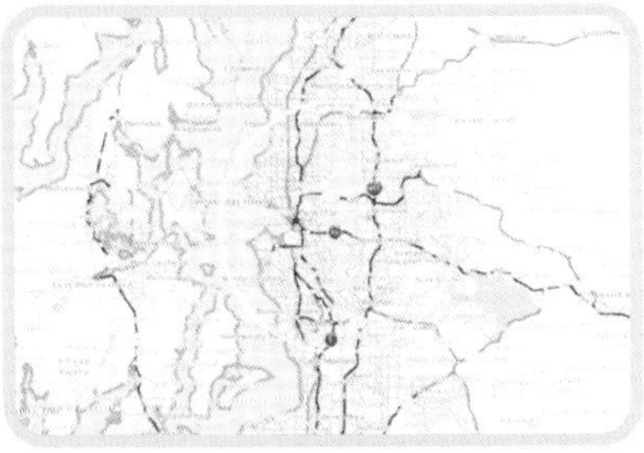	MANs provide private and/or global Internet access on a metropolitan scale.
Local Area Network (LAN) 10^3 meters 	LANs enable private and/or Global Internetwork ingress/egress on a campus scale.

Figure 8-17 (continued): RAAM Gate™ Calculation Basis to the Cosmic Computer and the Cosmic Switchboard

Name **Scale** **Form**	**Description** **Calculation Density**
Internet Data Center, Data Center 10^2 meters 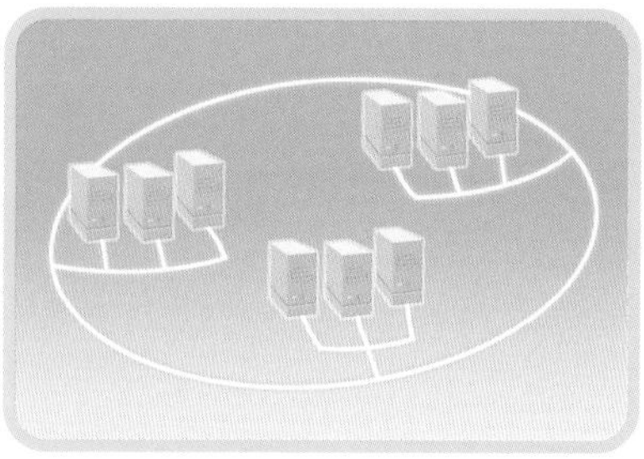	Data centers and Internet data centers are the physical infrastructure basis to enterprise- and carrier-class network computing.
SAN/NAS Server Farm 10^1 meters 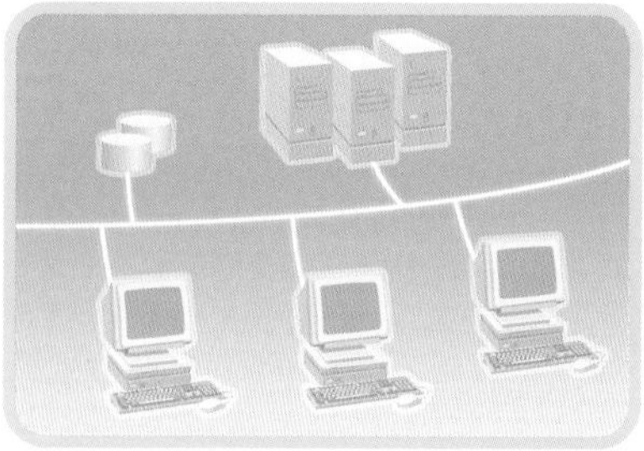	Storage Area Network (SAN)/Network-Attached Storage (NAS) server farms can each cache, mirror, Redundant Array of Independent Disks (RAID), stripe, and map greater than 10^{15} bytes (multi-petabytes) of data.
Server (Web, E-mail, Database, E-commerce, M-commerce, Security, NMS, and SAN/NAS) 10^0 meter 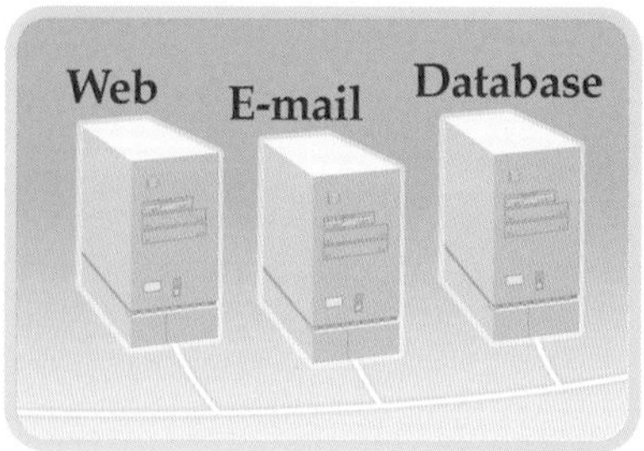 	**Description** Web, e-mail, database, e-commerce, mobile commerce (m-commerce), security, Network Management System (NMS), and SAN/NAS servers measure on the scale of one meter or a fraction thereof and provide the intelligent building blocks for network computing on a global scale. **Calculation Density** One meter is the path length traveled by light in a vacuum during a time interval of 1/299,792,458 of a second, where the speed of light, c, is 2.99792458×10^8 meters per second (m/s).

Figure 8-17 (continued): RAAM Gate™ Calculation Basis to the Cosmic Computer and the Cosmic Switchboard

Name **Scale** **Form**	**Description** **Calculation Density**
Visible Light-Based Transistor 10^{-6} meter 	Micron (μ) wavelength (λ) technologies are capable of frequencies of $10^{14} \leq Hz \leq 10^{15}$.
EUV Light-Based Transistor 10^{-7} meter 	Extreme Ultraviolet (EUV) is based on electromagnetic radiation whose λ, 10^{-7} m, is shorter than visible light and is capable of frequencies of $10^{15} \leq Hz \leq 10^{16}$. This is part of the basis of one-tenth micron (.1 $\mu = 10^{-7}$ m, sub-micron) technologies likely to yield a one billion transistor chip by 2010, which will be able to execute 100 billion instructions per second, or 100,000 Million Instructions Per Second (MIPS).
Nanotechnologies, Moletronics, Molecular Computing 10^{-9} meter 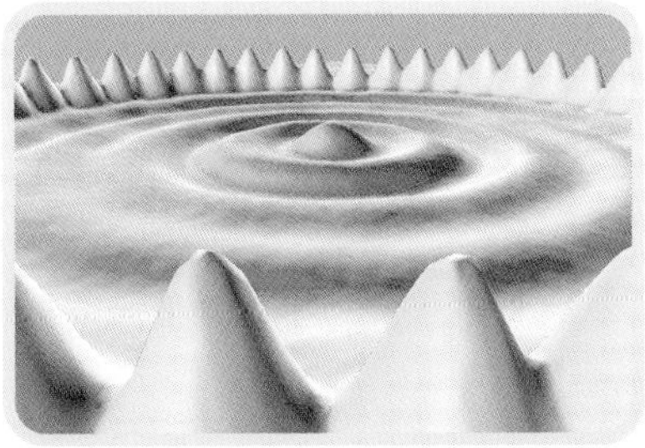	Molecular scale computing technologies (i.e., nanotubes, buckytubes) are theoretically capable of generating greater than 10^{16} Floating Point Operations Per Second (> 10 PetaFLOPS). Molecules are orderly collections of atoms. Light takes 3.3×10^{-18} second to traverse the molecular scale.

Figure 8-17 (continued): RAAM Gate™ Calculation Basis to the Cosmic Computer and the Cosmic Switchboard

Name **Scale** **Form**	**Description** **Calculation Density**
Single-Atom Bits and Introduction to Quantum Computing Scale 10^{-10} meter (Angstrom, Å) 	**Description** Atoms are orderly collections of elementary particles. **Calculation Density** The current estimated number of atoms in the universe is 10^{80}. Light takes 3.3×10^{-19} second to traverse the atomic scale.
Picotechnologies™ (10^{-12} m scale) Spintronics, Quantum Computing, and Networking Based upon Electron Spin Rather Than Charge **Femtotechnologies™ (10^{-15} m scale, the characteristic length of the Strong Force)** 10^{-12} meter to 10^{-15} meter 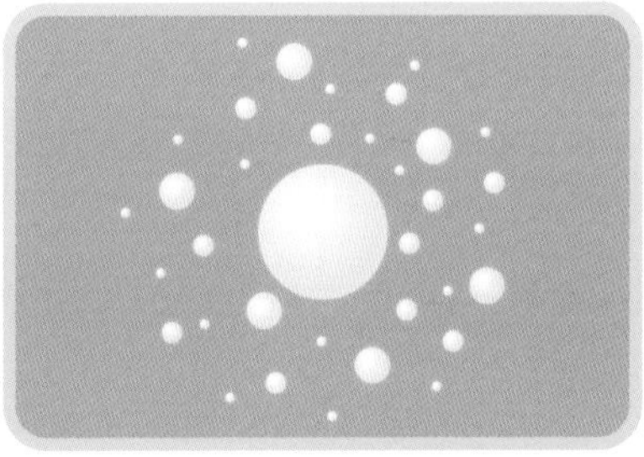	**Description** Picotechnologies and Femtotechnologies are intrinsic to quantum computing and quantum networking due to the quantum properties of superposition and quantum entanglement (the latter, where the spins of particles polarized together remain correlated even if spatially separated). The Single-Electron Transistor (SET, at a scale of 10^{-12} m) enables an electron to tunnel across an insulator onto a conducting island only if states are available to it on both sides, creating a periodic modulation called the Coulomb blockade in the charging current due to the integer number of electrons allowed on the island. This technology can also be applied to create a memory cell that stores a single electron. **Calculation Density** During the period 2010–2020 most computer and network subcomponent parameters will simultaneously reach physical limits encountered within classical space-time symmetry bounds. Non-quantum wires cannot be thinner than a single atom; classical (non-quantum) memories cannot have fewer than one electron, and, to retain economic viability, chip fabrication plants must cost less than the gross planetary product. All of this leads inevitably to the requirement for quantum computing and networking.

Figure 8-17 (continued): RAAM Gate™ Calculation Basis to the Cosmic Computer and the Cosmic Switchboard

Name **Scale** **Form**	**Description** **Calculation Density**
Elementary Particle Basis to Electronic Computing and Networking (Fermi-matter fields) **Attotechnologies™ (10^{-18} m scale, the characteristic length of the Weak Force)** **Zeptotechnologies™ (10^{-21} m scale)** **Yoctotechnologies™ (10^{-24} m scale)** 10^{-18} to 10^{-31} meter 	Elementary particles are resonant excitations of the fields; they are the smallest packets (quanta of energy) of the Unified Field. There are 24 fermionic elementary particles plus the bosonic elementary particles mediating the four forces. Light takes 3.3×10^{-27} to 10^{-40} second to traverse the elementary particle scale.
Force Field Basis to Optical Computing and Networking (Bose-force fields) **Attotechnologies™ (10^{-18} m scale)** **Zeptotechnologies™ (10^{-21} m scale)** **Yoctotechnologies™ (10^{-24} m scale)** 10^{-18} to 10^{-31} meters 	Quantum electrodynamics (QED) identifies photons as the "smallest bundles of light" and reveals their interactions with electrically charged particles such as electrons in a mathematically complete framework, providing a predictive basis for developments in optical computing and optical networking (laser injection, optical transmission, optical switching/routing, and optical network ingress). Force and matter fields are the initial relative expression of the Unified Field. There are four force fields and 24 matter fields.

Figure 8-17 (continued): RAAM Gate™ Calculation Basis to the Cosmic Computer and the Cosmic Switchboard

Name **Scale** **Form**	**Description** **Calculation Density**
Unified Field of All the Laws of Nature 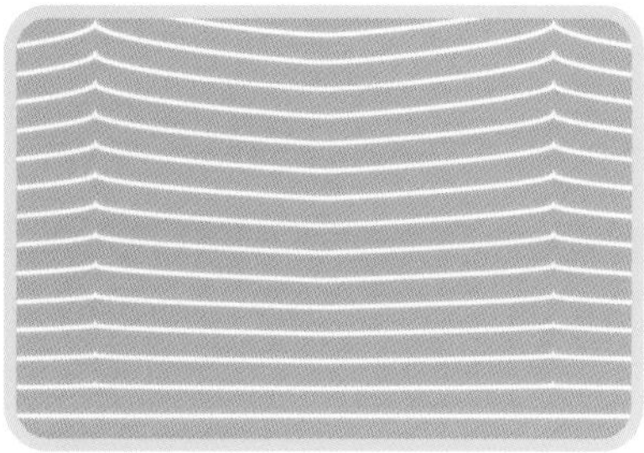	**Description** Supersymmetry fundamentally unifies particles of adjacent spin types (i.e., spin-0 fields with spin-1/2 fields, spin-1/2 fields with spin-1 fields), therein interlinking bosons (the basis of optical computing and networking) and fermions (the basis of electronic computing and networking) into a specialized form of Unified Field called a Superfield. Therefore, simple supersymmetry, $N = 1$ supersymmetry (refer to the Unified Field of physics lower portion of Figure 1-1 on pages 6 and 7), provides a degree of unification that is, in principle, capable of unifying force fields (spin-1 bosons) with matter fields (spin-1/2 fermions). There is one unbounded field. **Calculation Density** ***Planck scale:*** • Planck length = 10^{-33} cm = 10^{-35} m. • Planck time = 10^{-43} second, the time required for light to travel the Planck length. • Planck mass ≅ 10^{18} times the mass of a proton, which is equivalent to the mass of a vibrating supersymmetric string in string theory. • Planck tension ≅ 10^{39} tons, which is equivalent to the tension on a typical supersymmetric string in string theory. • Planck energy ≅ 10^{3} kilowatt hours, which is the energy necessary to probe the Planck length distance scale and the typical energy of a vibrating supersymmetric string in string theory. ***Sub-Planck scale:*** • Sub-Planck length is < 10^{-33} cm (< 10^{-33} m). • The Sub-Planck scale is the ultimate computational and networking basis of the *Sandhi (Atyanta-Abhāva* and *Anyonya-Abhāva)* of the Cosmic Computer and Cosmic Switchboard.

ATHARVA VEDA PRĀTISHĀKHYA—*Unfolding*—Quantum Network

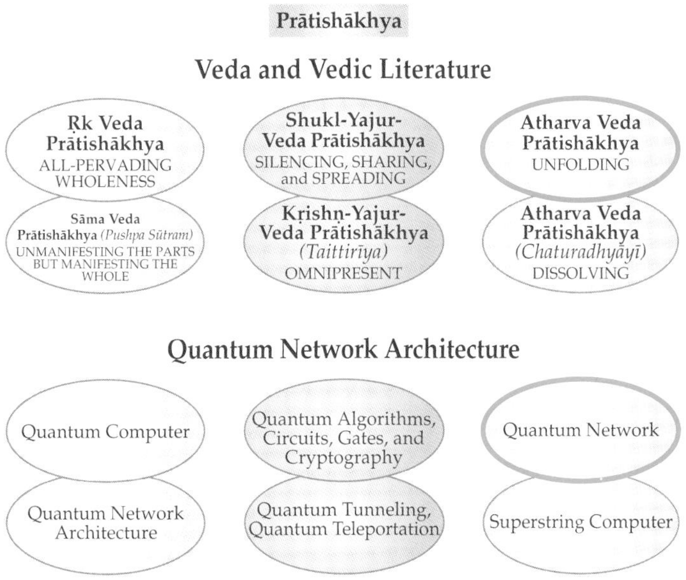

Atharva Veda Prātishākhya represents the *Unfolding* quality of consciousness. Atharva Veda represents Wholeness with reference to *Chhandas* value. It corresponds in Quantum Network Architecture to *Nodal Input/Output Systems.*

The highest-order level of this *Unfolding* quality of Quantum Network Architecture resides in Atharva Veda Prātishākhya as *Quantum Network*. It is also available within the *Atyanta-Abhāva* and *Anyonya-Abhāva* of the Cosmic Computer and Cosmic Switchboard and in every computational and network component of the Global Internetwork.

We discuss earlier in this chapter that there are two essential bases to quantum computer and network systems:

- *Fermions*, which have 1/2-integer spin and cannot be in the same state due to the Pauli exclusion principle, and
- *Bosons*, which have integer spin and can share the same state.

As stated earlier, electrons are fermions. Electronic computing and networking is ultimately fermion-based (refer to Figure 1-1 on pages 4–6, "Unified Field Chart for

Quantum Network Architecture"), where N_8 must be either 0 or 1 because there cannot be more than one fermion in a single state. This is shown by the *Fermi-Dirac distribution:*

$$\langle N_S \rangle = \frac{\sum_{N_S=0}^{1} N_S e^{-\beta E_S N_S + \beta\mu N_S}}{\sum_{N_S=0}^{1} e^{-\beta E_S N_S + \beta\mu N_S}} = \frac{0 + e^{-\beta E_S + \beta\mu}}{1 + e^{-\beta E_S + \beta\mu}} = \frac{1}{e^{\beta(E_S - \mu)} + 1}. \tag{8.42}$$

N = number of particles
S = macroscopic quantum state
μ = Fermion chemical potential

⇐ Where +1 is the quantum difference which arises due to particle indistinguishableness

As we introduced earlier, fermions—named after the Italian physicist Enrico Fermi—are particles whose spin is half of a whole (odd) number, and tend to give cancelling quantum-mechanical contributions. Photons are bosons (particles whose spin is a whole number) and are named after the Indian physicist Satyendra Bose. Optical computing and networking is ultimately boson-based (refer again to Figure 1-1) where, for bosons, the sum over N_8 runs from 0 to infinity, as shown in the *Bose-Einstein distribution* (Equation 8.43 on page 217).

Note that the final result to the Bose-Einstein distribution differs from that of the Fermi-Dirac distribution (Equation 8.42, above) by the presence of minus and plus signs, respectively, in the non-exponent portion of the denominator. When the quantum jitters of a boson are positive, those of a fermion tend to be negative, and vice versa. Since supersymmetry ensures that bosons and fermions occur in pairs, substantial cancellations occur from the outset—cancellations that ultimately calm the apparently frenzied quantum effects.

The quantum network is based on the general interface between quantum computation and quantum communications and is the foundation of distributed quantum computation (refer to Figure 3-10 on page 58, "Holistic Functioning of the Cosmic Computer and Cosmic Switchboard—First Three *Ṛichās* of Ṛk Veda—Quantum Computer Network Case"). Distributed quantum computation is also based in part upon quantum tunneling and quantum teleportation, as we discuss in the upcoming section entitled "Krishn-Yajur-Veda Prātishākhya *(Taittirīya)*—Quantum Tunneling, Quantum Teleportation," beginning on page 219.

$$\langle N_S \rangle = \frac{\sum_{N_S=0}^{\infty} N_S e^{-\beta E_S N_S + \beta\mu N_S}}{\sum_{N_S=0}^{\infty} e^{-\beta E_S N_S + \beta\mu N_S}}$$

N = number of particles

S = macroscopic quantum state

μ = Boson chemical potential

$$= \frac{\sum_{N_S=0}^{\infty} N_S C^{N_S}}{\sum_{N_S=0}^{\infty} C^{N_S}} \quad (C \equiv e^{-\beta E_S + \beta\mu})$$

$$= \frac{C\frac{d}{dC}\sum_{N_S=0}^{\infty} C^{N_S}}{\sum_{N_S=0}^{\infty} C^{N_S}} \qquad (8.43)$$

$$= \frac{C\frac{d}{dC}(1-C)^{-1}}{(1-C)^{-1}}$$

$$= \frac{C(1-C)^{-2}}{(1-C)^{-1}}$$

$$= \frac{1}{C^{-1}-1}$$

$$= \frac{1}{e^{\beta(E_S+\mu)}-1}.$$

⇐ Where −1 is the quantum difference which arises due to particle indistinguishableness

ATHARVA VEDA PRĀTISHĀKHYA *(Chaturadhyāyī)—Dissolving* Superstring Computer

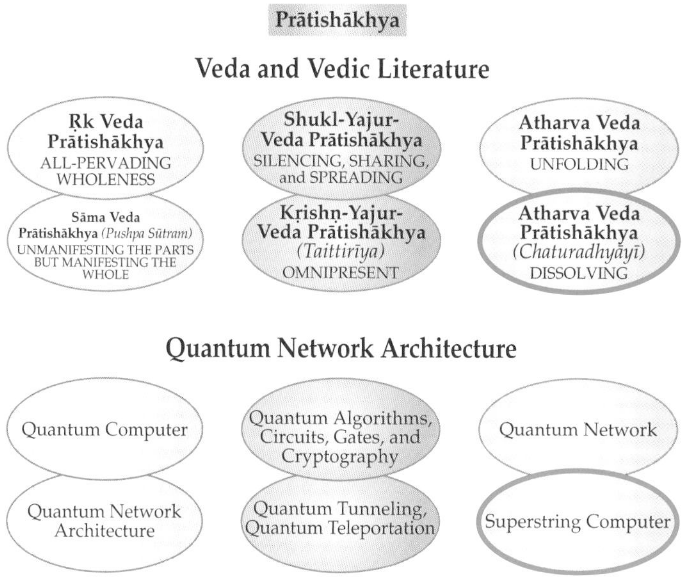

Atharva Veda Prātishākhya *(Chaturadhyāyī)* represents the *Dissolving* value of consciousness. Atharva Veda represents Wholeness with reference to *Chhandas* value. It corresponds in Quantum Network Architecture to *Nodal Input/Output Systems.*

This *Dissolving* quality of intelligence, available in the Vedic Literature in Atharva Veda Prātishākhya *(Chaturadhyāyī)* is found to be available in Quantum Network Architecture as *Superstring Computer*. It is also available within the *Atyanta-Abhāva* and *Anyonya-Abhāva* of the Cosmic Computer and Cosmic Switchboard and in every computational and network component of the Global Internetwork.

In the section of this chapter entitled "Shukl-Yajur-Veda Prātishākhya—Quantum Algorithms, Circuits, Gates, and Cryptography," we calculated the number of superstrings within the observable universe to be approximately 10^{105}.

The RAAM Gate is presented in this chapter as both a quantum and superstring network computational superfabric.

KRISHṆ-YAJUR-VEDA PRĀTISHĀKHYA *(Taittirīya)—Omnipresent—* Quantum Tunneling, Quantum Teleportation

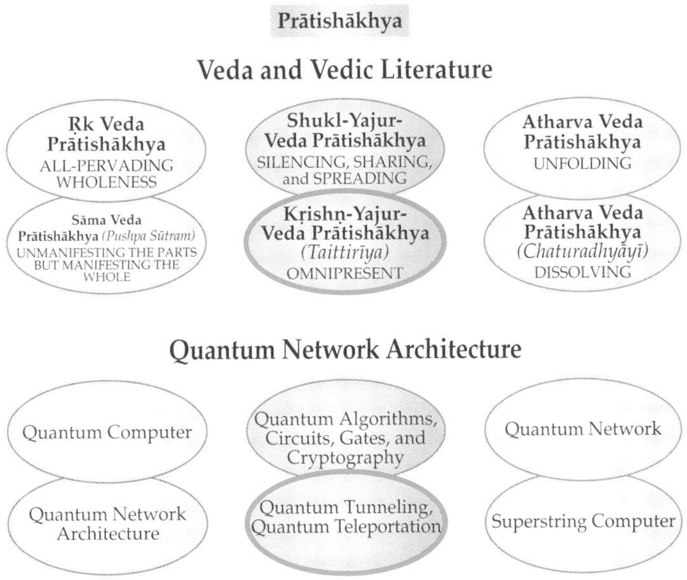

Krishṇ-Yajur-Veda Prātishākhya *(Taittirīya)* represents the *Omnipresent* value of consciousness. Yajur-Veda represents Wholeness with reference to *Devatā* value. Krishṇ-Yajur-Veda Prātishākhya *(Taittirīya)* represents the *Omnipresent* quality of intelligence and is available in Quantum Network Architecture as *Quantum Tunneling, Quantum Teleportation*. It is also available within the *Atyanta-Abhāva* and *Anyonya-Abhāva* of the Cosmic Computer and Cosmic Switchboard and in every computational and network component of the Global Internetwork.

Quantum Tunneling

Quantum tunneling is the characteristic of a particle wave in quantum mechanics of tunneling through classically unsurpassable barriers. This is possible because a particle wave can possess a probabilistic location. Figure 8-18 (on page 220) represents a quantum tunneling transistor (an on-off switch) that exploits an electron's ability to pass through normally impenetrable energy barriers. The transistor's contacts and gates adjust the voltage between the upper quantum well (top QW in the figure) and lower quantum well (bottom QW in the figure). Each well in this example is made of gallium

Figure 8-18: Quantum Tunneling Transistor

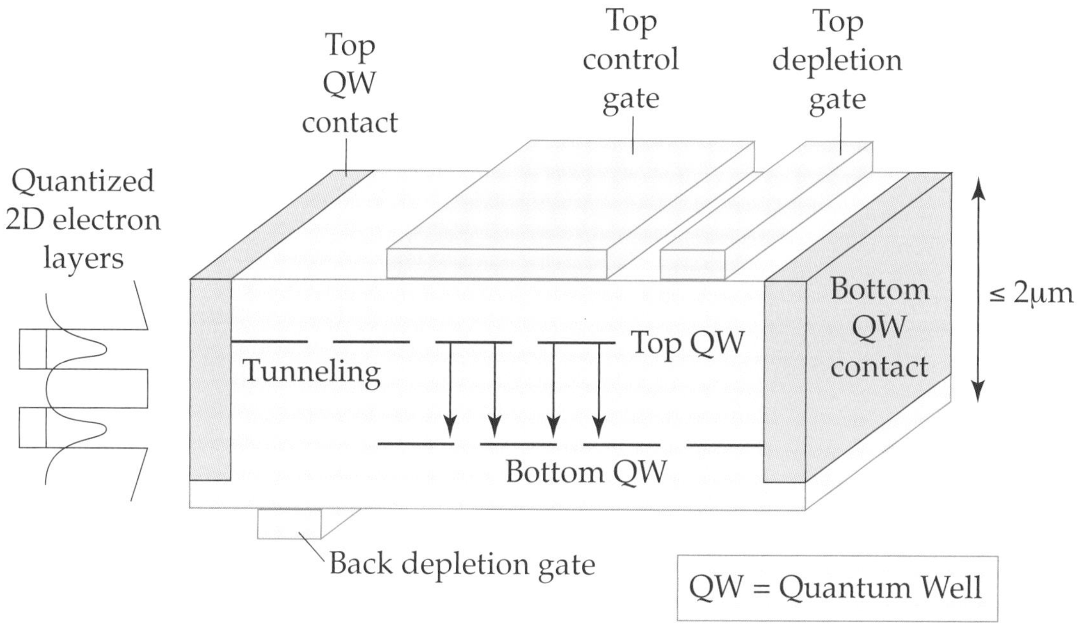

arsenide with thicknesses of 150 Angstroms (150×10^{-10} meters). Adjustments in voltage enable the electrons in the top QW to "tunnel through" an ordinarily insurmountable barrier made of aluminum gallium arsenide (shown as a sawtoothed energy barrier on the left side of the figure). Quantum tunneling occurs when the top QW and bottom QW accept electrons with the same energy and momentum states.

Quantum Teleportation

Quantum teleportation is a technique for moving quantum states between a sender and a receiver, even without a quantum communications channel linking the sender of the quantum state to the receiver. As we introduce in the section of this chapter entitled "Ṛk Veda Prātishākhya—Quantum Computer," a significant two-qubit state is the Bell state, or EPR pair, summarized as

$$|00\rangle + |11\rangle = \sqrt{2}. \tag{8.44}$$

This very important two-qubit state is the key component in quantum teleportation and superdense coding and is integral to the EPR effect (named after its discoverers Albert

Einstein, Boris Podolsky, and Nathan Rosen in 1935). The EPR effect describes an enduring interconnection (entanglement) maintained between pairs of quantum systems that have interacted in the past.

Quantum entangled states result from interactions between particles, such as when a pair of particles is created simultaneously and where certain particle attributes (such as spin or polarization) need to be conserved. Due to superpositionality, the exact state of each particle is not known until a measurement is made. Yet, due to quantum entanglement, their states are correlated. Therefore, whenever a measurement is made on one member of an entangled pair, the states of both particles become definite and usually opposite; at that moment the entanglement ceases. If, for example, the state of particle 1 of an entangled pair is

$$|\psi_1\rangle = \frac{1}{\sqrt{2}}(|0\rangle_1 + |1\rangle_1), \tag{8.45}$$

and the state of particle 2 of an entangled pair is

$$|\psi_2\rangle = \frac{1}{\sqrt{2}}(|0\rangle_2 + |1\rangle_2) \ , \tag{8.46}$$

then the joint state of the entangled pair will often be

$$|\psi_{12}\rangle = \frac{1}{\sqrt{2}}(|0\rangle_1 \otimes |1\rangle_2 - |1\rangle_1 \otimes |0\rangle_2). \tag{8.47}$$

Figure 8-19 (on page 222) provides an overview of a quantum teleportation circuit, initialized with Hadamard and CNOT gates to create an EPR pair from Bob's and Alice's qubits. In this example, Bob travels to the Sun and Alice remains on Earth. Alice wishes to transmit a new qubit to Bob but cannot measure or communicate its state classically because that would force the qubit into a measurement basis.

As the figure indicates, Alice chooses instead to use a second CNOT gate to entangle the qubit with her half of the EPR pair, which is instantly entangled with Bob's qubit. Alice accomplishes this in the reverse order of the original EPR circuit by following a CNOT with a Hadamard transform. She next performs a measurement to determine the state of her two qubits. Due to entanglement, the coefficients of Alice's qubit instantly teleport to

Figure 8-19: Quantum Teleportation Circuit

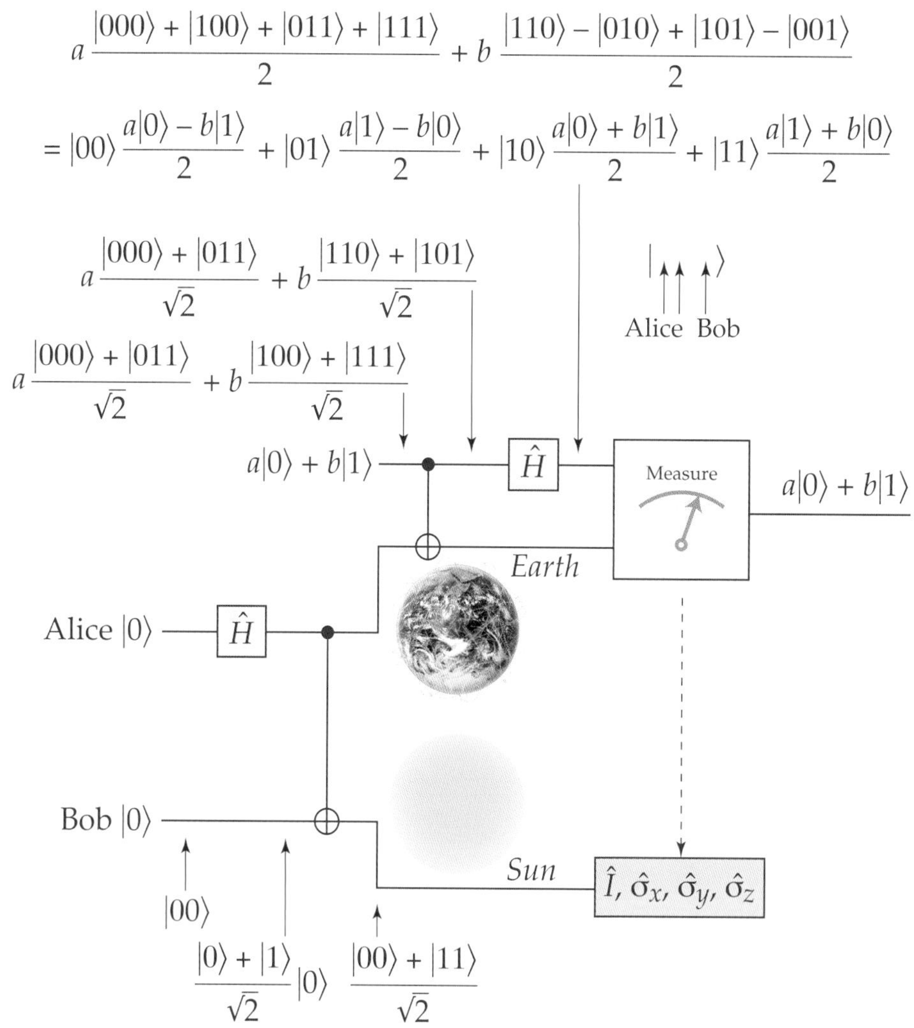

Bob's qubit. Alice can then utilize a classical or quantum communication channel to communicate to Bob which of four (in this example) possible outcomes she has obtained. Bob uses that information to swap the terms in his qubit or change its sign as shown in Equation 8.48:

$$
\begin{aligned}
|00\rangle &\rightarrow \hat{\sigma}_z = \begin{bmatrix} 1 & 0 \\ 0 & -1 \end{bmatrix} \\
|01\rangle &\rightarrow i\hat{\sigma}_y = \begin{bmatrix} 0 & 1 \\ -1 & 0 \end{bmatrix} \\
|10\rangle &\rightarrow \hat{I}_z = \begin{bmatrix} 1 & 0 \\ 0 & 1 \end{bmatrix} \\
|11\rangle &\rightarrow \hat{\sigma}_x = \begin{bmatrix} 0 & 1 \\ 1 & 0 \end{bmatrix}.
\end{aligned}
\tag{8.48}
$$

Upon completion of the terms swap or sign change in his qubit, Bob has Alice's coefficients. At that moment, Bob actually has Alice's qubit, as hers was consumed during measurement. All of Alice's quantum information is teleported to Bob instantly, regardless of distance.

Maharishi has stated that the phenomenon of quantum teleportation explains the inherent ability of *Yagya* (Vedic performances integral to Maharishi Jyotish that neutralize upcoming and foreseen difficulties) to produce the desired outcome instantaneously and at a distance.

> हेयं दुःखमनागतम् ।
>
> *Heyaṁ dhykham anāgatam.*
>
> *(Yog-Sūtra, 2.16)*
>
> *Avert the danger that has not yet come.*
>
> This means possess the supreme power of prevention. This level of invincibility is a level of life that is beyond reproach; it is the transcendental level of Being; it is the level of pure singularity—the eternal field of life devoid of duality; it is the field of the total potential of Natural Law, परमे व्योमन् *Parame vyoman*, the field of the Transcendent, यस्मिंन् देवा अधि विश्वे निषेदुः । *Yasmin Devā adhi vishwe nisheduḥ*, which is the home of all the administrators of the universe—that level of self-referral consciousness from where all the Laws of Nature administer the universe.

Performance from this level is the performance of the total potential of Natural Law—

यतीनां ब्रह्मा भवति सारथिः ।

Yatīnāṁ Brahmā bhavati sārathiḥ.

(Ṛk Veda, 1.158.6)

For those established in Self-referral consciousness, the infinite organizing power of the Creator becomes the charioteer of all action.

SĀMA VEDA PRĀTISHĀKHYA(*Pushpa Sūtram*)—*Unmanifesting the Parts But Manifesting the Whole* —Quantum Network Architecture

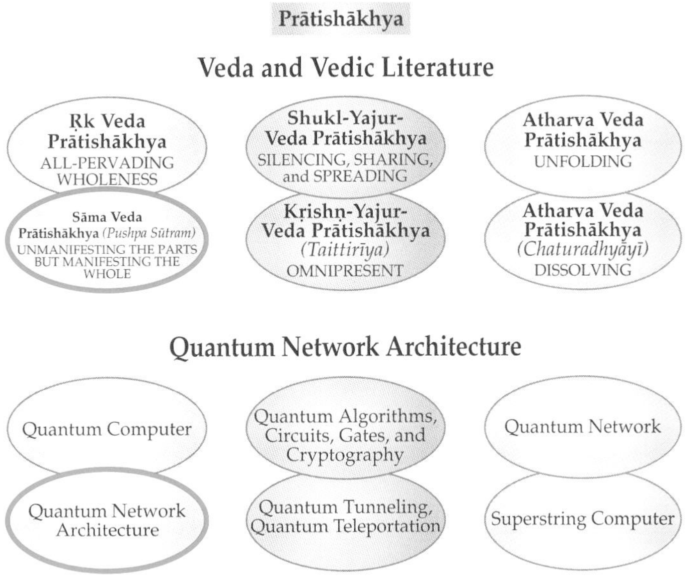

Sāma Veda Prātishākhya *(Pushpa Sūtram)* corresponds to the unmanifesting and manifesting values of consciousness—*Unmanifesting the Parts but Manifesting the Whole.* This quality of intelligence represents Wholeness with reference to the *Ṛishi* value and is available in Quantum Network Architecture as *Quantum Network Architecture* available within the *Atyanta-Abhāva* and *Anyonya-Abhāva* of the Cosmic Computer and Cosmic Switchboard. It is also available in every computational and network component of the Global Internetwork.

To completely express Quantum Network Architecture, we first note in Figure 8-20 (on page 226) that modern physics holds that all known Laws of Nature function through the Principle of Least Action.

In the seven formulae presented in Figure 8-20 by quantum physicist Dr. John Hagelin, Superstring Theory—the Theory of the Unified Field—is symbolized by the Lagrangian of the Superstring, $\mathcal{L}(x)^{\text{superstring}}$, which represents the most compact mathematical expression of the detailed structure of the Unified Field—its symmetries, components, and self-interaction (refer to Figure 1-1 on pages 4–6, "Unified Field Chart for Quantum

Network Architecture"). At more superficial levels of Quantum Field Theory, this Lagrangian sequentially gives rise to the Lagrangians at the Grand Unification level, the level of Electroweak Unification, and the level of the four forces, establishing that the Principle of Least Action is upheld throughout increasingly expressed levels of Nature.

Figure 8-21 (on page 227) depicts the RAAM Gate (from Figure 8-16 on pages 198 and 199) as a quantum network computational superfabric through its view of the Cosmic Computer and Cosmic Switchboard, where each of its three-in-one components, from the perspective of *Ṛishi*, is the *Saṁhitā* of *Ṛishi*, *Devatā*, and *Chhandas*.

Figure 8-20: Principle of Least Action from Classical Mechanics to Superstring Theory

Classical Mechanics of a Particle:

$$\int_1^2 dt[1/2mv^2 - V(x[t])] = \text{minimum}$$

Relativistic Motion:

$$\int_1^2 dt[-m_0c^2\sqrt{1-v^2/c^2} - q(\Phi - v \bullet A)] = \text{minimum}$$

General Relativity:

$$-(c^3/16\pi G)\int d^4x\sqrt{-g}\,R = \text{minimum}$$

Relativistic Quantum Mechanics:

$$\int d^4x\bar{\psi}(\gamma^\mu iD_\mu - m)\psi = \text{minimum}$$

Electromagnetic Field:

$$\int d^4x[1/4F_{\mu v}F^{\mu v} - F^{\mu v}(\partial_\mu A_v - \partial_v A_\mu)] = \text{minimum}$$

Quantum Field Theory (spin-0 field):

$$\int d^4x\{\partial_\mu\Phi\partial^\mu\Phi^* - \mu^2\Phi\Phi^* - \lambda(\Phi\Phi^*)^2\} = \text{minimum}$$

Superstring Theory—the Theory of the Unified Field:

$$\int d^nx\,\mathcal{L}(x)^{\text{superstring}} = \text{minimum}$$

Figure 8-21: Three-In-One Structure and Function of the Cosmic Computer and Cosmic Switchboard As Seen Through the RAAM Gate™ (Routt Addressable Absolute Memory Gate™)

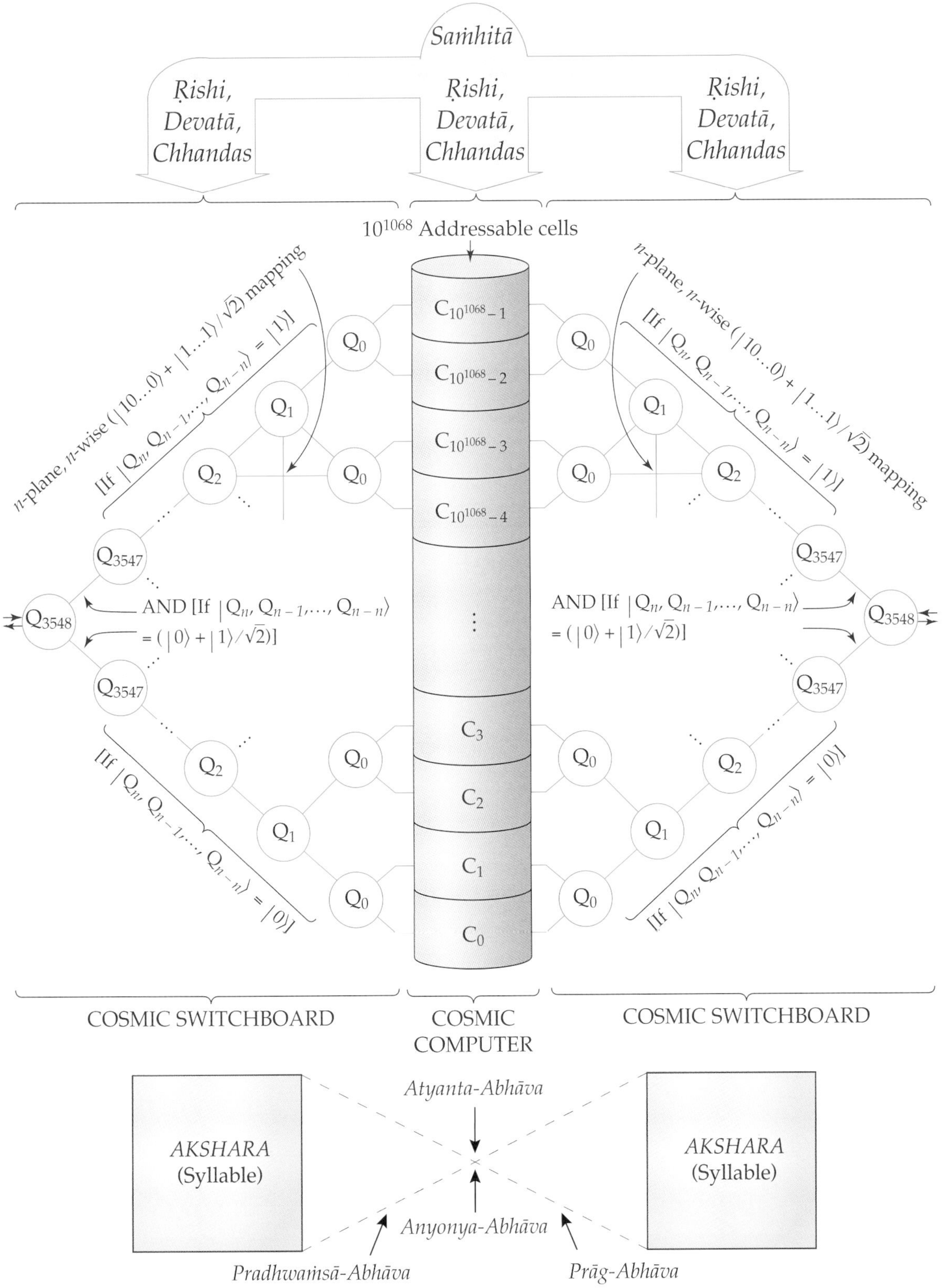

Reference: T.J. Routt, "Methods for Transmitting Data Across Quantum Interfaces and Quantum Gates Using Same," United States Patent Application Number US2004/0078421. Refer to Appendix D.

We found earlier in the Shukl-Yajur-Veda Prātishākhya section of this chapter that QKD networks have been successfully implemented and tested. Certainly, quantum cryptographic methodologies are baseline requirements within Quantum Network Architecture.

Quantum Network Architecture, in its highest expression, necessarily incorporates the following minimum characteristics:

- Continuous foundational self-referral in terms of the Cosmic Computer and Cosmic Switchboard:
  - Massively parallel network computation, wherein any intention or action contemplated or executed at any point within the infinity of creation—ranging, at a minimum, from the cosmic spectrum of the observable universe to that of the Planck scale—is instantly known
  - The computational basis for each succeeding step in the cosmic evolutionary process contained within the results from the previous cosmic network computation
  - Cosmic memory *(Smṛiti)*
  - Instantaneous and refreshed quantum and superstring network computation of cosmic counterparts throughout the spectrum of creation
  - Infinite and eternal fault tolerance
  - Perpetual availability
  - Mean Time Between Failures (MTBF) is infinite
  - Mean Time Between Outages (MTBO) is infinite
  - Zero access and processing latencies within the entire cosmic spectrum of creation
  - Absolute reliability
  - Infinite security
  - Hidden and eternally flawless operation

  – Automation of administration throughout the cosmic spectrum of creation

- Quantum specifications and protocols aligned to the OSI computer network architecture reference model, with quantum-specific Application Programming Interface (API) extensions for applications increasingly running within quantum computational platforms

- Quantum specification and implementation of a Quantum Security Architecture that incorporates QKD at multi-terabit and petabit rates, quantum end-to-end authentication and authorization, quantum End-System (ES) and Intermediate-System (IS) security processing, and quantum-specific implementations of IP security (IPsec) and IPv6 (including qubit time-to-live IP packet extensions).

- Quantum specifications to directly correspond to TCP Layer 4 connection-orientation, User Datagram Protocol (UDP) Layer 4 connectionless behavior, and IP Layer 3c connectionless, packet-mode service

- Quantum-specific extensions of a Cosmic Clock™, on the order of the description in the Shukl-Yajur-Veda Prātishākhya section of this chapter

- Short- and long-term buffered storage of n qubits, with Quality of Service (QoS) guaranteed thresholds for qubit decoherence time and non-regenerative qubit properties

- Massive scalability from manageable numbers of quantum ES and IS nodes ($2 < n \leq 30$), to arbitrarily large N. Increasingly dense and scalable interconnections could be achieved at $n(f+1)/2$, where, for any combination of node count n and fault tolerance f, $n - 1 > f > 0$. We now approach a K-cube-connected cycle where, to ensure a truly scalable network, we let the minimum node degree, $f + 1$, grow in proportion p_{wc} to the total number of nodes, n. We also assume irregular, partial mesh, and/or multi-tier topologies.

- Creation of the quantum Internet, quantum Web, and quantum Global Internetwork.

- Creation of a quantum, global grid network that supports 24 × 7 massively parallel virtual organizations, enabling instantaneous decision making based upon world-scale quantized probability amplitudes of superposed transitions, resulting from the summation of all possible computational trajectories achievable within any time t.

- Creation of a quantum-switchless Global Internetwork that reflects quantum macroscopic properties that neither depend on the history that led to any given present system state, nor on the state sojourn time

Figure 8-22 provides a view of a quantum network architecture that expresses these characteristics. Quantum database servers are running quantum search, QFFT, and quantum simulation applications invoked by clients and other servers through Quantum Application Programming Interface™ (QAPI™) and Quantum Finite State Machine™ (QFSM™) logic within a Quantum Operating System™ (QOS™) environment. One possible interconnection approach, as shown in the figure, is via quantum teleportation circuits.

These logical interconnections are structured atop QKD servers, which exchange quantum keys and authentication logic. These, in turn, are shown interfaced via quantum extensions to IP security (IPsec) protocols, and interconnected through photonic (optical) networks employing waveband-routed multi-tier topologies (as we describe in Chapter 3). ES (application hosts) and IS (switch/routers) contain photonic chips implementing embeded Native Optical Logic™ and Native Quantum Logic.™

Figure 8-22: Quantum Network Architecture

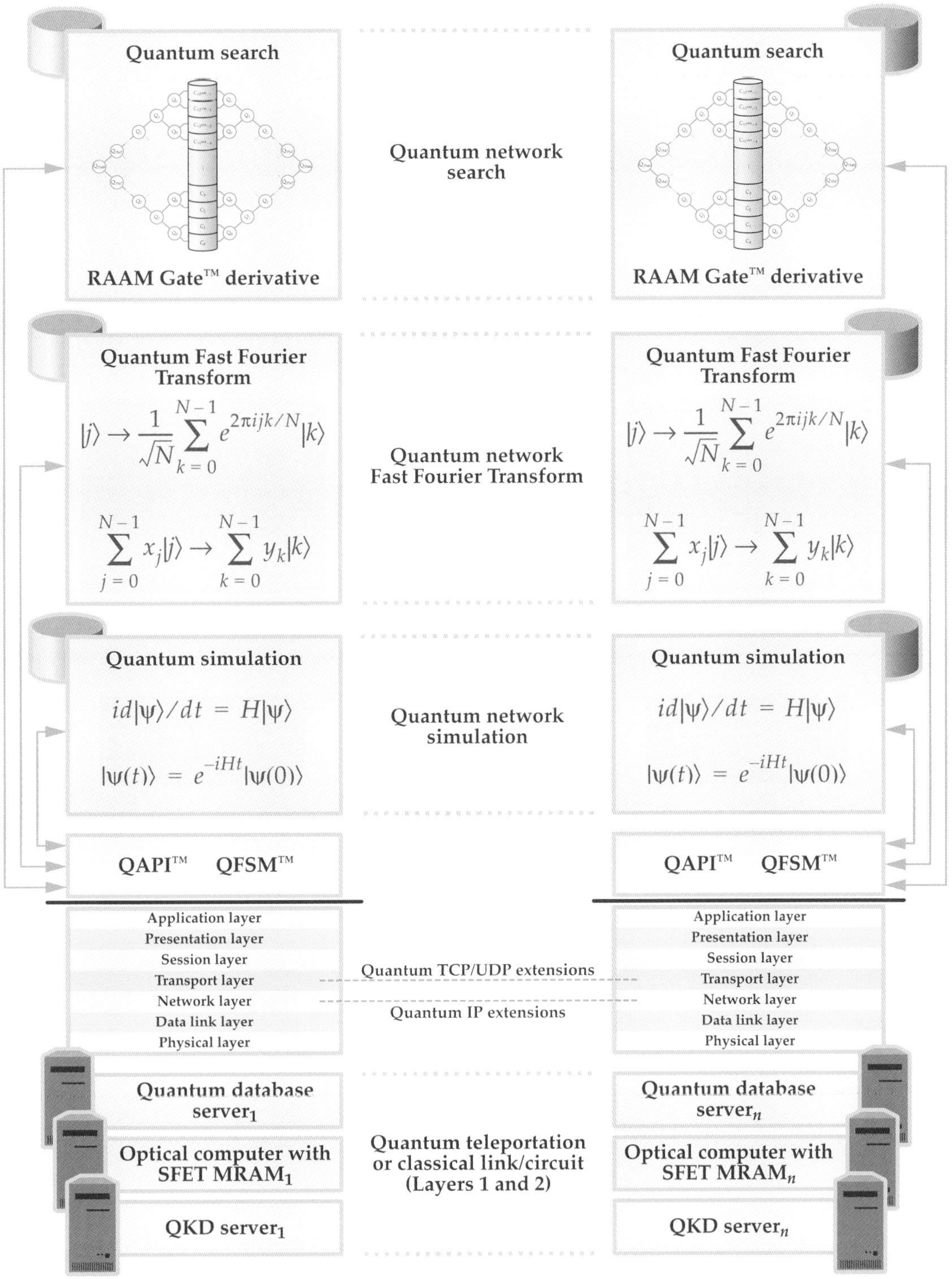

Legend

IP	Internet Protocol
MRAM	Magnetic Random Access Memory
QAPI™	Quantum Application Programming Interface
QFSM™	Quantum Finite State Machine
QKD	Quantum Key Distribution
RAAM Gate™	Routt Addressable Absolute Memory Gate™
SFET	Spin-Field Effect Transistor
TCP	Transmission Control Protocol
UDP	User Datagram Protocol

Reference: T.J. Routt, "Methods for Transmitting Data Across Quantum Interfaces and Quantum Gates Using Same," United States Patent Application Number US2004/0078421. Refer to Appendix D.

9: Vedic *Devatā* in Quantum Network Architecture

The Global Internetwork—the logical confluence of the Internet; the World Wide Web; and hundreds of thousands of intranets, extranets, and private computer networks, both in classical and Quantum Network Architecture™ expressions—is a celestial nervous system, that is, a celestial, self-referral superfabric, that collects, interprets, interconnects, and integrates enterprise, governmental, educational, and personal data throughout the world. Indeed, a portion of the Internet Protocol Version 6 (IPv6) address has already been defined and reserved to accommodate any emerging requirements for extra-planetary internetworking.

Previous chapters reveal the one-to-one correspondence between Maharishi's Vedic Science and Technology and Information Science and Technology. We have seen how the 40 aspects of Veda and the Vedic Literature are all available and lively throughout the theoretical and applied breadth and depth of Information Science and Technology—inclusive of the entire spectrum of classical and quantum computing and networking. This chapter will show how all the aspects of Natural Law described as *Devatā* in the Vedic Literature are also available within Quantum Network Architecture.

Maharishi has brought to light that the Vedic *Devatā* are the various aspects of Natural Law that organize the entire universe and maintain perfect order throughout ever-present processes of evolution throughout creation. They are the Laws of Nature, or collections of Laws of Nature, with specific administrative functions that provide for the creation, maintenance, and dissolution of the entire universe. The Vedic *Devatā* are the creative powers of cosmic dimension, permeating the whole of creation. All the *Devatā*—all the impulses of Creative Intelligence of Natural Law—are present in every point and throughout the entire field of creation.

The Vedic *Devatā* exercise their administrative role over every form and function in the universe. For example, the *Devatā* that administers silence is called Shiva, and the *Devatā* that administers dynamism is called Vishṇu.

Professor Tony Nader, MD, PhD (His Majesty Raja Nader Rām), in his landmark discovery and book entitled *Human Physiology—Expression of Veda and the Vedic Literature*, prepared under Maharishi's guidance, pointed out that the Vedic *Devatā* are not separate from the ultimate reality of the Self—*Ātmā*—the Unified Field of Natural Law. Every point of creation, manifest or unmanifest, animate or inanimate, Planck-scale or cosmological in dimension, is, in its ultimate reality, the Unified Field (refer to Chapters 1 and 8 for discussions of the Unified Field).

Professor Nader systematically revealed that the Vedic *Devatā* are integral aspects of our own human physiology, embodied in every human being with the same forms and functions described in the Vedic Literature. He further made clear that the *Devatā* are present in the physiology of everyone, regardless of one's race, belief system, religion, political affiliation, or geographic region of origin. They are not religious, philosophical, or poetic concepts, but a scientific reality throughout the nature of human physiology.

The Vedic *Devatā* are also found at every point and throughout the entire field of Information Science and Technology, as expressed at its foundation within Quantum Network Architecture and throughout the Global Internetwork.

Shiva in Quantum Network Architecture

Shiva represents pure silence, the Wholeness of Natural Law available in complete, full silence, and is traditionally represented in the form of a *Lingam*. The Quantum Network Architecture expression of the Global Internetwork as a whole represents Shiva in His *Lingam* form.

Shiva has also been represented in the celestial form indicated in Figure 9-1. The Vedic Literature provides a precise description of Shiva and the items surrounding Him. From Shiva's head, on which the crescent moon is placed, the Gangā river flows in three directions. On His forehead is a third eye. His hair has a knot tied by a string of Rudraksha beads. Around His neck is a great cobra. He has with Him a drum, water pot, and trident.

Figure 9-1: Shiva is Seated with Some of the Items Associated with Him, as Described in the Vedic Literature

Considered as one, the silence of Shiva is expressed in Quantum Network Architecture and the Global Internetwork as the *Atyanta-Abhāva* and *Anyonya-Abhāva* of the Hardware-Software Gap™. The *Flowing Wakefulness* and self-referral feedback systems of the Global Internetwork correspond to the flowing of the Gangā and the third eye on Shiva's forehead. The *Reverberating Wholeness* of Nodal Input/Output (I/O) systems corresponds to the crescent moon placed on Shiva's forehead. The *Offering and Creating* value of network processing systems corresponds to Shiva's *Rudrāksha* beads, drum, water pot, and trident. Quantum network security systems and subsystems correspond to the great cobra around Shiva's neck.

Gaṇesh in Quantum Network Architecture

Gaṇesh is one of the sons of Shiva and Pārvatī. He is said to sit at the entrance to Shiva's cave; nothing and no one can go in or out without passing Him—He is the gateway to Shiva. Gaṇesh is also called Gaṇapati and Gaṇādhipa. These names, as the name

Figure 9-2: Gaṇesh Along with Some of the Items Associated with Him, as Described in the Vedic Literature

Gaṇesh, mean "leader of the Gaṇas" and "king of Gaṇas" (the Gaṇas are the attendants of Shiva and are quantified points of infinite silence).

Within the Global Internetwork, security servers and appliances form the gateways to Intermediate Systems (IS)—the "great intermediate net" of switches, routers, and intermediate servers—and to End System (ES) application, database, file system, e-mail, directory, Web, and security servers. These "gateways" to the information quantum highway correspond to Gaṇesh (refer to Figure 9-2 on page 236).

Vishṇu in Quantum Network Architecture

Vishṇu, the all-pervading sustainer of the universe, is embodied as the quality of *Absolute Dynamism* as expressed through the network processing systems within the Global Internetwork. (See Figure 9-3 on page 238.)

Vishṇu is described in Veda and the Vedic Literature as having 10 incarnations: The Routt Addressable Absolute Memory Gate™ (RAAM Gate™), in its role of cognizing, calculating, and invoking the Cosmic Computer and Cosmic Switchboard of Quantum Network Architecture, corresponds to Rām Avatār, the seventh incarnation of Vishṇu.

1 Matsya Avatār — Vishṇu's incarnation as a fish

2 Kūrma Avatār — Vishṇu's incarnation as a tortise

3 Varāha Avatār — Vishṇu's incarnation as a boar

4 Narasiṁha Avatār — Vishṇu's incarnation as a half-lion, half-man

5 Vāman Avatār — Vishṇu's incarnation as a dwarf

6 Parashurām Avatār — Vishṇu's incarnation as Parashurām, embodiment of obeisance and sense of duty

7 Rām Avatār — Vishṇu's incarnation as Shrī Rām, embodiment of cosmic calculation

8 Kṛishṇa Avatār — Vishṇu's incarnation as Shrī Kṛishṇa, a full incarnation of Vishṇu

9 Buddha Avatār — Vishṇu's incarnation as Buddha, embodiment of restoration of life in accord with Natural Law

10 Kalki Avatār — Vishṇu's incarnation as Kalki, embodiment of revival of Total Knowledge

Figure 9-3: Vishṇu with Some of the Items Associated with Him, as Described in the Vedic Literature

Brahmā in Quantum Network Architecture

Brahmā is the *Devatā* whose quality is that of Creator. He is the progenitor of all living things in the world, having first created the seven *Ṛishis* and the Prajapatis. Brahmā created the universe totally from His mind. In the *Taittirīya* Upanishad it is said that Brahmā created the universe, then entered into it. In the Vedic Literature, Brahmā had the task of creating; yet whenever He tried to create, nothing happened. All of His efforts were fruitless. Vishṇu advised Him to transcend, to reach the silent source of creation within His awareness—the state of Totality, the state of simultaneity and coexistent sequentiality of quantum singularity and superpositionality—and then try to create. Brahmā practiced Tapas (transcending, or Transcendental Meditation) for 1000 Yugas (ages). After this, whatever He thought immediately manifested in concrete form. It is for this reason that the progenitors of the human races are said to have been born from the mind of Brahmā. The *Śrī Brahmā-Saṁhitā* also provides a detailed account of Brahmā's enlightenment and subsequent creation.

Brahmā Himself is born from the navel of Vishṇu (Narayana). He has four heads and holds all the knowledge of the Vedas in His hand. As depicted in Figure 9-4, Brahmā, the

Figure 9-4: The Four Heads of Brahmā Correspond to the Four Projected Levels of Quantum Network Creation

creative value, is embodied within Quantum Network Architecture as the four-fold set of projected and mapped logical and physical topologies:

1 Interactive mapped creation of quantum networks and internetworks

2 Cyberspace spatialization and mapped creation

3 End sytem-to-end system (ES-to-ES) logical associations

4 Physical infrastructure mapping and associations (trans-oceanic optical fiber cabling; campus, metropolitan, and wide-area topology; satellite orbitals)

Sūrya in Quantum Network Architecture

Sūrya, the Sun, is one of the Pancha *Devatā* (Shiva, Vishṇu, Devī, Gaṇesh, and Sūrya) upheld in the Vedic Tradition. Sūrya, as described in the section on Maharishi Jyotish (refer to Figure 4-1, page 103), corresponds to Central Processing Unit (CPU)/Network Processing Unit (NPU) in Quantum Network Architecture. The CPU, located in the center of classical or quantum computers and network nodes, orchestrates all network computational functions. On a cosmological scale, Sūrya corresponds to the central intelligence operating within the Cosmic Computer. As we will see in Figure 9-6 ("Crown of Chakravartī—the Cosmic Switchboard" on page 245), the Cosmic Computer is surrounded by a crown-like structure formed by the Cosmic Switchboard. This is the royal crown of the Sun King.

Chakravartī in Quantum Network Architecture

Chakravartī is the ruler of the universe in the Vedic Literature and, as such, is the vital organizer, administrator, and controller on a Cosmic scale. The functions of Chakravartī and the structure of the kingdom of Chakravartī are well defined. The Vedic Literature also provides a detailed description of the various aspects of His kingdom: the prescribed routines, methods for the coronation of kings, and the cycles and rituals involved in these functions.

The Cosmic Computer and Cosmic Switchboard provide the Chakravartī function in Quantum Network Architecture. The rituals, routines, and procedures undertaken by Chakravartī and the activities of his palace correspond to the cycles, rhythms, and administrative aspects of the Cosmic Computer and Cosmic Switchboard:

- The Cosmic Computer and Cosmic Switchboard are a quantum computer and quantum network at the cosmological scale and are eternally engaged in the massively parallel calculations and interconnections required to create and maintain all the Laws of Nature from point to infinity.
- The Cosmic Computer and Cosmic Switchboard are inextricably interlinked within a multi-tier, full-mesh fashion.
- RAAM Gate-based discovery of the Cosmic Computer and Cosmic Switchboard indicate that they are addressable through 10^{1068} memory cells, resulting in a 3548-quantum bit (qubit) quantum (2^{3548}-qubit) address structure.
- Ten *Maṇḍals* of Ṛk Veda generate a radix-10 exponentiation basis to the infinity-within-all-points and all-points-within-infinity eternal calculations of the Cosmic Computer and Cosmic Switchboard.
- The 1068-power exponent RAAM Gate quantum network computational amplitude basis corresponds to the approximately 1000 *Sūktas* (including the 97th *Sūkta—Avyakta Sūkta*—within the first and tenth *Maṇḍals*) of the 10 *Maṇḍals* of Ṛk Veda.
- The RAAM Gate enables any unitary operation to be approximated to arbitrary accuracy by 1-to-n quantum circuits (including quantum teleportation circuits) and is therefore a universal quantum network computational gate; that is, it is universally unitary.
- RAAM Gate is logically reversible and measurable.
- RAAM Gate is an n-qubit gate comprised of massively parallel quantum circuitry that operates on n qubits, and it therefore behaves in a state space characterized as a 2^n–10^n-dimensional complex Hilbert space.

- The RAAM Gate employs massive quantum parallelism intrinsic to processing quantum algorithms, enabling, for example, simultaneous evaluation of a function, $f(x)$, for n different values of x.
- Each cosmic calculation step within the Cosmic Switchboard contains self-referral, complete knowledge of all previous steps and its computational relationship to the Cosmic Computer.

Correspondence Between the Seven Quantum Network Architectural Layers and the Seven Chakravartī *Ṛishis*

Inextricable connections between the Cosmic Computer and Cosmic Switchboard are provided via seven longitudinal columns within the Cosmic Computer that function as a macroscopic quantum network (Cosmic Switchboard) interface on a cosmological scale. These columns function as the seven network architectural layers described in Chapter 3. Cosmological scale quantum network architectural layers, in turn, correspond to the seven *Ṛishis* in the Vedic Literature who are the seven hands of Chakravartī, and whose counterparts in the universe are the seven stars in the group of stars known as the Big Dipper, or the Great Bear, Ursa Major. Figure 9-5 (on page 243) presents the direct correspondence between the seven cosmologic scale quantum network architectural layers and the seven *Ṛishis*.

Quantum Network APIs and *Ṛishi* Agastya

In the Vedic Literature, *Ṛishi* Agastya, who is Himself an ocean of spiritual merit and power, is said to purify and protect the world from imbalances. For example, He purified the waters by drinking the ocean dry to expose demons lying at the bottom, and removed "the obstruction of the Sun's rays caused by a mountain that had grown too high."

These Vedic descriptions of *Ṛishi* Agastya correspond directly to the role of quantum network Application Programming Interfaces (APIs), which specify superpositional and non-superposed programmatic runtime, conversational, and transactional interfaces between applications executing quantum algorithms and the quantum Global Internetwork. These applications include the following:

Figure 9-5: Direct Correspondence between the Seven Cosmologic Scale Quantum Network Architectural Layers and the Seven Chakravartī *Ṛishis*

Seven Chakravartī Ṛishis	**Seven Quantum Network Architectural Layers**
Ṛishi Marīchi *Ṛishi Marīchi is described in the Bṛihat Saṁhitā as a controller of Gandharvans—celestial musicians and singers.*	**Application Layer** Provides application process interfaces into quantum network services, including quantum searching, quantum database, and Quantum Key Distribution (QKD).
Ṛishi Vasishta *Ṛishi Vasishta is described in the Bṛihat Saṁhitā as the controller of certain tribes of hermits and those areas in the world that are forested.*	**Presentation Layer** Presents and describes data structures to end-users in quantum computer-independent formats. Codes/formats data from sender-internal formats into a common transfer format and decodes to the required receiver representation.
Ṛishi Angiras *Ṛishi Angiras is described in the Bṛihat Saṁhitā as a controllers of Brahmāns, intelligent men, and scholars.*	**Session Layer** Enables quantum application process dialogs, information flows, and data flow synchronization.
Ṛishi Atri *Ṛishi Atri is described in the Vedic Literature as a controller of watery areas, oceans, rivers, and certain tribes.*	**Transport Layer** Specifies the logical interface between remote quantum end systems. Provides end-to-end information interchange and control. Orchestrates establishment, data transfer, and termination of quantum network logical connections.
Ṛishi Pulastya *Ṛishi Pulastya (the grandfather of Rāvaṇ, the demon in the Rāmāyaṇ) is described in the Bṛihat Saṁhitā as presiding over the races of demons, devils, giants, and serpents, all of whom are the perpetuators of sorrow and stress.*	**Network Layer** Selects quantum network switching, routing, and internetworking services. Defines datagram-based security access control. Segments and blocks network messages.
Ṛishi Pulaha *Ṛishi Pulaha is described in the Bṛihat Saṁhitā as a controller of food products that grow under the earth, such as roots, bulbs, radishes, and potatoes.*	**Data Link Layer** Initializes data links between adjacent network nodes. Transfers data across wide-area, metropolitan-area, and campus links. Delimits the flow of qubits from the physical layer, provides Data Terminal Equipment (DTE) flow control, and detects/corrects link transmission errors. Provides quantum error detection and correction. Disconnects data links between adjacent network nodes.
Ṛishi Kratu *Ṛishi Kratu is described in the Bṛihat Saṁhitā as a controller of Yagya and other Vedic performances that involve chanting the Vedas in a specifically prescribed manner.*	**Physical Layer** Activates, maintains, and deactivates physical interfaces (optical, opto-electronic, and electronic) and circuits (terrestrial and celestial) between DTE and Data Circuit-terminating Equipment (DCE). Provides local and remote network clocking and signaling.

- Quantum parallelism
- Quantum simulation
- Quantum Fast Fourier Transform (QFFT)
- Quantum factoring
- Quantum cryptography
- Quantum database search
- Quantum counting
- Quantum Internet (quantum extensions to Tranmission Control Protocol [TCP], User Datagram Protocol [UDP], Real-Time Protocol [RTP], and Internet Protocol [IP])
- Quantum extensions to World Wide Web services

The Seven Enclosures of the Palace of Chakravartī

The Vedic Literature describes Chakravartī's palace as having seven enclosures. There are seven corresponding enclosures within the global quantum Internetwork, from the center ("containing" the Cosmic Computer and Cosmic Switchboard), to the periphery:

1. Quantum gates, the RAAM Gate
2. Quantum algorithms
3. Quantum/Cosmic Clock™
4. Quantum memory (Smṛiti)
5. Quantum processor architecture
6. Quantum database
7. Quantum security, cryptography, and Quantum Key Distribution (QKD)

This Quantum Network Architecture is in accordance with Maharishi Sthāpatya Veda; therefore, the distance between the seven borders increases linearly in the following proportions: 1/2/3/4/5/1.5.

The Crown of Chakravartī and the Cosmic Switchboard

The Vedic Literature also describes the crown of Chakravartī. The Cosmic Switchboard corresponds directly to Chakravartī's crown and is shown in Figure 9-6, which, in turn, adds a few degrees of cosmological quantum interconnection density to the Cosmic Computer and Cosmic Switchboard rendering introduced in Chapter 8, Figure 8-16 (on pages 198 and 199). As is shown in Figure 9-6, the Cosmic Switchboard switching density is on the order of 2^{3546} quantum switching nodes, constituting the superdense, cosmic-scale, networked celestial fabric of the crown of Chakravartī.

Figure 9-6: Crown of Chakravartī—The Cosmic Switchboard

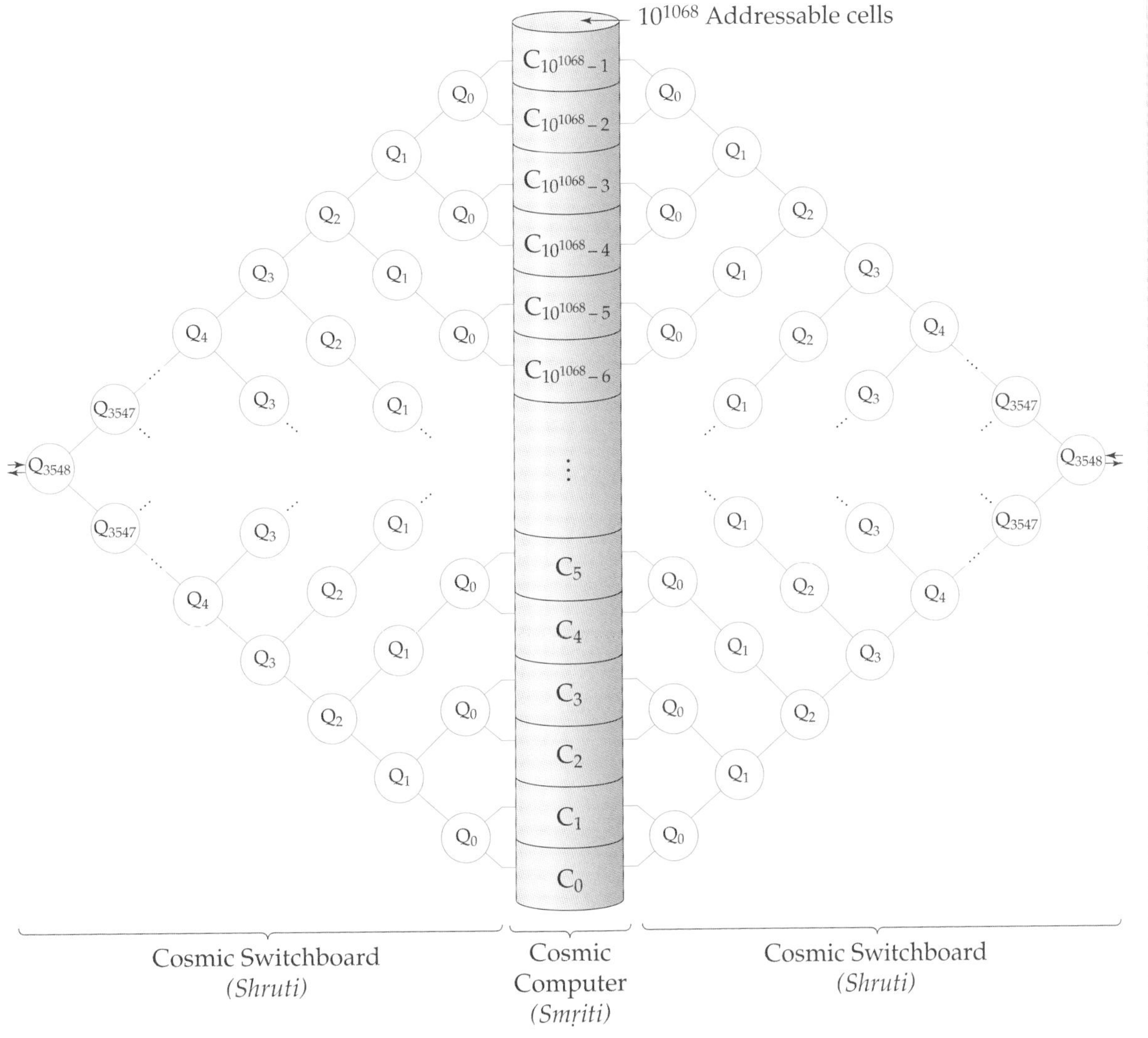

Cosmic-scale input qubits are routed to the Cosmic Computer database defined within the RAAM Gate by the Cosmic Switchboard at the sub-Planck time scale, where their states are changed or not, according to the contents of memory *(Smṛiti)*. Qubits are then routed into a definite, non-superposed location containing the retrieved information (the *Mantra, Akshara*). Qubits are subsequently routed back to their source via the Cosmic Switchboard defined within the RAAM Gate through the Cosmic Computer massively parallel quantum database at the sub-Planck time scale, into a precise (non-superposed) position containing retrieved information. This creates the memory (Smṛiti) basis of the massively parallel *Sandhi* throughout creation from which the succeeding *Akshara* is projected.

The Twelve *Rājadhāni*—Twelve *Rājā Maṇdals* of Chakravartī

The Vedic Literature also describes Chakravartī as controlling 12 *Rājadhāni*, or 12 *Rājā Maṇdals*. These 12 *Rājā Maṇdals* correspond to the following aspects of Quantum Network Architecture:

- Radix-10 RAAM Gate derivation of the number of addressable cells in the Cosmic Computer, which, in turn, correspond directly to the 10 *Maṇdals* of Ṛk Veda
- *Brahmāṇda*, the structure of this universe, derived in earlier calculations of the Cosmic Computer and Cosmic Switchboard (11th *Maṇdala*)
- *Bhu-Maṇdala* (12th *Maṇdala*), or the earthly planetary system described in the Fifth *Skanda* of *Śrīmad Bhāgavatam*, one of the 18 Mahā-Purāṇ, authored by Veda Vyāsa, who codified the Veda.

MERU and The Cosmic Computer

Śrimad Bhāgavatam—integral to the Vedic Literature—describes the cosmos as an unlimited ocean containing innumerable universes, or *Brahmāṇdas*, comparable to spherical bubbles of foam grouped in clusters. Each of these universal globes incorporates a series of spherical enclosures and an inner, inhabited portion. The most striking feature within our local *Brahmāṇda* is *Bhu-Maṇdala*, or the earthly planetary system. *Bhu-Maṇdala* resembles a lotus flower, and its concentric islands resemble the whorl of that flower.

Dimensions of the universe are provided in both the *Śrimad Bhāgavatam* and the *Sūrya Siddhānta* in units of *yojanas*. Various definitions of a *yojana* are found in the Vedic Literature. One standard and recurring definition is that one *yojana* equals 8000 *nr*, or heights of a man. Applying eight miles per *yojana* and 5280 feet per mile, the height for a man is derived as 5.28 feet, which is within the range of acceptability. Aryabhata, a Vedic astronomer, provided a figure of 1050 *yojanas* for the diameter of earth which, when divided into the currently accepted figure of 7928 miles, results in 7.55 miles per *yojana*. *Sūrya-Siddhānta* presents a diameter of earth of 1600 *yojanas*, yielding approximately five miles per *yojana*, however eight miles per *yojana* appears more prevalently in the Vedic Literature.

Śrīmad Bhāgavatam provides a figure of 500 million *yojanas* (four billion miles) as the diameter of the universe, a dimension that can accommodate the orbit of *Shani* (Saturn) around *Sūrya* (the Sun), but that is smaller than the orbital diameters of the outer planets within our presently known Solar System. *Sūrya Siddhānta* states that the circumference of the sphere of the *Brahmāṇda* in which the sun's rays spread is 18,712,080,864,000,000 *yojanas* (18.712 quadrillion *yojanas*, or approximately 150 quadrillion miles), which equates to a diameter of approximately 5.956 quadrillion *yojanas*, a number over six magnitudes greater than the diameter of 500 million yojanas provided in *Śrīmad Bhāgavatam*.

This apparent discrepancy is reconciled in the Fifth *Skandha*, Chapter 20 of *Śrīmad Bhāgavatam* in the description of the mountain known as Lokāloka (called by this name because it stands between Loka, seen worlds, and Aloka, worlds that cannot be seen). Lokāloka is the boundary mountain placed as the limit of the three worlds—Bhūr-Loka, Bhuvaḥ Loka, and Svaḥ Loka—to control the rays of the sun throughout the universe. All the luminaries, from the sun, up to Dhruvaloka (the pole star), distribute their rays throughout the three worlds, but only within the boundary formed by the great mountain Lokāloka.

The diameter of Lokāloka Mountain is also stated in *Śrīmad Bhāgavatam* to be half the diameter of the universe, suggesting that the rays of the sun and other luminaries spread to a radial distance of approximately 2.978 quadrillion *yojanas* and are there blocked in all directions by an enormous mountain, which lies at the midpoint between the sun and the outer coverings of the universe. Calculations on this basis indicate the radial distance from the sun to the coverings of the universe to be approximately 5077 light years.

Sūrya Siddhānta also gives the rule that to find the circumference of the *Brahmāṇda*, or universe, multiply the number of revolutions of *Chandra* (the moon) in a *Kalpa* (equal to the time of fourteen Manus or Manvantaras, each of which comprises seventy-one Chaturyugis, each of which in turn comprises the total span of four Yugas; these relationships are more fully explained in the upcoming section entitled "Devī Gāyatrī's Abode") by the moon's orbit; the product is equal to the orbit of heaven (the outermost circumference of the *Brahmāṇda*). Calculations indicate this value to be approximately 18.712 quadrillion *yojanas*.

The Fifth *Skandha* of *Śrīmad Bhāgavatam* provides further calculations as to the size, shape, and position of several of the geographic structures of *Bhu-Maṇdala*. Perhaps most striking in this regard is that while the descriptions utilize names for familiar features of earthly geography—mountains, oceans, islands—they are all on the cosmic scale of *Bhu-Maṇdala* itself. For example, several mountains on *Bhu-Maṇdala* are 2000 *yojanas*, or 16,000 miles in height, several are 10,000 *yojanas* or 80,000 miles in height, and many more are as high as 84,000 *yojanas* or 672,000 miles.

Calculations based on the distances and proportions presented in the Fifth *Skanda* of *Śrīmad Bhāgavatam* indicate that when viewing *Bhu-Maṇdala* from a great distance (75 million *yojanas* or 600 million miles), five ring-shaped structures are discernable surrounding a central region. Moving from the outermost region inward, we encounter the *Dvīpas*, or islands, named Puṣkaradvīpa, Śākadvīpa, Krauñcadvīpa, Kuśadvīpa, and Śalmalīdvīpa. These *Dvīpas* appear at this distance as concentric rings. Inter-*Dvīpa* intervals are occupied by oceans, each of which has the same width as the *Dvīpa* that it encircles.

Further calculations based upon the distances and proportions presented in the *Śrīmad Bhāgavatam* indicate that the central island of *Bhu-Maṇdala*, Jambūdvīpa, is discernable at a distance of approximately 1,875,000 *yojanas* (150 million miles). Jambūdvīpa is described in he Fifth *Skanda* of *Śrīmad Bhāgavatam* as a disc-shaped island that is 100,000 *yojanas* (800,000 miles) in diameter.

Jambūdvīpa incorporates nine divisions—or *varṣas*—of land, each with a length of 9000 *yojanas* (72,000 miles), with eight mountains that demarcate the boundaries of these divisions. Ilāvarta-varṣa is the central *varṣa* of Jambūdvīpa and is situated in the center of the whorl of that lotus.

The most striking feature of Jambūdvīpa is the central structure of Ilāvarṭa called Mount Meru (MERU), which is made of gold. The elevation of MERU is equal to the width of Jambūdvīpa, or 100,000 *yojanas* (800,000 miles), of which 16,000 *yojanas* (128,000 miles) are within the earth and 84,000 *yojanas* (672,000 miles) are above the earth. MERU is 32,000 *yojanas* (256,000 miles) across at its summit and 16,000 *yojanas* (128,000 miles) across at its base (Fifth *Skanda,* Chapter 16, *Śrīmad Bhāgavatam*).

MERU is surrounded by eight principal mountains, two in each of the cardinal directions. On the eastern side of MERU are two mountains named Jaṭhara and Devakūṭa, which extend to the north and south for 18,000 *yojanas*. On the western side of MERU are two mountains named Pāvana and Pāriyātra, which also extend north and south for 18,000 *yojanas*. On the northern side of MERU are the two mountains named Triśṛṅga and Makara, and on the southern side of MERU are two mountains named Kailāsa and Karavīra, all four of which extend for 18,000 *yojanas* to the east and west.

Śrīmad Bhāgavatam states that in the center of the summit of MERU is Brahmāpurī, the golden city (Śātakaumbhī) of Lord Brahmā, the Self-created one, in the shape of a square, covering 10 million *yojanas* (80 million miles). Surrounding Brahmāpurī in all directions are the cities belonging to eight other *Devatās* including Indra. Four mountains, Mandara, Merumandara, Supārśva, and Kumuda, each 10,000 *yojanas* (80,000 miles) in elevation and width, are placed on the four sides of MERU and its embankments.

Based on calculations from the *Śrīmad Bhāgavatam,* Figure 9-7 (on page 250) presents a view of Jambūdvīpa showing MERU as the principal feature and surrounding mountain ranges forming the boundaries of the nine *varsas* of Jambūdvīpa. MERU is the central whorl of the lotus-like *Bhu-Maṇdala Brahmāṇda* and, as such, is the source, course, and goal of Natural Law within the universe. MERU is the cosmic fountainhead of computational intelligence within the universe, and therefore corresponds directly to the Cosmic Computer. The Cosmic Computer, as the central cone shown in Figure 9-7, corresponds to MERU towering on a cosmic scale above Jambūdvīpa:

> *In the center of Jambūdvīpa is the region known as Ilāvarṭa, which is the most interior of all regions. In the middle of Ilāvarṭa is situated Mahameru, the king of the mighty mountains. This golden mountain is like a central pistil to the earth-lotus.*
>
> *Śrīmad Bhāgavatam, 5.16.7*

Figure 9-7: MERU As the Cosmic Computer

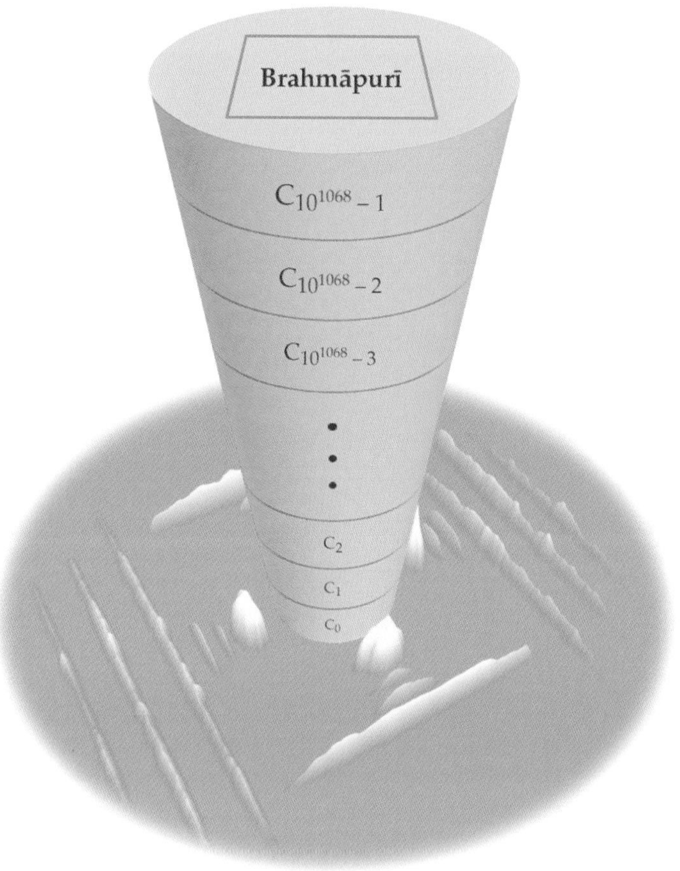

MERU is shown as the Cosmic Computer and depicts the 10^{1068}-cell quantum memory (*Smṛiti*) infinity-point calculation density matrix introduced with the RAAM Gate™ in Figure 8-16, page 198. MERU is also associated with *Merudaṇḍa* in the human physiology. *Śrīmad Devī Bhāgavatam*, Seventh *Skandha*, states that *Merudaṇḍa* is situated in the center of the spinal cord and is the foremost of thirty million *nāḍīs* (subtle avenues of circulation). *Merudaṇḍa* and the brain function as an individualized infinity-point calculation network of the Cosmic Computer and Cosmic Switchboard.

Mother Divine in Quantum Network Architecture

Pārvatī (Figure 9-8) represents the fundamental aspect of Mother Divine. She is the source of all that there is in creation. Nothing takes shape without Her; nothing can have a manifest form or a structure without Her. In Quantum Network Architecture, Pārvatī represents all that provides structure and form—ranging from qubit interactions at quantum scales, to quantum network *N*-node scalability, to the measured results of quantum network algorithmic execution.

Figure 9-8: Pārvatī Sustains All Structures

The three traditional, main aspects of Mother Divine—Lakshmī, Saraswatī, and Dūrgā—are always said to be together. Lakshmī is the nourishing and wealth-giving value; Saraswatī is the knowledge value; and Dūrgā is the energy and power value. Mother Divine is seen residing in these three manifestations in every aspect of Quantum Network Architecture.

Saraswatī

Saraswatī, representing knowledge, is located in the four mentally-projected levels of quantum network creation. Her four arms, in the form of the four projected levels of quantum network creation, represent the seat of all knowledge, experience, and action. Saraswatī is the consort of Brahmā, who has four heads, and She is also represented as the four projected levels of quantum network creation. Figure 9-9 (on page 252) depicts the relationship of the four arms of Saraswatī to the four projected levels of Quantum Network Architecture. Saraswatī, in Her embodiment of knowledge, also resides within four

Figure 9-9: The Four Arms of Saraswatī Correspond to the Four Projected Levels of Quantum Network Creation

guiding theories of Quantum Network Architecture (introduced in Figure 3-1, on pages 41–43):

1 Quantum Information Theory

2 Classical Information Theory

3 Sampling Theory

4 Analytic Queueing Theory

Lakshmī

Lakshmī, representing wealth, health, and the nourishing power of Mother Divine, resides in the four major elements of Quantum Network Architecture:

1 Quantum switching and routing

2 Secure qubit network infrastructure

3 Network quantum storage

4 *N*-node scalability

Figure 9-10 depicts the relationship of the four hands of Lakshmī to the four elements of Quantum Network Architecture.

Figure 9-10: The Four Hands of Lakshmī Correspond to the Four Major Elements of Quantum Network Architecture

1 Quantum switching/routing

2 Secure qubit network infrastructure

3 Network quantum memory

4 *N*-node scalability

Dūrgā

Dūrgā represents power, or *Shakti*. In the Vedic Literature, the lower tip of the human spinal cord is seen as the seed source of energy—*Shakti*. That region of the physiology is associated with *Mūla,* the root. This area corresponds in Quantum Network Architecture to secure root access and all associated security policies and taxonomies, which function as the outermost protective layer of mission-critical enterprise and personal information assets. Figure 9-11 depicts the relationship of the eight arms of Dūrgā to the eight components of quantum network security.

Figure 9-11: The Eight Arms of Dūrgā Correspond to the Eight Quantum Network Security Components

1. Perimeter security
2. Root access and access control
3. Authentication, authorization, auditing
4. Content and liability management
5. Virtual Private Network (VPN)
6. Public Key Infrastructure (PKI)
7. Intrusion Detection System (IDS) and response
8. User management and policy enforcement

Devī Gāyatrī's Abode

The *Śrīmad Devī Bhāgavatam* is a key Vedic text that presents a detailed analysis of the abode of Devī Gāyatrī, or Mother Divine. In order to illustrate more precisely the relationships among the *Devatā*, the Vedic texts, and Quantum Network Architecture—embodied as the Global Internetwork and Information Science and Technology—we present here an analysis of the abode of Devī Gāyatrī, or Mother Divine. His Holiness Maharishi Mahesh Yogi has described the eternal nature of Mother Divine within his commentary to Chapter 4, Verse 1 of The *Bhagavad Gita* as follows:

> Time is a conception to measure eternity. Indian historians base their conception of time on eternal Being; for them eternity is the basic field of time.
>
> To arrive at some conception of the eternal, the best measure will be the life-span of something that has the greatest longevity in the relative field of creation. This, according to the enlightened vision of Vyāsa, is the Divine Mother, the Universal Mother, who is ultimately responsible for all that is, was, and will be in the entire cosmos.
>
> The eternity of the eternal life of absolute Being is conceived in terms of innumerable lives of the Divine Mother, a single one of whose lives encompasses a thousand life-spans of Lord Shiva. One life of Lord Shiva covers the time of a thousand life-spans of Lord Vishṇu.
>
> One life of Lord Vishṇu equals the duration of a thousand life-spans of Brahmā, the Creator. A single life-span of Brahmā is conceived in terms of one hundred years of Brahmā; each year of Brahmā comprises 12 months of Brahmā, and each month comprises thirty days of Brahmā. One day of Brahmā is called a Kalpa. One Kalpa is equal to the time of fourteen Manus.
>
> The time of one Manu is called a Manvantara. One Manvantara equals seventy-one Chaturyugis. One Chaturyugi comprises the total span of four Yugas, i.e. Sat-yuga, Tretā-yuga, Dvāpara-yuga and Kali-yuga. The span of the Yugas is conceived in terms of the duration of Sat-yuga. Thus the span of Tretā-yuga is equal to three quarters of that of Sat-yuga; the span of Dvāpara-yuga is half that of Sat-yuga, and the span of Kali-yuga one quarter that of Sat-yuga. The span of of Kali-yuga equals 432,000 years of man's life.

Book 12, Chapters 10–12 of the *Śrīmad Devī Bhāgavatam,* presents a detailed description of Devī Gāyatrī's abode, known as *Sarvaloka,* and identifies 19 enclosures, each with specific characteristics. These enclosures are found to correspond to 19 distinct enclosures within Quantum Network Architecture and the Global Internetwork.

Maharishi has brought to light the significance of the 19 enclosures of Devī's abode following the discovery of Veda and the Vedic Literature in human physiology by Professor Tony Nader, MD, PhD (His Majesty Raja Nader Rām). The first 16 enclosures are related to the eight outward and eight inward values of the eight *Prakṛiti* (see Figure 3-11 on page 59, "Direct Correspondence of the eight Gap *Prakṛiti* to Eight Computer Network Architectural Interfaces and Layers," for a descriptive overview of the eight *Prakṛiti*), or fundamental aspects of Natural Law. The last three of the 19 enclosures are transcendental with respect to the previous 16 and represent the transcendental aspects of *Ṛishi, Devatā,* and *Chhandas.*

The 19 enclosures, or layers of Devī's abode, represent the values of *Ṛishi, Devatā,* and *Chhandas,* each with six distinct aspects, creating 3 values × 6 distinct aspects = 18 enclosures, with the nineteenth enclosure representing the *Saṁhitā* value. This interpretation is also supported in the corresponding elaborations of Quantum Network Architecture and the Global Internetwork found in Figure 9-13 (on page 259) and elaborated in Figure 9-14 (pages 260–286). The first six outer layers of the Global Internetwork have a fundamentally protective, covering, and hiding function, which corresponds to *Chhandas.* The next six layers are involved in the functions of interconnecting, processing, and nourishing the network—functions associated with the *Devatā* quality. The final six layers lie within the inner core of the network and represent the inner quality of *Ṛishi.* The last layer or enclosure, the nineteenth aspect, contains the Cosmic Computer and Cosmic Switchboard and represents the sum total of everything as the *Saṁhitā* quality. Figure 9-12 depicts Devī Gāyatrī, or Mother Divine, with some of the items associated with Her, as described in the Vedic Literature.

Śrīmad Devī Bhāgavatam describes all 19 enclosures of Devī's abode in great detail. These are summarized at a high level in Figure 9-13, then elaborated in detail in Figure 9-14. The first eight enclosures of Devī's abode are made of metal and are either seven *yojanas* high, seven *yojanas* long, or seven *yojanas* wide.

Figure 9-12: Devī Gāyatrī Along with Some of the Items Associated with Her, as Described in the Vedic Literature

The second eight enclosures of Devī's abode are made of gems and are 10 *yojanas* high. The seventeenth enclosure is 100 *yojanas* in height, the eighteenth is higher, and the nineteenth enclosure is 1000 *yojanas* high. The last three enclosures are made respectively of coral, *Navaratna* (nine gems), and *Chintāmaṇi* gems (gems of mind or consciousness).

The 8/8/3 organizational pattern presented above corresponds to the organization brought to light by Maharishi in terms of eight outer *Prakṛiti*, eight inner *Prakṛiti*, and the transcendental expression of *Ṛishi, Devatā, Chhandas*. The first eight enclosures are made of metal, reflect light in the outward direction, and correspond to the outer expression of the eight *Prakṛiti.*

The second eight enclosures (9 through 16) are made of gems, generally take light within themselves, shine with brilliance from within, and therefore correspond to the eight inner *Prakṛiti.*

The remaining three enclosures (17 through 19) are made of gems, reflecting three levels of subtlety. The seventeenth enclosure is made of red coral, an opaque gem corresponding to the hiding value of *Chhandas.* The eighteenth enclosure is made of *Navaratnas,* or special groupings of the nine principal gems in Maharishi Jyotish. The *Navaratnas* represent the field of all possibilities—all possible dynamics and transformations corresponding to the *Devatā* value with its organizing and transforming power. The nineteenth enclosure is made of *Chintāmaṇi,* or gems made of mind or consciousness, corresponding to the *Ṛishi* quality, the innocent witnessing value.

Figure 9-14 (pages 260–286) provides a detailed description of the nineteen enclosures of Devī Gāyatrī, Mother Divine, and elaborates their direct correspondences in Information Science and Technology, as expressed by the Global Internetwork and Quantum Network Architecture.

Figure 9-13: Summary of the Nineteen Enclosures of Devī Gāyatrī's Abode and Their Correspondence in Information Science and Technology, as Expressed in the Global Internetwork and Quantum Network Architecture

		Enclosures of Devī Gāyatrī's Abode	**Enclosures of the Global Internetwork and Quantum Network Architecture**
		General description of Sarvaloka, the abode of Mother Divine	General Description of Information Science and Technology
		Sudhā Samudra Ocean	Global Internetwork
The first 8 enclosures: • *Made of metal* • *Reflect light in the outward direction* • *Correspond to the outer expression of the 8 Prakṛiti*	*Chhandas*	1 *Iron Enclosure Wall*	Security Policies, Taxonomies, and Architecture
		2 *White Copper Metal Enclosure Wall*	Security Subsystems
		3 *Wall of Copper*	Remote Authentication
		4 *Wall of Lead*	Access Control
		5 *Wall of Brass*	Identity and Credential Subsystem
		6 *Wall of Five-Fold Irons*	Physical Network Topology, Backbone Network
	Devatā	7 *Silver Enclosure Wall*	Directory Server
		8 *Molten Gold Enclosure Wall*	Domain Name System
The second 8 enclosures: • *Made of gems* • *Take light within themselves and shine with brilliance from within* • *Correspond to the 8 inner Prakṛiti*		9 *Pushparāgamaṇi (Red Kum Kum—Saffron) Enclosure Wall*	Logical Network Topology and Association
		10 *Padmarāgamaṇi (Ruby) Enclosure Wall*	Network Time Server, Network Master Clock
		11 *Gomedamaṇi (Gomed, a gem associated with Rahu) Enclosure Wall*	Web Server and Services
		12 *Diamond Enclosure Wall*	Database Server, Data Repository
	Ṛishi	13 *Vaidūryamaṇi (Lapiz Lazuli) Enclosure Wall*	Operating System, Network Operating System
		14 *Indranīlamaṇi (Blue Sapphire) Enclosure Wall*	Storage Area Network (SAN), Network Attached Storage (NAS)
		15 *Mukta (Pearl) Enclosure Wall*	Classical Computer, Classical Network
		16 *Marakata (Emerald) Enclosure Wall*	Classical Algorithms and Gates
The three final enclosures: • *Made of gems* • *Reflect three levels of subtlety* • *Transcendental Aspects of Ṛishi, Devatā, Chhandas*		17 *Prabala (Red Coral) Enclosure Wall (Chhandas)*	Quantum Computer, Quantum Network
		18 *Navaratna (the Nine jewels) Enclosure Wall (Devatā)*	Quantum Algorithms and Gates
	Saṁhitā	19 *Chief and crowning palace of Shrī Devī, built of Chintāmaṇi gems (Ṛishi)*	Cosmic Computer and Cosmic Switchboard

Figure 9-14: Elaboration of Gāyatrī's Abode with Direct Correspondences in Information Science and Technology, as Expressed in the Global Internetwork and Quantum Network Architecture

Enclosures of Devī Gāyatrī's Abode	**Enclosures of the Global Internetwork and Quantum Network Architecture**
General Description of Sarvaloka, the abode of Mother Divine: *O King Janamejaya, what is known in the Shrutis, in the Shubala Upanishad, as the Sarvaloka over the Brahmāloka, that is Maṇidwīpa (island of gems). Here the Devī resides. This region is superior to all the other regions. Hence it is named Sarvaloka. (In the very beginning) Devī built this place according to Her will to serve as Her residence…Verily no other place in this universe can stand before it. Hence it is called Maṇidwīpa, or Sarvaloka, as superior to all other Lokas.* *This Maṇidwīpa is situated at the top of all the regions, and resembles an umbrella. Its shadow falls on the Brahmāṇda (universe) and destroys the pains and suffering of the world.* *Śrīmad Devī Bhāgavatam, 12.10.1–20*	**General Description of Information Science and Technology:** We are living in the Information Age and Knowledge Age, expressed by Information Science and Technology (IS&T). IS&T has more than doubled its proportion of worldwide gross product during the past two decades within the following six fundamental areas: **1** Electronic and optical components and semiconductors **2** Computer hardware and office equipment **3** Communications equipment **4** Household audio and video **5** Telecommunications and broadcast services **6** Computer and data processing services (including software) The IS&T sector commands a Compound Annual Growth Rate (CAGR) of 10 percent and is growing more rapidly than the global economy. This is a worldwide phenomenon, as all major nations in the world are increasingly creating and supporting the policy frameworks, infrastructures, capital pools, partnerships, education, skills bases, and applications necessary to facilitate IS&T growth, even those nations experiencing financial and economic constraint. IS&T is the single largest exporting sector of developed and developing nations and is central to the current exponentially evolving Information Economy and Information Age: *this region is superior to all the other regions;* and *verily no other place in the universe can stand before it.* IS&T—in its complete theoretical and expressed breadth and depth—synthesizes the following 19 core competencies: • Quantum information theory • Quantum information logic and algorithms • Computer science • Electrical engineering • Electronic engineering

Figure 9-14 (continued): Elaboration of Gāyatrī's Abode with Direct Correspondences in Information Science and Technology, as Expressed in the Global Internetwork and Quantum Network Architecture

Enclosures of Devī Gāyatrī's Abode	**Enclosures of the Global Internetwork and Quantum Network Architecture**
General Description of Sarvaloka, the abode of Mother Divine (continued)	**General Description of IS&T (continued):** • Data communications • Telecommunications • Optical engineering • Laser technology • Video engineering • Voice engineering • Wireless technology • Bandwidth engineering • Quantum and superstring physics • Classical physics • Linear programming • Mathematical programming • Analytic queueing • Simulation IS&T falls on, or influences, the automation of administration of the world and guides it to avoid pain and suffering, to the extent that nations most heavily invested in IS&T are the recipients of maximum abundance during economic upturns and experience the mildest effects of economic downturns: *its shadow falls on the Brahmāṇda (universe) and destroys the pains and suffering of this world.*
Sudhā Samudra Ocean: *Surrounding this Maṇidwīpa exists an ocean called the Sudhā Samudra (ocean of nectar), many yojanas wide and many yojanas deep. Many waves arise in it due to winds. Various fishes and conches and other aquatic animals play here and the beach is full of clear sand-like gems. The sea shores are always kept cool by the splashes of the waves of water striking the beach. Various ships decked with various nice flags are plying to and fro. Various trees bearing gems are adorning the beach.* *Śrīmad Devī Bhāgavatam, 12.10.1–20*	***Sudhā Samudra* corresponds to the Global Internetwork:** At the beginning of the account of *Sarvaloka*, the *Śrīmad Devī Bhāgavatam* presents a description of *Sudhā Samudra*, an ocean which surrounds the 19 enclosures. *Sudhā Samudra* corresponds to the Global Internetwork. The Global Internetwork—as the worldwide expression of IS&T—is the physical, logical, and ubiquitous confluence of the Internet, World Wide Web, intranets, extranets, and private computer networks, and is a global, self-referral, celestial nervous system, or celestial conscious superfabric,

Figure 9-14 (continued): Elaboration of Gāyatrī's Abode with Direct Correspondences in Information Science and Technology, as Expressed in the Global Internetwork and Quantum Network Architecture

Enclosures of Devī Gāyatrī's Abode	**Enclosures of the Global Internetwork and Quantum Network Architecture**
Sudhā Samudra Ocean (continued)	***Sudhā Samudra* corresponds to the Global Internetwork (continued):** that continually collects, interprets, processes, interconnects, and integrates enterprise and personal data throughout the world. Networked information is the nucleus of our interconnected world. At any given moment, a billion people are interacting with hundreds of millions of applications through a trillion interconnected, intelligent devices: *various fishes and conches and other aquatic animals play here* (in the ocean); and *ships decked with various nice flags.* The movement of networked information throughout the Global Internetwork is on the basis of signaling sine waves containing characteristic wavelength-, velocity-, and frequency-based waveforms: *waves arise in it due to winds.* Signal processing and sampling are orchestrated through stochastic gradient, least squares, multipath equalization, cross-relation, direct symbol estimation, space-time signal processing, and orthogonally anchored algorithms; signal models; and audio/video compression all based upon tree-like sampling and branching logic: *trees bearing gems are adorning the beach.* Classical digital information flow proceeds through bit transitions; classical analog information flow proceeds through transitions relative to references waveform amplitudes; and the flow of quantum information proceeds through quantized probability amplitudes of superposed transitions resulting from the summation (cooling) of all possible computational trajectories over time into quantum bits (qubits): *the sea shores are always kept cool by the splashes of the waves of water striking the beach.*

Figure 9-14 (continued): Elaboration of Gāyatrī's Abode with Direct Correspondences in Information Science and Technology, as Expressed in the Global Internetwork and Quantum Network Architecture

Enclosures of Devī Gāyatrī's Abode	**Enclosures of the Global Internetwork and Quantum Network Architecture**
The First Enclosure: *Iron Enclosure Wall* *Across this ocean there is an iron enclosure, very long and seven yojanas wide, very high so as to block the heavens. Within this enclosure wall the military guards skilled in war and furnished with various weapons are running gladly to and fro.* *There are four gateways or entrances; at every gate there are hundreds of guards and various hosts of the devotees of the Devī. Whenever any Deva comes to pay a visit to the Jagadīshwarī, their vāhanas (carriers) and retinue are stopped here.* *This place resounds with the chiming of the bells of hundreds of chariots of the Devas and the neighing of their horses and the sounds of their hoofs. The Devīs walk here and there with canes in their hands, chiding at intervals the attendants of the Devas.* *This place is so noisy that no one can hear clearly another's word. Here are seen thousands of houses adorned with trees of gems and jewels, and tanks filled with plenty of tasteful, good sweet waters.* *Śrīmad Devī Bhāgavatam, 12.10.1–20*	**Security Policies, Taxonomies, and Architecture** The first enclosure in the Global Internetwork is the set of security policies, taxonomies, and architecture, which function as the outermost protective layer of mission-critical information assets. Security policy, taxonomy, and architecture integrates the following: • Perimeter security • Access control and services (external and internal) • Authentication, authorization, auditing • Content and liability management (application security control, email filtering, content control, and virus protection) • Virtual Private Network (VPN) services • Public Key Infrastructure (PKI) • Intrusion detection and response services • User management and policy enforcement *Within this enclosure wall the military guards skilled in war and furnished with various weapons are running gladly to and fro...* Secure flow of information requires that the four following "gateway" protections are in place: 1 Security policies, taxonomies, and guidelines 2 Security architecture 3 Perimeter security 4 Trusted third-party user identification and authentication *There are four gateways or entrances; at every gate there are hundreds of guards and various hosts of the devotees of the Devī. Whenever any Deva comes to pay a visit to the Jagadīshwarī, their vāhanas (carriers) and retinue are stopped here.*

Figure 9-14 (continued): Elaboration of Gāyatrī's Abode with Direct Correspondences in Information Science and Technology, as Expressed in the Global Internetwork and Quantum Network Architecture

Enclosures of Devī Gāyatrī's Abode	**Enclosures of the Global Internetwork and Quantum Network Architecture**
The Second Enclosure: *White Copper Metal Enclosure Wall* *After this there is a second enclosure wall, very big and built of white copper metal (an amalgam of zinc or tin and copper); it is so very high that it almost touches the Heavens. It is a hundred times more brilliant than the preceding enclosure wall; there are many principal entrance gates and various trees here.* *What to speak of the trees…all the trees that are found in this universe are found here, and they bear always flowers, fruits and new leaves! All quarters are scented with their sweet fragrance! The place is interspersed with various forests and gardens.* *At intervals there are wells and tanks. The cuckoos are perching on every tree and cooing sweetly; the bees are drinking the honey and humming all around. The trees are casting nice cool shadows. The trees of all seasons are seen here (on the tops of which are many birds).* *There are rivers flowing at intervals carrying many juicy liquids. The flamingoes, swans, and other aquatic animals are playing in them.* *The breeze is stealing away the perfumes of the flowers and carrying it all around. The deer are following this breeze, the wild, mad peacocks are dancing with madness, and the whole place looks very nice, lovely, and charming.* *Śrīmad Devī Bhāgavatam, 12.10.1–20*	**Security Subsystems** The second enclosure is the security subsystem environment, containing copper and zinc (present in copper security Application-Specific Integrated Circuits—ASICs): *there is a second enclosure wall, very big and built of white copper metal (an amalgam of zinc or tin and copper).* There are five principal security subsystems and these are integrated within a closed-loop control system. Each subsystem consists of a managing process incorporating a default idle state and multiple execution pathways (*…There are many principal entrance gates…There are rivers here flowing at intervals carrying many juicy liquids. The flamingoes, swans, and other aquatic animals are playing in them…*) that can be invoked either by an asynchronous request signaled by another security subsystem, or by a synchronized request from a non-security process. *At intervals there are wells and tanks.* The five principal security subsystems are: 1 Identity or credential subsystem 2 Access control subsystem 3 Information flow control subsystem 4 Solution integrity subsystem 5 Security audit subsystem *…the whole place looks very nice, lovely, and charming…it is a hundred times more brilliant than the preceding enclosure wall.*

Figure 9-14 (continued): Elaboration of Gāyatrī's Abode with Direct Correspondences in Information Science and Technology, as Expressed in the Global Internetwork and Quantum Network Architecture

Enclosures of Devī Gāyatrī's Abode	**Enclosures of the Global Internetwork and Quantum Network Architecture**
The Third Enclosure: *Wall of Copper* *Next to this Kamsya enclosure comes the third enclosure, a wall of copper. It is square-shaped and seven yojanas high. Within this are forests of Kalpavṛikshas (wish fulfilling trees), bearing golden leaves and flowers and fruits like gems. Their perfumes spread 10 yojanas and gladden things all around.* *The king of the seasons always preserves this place. The king's seat is made of flowers; his umbrella is of flowers; ornaments are made of flowers; he drinks the honey of the flowers...the Gandharvans, the celestial musicians, live here with their wives. The places around this are filled with the beauties of the spring and with the cooing of cuckoos.* *Śrīmad Devī Bhāgavatam, 12.10.21–40*	**Remote Authentication** The third enclosure is the remote authentication system, which lies directly beneath the security subsystem environment. Root and branching logic pervades the four major authentication technologies: *within are forests*. These are implemented on copper chips and their substrates: *a wall of copper*. These chips are square-shaped: *it is square-shaped*. Reliable user authentication is a critical component in the Web-enabled world to the extent that an insecure authentication system can lead to serious, even catastrophic consequences, including loss of confidential information, denial of service, and compromised data integrity. Prevailing user authentication techniques encompass the following: • What the requesting user knows: user identifiers (user IDs), Personal Identification Numbers (PINs), and passwords • What the requesting user has: cards, badges, key • Combinations of what one knows and what one has, i.e., Automated Teller Machine (ATM) card plus PIN • Unique user biometric characteristics: anatomic, fingerprint, iris, voiceprint, phrenology, and/or physiognomy. Automated biometrics generally provide highly accurate and reliable user authentication relative to reliance upon what one knows (usually shared, several passwords are straightforward to guess, and many are forgotten), and what one has (cards, badges, and keys are often shared, and can be duplicated, lost, or stolen). Reliable network authentication provides users access to desired resources: *forests of Kalpavṛikshas (wish fulfilling trees)...gladden things all around.*

Figure 9-14 (continued): Elaboration of Gāyatrī's Abode with Direct Correspondences in Information Science and Technology, as Expressed in the Global Internetwork and Quantum Network Architecture

Enclosures of Devī Gāyatrī's Abode	**Enclosures of the Global Internetwork and Quantum Network Architecture**
The Fourth Enclosure: *Wall of Lead* *Next comes the enclosure wall made of lead. Its height is seven yojanas. Within this enclosure there is the garden of the Santānaka tree (a Kalpavṛiksha tree), one of the five trees in Indra's Heaven. The fragrance of its flowers extends to 10 yojanas. The flowers look like gold and are always in full bloom.* *Its fruits are very sweet; they seem to be imbued with nectar drops. In this garden resides the Summer Season with his two wives, Shukra Shrī and Shuchi Shrī.* *The inhabitants of this place always remain under the trees; otherwise they would be scorched by summer rays. Various Siddhas and Devas inhabit this place. The water here is very cool and refreshing.* *Śrīmad Devī Bhāgavatam, 12.10.41–60*	**Access Control** The fourth enclosure of *Sarvaloka* corresponds to networked application access control, and is the final major "wall" protecting privileged system root-level access. It is therefore associated with the "heaviest" component of trusted privilege: *made of lead*. Information security requires that networked systems provide five essential services: 1 Authentication 2 Access control 3 Integrity (operational, physical, and semantic) 4 Confidentiality 5 Non-repudiation As such, access control (both external and internal) is one of the five essential information security functions: *Within this enclosure there is the garden of the Santanaka tree (a Kalpavṛiksha tree), one of the five trees in Indra's Heaven.* Role-Based Access Control (RBAC) is a key mechanism for administering access control, both inside and outside of workflow environments. RBAC is integral to separation of duty, or separation of privilege, based on the observation that a networked information system with two keys is more robust and flexible than one that only requires a single key: *In this garden resides the Summer Season with his two wives, Shukra Shrī and Shuchi Shrī.* Privileged root access is also integral to access control: *The inhabitants of this place always remain under trees.*

Figure 9-14 (continued): Elaboration of Gāyatrī's Abode with Direct Correspondences in Information Science and Technology, as Expressed in the Global Internetwork and Quantum Network Architecture

Enclosures of Devī Gāyatrī's Abode	**Enclosures of the Global Internetwork and Quantum Network Architecture**
The Fifth Enclosure: *Wall of Brass* *Next to this enclosure comes the wall made of brass, the fifth enclosure wall. It is seven yojanas long. In the center is situated the garden of Harichandana trees. Its ruler is the Rainy Season...The lightnings are his auburn eyes, the clouds are his armour, the thunder is his voice, and the rainbow is his arrow. Surrounded by his hosts he rains incessantly. He has 12 wives...All the trees here are always seen with new leaves and entwined with new creepers.* *The whole site is covered all over with fresh green leaves and twigs. The rivers here always flow full and the current is strong indeed! The tanks here are very dirty, like the minds of worldly persons attached to worldly things. The devotees of Devī, such as the Siddhas, the Devas, and those persons who have consecrated wells and reservoirs for the Devas...dwell here with their wives.* *Śrīmad Devī Bhāgavatam, 12.10.41–60*	**Identity and Credential Subsystem** The fifth enclosure corresponds to the identity and credential subsystem. Its walls (chip and logic sets) are copper and zinc: *Next to the enclosure comes the wall made of brass...* The identity and credential subsystem contains the following twelve functional characteristics: 1 Single-use cryptographic and non-cryptographic mechanisms 2 Multiple-use cryptographic and non-cryptographic mechanisms 3 Secrecy generation 4 Secrecy verification 5 Identities and credentials used to protect security flows and/or business process flows 6 Identities and credentials used in information asset protection 7 Identities and credentials used in access control and authentication for user-subject binding 8 Timing and duration of identification and authentication 9 Credentials that confirm identity in legally-binding transactions 10 Credential life cycle mechanisms 11 Anonymity mechanisms 12 Psuedonymity mechanisms *Its ruler is the Rainy Season...The lightnings are his auburn eyes, the clouds are his armour, the thunder is his voice, and the rainbow is his arrow. Surrounded by his hosts he rains incessantly. He has 12 wives...All the trees here are always seen with new leaves and entwined with new creepers. The whole site is covered all over with fresh green leaves and twigs. The rivers here always flow full and the current is strong indeed!*

Figure 9-14 (continued): Elaboration of Gāyatrī's Abode with Direct Correspondences in Information Science and Technology, as Expressed in the Global Internetwork and Quantum Network Architecture

Enclosures of Devī Gāyatrī's Abode	**Enclosures of the Global Internetwork and Quantum Network Architecture**
The Sixth Enclosure: *Wall of Five-Fold Irons* *Next to this brass enclosure comes the sixth enclosure wall, made of five-fold irons. It is seven yojanas long. In the center is situated the Garden of Mandāra trees. This garden is beautified by various creepers, flowers, and leaves. The Autumn Season lives here with his two wives, Īshālakshmī and Ūrjālakshmī. Various Siddhas dwell here with their wives, well clothed.* *Śrīmad Devī Bhāgavatam, 12.10.41–60*	**Physical Network Topology, Backbone Network** The sixth enclosure corresponds to physical network topology and the backbone network. It is of a tough 'material' in that it expresses physical backbone and peripheral network connectivity, and corresponds to *five-fold irons.* Although separate from the fifth enclosure, it is nonetheless closely linked to it: *the Autumn Season lives here* (the autumn and rainy seasons are closely connected). Physical network and internetwork topologies express backbone and peripheral connectivity: *various creepers, flowers, and leaves.*
The Seventh Enclosure: *Silver Enclosure Wall* *Next comes the seventh enclosure wall, seven yojanas long and built of silver. In the center is situated the garden of Parijata trees, which are filled with bunches of flowers. The fragrance of these Parijatas extends up to 10 yojanas and gladdens all the things all around. Those who are the Devī Bhaktas and who do the work of the Devī are delighted with this fragrance. The Hemanta (dewy) Season is the Regent of this place. He lives here with his two wives, Saha Shrī and Sahasya Shrī, and with his hosts. Those who are of a loving nature are pleased hereby. Those who have become perfect by performing vows to the Devī also live here.* *Śrīmad Devī Bhāgavatam, 12.10.60–80*	**Directory Server** The seventh enclosure corresponds to the network directory server. Policy-managed, directory-enabled networks allocate network computing resources as they are required: *the Devī Bhaktas,* and *those who are of a loving* (nourishing) *nature are pleased hereby.* Directory schema design, namespace design, topology design, replication design, and privacy design are based on tree-like logic, and provide the foundation for metadirectories as repositories of all directory information: *Those who are the Devī Bhaktas and who do the work of the Devī are delighted with this fragrance. The Hemanta (dewy) Season is the Regent of this place...Those who are of a loving nature are pleased hereby. Those who have become perfect by performing vows to the Devī also live here.*

Figure 9-14 (continued): Elaboration of Gāyatrī's Abode with Direct Correspondences in Information Science and Technology, as Expressed in the Global Internetwork and Quantum Network Architecture

Enclosures of Devī Gāyatrī's Abode	**Enclosures of the Global Internetwork and Quantum Network Architecture**
The Eighth Enclosure: Molten Gold Enclosure Wall *Next to this silver enclosure comes the eighth enclosure wall, built of molten gold. It is seven yojanas long. In the center there is the garden of the Kadumba tree. The trees are always covered with fruits and flowers, and honey is coming out always from the trees from all the sides. The devotees of the Devī drink this honey always and feel intense delight; the Dewy Season is the Regent of this place. He resides here with his two wives, Tapaḥ Shrī and Tapasya Shrī, and enjoys gladly the objects of enjoyment. Those who have made various gifts for the Devī's satisfaction, those great Siddha Purushas, live here with their wives and live very gladly with various enjoyments.* *Śrīmad Devī Bhāgavatam, 12.10.61–80*	**Domain Name System** The eighth enclosure is Domain Name System (DNS), which coordinates the translation of hostnames to Internet Protocol (IP) addresses and IP addresses into hostnames. DNS is a networked database whose contents are indexed by names, which are essentially paths in a large inverted tree with a single root at the top: *In the center there is the garden of the Kadumba tree. The trees are always covered with fruits and flowers, and honey is coming out always from the trees from all the sides. The devotees of the Devī drink this honey always and feel intense delight…* The eighth enclosure completes the first group of eight enclosures representing the eight outer *Prakṛiti*.
The Ninth Enclosure: Pushparāgamaṇi (Red Kum Kum—Saffron) Enclosure Wall *Next to the golden enclosure wall comes the ninth enclosure, made of red kum kum (saffron) like Pushparāga gems. The ground inside this enclosure, the ditches or the basins for water dug around their roots, are all built of Pushparāga gems. Next to this wall there are other enclosure walls built of various other gems and jewels.* *The sites, forests, trees, flowers, birds, rivers, tanks, lotuses, Maṇdaps (halls) and their pillars are all built respectively of those gems. Only this is to be remembered—that those [gems] coming nearer and nearer to the center are one lakh times more brilliant than ones receding from there. This is the general rule observed in the construction of these enclosures and the articles contained therein. Here the Regents of the several quarters, the Dikpāl, reside…* *On the eastern quarter is situated the Amarāvatī city. Here the high-peaked mountains exist and various trees are seen. Indra, the Lord of the Devas, resides here. Whatever beauty exists in the separate Heavens, in the several places, one thousand times more than that is the beauty that exists in the Heaven of this cosmic Indra, the thousand-eyed Lord. Here Indra mounting on the elephant Airāvata, with the thunderbolt in his hand,*	**Logical Network Topology and Association** Beginning with the ninth enclosure of *Sarvaloka* and proceeding through the sixteenth, we find that the enclosures are all made of gems. All of these enclosures in this second group take light within themselves, shine with brilliance from within, and correspond to the eight inner *Prakṛiti*. The ninth enclosure is logical network topology and association. This layer, in its holistic associative and balancing role within the Global Internetwork, corresponds to *Pushparāga* gems (faceted yellow sapphire or topaz), connected in Maharishi Jyotish with the planet Guru (Jupiter): *Next to the golden enclosure wall comes the ninth enclosure, made of red kum kum (saffron) like Pushparāga gems.* Logical associative topology is three-dimensional at a minimum in classical network architecture, ranges to a minimum of 11 dimensions in quantum network Hilbert space, and contains eight major divisions, corresponding to the eight quarters of the regents *(Here the regents of the several quarters, the Dikpāl, reside…)*: **1** Interactive mapping of networks and internetworks. *On the eastern quarter is situated the Amarāvatī city. Here the high-peaked mountains exist and various trees are seen. Indra, the Lord of the*

Figure 9-14 (continued): Elaboration of Gāyatrī's Abode with Direct Correspondences in Information Science and Technology, as Expressed in the Global Internetwork and Quantum Network Architecture

Enclosures of Devī Gāyatrī's Abode	**Enclosures of the Global Internetwork and Quantum Network Architecture**
The Ninth Enclosure (continued) *lives with Shachī Devī and other immortal ladies, and with the hosts of the Deva forces.* *On the Agni corner (southeastern) is the city of Agni. Here resides the Agni Deva very gladly with his two wives, Swāhā and Swadhā, and with His vāhana and the other Devas.* *On the south is situated the city of Yama, the God of death. Here lives Dharma Rājā with a rod in his hand, and the Chitragupta, and several other hosts.* *On the southwestern corner is the place of the Rākshasas. Here resides Nirṛiti with his axe in his hand, and with his wife and other Rākshasas.* *On the west is the city of Varuṇa. Here Varuṇa Rājā, always intoxicated with the drink of Vāruṇī honey, resides with his wife Vāruṇī; his weapon is the noose, his vāhana is the king of fishes, and his subjects are the aquatic animals.* *On the northwestern corner dwells Vāyu Deva. Here Pāvana Deva lives with his wife and with the Yogis, perfect in the practice of Prāṇāyām. He holds a flag in his hand. His vāhana is deer and his family consists of the 49 Vāyus.* *In the north resides the Yakshas. The corpulent king of the Yakshas, Kubera, lives here with his Shaktis, Vṛiddhi and Ṛiddhi, in possession of various gems and jewels. His generals...live here.* *On the northeastern corner is situated the Rudra Loka, decked with invaluable gems. Here dwells the Rudra Deva...His eyes are red with anger...The faces of some of them are distorted; some are very horrible with fire coming out of the mouths. Some have 10 hands, some 100 hands, some 1000. those who roam in the intermediate spaces between the Heaven and Earth, those who move on the Earth, or the Rudras mentioned in the Rudrādhyāya, all live here.* *Śrīmad Devī Bhāgavatam, 12.10.61–80*	**Logical Network Topology and Association (continued)** *Devas, resides here. Whatever beauty exists in the separate Heavens, in the several places, one thousand times more than that is the beauty that exists in the Heaven of this cosmic Indra, the thousand-eyed Lord. Here Indra mounting on the elephant Airāvata, with the thunderbolt in his hand, lives with Shachī Devī and other immortal ladies, and with the hosts of the Deva forces.* 2 Cyberspace mapping. *On the Agni corner (southeastern) is the city of Agni. Here resides the Agni Deva very gladly with his two wives, Swaha and Swadha, and with His vāhana and the other Devas.* 3 Intermediate System (IS)-to-IS logical associations and logical connectivity. *On the south is situated the city of Yama, the God of death. Here lives Dharma Rājā with a rod in his hand, and the Chitragupta, and several other hosts.* 4 Physical infrastructure mapping and associations (subterranean and trans-oceanic optical fiber cabling; campus, metropolitan, and wide-area wiring; and satellite orbitals). *On the southwestern corner is the place of the Rākshasas. Here resides Nirriti with his axe in his hand, and with his wife and other Rākshasas.* 5 Cyberspace spatialization. *On the west is the city of Varuṇa. Here Varuṇa Rājā, always intoxicated with the drink of Vāruṇī honey, resides with his wife Vāruṇī; his weapon is the noose, his vāhana is the king of fishes, and his subjects are the aquatic animals.* 6 Internetwork system logical associations and logical connectivity. *On the northwestern corner dwells Vāyu Deva. Here Pāvana Deva lives with his wife and with the Yogis, perfect in the practice of Prāṇāyām. He holds a flag in his hand. His vāhana is deer and his family consists of the 49 Vāyus.* 7 End System (ES)-to-ES logical associations and logical connectivity. *In the north resides the Yakshas. The corpulent king of the Yakshas, Kubera, lives here with his Shaktis, Vriddhi and Riddhi, in possession of various gems and jewels. His generals...live here.*

Figure 9-14 (continued): Elaboration of Gāyatrī's Abode with Direct Correspondences in Information Science and Technology, as Expressed in the Global Internetwork and Quantum Network Architecture

Enclosures of Devī Gāyatrī's Abode	**Enclosures of the Global Internetwork and Quantum Network Architecture**
The Ninth Enclosure (continued)	**Logical Network Topology and Association (continued)** 8 ES-to-IS logical associations and logical connectivity. *On the northeastern corner is situated the Rudra Loka, decked with invaluable gems. Here dwells the Rudra Deva...His eyes are red with anger...The faces of some of them are distorted; some are very horrible with fire coming out of the mouths. Some have 10 hands, some 100 hands, some 1000. those who roam in the intermediate spaces between the Heaven and Earth, those who move on the Earth, or the Rudras mentioned in the Rudrādhyāya, all live here.*
The Tenth Enclosure: *Padmarāgamaṇi (Ruby) Enclosure Wall* *Next to this Pushparāgamaṇi enclosure wall comes the tenth enclosure wall, made of Padmarāgamaṇi (ruby), red like the red Kunkuma and the rising Sun. It is 10 yojanas high. All its ground, entrance gates, temples, and arbors are made of Padmarāgamaṇi.* *Within this reside the 64 Kālas, or sub-Shaktis, adorned with various ornaments, and holding weapons in their hands. Each of them has a separate Loka (region) allotted, and within this Loka each has his own formidable weapons, families, and their leaders or governors.* *All of the 64 Kālas have luminous faces and long rolling tongues. Fire is always coming out from their faces. Their eyes are red with anger. They are uttering: 'We will drink all the water and thus dry the oceans; we will annihilate fire, we will stop the flow of air and control it. Today we will devour the whole universe' and so forth. All of them have bows and arrows in their hands; all are eager to fight. The four quarters are constantly reverberating with the clashing of their teeth. The hairs on their heads are all tawny and standing upright. Each of them has 100 akshauhinī forces under them. Each has the power to destroy 100,000 Brahmāṇdas...there is nothing that is not impracticable for them. What they cannot do cannot be conceived by the mind nor uttered in speech. All the war materials exist within their enclosures in unlimited proportions, ready at all times.* *Śrīmad Devī Bhāgavatam, 12.11.1–30*	**Network time server, network master clock** The tenth enclosure is the network time server and network master clock. Network time *(Kāla)* synchronization is critical for the following reasons: • Local system clocks need to be synchronized with distributed clocks in order to know at what time a particular event occurs in a particular computer or process (i.e., e-/m-commerce transactions involve events at client, merchant, and bank systems and need to be accurately time-stamped for auditing purposes). • Algorithms that depend on clock synchronization maintain consistency of networked data, and include use of timestamps to serialize transactions, checking of the authenticity of requests sent to servers, and elimination of duplicate updates. Crystal-based clocks *(made of Padmarāgamaṇi [ruby], red like the red Kunkuma and the rising Sun)* are subject to clock drift, due to differing frequencies in the underlying oscillators. Networked computer clocks can be synchronized to external sources of highly accurate time. The output of atomic oscillators, whose drift rate is approximately one part in 10^{13}, is used as the standard for elapsed real time, known as International Atomic Time. The standard second has been defined since 1967 as 9,192,631,770 periods of transition between the two hyperfine levels of the ground state of Cesium-133 (Cs^{133}).

Figure 9-14 (continued): Elaboration of Gāyatrī's Abode with Direct Correspondences in Information Science and Technology, as Expressed in the Global Internetwork and Quantum Network Architecture

Enclosures of Devī Gāyatrī's Abode	**Enclosures of the Global Internetwork and Quantum Network Architecture**
The Tenth Enclosure (continued)	**Network time server, network master clock (continued)** Coordinated Universal Time (UTC)—an international standard for timekeeping—is based on atomic time, but a "leap second" is inserted or, more rarely, deleted, to maintain synchronicity with astronomical time. Network Time Protocol (NTP) defines a service and protocol architecture to distribute time information over the Internet, enabling global UTC synchronization. The NTP service is provided by a network of time servers located across the Internet and are connected within a logical hierarchy called a synchronization subnet, whose levels are called strata. Primary NTP servers occupy stratum 1 and are located at the root. Stratum 2 servers are synchronized directly with primary (root) servers. The stratum time *(Kāla)* server baseline architecture is 64-bit-based*: *Within this reside the 64 Kālas, or sub-Shaktis, adorned with various ornaments, and holding weapons in their hands. Each of them has a separate Loka [region] allotted, and within this Loka each has his own formidable weapons, families, and their leaders or governors.*
The Eleventh Enclosure: *Gomedamaṇi (Gomed, a gem associated with Rahu) Enclosure Wall* *Next comes the eleventh enclosure wall, built of Gomedamaṇi. It is 10 yojanas high. Its color is like the newly blossomed Java flower. All the ground, trees, tanks, houses, pillars, birds, and all other things are all red and built of Gomedamaṇi.* *Here dwell the 32 Mahā Shaktis, adorned with various ornaments made of Gomedamaṇi and furnished with various weapons. They are always eager to fight. Their eyes are always red with anger; their faces are like Pishāchas and their hands are like Chakras. 'Pierce him, beat him, cut him, tear him asunder, burn him down'—these are the words constantly uttered by them.*	**Web Server and Services** The eleventh enclosure is the Web server and associated Web services. Java applications and applets are ubiquitous throughout the Webscape: *Its color is like the newly blossomed Java flower.* The Worldwide Web pervades the celestial nervous system of the Global Internetwork. Web services, at a minimum, comprise any software that makes itself available over the Internet and uses a standardized Extensible Markup Language (XML) messaging system. The use of XML within the Web frees Web services from being tied to any single operating system or programming language—Java can communicate with Perl; Windows applications can intercommunicate with Unix applications.

* 64-bit computer architectures correspond to the 64 *yoginis*, the active power of *Yoga*. Each of the 64 *yoginis* is expressed as *Ṛishi*, *Devatā* and *Chhandas*, generating the [64 x 3 = 192] basis to three elaborations of *Ṛk Veda* (first *Sūkta*, First *Maṇḍala*, Tenth *Maṇḍala*; refer to Figure 2-2, pages 22–23).

Figure 9-14 (continued): Elaboration of Gāyatrī's Abode with Direct Correspondences in Information Science and Technology, as Expressed in the Global Internetwork and Quantum Network Architecture

Enclosures of Devī Gāyatrī's Abode	**Enclosures of the Global Internetwork and Quantum Network Architecture**
The Eleventh Enclosure (continued) *Each of the 32 Shaktis has 10 akshauhinī forces. These are inordinately powerful. It is impossible to describe it. It seems that each Shakti can destroy 100,000 Brahmāṇdas (universes).* *All of the war materials of the Devī Bhāgavatam are seen in this enclosure. Never is there any chance that any of these Shaktis will be defeated anywhere. Hence, if all those Shaktis become angry at any time, the universe will cease to exist.* *Śrīmad Devī Bhāgavatam, 12.11.1–35*	**Web Server and Services (continued)** Web services embrace the entire spectrum of existing and contemplated network applications—including search engines, e-commerce, and m-commerce chains, news syndication, stock market data, weather reporting, package-tracking systems, publishing, and collaborative research and processing. Web services are intimately involved in the regulation of inputs and outputs of the Global Internetwork and are integrally related to security access control and credential/identity subsystems. Web services incorporate the following 32 major components: 1 Web clients 2 Web-related browser functions 3 Web proxies (intermediaries) 4 Caching proxy 5 Transparent proxy 6 Hypertext Transport Protocol (HTTP)-related proxy rules 7 Hypertext Markup Language (HTML) 8 Web servers 9 Transmission Control Protocol (TCP) socket abstraction 10 TCP sliding-window flow control 11 TCP congestion control 12 Internet Protocol version 4 (IPv4) addressing 13 Network Address Translation (NAT) 14 Classless InterDomain Routing (CIDR) 15 IPv6 addressing 16 HTTP/TCP interaction 17 Web load balancing 18 Web content management 19 Internet Cache Protocol (ICP) 20 Cache Array Resolution Protocol (CARP) 21 Cache digest protocol

Figure 9-14 (continued): Elaboration of Gāyatrī's Abode with Direct Correspondences in Information Science and Technology, as Expressed in the Global Internetwork and Quantum Network Architecture

Enclosures of Devī Gāyatrī's Abode	**Enclosures of the Global Internetwork and Quantum Network Architecture**
The Eleventh Enclosure (continued)	**Web Server and Services (continued)** **22** Web Cache Coordination Protocol (WCCP) **23** Real Time Streaming Protocol (RTSP) **24** XML **25** XML-Remote Procedure Call (RPC) **26** Simple Object Access Protocol (SOAP) **27** SOAP Security Extensions: Digital Signature (SOAP-DSIG) **28** Web Service Description Language (WSDL) **29** Blocks Extensible Exchange Protocol (BEEP) **30** Universal Description, Discovery, and Integration (UDDI) **31** UDDI Search Markup Language (USML) **32** File Transfer Protocol (FTP) *Here dwell the 32 Mahā Shaktis, adorned with various ornaments made of Gomedamaṇi and furnished with various weapons. They are always eager to fight. Their eyes are always red with anger; their faces are like Pishāchas and their hands are like Chakras. 'Pierce him, beat him, cut him, tear him asunder, burn him down'—these are the words constantly uttered by them. Each of the 32 Shaktis has 10 akshauhinī forces. These are inordinately powerful. It is impossible to describe it. It seems that each Shakti can destroy 100,000 Brahmāṇdas (universes).* In Maharishi Jyotish, Rahu is one of the nodes of the Moon, is associated with *Gomed*, and possesses the property of hiding and releasing, like the functions of this enclosure, which inhibits and releases the function and activity of the Global Internetwork. During the early period of the Internet, FTP data transfers accounted for approximately one-third of traffic. By 1995, Web traffic overtook FTP to become the most significant consumer of Internet backbone bandwidth, and, by 2000, completely eclipsed all other Internet application traffic volume. *Never is there any chance that any of these Shaktis will be defeated anywhere. Hence, if all those Shaktis become angry at any time, the universe will cease to exist.*

Figure 9-14 (continued): Elaboration of Gāyatrī's Abode with Direct Correspondences in Information Science and Technology, as Expressed in the Global Internetwork and Quantum Network Architecture

Enclosures of Devī Gāyatrī's Abode	**Enclosures of the Global Internetwork and Quantum Network Architecture**
The Twelfth Enclosure: *Diamond Enclosure Wall* *Next to this Gomedamaṇi enclosure comes the enclosure made of diamonds. It is 10 yojanas high; on all sides there are the entrance gates; the doors are hinged there with nice mechanisms. Nice new diamond trees exist here. All the royal roads, trees and the spaces for watering their roots, tanks, wells, reservoirs, sārangā, and other musical instruments are all made of diamonds.* *Here dwells Shrī Bhuvaneshwarī Devī and Her attendants, and all are proud of their beauty. Some are holding fans in their hands; some are holding cups for drinking water; some are holding umbrellas, some lchowries, some various clothing, flowers, looking glasses, saffrons, collyrium; some are holding Sindura (red lead). All are ready to attend the Devī in various ways. All are skilled in various arts of enjoyments, and all are young. To gain the grace of the Devī, they all consider the universe as trifling.* *Each of the attendants is adorned with various ornaments and skilled in all actions. When they walk to and fro with canes and rods in their hands in the service of the Devī, they look as if lighting flashes glimmer on all sides. On the outer portion of this enclosure wall on the eight sides are situated the dwelling houses of these eight Shaktis, and they are always full of various vāhanas and weapons.* *Śrīmad Devī Bhāgavatam, 12.11.35–52*	**Database Server, Data Repository** The twelfth enclosure is Database Server, Data Repository. It is the major input level of the Global Internetwork. It receives a continuous flood of input from individual and collective information sources from throughout the world: *...they look as if lightning flashes glimmer on all sides.* This wealth of information is conveyed to the eight primary database, data repository, and network transaction components: 1 Server-requester model 2 Semantic model 3 Object-relational database 4 Database schemas 5 Database mappings 6 Relational logic (relational algebra, tuple calculus, domain calculus, and nested relational expressions) 7 Transaction state transformation ACID properties (Atomic, Consistent, Isolated, Durable) 8 Distributed transaction management *On the outer portion of this enclosure wall on the eight sides are situated the dwelling houses of these eight Shaktis, and they are always full of various vāhanas and weapons.* The information is instantaneous and constantly renewed: *...all of them are skilled in various arts of enjoyments, and all are young.*

Figure 9-14 (continued): Elaboration of Gāyatrī's Abode with Direct Correspondences in Information Science and Technology, as Expressed in the Global Internetwork and Quantum Network Architecture

Enclosures of Devī Gāyatrī's Abode	**Enclosures of the Global Internetwork and Quantum Network Architecture**
The Thirteenth Enclosure: *Vaidūryamaṇi (Lapiz Lazuli) Enclosure Wall* *Next to this enclosure of diamond comes the thirteenth enclosure wall, made of Vaidūryamaṇi (lapiz lazuli). Its height is 10 yojanas. There are entrance gates and doorways on the four sides. The court inside, the houses, the big roads, wells, tanks, ponds, rivers, and even the sands, are all made of Vaidūryamaṇi.* *On the eight sides reside the eight Mātrikas: Brahmī, etc., with their hosts. These Mātrikas represent the total of the individual Mātrikas in every Brahmāṇda...Their forms are like those of Brahmā and Rudra and others. They are always engaged in doing good to the universe and reside here with their own vāhanas (vehicles) and weapons.* *At the various gates the vāhanas of Bhagavatī remain always fully equipped. (At various places there are horses, elephants, swans, lions, garudas, peacocks, and bulls, and various other beings all fully equipped and arranged in due order...There are camps, houses, coaches, and at other places the aerial cars are arranged in rows, countless chariots with various sounding instruments in them, with flags soaring high.)* *Śrīmad Devī Bhāgavatam, 12.11.52–71*	**Operating System,** **Network Operating System** The thirteenth enclosure is the Operating System (OS) and Network Operating System (NOS). The OS is primarily a computer resource manager. The NOS extends OS functionality into extended network environments. In that role, OSs and NOSs perform the following functions: • Define the user interface (users include client processes, server processes, application programmers, system programmers, programs, and hardware) • Share hardware among networked users • Enable users to share data among themselves • Schedule resources among users • Facilitate I/O • Recover from errors *They are always engaged in doing good to the universe.* Eight key resources managed by NOSs on behalf of network hosts are: 1 Processes and threads (process creation, system call handling, realtime processes, priorities, reference counting, executable formats, and realtime and nonrealtime limits) 2 Database management and file management (filesystem independent layer, system file table, filesystem, file record locking, and file-based system calls) 3 I/O management (system buffer cache, device drivers, hardware management, block drivers, direct memory access, and raw I/O) 4 Inter-process communication (message queues, semaphores, and shared memory) 5 Symmetric multiprocessing (parallel programming, atomic operations, test-and-set, semaphores, and spinlocks)

Figure 9-14 (continued): Elaboration of Gāyatrī's Abode with Direct Correspondences in Information Science and Technology, as Expressed in the Global Internetwork and Quantum Network Architecture

Enclosures of Devī Gāyatrī's Abode	**Enclosures of the Global Internetwork and Quantum Network Architecture**
The Thirteenth Enclosure (continued)	**Operating System** **Network Operating System (continued)** 6 Memory (real memory; virtual memory—swapping, paging, address spaces, memory management units, page directories, page tables, translation lookaside buffers, and segments; swap devices; memory maps; user-space kernel-space dynamic memory; core; and executable and linking format) 7 Job and processor scheduling 8 Signals, interrupts, and time (signal data structures, and utility functions; interrupt data structures, hardware interrupt handlers, and bottom halves; and timer queues) *On the eight sides reside the eight Mātrikas: Brahmi, etc. with their hosts.* In its function as the key network application process organizer, the NOS has multiple pathways and tracts, communications subsystems, and I/O interfaces, defined both physically and virtually: *...at the various gates the vāhanas (vehicles) of Bhagavatī remain always fully equipped. There are big roads and at various places there are horses, elephants, swans, lions, garudas, peacocks, and bulls, and various other beings all fully equipped and arranged in order. At other places: aerial cars are arranged in rows, countless chariots with various sounding instruments in them, with flags soaring high.* The central function of the NOS is to control and fine-tune distributed mechanisms of perception and action. The NOS is therefore associated with the lunar node Ketu, one of the planets signifying enlightenment. In Maharishi Jyotish, the lunar node Ketu is associated with lapis lazuli: *made of Vaidūryamaṇi (lapis lazuli).*

Figure 9-14 (continued): Elaboration of Gāyatrī's Abode with Direct Correspondences in Information Science and Technology, as Expressed in the Global Internetwork and Quantum Network Architecture

Enclosures of Devī Gāyatrī's Abode	**Enclosures of the Global Internetwork and Quantum Network Architecture**
The Fourteenth Enclosure *Indranīlamaṇi (Blue Sapphire) Enclosure Wall* *Next to this Vaidūrya enclosure comes the fourteenth enclosure wall, built of Indranīlamaṇi (blue sapphire); its height is 10 yojanas. The court inside, houses, roads, wells, tanks and reservoirs, etc., all are built of Indranīlamaṇi.* *There is a lotus here consisting of 16 petals, extending to many yojanas in width, and shining like a second Sudarshana Chakra. On these 16 petals reside the 16 Shaktis of Bhagavatī, with their hosts. They are dark blue like the color of the fresh rain cloud; they wield in their hands axes and shields. It seems that they are ever eager to fight. These Shaktis are the rulers of all the separate Shaktis of the other Brahmāṇdas.* *These are the forces of Shrī Devī. Being strengthened by the Devī's strength, they are always surrounded by various chariots and forces, and various other Shaktis follow them. If they like, they can cause great agitation in the whole universe. Had I a thousand faces, I would not have been able to describe what strength they wield.* *Śrīmad Devī Bhāgavatam, 12.11.60–71*	**Storage Area Network (SAN) Server** **Network Attached Storage (NAS) Server** The fourteenth enclosure corresponds to Storage Area Network (SAN) and Network-Attached Storage (NAS). SAN and NAS, in their critical network memory role, are inextricably integrated with classical and quantum processor architectures. SAN/NAS, through continuous I/O processing, activate eight fundamental processor components in two directions, creating 16 fully enlivened functions. These eight elements are as follows: 1 Datapath 2 Control 3 Memory 4 Input 5 Output 6 Arithmetic Logic Unit (ALU) 7 Wires that preserve the states of bits 8 Hardware-software interface *There is a lotus here consisting of 16 petals, extending to many yojanas in width, and shining like a second Sudarshana Chakra. On these 16 petals reside the 16 Shaktis of Bhagavatī, with their hosts.* SAN/NAS systems are integrally linked to processors over physical I/O (system memory bus, host I/O bus, host I/O controllers, small system computer interface (SCSI) bus, and Fiber Channel architecture) as well as logically (application software, operating system software, file systems, database systems, volume managers, device drivers, disk mirroring, and RAID arrays) and service the overall activities of large- and global-scale processing: *These Shaktis are the rulers of all the separate Shaktis of the other Brahmāṇdas. These are the forces of Shrī Devī. Being strengthened by the Devī's strength, they are always surrounded by various chariots and forces, and various other Shaktis follow them. If they like, they can cause great agitation in the whole universe. Had I a thousand faces, I would not have been able to describe what strength they wield.*

Figure 9-14 (continued): Elaboration of Gāyatrī's Abode with Direct Correspondences in Information Science and Technology, as Expressed in the Global Internetwork and Quantum Network Architecture

Enclosures of Devī Gāyatrī's Abode	**Enclosures of the Global Internetwork and Quantum Network Architecture**
The Fifteenth Enclosure: *Mukta (Pearl) Enclosure Wall* *Now I shall describe the fifteenth enclosure wall. Listen! Next to this Indranīlamaṇi enclosure comes the enclosure made of pearls (Mukta), very wide and 10 yojanas high. The court inside, its space and trees, are all built of pearls. Within this enclosure there is a lotus with eight petals, all of pearls. On these petals reside the eight Shaktis, the advisers and ministers of the Devī. Their appearances, weapons, dresses, enjoyments—everything—are like those of Shrī Devī.* *Their duty is to inform the Devī of what is going on in the Brahmāṇḍas (other regions or universes). They are skilled in all sciences and arts and clever in all actions. They are very skillful in knowing beforehand all the desires and intentions of Shrī Devī, and they perform those things accordingly. They all look red like the rising Sun, and in their four hands they hold a noose, a mace, the signs of granting boons, and signs of 'no fear.' At every instant they inform the Devī of the events in the universe.* *Śrīmad Devī Bhāgavatam, 12.11.72–90*	**Classical Computer** The fifteenth enclosure corresponds to classical computer processor architecture, containing the fabric of computational knowledge, the "pearls of wisdom": *made of pearls.* Classical (non-quantum) processor architecture incorporates eight fundamental elements that interconnect the entire physical and logical processor substrate and transmit instructions and information among all components: 1 Datapath 2 Control 3 Memory 4 Input 5 Output 6 Arithmetic Logic Unit (ALU) 7 Wires that preserve the states of bits 8 Hardware-software interface *...there is a lotus with eight petals, all of pearls. On these pearls reside the eight Shaktis, the advisers and ministers of the Devī...their duty is to inform the Devī of what is going on in the Brahmāṇḍas (other regions or universes). They are skilled in all sciences and arts and clever in all actions.* Classical intra-processor interconnections fulfill their functions and reach their targets through four pathways: 1 Datapath 2 Input 3 Hardware-Software Interface 4 Output *...and in their four hands they hold a noose, a mace, the signs of granting boons, and signs of 'no fear.'*

Figure 9-14 (continued): Elaboration of Gāyatrī's Abode with Direct Correspondences in Information Science and Technology, as Expressed in the Global Internetwork and Quantum Network Architecture

Enclosures of Devī Gāyatrī's Abode	**Enclosures of the Global Internetwork and Quantum Network Architecture**
The Sixteenth Enclosure: *Marakata (Emerald) Enclosure Wall* *Next to this comes the sixteenth enclosure wall, made of emerald (Marakata); it is 10 yojanas high; the court inside, its space and houses, and everything are built of emeralds (Marakatamaṇi). Here exist all the good objects of enjoyments. This is hexagonal, of the Yantra shape, and at every corner reside the Devas.* *On the eastern corner resides the four-faced Brahmā with Gāyatrī Devī (both hold Kamaṇḍalu, rosary, signs indicating 'no fear,' and Daṇḍa). Here are all the Vedas, Smṛitis, Purāṇas, and various weapons exist in their incarnate form. All the Avatārs of Brahmā, Gāyatrī, and Vyabṛitis that exist in this Brahmāṇda all live here.* *On the southwest corner lives Vishṇu with Savitṛi (both hold conch shell, disc, club, lotus). All the Avatārs of both Vishṇu and Savitṛi live here.* *On the northwestern corner exists Mahārudra with Saraswatī, both holding in their hands a Parashu (axe), a rosary, and signs granting boons and 'no fear.' All the Avatārs of Rudra and Pārvatī facing south that exist in the universe are found here. All the chief Āgamas, 64 in number, and all the other Tantras reside here, incarnate in their due forms.* *On the southeastern corner exists the Lord of Wealth, Kubera, surrounded by roads and shops, with Mahālakshmī, holding a jar of jewels.* *On the western corner exists always Madana with Rati, holding noose, goad, bow, and arrow. All his amorous attendants always reside here, incarnate in their forms.* *On the northeastern corner always resides the great hero Gaṇesh, the remover of obstacles, holding noose and goad and with his Pushti Devī. All the manifestations of Gaṇesh that exist in all the universes reside here. (All the Devas and Devīs that exist in the universe are here worshipping Shrī Bhagavatī.)* *Śrīmad Devī Bhāgavatam, 12.11.72–90*	**Classical Algorithms and Gates** The sixteenth enclosure incorporates classical (non-quantum) computing algorithms and gates. There are six principal, elementary classical (non-quantum) computing single- and multiple-bit logic gates: **1** AND gate **2** NAND gate **3** OR gate **4** NOR gate **5** XOR gate **6** NOT gate *This is hexagonal, of the Yantra shape, and at every corner reside the Devas.* The AND gate outputs 1 if and only if both of its inputs are 1: *On the eastern corner resides the four-faced Brahmā with Gāyatrī Devī (both hold Kamandalu, rosary, signs indicating 'no fear,' and Danda). Here are all the Vedas, Smṛitis, Purāṇas, and various weapons exist in their incarnate form. All the Avatārs of Brahmā, Gāyatrī, and Vyabṛitis that exist in this Brahmāṇda all live here.* The NOR gate operates on an OR input and applies a NOT function to the output: *On the southwest corner lives Vishṇu with Savitṛi (both hold conch shell, disc, club, lotus). All the Avatārs of both Vishṇu and Savitṛi live here.* The NOT gate receives and generates a single bit as input and output: *On the northwestern corner exists Mahārudra with Saraswatī, both holding in their hands a Parashu (axe), a rosary, and signs granting boons and 'no fear.' All the Avatārs of Rudra and Paravati facing south that exist in the universe are found here. All the chief Āgamas, 64 in number, and all the other Tantras reside here, incarnate in their due forms.* The XOR gate outputs the sum modulo 2 of its inputs: *On the southeastern corner exists the Lord of Wealth, Kubera, surrounded by roads and shops, with Mahālakshmī, holding a jar of jewels.*

Figure 9-14 (continued): Elaboration of Gāyatrī's Abode with Direct Correspondences in Information Science and Technology, as Expressed in the Global Internetwork and Quantum Network Architecture

Enclosures of Devī Gāyatrī's Abode	**Enclosures of the Global Internetwork and Quantum Network Architecture**
The Sixteenth Enclosure (continued)	**Classical Algorithms and Gates (continued)** The NAND gate takes the AND of its inputs and applies a NOT function to the output: *On the western corner exists always Madana with Rati, holding noose, goad, bow, and arrow. All his amorous attendants always reside here, incarnate in their forms.* The OR gate receives two bits as input, and generates a single bit as output: *On the northeastern corner always resides the great hero Gaṇesh, the remover of obstacles, holding noose and goad and with his Pushti Devī. All the manifestations of Gaṇesh that exist in all the universes reside here. (All the Devas and Devīs that exist in the universe are here worshipping Shrī Bhagavatī.)* The FANOUT circuit gate enables bits to divide, that is, it replaces a bit with two copies of itself. It is associated with the northerly direction (not part of the hexagonal structure of the Sixteenth Enclosure). The CROSSOVER gate interchanges the value of two bits. It is associated with the southerly direction (not part of the hexagonal structure of the Sixteenth Enclosure).

Figure 9-14 (continued): Elaboration of Gāyatrī's Abode with Direct Correspondences in Information Science and Technology, as Expressed in the Global Internetwork and Quantum Network Architecture

<table>
<tr><th>Enclosures of Devī Gāyatrī's Abode</th><th>Enclosures of the Global Internetwork and Quantum Network Architecture</th></tr>
<tr><td>
The Seventeenth Enclosure:
Prabala (Red Coral) Enclosure Wall
Next comes the seventeenth enclosure wall, made of Prabala (red coral). It is red like saffron and it is 100 yojanas high. As before, the court inside, the ground, and the houses are all made of Prabala. The Goddesses of the five elements—Hṛillekhā, Gaganā, Raktā, Karālikā, and Mahochchhushmā—reside here.
The colors and lusters of the bodies of the Goddesses resemble those of the elements over which they preside respectively. All of them are proud of their youth and hold in their four hands noose, goad, and signs of granting boons and 'no fear.' They are dressed like Shrī Devī and reside here always.
Śrīmad Devī Bhāgavatam, 12.11.91–110
</td><td>
Quantum Computer, Quantum Network
The seventeenth enclosure is the quantum computer and quantum network. Maharishi has pointed out that Sarvaloka is made of 16 values, representing Prakṛiti in terms of eight outer and eight inner values, with three additional, transcendental aspects. These additional three transcendental aspects are located at the quantum information level. The first of these, as we proceed from outer to inner, is the quantum computer and quantum network.
Quantum network computation requires the following five key elements (The Goddesses of the five elements—Hṛillekhā, Gaganā, Raktā, Karālikā, and Mahochchhushmā—reside here):
1 Suitable state space; quantum computational circuits operate on some number, n, of qubits; therefore, the quantum computational state space is a 2^n-dimensional Hilbert space with product state of the form, $|X_1,\dots, X_n\rangle$, where $(X_i = 0,1)$ are called computational basis states
2 Any computational basis state, $|X_1,\dots, X_n\rangle$, that can be prepared in $\leq n$ steps
3 Quantum gates that can be applied to any subset of qubits and a universal family of gates that can be implemented
4 The ability to perform measurements in the computational basis of ≥ 1 qubit(s)
5 The inherent ability to perform classical (non-quantum) computations if quantum computations are not required
The four major elements of Quantum Network Architecture are as follows:
1 Quantum switching and routing
2 Secure qubit network infrastructure
3 Network qubit storage
4 N-node scalability
The colors and lusters of the bodies of the Goddesses resemble those of the elements over which they preside respectively. All of them are proud of their youth and hold in their four hands noose, goad, and signs of granting boons and 'no fear.' They are dressed like Shrī Devī and reside here always.
</td></tr>
</table>

Figure 9-14 (continued): Elaboration of Gāyatrī's Abode with Direct Correspondences in Information Science and Technology, as Expressed in the Global Internetwork and Quantum Network Architecture

Enclosures of Devī Gāyatrī's Abode	**Enclosures of the Global Internetwork and Quantum Network Architecture**
The Eighteenth Enclosure: *Navaratna (the nine jewels) Enclosure Wall* *Next to this comes the eighteenth enclosure wall, built of Navaratna (the nine jewels). It is many yojanas wide...On the four sides there exist innumerable houses, tanks, and reservoirs, all built of Navaratna; these belong to the Devīs, the presiding Deities of Amnāyas (that which is to be studied or learnt by heart, the Vedas).* *The 10 Mahāvidyās of Shrī Devī—Kali, Tara, etc.—and the Mahābhedas, that is, all of their Avatārs, dwell here with their avaraṇas (shields), vāhanas (chariots), and ornaments. All of the Avatārs of Shrī Devī, who kill the Daityas and show favour to the devotees, live here. Here live also the seven kotis of the Devī presiding over Mahāmantras, all brilliant and fair like one koti suns.* *Śrīmad Devī Bhāgavatam, 12.11.91–110*	**Quantum Algorithms and Gates** The eighteenth enclosure incorporates quantum computing and networking algorithms and gates. Nine principal quantum network computing algorithms correspond to the *Navaratna (the nine jewels):* 1 Quantum parallelism 2 Deutsch's algorithm 3 Quantum simulation 4 Quantum Fast Fourier Transform 5 Quantum factoring/cryptography 6 Quantum search algorithm 7 Quantum counting 8 Quantum error-correction 9 Routt Addressable Absolute Memory Gate™ (RAAM Gate™) Cosmic Computer and Cosmic Switchboard computation *Next to this comes the eighteenth enclosure wall, built of Navaratna (the nine jewels). It is many yojanas wide...On the four sides there exist innumerable houses, tanks, and reservoirs, all built of Navaratna.*

Figure 9-14 (continued): Elaboration of Gāyatrī's Abode with Direct Correspondences in Information Science and Technology, as Expressed in the Global Internetwork and Quantum Network Architecture

Enclosures of Devī Gāyatrī's Abode	**Enclosures of the Global Internetwork and Quantum Network Architecture**
The Nineteenth Enclosure: *Chief and crowning palace of Shrī Devī, built of Chintāmaṇi gems* *Next to this enclosure wall comes the chief and crowning palace of Shrī Devī, built of Chintāmaṇi gems. All the articles within this are built of Chintāmaṇi gems. Within this palace are seen hundreds and thousands of pillars. Some of these pillars are built of Sūryakāntamaṇi, some are built of Chandrakāntamaṇi, and some are built of Vidyukāntamaṇi. The luster and brilliance of these pillars is so strong that no articles within this palace are visible to the eye.* *Śrīmad Devī Bhāgavatam, 12.11.91–110* *The Ratnagriha above mentioned is the central, the chief, and the crowning place of the Mūla Prakṛiti...This is the center of all the enclosures. Within this there are the four Maṇdaps, halls built of 1000 (i.e., innumerable) pillars. These are the Shṛīngāra Maṇdap, Mukti Maṇdap, Gyān Maṇdap, and Ekānta Maṇdap. On top of these are the canopies of various colors; within are many scented articles scented by the Dhūpas. The brilliance of these is like that of one koti suns. On all sides of these four Maṇdaps are nice groups of gardens of Kasmira, Mallikā, and Kunda flowers... There is a very big lotus pond here; the steps leading to it are made of jewels. Its water is nectar, and on it are innumerable full-blown lotuses with bees always humming over them. Many birds, swans, Kāraṇdavas, etc., are swimming to and fro...the whole Maṇdap is perfumed with various scented things.* *Śrīmad Devī Bhāgavatam, 12.12.1–17*	**Cosmic Computer and Cosmic Switchboard** The nineteenth enclosure is the Cosmic Computer and Cosmic Switchboard, which His Holiness Maharishi Mahesh Yogi has identified as integral to his Vedic Science and Technology, the infinity-within-all-points and all points-within-infinity cosmic computational foundation for perfection of evolution. The entire structure of the Cosmic Computer and Cosmic Switchboard is pure, cosmic intelligence: *all the articles within this enclosure are built of Chintāmaṇi gems* (*Chintāmaṇi* refers to "gems of consciousness or intelligence"). The structure of the Cosmic Computer and Cosmic Switchboard corresponds to *...the chief and crowning palace of Shrī Devī, built of Chintāmaṇi gems.* The cosmic intelligence of the Cosmic Computer and Cosmic Switchboard is identical to *...the Devī Bhagavatī is situated in the center on an Āsana.* RAAM Gate quantum network computational density for the Cosmic Computer and Cosmic Switchboard is on the order of 10^{1068} quantum computations and interconnections at every cosmic moment and point throughout the universe (calculated in Chapter 8). RAAM Gate radix-10 component of the cosmic computational and network basis states corresponds to the 10 *Maṇdals* of Ṛk Veda, which in turn constitute the dynamics of *Anyonya-Abhāva* in the silent nature or *Atyanta-Abhāva*, the self-referral, self-looping nature of Ṛk Veda. Each of the 10 *Maṇdals* of Ṛk Veda is associated with a successive calculation radix from which to fully apprehend and incorporate the Cosmic computational and network scale of Natural Law. The 1068-power exponent result corresponds to the approximately 1000 Sūktas, (including the 97th *Sūkta—Avyakta Sūkta*—within the first and tenth *Maṇdals*) of the 10 *Maṇdals* of Ṛk Veda. Ṛk Veda is the principal of the four Veda (Ṛk Veda, Sāma Veda, Yajur Veda, and Atharva Veda): *...within this there are the four Maṇdaps, halls built of 1000 (i.e., innumerable) pillars.*

Figure 9-14 (continued): Elaboration of Gāyatrī's Abode with Direct Correspondences in Information Science and Technology, as Expressed in the Global Internetwork and Quantum Network Architecture

Enclosures of Devī Gāyatrī's Abode	**Enclosures of the Global Internetwork and Quantum Network Architecture**
The Nineteenth Enclosure (continued) *Within the Shṛingāra Maṇdap, the Devī Bhagavatī is situated in the center on an Āsana, and She hears the songs sung in tune by the other Devīs along with the other Devas.* *Similarly, sitting on the Mukti Maṇdap, She frees the Jīvas from the bondage of the world. Sitting on the Gyān Maṇdap, She gives instructions on Gyān. Sitting on the fourth, the Ekānta Maṇdap, She consults with Her ministers, the Sakhis, Ananga, Kusuma, etc., on the creation, preservation, and destruction of the universe.* *Now I shall describe the main Khās room of Shrī Devī. Listen! The Khās Mahal palace of the Devī Bhagavatī is named Shrī Chintāmaṇi Gṛiha. Within this is placed a raised platform, the dais and sofa whereon the Devī taketh Her honorable seat. The 10 Śakti-tattvas form the staircases. The four legs are: (1) Brahmā, (2) Vishṇu, (3) Rudra, and (4) Maheśvara. Sadāśiva forms the upper covering plank. Over this Shrī Bhuvaneshwara Mahā Deva, the Supreme Architect of the Universe, is reigning...* *The beauty of [Shrī Devī's] forehead vies with, or defies the moon of the eighth bright lunar day...The divine crown on Her forehead is beautified with the sun and moon made of jewels...Her lotus face is beautified with alakā...She has three eyes like lotus leaves; the luster of Her body is bright like Padmarāgamaṇi cut and carved and sharpened on stone. The bracelets are adorned with jewel tinkling bells; Her neck ornaments and medals are studded with gems and jewels. Her hands are resplendent with the luster of the jewels on Her fingers; the braid of Her head is wreathed with a garland of Mallikā flowers...* *On the side of the Devī are the two oceans of treasures; from these streams of Navaratna, gold, and seven Dhatus go out and assume the forms of rivers and fall into the ocean of Sudhā Sindu...* *O King, now I will describe the dimensions of the Chintāmaṇi Gṛiha. It is 1000 yojanas wide; its center is very big; the rooms situated further and further are twice those preceding them. It lies in Antarīksa (the intervening space) without any support.*	**Cosmic Computer and Cosmic Switchboard (continued)** The Cosmic Computer and Cosmic Switchboard have been discovered through the doorway of the RAAM Gate (refer to Chapter 8). As that quantum network computational gate is directly interfaced to the Unified Field, there are four fundamental components of the RAAM Gate: 1 *n*-qubit addressability 2 Unitarity 3 Quantum computational reversibility and measurability 4 Eternal operation at the Hardware-Software Gap™ (refer to Chapter 3) *These (the four Maṇdaps) are the Shṛīngāra Maṇdap (love, desire, enjoyment), Mukti Maṇdap (liberation or enlightenment), Gyān Maṇdap (knowledge), and Ekānta Maṇdap (unified awareness).* The Cosmic Computer and Cosmic Switchboard permeate and flow through all points and the entire field of the universe: *rivers are flowing, some of ghee, some of milk, curd, honey, nectar, pomegranate juice; and some of mango juice and sugarcane juices are flowing on all sides.* The Cosmic Computer and Cosmic Switchboard permeate the *Atyanta Abhāva* and *Anyonya-Abhāva* of the *Sandhis* (the self-referral, massively parallel nexuses of infinity-within-all-points, all-points-within-infinity): *It (the Chintāmaṇi Gṛiha, a house made of gems of consciousness) lies in Antariksha (the intervening space) without any support. At the times of dissolution and creation, it contracts and expands like a cloth.* RAAM Gate calculations indicate that all the intelligence, knowledge, and organizing power of IS&T has its source in the intelligence and organizing power of the Cosmic Computer and Cosmic Switchboard. The wholeness of intelligence resides here: *The luster of this Chintāmaṇi Gṛiha is comparatively far more bright and beautiful than that of other enclosure walls. Shrī Devī Bhagavatī dwells always in this place. All the great Bhaktas of the Devī in every Brahmāṇda, in the*

Figure 9-14 (continued): Elaboration of Gāyatrī's Abode with Direct Correspondences in Information Science and Technology, as Expressed in the Global Internetwork and Quantum Network Architecture

Enclosures of Devī Gāyatrī's Abode	**Enclosures of the Global Internetwork and Quantum Network Architecture**
The Nineteenth Enclosure (continued) *At the times of dissolution and creation it contracts and expands like a cloth. The luster of this Chintāmaṇi Gṛiha is comparatively far more bright and beautiful than that of other enclosure walls. Shrī Devī Bhagavatī dwells always in this place. All the great Bhaktas of the Devī in every Brahmāṇda, in the Devaloka, in Nāgaloka, in the world of men or in any other loka, all those who were engaged in meditation of the Devī in the sacred places of the Devī and died there, all come here and reside with the Devī in great joy and festivity.* *On all sides rivers are flowing; some of ghee; some of milk, curd, honey, nectar, pomegranate juice, jambu juice, and some of mango juice and sugercane juices are flowing on all sides. The trees here yield fruits according to one's desires, and the wells and tanks yield water also as people desire. Never is there any want felt here for anything. Never are seen here diseases, sorrow, old age, decrepitude, anxiety, anger, jealously, envy, or other lower emotions. All the inhabitants of this place are full of youth and look like 1000 suns. All enjoy with their wives and worship Shrī Bhuvaneshwarī...The seven koti Mahāmantras and Mahāvidyās here assume forms and worship the Mahā Māyā Shrī Bhagavatī, Who is of the nature of Brahmā.* *Śrīmad Devī Bhāgavatam, 12.12.1–59*	**Cosmic Computer and Cosmic Switchboard (continued)** *Devaloka, in Nāgaloka, in the world of men or in any other loka, all those who were engaged in meditation of the Devī in the sacred places of the Devī and died there, all come here and reside with the Devī in great joy and festivity.* The Cosmic Computer and Cosmic Switchboard eternally provide the computational superfabric for the Computational Constitution of the Universe which exhibit the following lively characteristics: • Massively parallel network computation, wherein any intention or action contemplated or executed at any point within the infinity of creation—ranging, at a minimum, from the cosmic spectrum of the observable universe to that of the Planck scale—is instantly known • The computational basis for each succeeding step in the cosmic evolutionary process is contained within the results from the previous cosmic network computation • Cosmic memory *(Smṛiti)* • Instantaneous and refreshed quantum and superstring network computation of cosmic counterparts throughout the spectrum of creation • Infinite and eternal fault-tolerance • Perpetual availability • Mean Time Between Failures (MTBF) is infinite • Mean Time Between Outages (MTBO) is infinite • Zero access and processing latencies within and among the entire cosmic spectrum of creation • Absolute reliability • Infinite security • Hidden and eternally flawless operation • Automation of administration throughout the cosmic spectrum of creation *All the inhabitants of this place are full of youth and look like 1000 suns; and never are seen here diseases, sorrow, old age, or decrepitude.*

Summary and Conclusion

We have seen through the preceding references and examples in Veda and the Vedic Literature that all the *Devatā*, the *Ṛishis*, in fact all the aspects of Natural Law available in the universe, are embodied in Quantum Network Architecture. All the events and stories that occur in Itihās, Purāṇ, Upanishad, and in the whole of the Vedic Literature are an all-time reality, taking place at every moment both within the human physiology and within Quantum Network Architecture.

Quantum Network Architecture, in its complete extent throughout the Global Internetwork, is a global, self-referral, celestial nervous system, or celestial conscious superfabric, that continually collects, interprets, processes, interconnects, and integrates enterprise and personal data throughout the world.

We find and have elaborated the Holistic functioning of the Cosmic Computer and Cosmic Switchboard to be equivalent to Ṛk Veda, the Cosmic Network of Consciousness. Quantum Network Architecture contains and is the expression of Veda and the Vedic Literature, the Computational Constitution of the Universe; therefore, it is the field of all possibilities from which to enrich and fulfill the highest aspirations of this generation in the Information Age, the Knowledge Age.

This elaboration of Quantum Network Architecture as the expression of Veda and the Vedic Literature is dedicated to His Holiness Maharishi Mahesh Yogi and his Vedic Science and Technology, from whom we have this wisdom of integration of life, the Guiding Light of the discovery of the Cosmic Computer and Cosmic Switchboard, and of the one-to-one correspondence between Information Science and Technology and Maharishi's Vedic Science and Technology.

His Holiness Maharishi Mahesh Yogi has revealed that Wholeness is available in the most concentrated value of Natural Law in the *Last Expression—Last Sūkta* of Ṛk Veda, the *Last Expression*—Last Song of Sāma Veda, the *Last Expression—Last Mantra* of Yajur-Veda, and the *Last Expression—Last Mantra* of Atharva Veda. Following are excerpts regarding the significance of the *Last Expressions* of Ṛk Veda, Sāma Veda, Yajur-Veda, and Atharva Veda, drawn from Maharishi's *Constitution of India Fulfilled Through Maharishi's Transcendental Meditation.*

Ṛk Veda—*Last Sūkta*

संस॒मिद्यु॑वसे वृष॒न्नग्ने॒ विश्वा॑न्य॒र्य आ
इ॒ळस्प॒दे समि॑ध्यसे॒ स नो॒ वसू॒न्या भ॑र
सं ग॑च्छध्वं॒ सं व॑दध्वं॒ सं वो॒ मनां॑सि जानताम्
दे॒वा भा॒गं यथा॒ पूर्वे॑ सं॑ञ्जाना॒ना उ॒पासते
स॒मा॒नो मन्त्रः॒ समि॑तिः सं॑मा॒नी सं॑मा॒नं मनः॑ स॒ह चि॒त्तमे॑षाम्
स॒मा॒नं मन्त्र॑म॒भि मं॑त्रये वः समा॒नेन॑ वो ह॒विषा॑ जुहोमि
स॒मा॒नी व॒ आकू॑तिः समा॒ना हृद॑यानि वः
स॒मा॒नम॑स्तु वो॒ मनो॒ यथा॑ वः॒ सुस॒हास॑ति

(Ṛk Veda, 10.190.1–4)

Agni—showerer (of all life, of all benefits), *thou who art the supreme source, course, and goal of all creation, thou verily combinest with all creatures, thou art kindled upon the footmark of ILA* (the unmanifest dynamism [of इ *(I)*]—the dymanic basis of all life); *bring unto us riches.*

Go together, speak together, know your minds to be functioning together from a common source in the same manner as the impulses of Creative Intelligence, in the beginning, remain together united near the source.

Integrated is the expression of knowledge, as assembly is significant in unity; united are their minds in the silent dynamism of all possibilities. For you (says the seer Samvanana) *I make use of the integrated expression of knowledge. By virtue of unitedness, and by means of that which is to be united, I perform action to generate Wholeness of life;* (this means that the consciousness of the seer Samvanana, whose qualities are illustrated by the letters of his name, reverberating in the form of this hymn and producing the cognition, proclaims that consciousness, or the pure nature of life, continues to create newer and newer Wholeness, newer and newer Ṛk—all the time maintaining Wholeness—all the time united in one grand Wholeness).

United by your purpose, harmonious be your feelings, collected by your mind, in the same way as all the various aspects of the universe exist in togetherness, Wholeness.

This is the characteristic of the infinitely diversified galactic structures of the universe. Galaxies always perform in synchrony with each other; they "go together." Similar is the nature of the performance of the numberless neurons in the human brain physiology, because it is the same Natural Law that functions here, there, and everywhere.

Ṛk Veda, being the total Constitution of the Universe, the Constitution of Natural Law, culminates in the expression that all the diversified values of different Laws of Nature, all by habit function in perfect order—they "go together," naturally displaying order in their own cycles of evolution.

Going together means move as a whole: it culminates in the expression of the move of Wholeness. Transcendental Meditation, being the innocent procedure of Natural Law, displaying the natural, holistic performance of Natural Law, skillfully takes the conscious mind to increasingly refined levels of Wholeness, upheld by total Natural Law at every stage, arriving at the pinnacle of evolution in the unbounded, unmanifest field of immortality expressed by *Aṇoraṇiyān Mahato-mahīyān* (finer than the finest is bigger than the biggest)—eternally lively absolute wakefulness ranging from POINT to infinity.

This field of intelligence is the reality of the supreme state of Totality—*Brahm*—from which and within which all the Laws of Nature and all their innumerable expressions abide. The call of Ṛk Veda, the call of the Constitution of the Universe, is to realize this level of intelligence in our awareness and let that be the lively basis of our daily life.

Let us all be the custodians of the total potential of Natural Law; let us all enjoy mastery over Natural Law and enjoy the fruit of all knowledge—all possibilities on the lively ground of Natural Law. Now that Ṛk Veda has been discovered within the structure and function of the human physiology, this total intelligence of Natural Law is within the reach of everyone…

> तत्सन्निधौ वैरत्यागः
> *Tat sannidhau vairatyāgaḥ*
> *(Yog-Sūtra, 2.35)*
> *In the vicinity of coherence (Yoga), hostile tendencies are eliminated;*

वसुधैव कुटुम्बकम्
Vasudhaiva kutumbakan
(Manu Smṛiti, 11.12.22)
The world is a family;

ज्ञानविज्ञानतृप्तात्मा
Gyān vigyān tṛipt-Ātmā
(Bhagavad Gītā, 6.8)
Knowledge and experience bring contentment,

दृढभूमिः
Dṛidh bhūmiḥ
(Yog-Sūtra, 1.14)
Well-founded state—established state.

Individual action will be united with Cosmic Action; it will be in harmony with Cosmic Order; and with a collected mind—unbounded Bliss Consciousness—it will be invincible…

पूर्णमदः पूर्णमिदं पूर्णात् पूर्णमुदच्यते
पूर्णस्य पूर्णमादाय पूर्णमेवावाशिष्यते
Pūrṇam adaḥ pūrṇam idaṃ pūrṇāt pūrṇam udachyate
pūrṇasya pūrṇam ādāya pūrṇam evāvashishyate
(Shāntipāth, Kena Upanishad, 5.1.1)
That is full; this is full; from fullness, fullness comes out; taking fullness from fullness, what remains is fullness.

This is the clarion call of this last *Sūkta* of Ṛk Veda for everyone.

It is the delight of Vedic Scholars…to locate and study this level of intelligence in the last expressions of every aspect of the Vedic Literature because every aspect of the Vedic Literature follows the sequential evolution of Ṛk Veda—the Constitution of the Universe; every aspect of the Vedic Literature is a sequentially developing, perfect theme of knowledge that upholds the natural, evolutionary stream of life to encompass the full range of performance of Natural Law, from point to infinity, at every step of evolution.

The fulfillment…through Transcendental Meditation is really absolute fulfillment because the Transcendental Meditation program takes human awareness to the absolute level of transcendence, the intelligence of *"Aṇoraṇīyān"*—point of point, क् (K)—which is *"Mahato-mahīyān"*—bigger than the biggest, unbounded infinity, अ (A). This is the full awakening of all knowledge, all organizing power of knowledge—total Natural Law.

This phenomenon of the point, क् (K), expanding to infinity, अ (A), is *Shruti*—sound emerging from the phenomenon of the self-referral process within Wholeness, as it shifts from its point value to its unbounded state. Even though this shift "being unmanifest" is only the reality of a notion; it is this notion that renders Veda, the Constitution of the Universe, a total concept on the unmanifest level of reality at the basis of all creation. That is why transcending is a Vedic phenomenon, a Vedic process, which culminates in the point and infinity within the point—the total range of intelligence which makes human awareness the embodiment of total Veda—total knowledge, total Natural Law, total Constitution of the Universe—rendering the conceptual individual life to be the reality of Cosmic Life—the embodiment of the total organizing power of Natural Law and its expression, the ever-expanding material universe.

Maharishi's Transcendental Meditation is the practice of *Nivartadhwam*—the Vedic Practice of *return*—return from concept to reality, which presents the dynamics of total knowledge—Ṛk, Sāma, Yajur, and Atharva—in the unified structure of Ṛk Veda. If the principle of *Nivartadhwam* is applied to this last *Sūkta* of Ṛk Veda, it demonstrates the structure of perpetual flow of self-referral intelligence, which means that it gives a structure to Sāma Veda (flowing wakefulness); it also demonstrates the supremely evolved state of *Yagya* in Yajur-Veda, the dynamics of creation, and meaningfully actualizes Atharva—reverberating Wholeness.

These last expressions of all the Veda express the supreme level of evolution of intelligence; they stand for the total value of Veda and Vedānt—the total value of knowledge and its infinite organizing power inherent in everyone's Transcendental Consciousness—and lead to the complete unfoldment of life through the study and programs of Maharishi Mahesh Yogi Vedic Vishwavidyalaya, which will be made available to all nations.

Every nation will enjoy the friendship of all nations, and there will be a compact Wholeness of all nations. This is the phenomenon that is portrayed in the last expressions of Ṛk Veda, Sāma Veda, Yajur-Veda, and Atharva Veda.

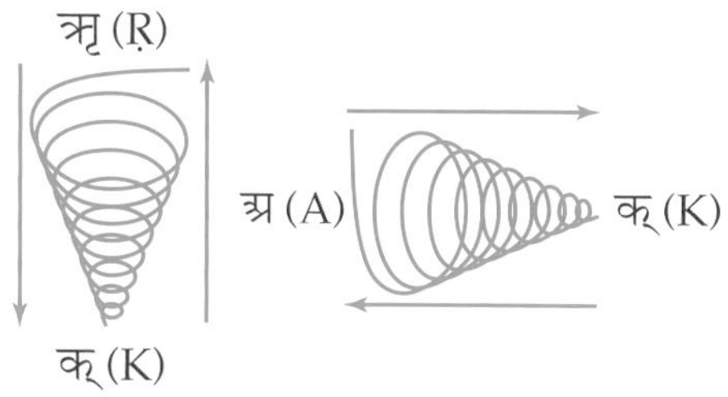

Flow (अ [A] ⟶ क् [K]) demonstrates Sāma (elaborated in Sāma Veda) within the structure of अक् (Ak), which is the concentrated expression of Ṛk Veda. When the point returns to infinity (अ [A] ⟵ क् [K]), when the point offers itself to infinity, it demonstrates the supreme performance of *Yajur*—one side surrendering to the other side, and the process of surrender returning from the point (अ [A] ⇄ क् [K]) demonstrating the eternal process of *Yajan,* which is elaborated in Yajur-Veda. Close observation of the process of return at the point (⇄) reveals Atharva—the *Tharva* of अ (A)—the wakefulness of Wholeness at its minutest scale—ever-wakeful *Atharva.*

All this analysis of letters and gaps between letters in the sequentially evolving structure of Ṛk Veda has been mentioned here in detail to actualize the proper understanding of *Shruti*—the sequentially developing structure of Natural Law.

Sāma Veda—*Last Song*

भद्रं कर्णेभिः शृणुयाम देवा भद्रं पश्येमाक्षभिर्यजत्राः
स्थिरैरङ्गैस्तुष्टुवाँ सस्तनूभिर्व्यशेमहि देवहितं यदायु
स्वस्ति न इन्द्रो वृद्धश्रवाः स्वस्ति नः पूषा विश्ववेदाः
स्वस्ति नस्तार्क्ष्यो अरिष्ठनेमिः स्वस्ति नो बृहस्पतिर्दधातु
ओ३म् स्वस्ति नो बृहस्पतिर्दधातु

(Sāma Veda, 2.9.3.9)

May the Devatā of our ears—the vibrating intelligence of the Veda, Natural Law, that structures the auditory system—hear that which is auspicious; may the Devatā of our eyes—the vibrating intelligence of the Veda, Natural Law, that structures the sense of sight—see that which is auspicious.

Realize the holistic integration of the limbs of the body, Vedānga, to be established in Veda, so that the Āngas (parts) are not isolated and separated from each other; they remain connected and integrated with the wholeness of their source.

Realize that level of lifespan that is nourishing to the Devatā—the intelligence, Laws of Nature—so that they are continually in time with the whole (Brahm); that means live Wholeness of Āyu—immortality. The picture is to support the eternal dynamism of life with eternal silence and evolve to a level of unity of dynamism and silence; materialize Ṛk in the flow of Sāma—materialize or actualize Ṛk, which is the enlivenment of the total potential of dynamism in the nature of Ātmā; actualize आत्मैवेदं सर्वम् *Ātmai Vedaṁ Sarvam—All this is Ātman only;* सव खलु इदं ब्रह्म *Sarvaṁ Khalu Idaṁ Brahm (Chhandogya Upanishad, 3.14.1)—All this is Brahm—Totality, Wholeness;* अहं ब्रह्मास्मि *Ahaṁ Brahmāsmi (Bṛihadāraṇyak Upanishad, 1.4.10)—I am Totality, and render the Wholeness of Ātmā to be a living reality of daily life.*

This eternal flow (Sāma—Aṇoraṇīyān Mahato-mahīyān) be auspicious to us; Totality, the basis of all life be at our disposal; total potential of Sāma (flow of Soma, integrating Wholeness) be at our disposal; may Indra—the ruling intelligence of the universe—the infinite organizing power of Natural Law—Totality—Brahm—be our reality; may Pūshan—the nourishing potential of Sāma, or Soma—be our reality; Bṛihaspati—total potential of the nourishing quality of intelligence—Sāma, or Soma—be our reality; Bṛihaspati—total potential of

> *the nourishing quality of intelligence—Sāma, or Soma—be our reality; Bṛihaspati bestow on us that level of reality where Ātmā is; where Wholeness is; where self-referral, eternal harmony prevails—*आत्मैवेदं सर्वम् *Ātmai Vedaṁ Sarvam—*सर्दं खलु इदं ब्रह्म *Sarvaṁ Khalu Idaṁ Brahm—*अहं ब्रह्मास्मि *Ahaṃ Brahmāsmi.*

The effect of this *Shruti* (Sāma song) is that the senses of perception perceive the total range of the evolution of the object—from gross to subtle—so that the gross value of the object does not overshadow (hide) the unifying *(Soma)* value of the object.

There the sensory level of intelligence is being inspired to awake to its total creative potential in order that when it perceives differences, it is competent to comprehend the underlying, unifying, harmonizing *Sāma* level of the object—*Sāma* level of dynamism at the most fundamental level of the dynamics of consciousness.

Harmonize means in this case that the sense of sight sees the gross and continues to see (through the harmonizing influence of sound—*Sāma*) all the finer levels of the object until the vision comprehends the *Baikharī, Madhyamā, Pashyantī,* and finally *Parā* level.

Sāma inspires harmony that permeates all the expressed levels of intelligence, or consciousness it enlivens the full creative potential of intelligence at the basis of the senses.

This is the complete enlivenment of the *Sāma* level of consciousness where the object is perceived a complete expression of the non-expressed, unmanifest *Saṁhitā* level of self-referral consciousness, covering the whole range of the evolution of life from unmanifest to the whole range of the manifest, ever-expanding universe; and this total reality is comprehended by the fully awakened, fully alert, self-referral intelligence and its subjective means of perception, the senses—the whole range of objectivity and the whole range of subjectivity and the sensory level that connects the two are all fully developed.

The effect is that the observer should appreciate the subjective level of intelligence within the object: his senses should be so refined as to experience all levels of the object, from gross to subtle, and ultimately comprehend the transcendental level of the object—pure subjectivity, the field of pure Bliss Consciousness—and live the total reality on the sensory level of daily ife where every perception—every thought, speech, and action—comprehends the total reality of the object of the senses and resonates on that holistic, divine level of subjectivity within every object.

In this state (of Unity Consciousness) where *Soma* is always flowing, every perception is a wave of bliss, fulfilling the exhortation of Maharishi Yāgyavalkya—

> आत्मा वा अरे द्रष्टव्यः श्रोतव्यः मन्तव्यः निदिध्यासितव्यः
> *Ātmā vāre drashtavyaḥ shrotavyaḥ mantavyaḥ nididhyāsitavyaḥ*
> *(Bṛihadāraṇyak Upanishad, 2.4.5)*

and materializing the vision of Maharishi Vasishta—

> दूरे दृशं गृहपतिम् अथर्युम्
> *Dūrē dṛishaṁ gṛihapatim atharyum*
> *(Ṛk Veda, 7.1.1)*

Yajur-Veda—Last Mantra

अग्ने॒ नय॑ सु॒पथा॑ रा॒ये अ॒स्मान्विश्वा॑नि देव व॒युना॑नि वि॒द्वान्

युयो॒ध्यस्म॒ज्जुहु॑रा॒णमेनो॒ भूयि॑ष्ठां ते॒ नम॑ उ॒क्तिं विधेम

हि॒रण्म॑ये॒न पात्रे॑ण स॒त्यस्यापि॑हितं मुख॑म्

यो॒ऽसावा॑दि॒त्ये पुरु॑ष॒: । ओ३म् खं ब्रह्म सोऽसावहम्

(Yajur-Veda Saṁhitā, 40.16–17)

By goodly path lead us to riches. Agni, thou God who knowest all our works and wisdom. Remove the obstacles that make us stray and wander: most ample adoration will we bring thee.

The real face is hidden by a vessel formed of golden light. The Spirit yonder in the Sun, the Spirit dwelling there am I. Om! Heaven! Brahmā!

This commonly understood translation only scratches the superficial surface value of the script, which, being the last expression, is the most concentrated expression of Yajur-Veda—the eternal continuum of the process of *Yajan*—the eternal process of sacrificing, or offering Wholeness to itself—Wholeness offering to Wholeness—Wholeness performing—*Yajan, Yagya,* resulting in new Wholeness all the time—नवो नवो भवति जायमान: *Navo-Navo bhavati jāyamānaḥ* (Ṛk Veda, 10.85.19).

The sound emerging from the self-interacting dynamics of consciousness—*Shruti*—at the unmanifest basis of creation, demonstrates the eternal process of *Yagya.* [This is *Shruti,* that which is heard]; the self-interacting dynamics of consciousness is expressing its nature in terms of *Yagya;* Wholeness is emerging as a result of Wholeness performing (*Yagya*) within itself; through the eternal *Yagya,* the self-interacting dyamics or consciousness, *Apurva* (that which was not there before) is being created—मवो नवो भवति जायमानो *Navo-Navo bhavati jāyamānaḥ* (Ṛk Veda, 10.85.19)—new Wholeness is created.

New Wholeness is eternally emerging (from *Parā,* to *Pashyantī,* to *Madhyamā,* to *Baikharī*); what is emerging at every step of evolution is Wholeness—Totality—*Brahm.* In the ultimate analysis, *Brahm* is performing; Totality is performing; Wholeness is performing.

This performance is the performance of *Ātmā*, and that I am—in me, the eternal *Yagya*, my self-interacting dynamics—आत्मैव आत्मनो द्रष्टा *Ātmaiva Ātmano Drashtā;* आत्मैवेदं सर्वम् *Ātmai Vedaṁ Sarvam;* सर्वं खलु इदं ब्रह्म *Sarvaṁ Khalu Idaṁ Brahm (Chhāndogya Upanishad, 3.14.1);* अहं ब्रह्मास्मि *Ahaṁ Brahmāsmi (Bṛihadāraṇyak Upanishad, 1.4.10.)*

The whisper is that all that is going on is *Yagya*—all levels of creation and evolution is *Yagya* continuum, and in all these *Yagyas* it is the "I" that is real—self-interacting dynamics is all that there is—I am *Yagya;* I am performer; I am *Apurva* and *Purva*—actor, action, and the result of action—*Saṁhitā* of *Ṛishi, Devatā, Chhandas—Ātmā, Veda, Vishwa, Brahm—Yagya,* Yajur-Veda am I.

This is the total reality of *Yajan*. This eternal continuum of the reality of *Yajan* is expressed in these last words of Yajur-Veda. The call is for life to be the reality of the *Cosmic Yagya* where the point of the point (mainifest creation) is infinity (unmanifest reality) through the eternally continuing process of *Yagya* giving rise to the evolution of everything.

It is a delight to see *Shruti* (that which is heard) and *Smṛiti* (memory that leads *Shruti* to progress and evolve eternally in the same direction) both simultaneously engaged in promoting the process of evolution through the process of *Yajan—Yagya*.

The process of *Yajan* is available in the expression ऋक् (Ṛk), where the dynamism of ऋ (Ṛ) is offering itself to the silence of क् (K), and the silence of क् (K) in turn offers itself to अ (A). This is the phenomenon of *Yajan*. The process of *Yajan* is already expressed in the syllable ऋक् (Ṛk), where dynamism, ऋ (Ṛ), sacrifices itself to its point, क् (K), and the point of the point, क् (K), demonstrates *Yajan* expanding to infinity—अ (A)—expressing the phenomenon of *Yajan* in the whole name and form of Ṛk. Similarly, Sāma and Atharva have their reality within the structure of ऋक् (Ṛk).

Thus it is clear that the four Veda express the qualities of intelligence of *Ātmā*, the Self of everyone, and in the full awakening of *Ātmā*, the full awakening of Natural Law, the spontaneous result is यो जागार तम् ऋचः कामयन्ते *Yo jāgār tam ṛichaḥ kāmayante (Ṛk Veda, 5.44.14)*—fully awake *Ātmā* is already the lively ground of Veda—Ṛk Veda, Sāma Veda, Yajur-Veda, and Atharva Veda.

Atharva Veda—Last Mantra

मधुंमतीरोषंधीर्द्याव आपो मधुंमन्नो भवत्वन्तरिंक्षम्
क्षेत्रंस्य पतिर्मधुंमान्नो अस्त्वरिंष्यन्तो अन्वेंनं चरेम
पनाय्यं तदंश्विना कृतं वां वृषभो दिवो रजंसः पृथिव्याः
सहस्रं शंसां उत ये गविंष्टौ सर्वाँ इत् ताँ उपं याता पिबंध्यै

(Atharva Veda, 20.143.8–9)

Sweet be the plants for us, the heavens, the waters, and full of sweets for us be air's mid-region! May the Field's Lord for us be full of sweetness, and may we follow after him uninjured.

Ashwins, that work of yours deserves our praise, the Lord of firmament and earth and heaven; Yes, and your thousand victories in battle. Come near to all these men and shower your grace on all of us.

These last expressions of Atharva Veda are the momentum of the infinite organizing power of Natural Law that displays *Atharva*—the *Tharva* of "A"—the self-interacting dynamics of Wholeness—the impulse of Wholeness which eternally remaining Wholeness, expresses itself in newer and newer WholenessES—the self-interacting dynamics of Atharva Veda—the self-interacting dynamics of that last stage of evolution of Wholeness which renders Wholeness to be a continuum.

The call is for life to display Wholeness at every stage of its evolution because the reality of the minuter than the minutest, the reality of point of the point, the reality of the impulse of the unmanifest, is in the magnitude of the enormous, infinite unboundedness.

The phenomenon of *Atharva* is the phenomenon at that level of creation where the total range of evolution is concentrated as a little delicate frequency between a point of infinity and its point. The picture is clear when one's intellect attends to the phenomenon at the point where the total range of evolution is available in its most concentrated state, and when and where the point transcends its existence and expands into unboundedness—अणोरणीयान् महतो महीयान् *Aṇoraṇīyān Mahato-mahīyān;* also where the name of Veda—ऋक् (Ṛk)—turns into the form of ऋक् (Ṛk)—अक् (Ak)—the fine point of transformation of क् (K) into अ (A)—the reality of the point of dynamism transcending and gaining the status of a point of a point—point becoming infinity. This transformation is available in the phenomenon of क् (K). क् (K) + अ (A) = dynamism at a point—क् (K) evolving into the eternal continuum of silence in अ (A). This is *Tharva* (impulse) of अ (A), from where अ (A) expands into *Aknim īle*—the whole Ṛk Veda.

The last *Kaṇḍika* of Atharva Veda, expressed in these words, demonstrates Totality in the delicate *Tharva* of अ (A)—in the reality of eternal silence, which, in terms of *Atharva,* is eternal dynamism.

The call is for life to be what it actually is—Wholeness—perpetually evolving Wholeness.

सं गच्छध्वम्—Go Together

A: Sanskrit Alphabet, Transliteration, and Pronunciation

The Sanskrit alphabet, transliteration, and pronunciation presented in this Appendix are based in part upon *Introduction to Sanskrit: Part One* by Thomas Egenes, Motilal Publishers, Pvt. Ltd., Delhi, India, 1989, authored under the guidance of His Holiness Maharishi Mahesh Yogi.

Maharishi Mahesh Yogi describes Sanskrit as the Language of Nature, the language of the impulses within pure consciousness, the Self. Maharishi explains that the ancient Vedic Rishis of the Himalayas, fathoming the silent depth of their pure consciousness, cognized these impulses. These cognitions were recorded in the Vedic Literature, a vast body of beautiful expressions that embodies the mechanics of evolution in every field of life.

Maharishi has emphasized the value of learning the Sanskrit alphabet and learning to read the Vedic Literature in the original script. Calling it a "formula for perfection," Maharishi has explained that pronouncing the sounds of the Vedic Literature produces a corresponding quality in consciousness and, through consciousness, in the physiology and environment. The proper, sequential pronunciation of the Vedic Literature strengthens the impulse of evolution, causing all thoughts, desires, and intentions to be more in the direction of Natural Law.

From the Vedic Tradition, Maharishi has brought to light practical procedures for experiencing pure consciousness and promoting evolution in everyday life—the Maharishi

Transcendental Meditation and TM-Sidhi programs. These simple, natural, effortless programs have brought happiness and fulfillment to millions of people around the world. More than 600 scientific studies conducted and published in over 30 countries have verified the benefits of Transcendental Meditation and TM-Sidhi programs in every area of life—developing mental potential, improving health, improving personal relationships, and improving the quality of life for society as a whole. Maharishi has provided a means for removing stress and suffering and for unfolding the full potential of within every individual—for creating perfect health, progress, prosperity, and peace—Heaven on Earth.

Over the years, Maharishi has emphasized the most significant passages from the Veda and Vedic Literature, of which many have been included in this book to both describe and comment upon the process of evolution lively throughout the fabric of creation, and to describe the fundamental mechanics of direct correspondence between Quantum Network Architecture—the complete expression of Information Science and Technology—and Maharishi's Vedic Science and Technology. The knowledge contained within these expressions can also be found at the foundation of every culture and tradition.

Sanskrit Alphabet

Sanskrit (*Saṁskṛta*) is written in the devanagari script. The word devanagari mean the "city (nagari) of immortals (deva)." There are no capital letters.

Vowels

अ a	आ ā	
इ i	ई ī	
उ u	ऊ ū	
ऋ ṛ	ॠ ṝ	ऌ ḷ
ए e	ऐ ai	
ओ o	औ au	
अं aṃ—ṃ or ṇ (anusvāra)	अः aḥ—ḥ (visarga)	

Consonants

Velar (kaṇṭhaya)	क ka	ख kha	ग ga	घ gha	ङ ṅa
Palatal (tālavya)	च ca	छ cha	ज ja	झ jha	ञ ña
Retroflex (mūrdhanya)	ट ṭa	ठ ṭha	ड ḍa	ढ ḍha	ण ṇa
Dental (dantya)	त ta	थ tha	द da	ध dha	न na
Labial (oṣṭhya)	प pa	फ pha	ब ba	भ bha	म ma
Semi-vowels	य ya	र ra	ल la	व va	
Sibilants	श śa	ष ṣa	स sa		
Aspirate	ह ha				

Sanskrit Pronunciation

All Sanskrit sounds are pronounced at one of five different points of contact in the mouth, as indicated in the diagram below:

Sanskrit Pronunciation Points of Contact

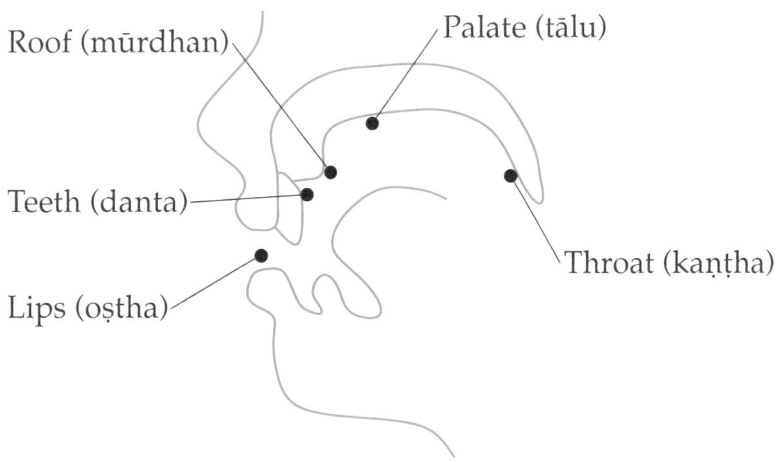

The first 25 consonants are listed below. Each row lists all the sounds that are said at a given point of contact in the mouth. The *a* is added for the sake of pronunciation.

The First 25 Consonants

			Voiced		
		Aspirated[a]		**Aspirated**	**Nasal**
Velar (kaṇṭhya)[b]	ka	kha	ga	gha	ña
Palatal (tālavya)[c]	ca	cha	ja	jha	ña
Retroflex (mūrdhahnya)[d]	ṭa	ṭha	ḍa	ḍna	ṇa
Dental (dantaya)[e]	ta	tha	da	dha	na
Labial (oṣṭhya)[f]	pa	pha	ba	bha	ma

a. The *h* following a consonant indicates aspiration, the addition of air. thus, *th* should not be confused with the *th* in the word then.

b. The first row lists all the sounds said in the throat, referred to as "velar."

c. The second row lists all the sounds said with the tongue touching the soft palate (palatal), at the top of the mouth.

d. The third row lists the "retroflex" sounds, so called because they curl the tip of the tongue upward toward the head, with the tongue touching the hard palate—the ridge behind the upper teeth.

e. The sounds in the fourth row (dental) are pronounced with the tongue flat and the tip of the tongue touching the point at which the upper teeth meet the gums.

f. The sounds in the fifth row are pronounced with the lips (labial).

In Sanskrit, each letter represents one and only one sound *(varṇa)*. There are two basic divisions to the alphabet: (1) Vowels (*svara*, or sounded); and (2) Consonants (*vyanjana*, or manifesting).

Vowels

Vowels can be either short *(hrasva)* or long *(dīrgha)*. Short vowels are held for one count (mātrā), and long vowels are held for two counts. Long-count vowels are marked like *ā*. Some vowels are called simple *(śuddha)*, and some are called complex *(saṃyukta)*.

The lines and dots are called "diacritics," or "diacritical marks," and are used because the Sanskrit alphabet contains more letters than the English alphabet. Diacritics are combined with roman letters to represent new sounds.

A vowel by itself, or a consonant or group of consonants followed by a vowel, is called a syllable *(akshara)*.

Vowels

Devanagari Script	Romanized Transliteration	Sounds Like	Example
अ	a	*a* like the "a" in America	agni
आ	ā	*ā* like the "a" in father	ātman
इ	i	*i* like the "ea" in heat	agni
ई	ī	*ī* like the "e" in he	Gītā
उ	u	*u* like the "u" in suit	guru
ऊ	ū	*ū* like the "oo" in pool	sūrya
ऋ	ṛ	*ṛ* like the "ri" in river (usually not rolled)	ṛk
ॠ	ṝ	*ṝ* like the "ree" in reed (held longer than ṛ)	dātṝn
ऌ	ḷ	*ḷ* like the "lry" in jewelry	kḷp
ए	e	*e* like the "e" in they	devatā
ऐ	ai	*ai* like the "ai" in aisle	vaidya
ओ	o	*o* like the "o" in pole	ojas
औ	au	*au* like the "ou" in loud	apaurusheya
अं	aṃ	The ṃ is called anusvāra. It causes the last portion of the vowel before it to be nasal. For example, गं = gaṃ, तं = taṃ, सं = sam	saṃkhyā
अः	aḥ	The (ḥ) is called visarga. It an unvoiced breathing, usually at the end of a word.	yogasthaḥ

Consonants

Velar (Kaṇthya) Consonants[a]

Devanagari Script	Romanized Transliteration	Sounds Like	Example
क	ka	*ka* like the "k" in skate (In writing this letter in Devanagari script, the **a** is automatically included, it is not written additionally.	kavi
ख	kha	*kh* like the "kh" in bunkhouse	sukham
ग	ga	*g* like the "g" in garland	Gaṅgā
घ	gha	*gh* like the "gh in loghouse	ghoṣavat
ङ	ṅa	*ṅ* like the "n" in sing	Gaṅgā

a. Velar (kaṇthya) consonants are sounded in the throat.

Palatal (Tālavya) Consonants[a]

Devanagari Script	Romanized Transliteration	Sounds Like	Example
च	ca	*c* like the "c" in cello	cit
छ	cha	*ch* like the "ch" in charm (using more breath)	chāya
ज	ja	*j* like the "j" in just	jalam
झ	jha	*jh* like the "j" in just (using more breath)	jhaṭ
ञ	ña	*ñ* like the "n" in enjoyable	Patañjali

a. Palatal (tālavya) consonants are sounded with the tongue touching the soft palate, at the top of the mouth.

Retroflex (Mūrdhanya) Consonants[a]

Devanagari Script	Romanized Transliteration	Sounds Like	Example
ट	ṭa	*ṭ* like the "t" in stable	dṛṣṭi
ठ	ṭha	*ṭh* like the "t" in table (using more breath)	haṭh
ड	ḍa	*ḍ* like the "d" in dynamic	paṇḍit
ढ	ḍha	*ḍh* like the "dh" in redhead	vyūḍham
ण	ṇa	*ṇ* like the "n" in gentle	Pāṇḍu

a. Retroflex (mūrdhanya) consonants are sounded with the tip of the tongue upward toward the head, with the tongue touching the hard palate—the ridge behind the upper teeth.

Dental (Dantya) Consonants[a]

Devanagari Script	Romanized Transliteration	Sounds Like	Example
त	ta	*t* like the "t" in stable	tat
थ	tha	*th* like the "t" in table (using more breath)	Sthāpatya
द	da	*d* like the "d" in dynamic	devatā
ध	dha	*dh* like the "dh" in redhead	dhātu
न	na	*n* like the "n" in gentle	namaste

a. Dental (dantya) consonants are sounded with the tongue flat and the tip of the tongue touching the point at which the upper teeth meet the gums.

Labial (Oṣṭhya) Consonants[a]

Devanagari Script	Romanized Transliteration	Sounds Like	Example
प	pa	*p* like the "p" in spin	Patañjali
फ	ph	*ph* like the "ph" in shepherd	phalam
ब	ba	*b* like the "b" in beautiful	buddhi
भ	bha	*bh* like the "bh" in clubhouse	Bhagavad
म	ma	*m* like the "m" in mother	māyā

a. Labial (oṣṭhya) consonants are sounded at the lips.

Semi-Vowels

Devanagari Script	Romanized Transliteration	Sounds Like	Example
य	ya	*y* like the "y" in yes	Yajur
र	ra	*r* like the "r" in red	rajas
ल	la	*l* like the "l" in law	līlā
व	va	*v* like the "v" in victory (but closer to a "w")	vāk

Sibilants

Devanagari Script	Romanized Transliteration	Sounds Like	Example
श	śa	*ś* like the "sh" in shine (pronounced at the same point of contact as **ca**)	śānti
ष	ṣa	*ṣ* like the "c" in efficient (pronounced at the same point of contact as **ṭa**)	puruṣa
स	sa	*s* like the "s" in sweet	Sītā

Aspirate

Devanagari Script	Romanized Transliteration	Sounds Like	Example
ह	ha	*h* like the "h" in <u>h</u>ero	Hanumān

Special Characters

Devanagari Script	Romanized Transliteration	Sounds Like	Example
ज्ञ	jñ	a nasalized sound like gya or jya	
क्ष	ksh		

Conventions

- As a rule, the root forms of Sanskrit words are used (without case endings).
- Geographical names, e.g., *Himalaya*, are marked with diacriticals only as main lexicon entries.

B: Units of Measurement and Orders of Magnitude—Powers of Ten and Two

Prefix	Symbol	Power of 10 Factor	Decimal	Name[a]	Power of 2 Factor	Bytes as Example Unit[b]
Yotta	Y	10^{24}	1,000,000,000,000,000,000,000,000	Septillion	2^{80}	Yottabyte (YB)
Zetta	Z	10^{21}	1,000,000,000,000,000,000,000	Sextillion	2^{70}	Zettabyte (ZB)
Exa	E	10^{18}	1,000,000,000,000,000,000	Quintillion	2^{60}	Exabyte (EB)
Peta	P	10^{15}	1,000,000,000,000,000	Quadrillion	2^{50}	Petabyte (PB)
Tera	T	10^{12}	1,000,000,000,000	Trillion	2^{40}	Terabyte (TB)
Giga	G	10^{9}	1,000,000,000	Billion	2^{30}	Gigabyte (GB)
Mega	M	10^{6}	1,000,000	Million	2^{20}	Megabyte (MB)
Kilo	k	10^{3}	1,000	Thousand	2^{10}	Kilobyte (KB)
Hecto	h	10^{2}	100	Hundred		
Deca	da	10^{1}	10	Ten		
		10^{0}	1	One		
Deci	d	10^{-1}	1/10	Tenth		
Centi	c	10^{-2}	1/100	Hundredth		
Milli	m	10^{-3}	1/1,000	Thousandth		
Micro	μ	10^{-6}	1/1,000,000	Millionth		
Nano	n	10^{-9}	1/1,000,000,000	Billionth		
Pico	p	10^{-12}	1/1,000,000,000,000	Trillionth		
Femto	f	10^{-15}	1/1,000,000,000,000,000	Quadrillionth		
Atto	a	10^{-18}	1/1,000,000,000,000,000,000	Quintillionth		
Zepto	z	10^{-21}	1/1,000,000,000,000,000,000,000	Sextillionth		
Yocto	y	10^{-24}	1/1,000,000,000,000,000,000,000,000	Septillionth		

See following page for notes.

a. One billion is one thousand million (1,000,000,000, or 10^9); however, in the British system it has also been one million million (one bi-million, 1,000,000,000,000, or 10^{12}). Similar distinctions occur for one trillion (tri-million or 10^{18} in the British system), quadrillion (quad-million or 10^{24} in the British system), one quintillion (quint-million or 10^{30} in the British system), one sextillion (sext-million or 10^{36} in the British system), one septillion (sept-million or 10^{42} in the British system).

b. 1 YB = 1,208,925,819,614,629,174,706,176 bytes
1 ZB = 1,180,591,620,717,411,303,424 bytes
1 EB = 1,152,921,504,606,846,976 bytes
1 PB = 1,125,899,906,842,624 bytes
1 TB = 1,099,511,627,776 bytes
1 GB = 1,073,741,824 bytes
1 MB = 1,048,576 bytes
1 KB = 1,024 bytes

C: Mathematical and Quantum Information Symbols, Notation, and Operations

Greek Alphabet

A	α		alpha	N	ν		nu
B	β		beta	Ξ	ξ		xi
Γ	γ		gamma	O	o		omicron
Δ	δ		delta	Π	π	ϖ	pi
E	ε		epsilon	P	ρ		rho
Z	ζ		zeta	Σ	σ	ς	sigma
H	η		eta	T	τ		tau
Θ	θ	ϑ	theta	Υ	υ		upsilon
I	ι		iota	Φ	ϕ	φ	phi
K	κ		kappa	X	χ		chi
Λ	λ		lambda	Ψ	ψ		psi
M	μ		mu	Ω	ω		omega

Mathematical Notation

scalars	a	general vectors	a
unit vectors	$\hat{a}$	scalar product	$a \cdot b$
vector cross-product	$a \times b$	gradient operator	∇
Laplacian operator	∇^2	derivative	$\frac{df}{dx}$, etc.
parital derivatives	$\frac{\partial f}{\partial x}$, etc	derivative of r with respect to t	$\dot{r}$
nth derivative	$\frac{d^n f}{dx^n}$	closed loop integral	$\oint_L dl$
closed surface integral	$\oint_s ds$	matrix	$\mathbf{A}$ or a_{ij}
mean value (of x)	$\langle x \rangle$	binomial coefficient	$\binom{n}{r}$
factorial	!	unit imaginary ($\mathbf{i}^2 = -1$)	$\mathbf{i}$
exponential constant	e	modulus (of x)	$\|x\|$
natural logarithm	ln	log to base 10	$\log_{10}$
less than	$<$	exponentiation	exp
less than or equal to	$\leq$	approaches	$\rightarrow$
probability	Pr	addition modulo 2	$\oplus$
function of variable x	$f(x)$	tensor product	$\otimes$
logarithm	log	spin	S
absolute value of variable x	$\|x\|$	angular momentum	J
Planck constant	h	cosine	cos
$h/(2\pi)$	h	sine	sin
wave function	ψ	complex number, fine-structure constant	α
complex number, fine-structure constant	β	weight, complex number, angular velocity	ω
summation	Σ	quantum bit (qubit) notation	$\|0\rangle$, $\|1\rangle$

Mathematical Notation

greater than	$>$	eigenstate, state vector	$\|\psi\rangle$
greater than or equal to	$\geq$	variable	n
variable	m	micro	μ
change	Δ	speed of light	c
wavelength	λ	frequency	f
nanometer	nm	optical input signal wavelength	λ_s
optical pump wavelength	λ_p	optical converted wavelength	λ_c
Markovian/exponential	M	general	G
infinity	∞	Lagrangian	$\mathcal{L}$
Hamiltonian	H	perturbation Hamiltonian	H'
Permittivity	ε	Permittivity of free space	ε_0
ohm	Ω	Angstrom	Å
integral, integration	$\int$	pi	π

Matrix Algebra Definitions and Operations

Matrix definition	$\mathbf{A} = \begin{bmatrix} a_{11} & a_{12} & \dots & a_{1n} \\ a_{21} & a_{22} & \dots & a_{2n} \\ \dots & \dots & \dots & \dots \\ a_{m1} & a_{m2} & \dots & a_{mn} \end{bmatrix}$	$\mathbf{A}$ a_{ij}	m by n matrix matrix elements
Matrix addition	$\mathbf{C} = \mathbf{A} + \mathbf{B}$ if $c_{ij} = a_{ij} + b_{ij}$		
Matrix multiplication	$\mathbf{C} = \mathbf{AB}$ if $c_{ij} = a_{ik}b_{kj}$ $(\mathbf{AB})\mathbf{C} = \mathbf{A}(\mathbf{BC})$ $\mathbf{A}(\mathbf{B} + \mathbf{C}) = \mathbf{AB} + \mathbf{C}$		
Transpose matrix	$\tilde{a}_{ij} = a_{ji}$ $(\widetilde{\mathbf{AB}\dots\mathbf{N}}) = \tilde{\mathbf{N}}\dots\tilde{\mathbf{B}}\tilde{\mathbf{A}}$	$\tilde{a}_{ij}$	transpose matrix (sometimes a^{T}_{ij}, or a'_{ij})
Adjoint matrix	$\mathbf{A}^{\dagger} = \tilde{\mathbf{A}}^{*}$ $(\mathbf{AB}\dots\mathbf{N})^{\dagger} = \mathbf{N}^{\dagger}\dots\mathbf{B}^{\dagger}\mathbf{A}^{\dagger}$	$*$ $\dagger$	complex conjugate (of each component) adjoint (or Hermitian conjugate)
Hermitian matrix	$\mathbf{H}^{\dagger} = \mathbf{H}$	$\mathbf{H}$	Hermitian (or self-adjoint) matrix

Examples:

$$\mathbf{A} = \begin{bmatrix} a_{11} & a_{12} & a_{13} \\ a_{21} & a_{22} & a_{23} \\ a_{31} & a_{32} & a_{33} \end{bmatrix} \qquad \mathbf{B} = \begin{bmatrix} b_{11} & b_{12} & b_{13} \\ b_{21} & b_{22} & b_{23} \\ b_{31} & b_{32} & b_{33} \end{bmatrix}$$

$$\tilde{\mathbf{A}} = \begin{bmatrix} a_{11} & a_{21} & a_{31} \\ a_{12} & a_{22} & a_{32} \\ a_{13} & a_{23} & a_{33} \end{bmatrix} \qquad \mathbf{A} + \mathbf{B} = \begin{bmatrix} a_{11} + b_{11} & a_{12} + b_{12} & a_{13} + b_{13} \\ a_{21} + b_{21} & a_{22} + b_{22} & a_{23} + b_{23} \\ a_{31} + b_{31} & a_{32} + b_{32} & a_{33} + b_{33} \end{bmatrix}$$

$$\mathbf{AB} = \begin{bmatrix} a_{11}b_{11} + a_{12}b_{21} + a_{13}b_{31} & a_{11}b_{12} + a_{12}b_{22} + a_{13}b_{32} & a_{11}b_{13} + a_{12}b_{23} + a_{13}b_{33} \\ a_{21}b_{11} + a_{22}b_{21} + a_{23}b_{31} & a_{21}b_{12} + a_{22}b_{22} + a_{23}b_{32} & a_{21}b_{13} + a_{22}b_{23} + a_{23}b_{33} \\ a_{31}b_{11} + a_{32}b_{21} + a_{33}b_{31} & a_{31}b_{12} + a_{32}b_{22} + a_{33}b_{32} & a_{31}b_{13} + a_{32}b_{23} + a_{33}b_{33} \end{bmatrix}$$

Commutators

Commutator definition	$[\mathbf{A},\mathbf{B}] = \mathbf{AB} - \mathbf{BA} = -[\mathbf{B},\mathbf{A}]$	$[\cdot,\cdot]$	commutator
Adjoint	$[\mathbf{A},\mathbf{B}]^\dagger = [\mathbf{B}^\dagger,\mathbf{A}^\dagger]$	$\dagger$	adjoint
Distribution	$[\mathbf{A}+\mathbf{B},\mathbf{C}] = [\mathbf{A},\mathbf{C}] + [\mathbf{B},\mathbf{C}]$		
Association	$[\mathbf{AB},\mathbf{C}] = \mathbf{A}[\mathbf{B},\mathbf{C}] + [\mathbf{A},\mathbf{C}]\mathbf{B}$		
Jacobi identity	$[\mathbf{A},[\mathbf{B},\mathbf{C}]] = [\mathbf{B},[\mathbf{A},\mathbf{C}]] - [\mathbf{C},[\mathbf{A},\mathbf{B}]]$		

Rotation Matrices

Rotation about x_1	$\mathbf{R}_1(\theta) = \begin{bmatrix} 1 & 0 & 0 \\ 0 & \cos\theta & \sin\theta \\ 0 & -\sin\theta & \cos\theta \end{bmatrix}$	$\mathbf{R}_i(\theta)$	matrix for rotation about the ith axis
Rotation about x_2	$\mathbf{R}_2(\theta) = \begin{bmatrix} \cos\theta & 0 & -\sin\theta \\ 0 & 1 & 0 \\ \sin\theta & 0 & \cos\theta \end{bmatrix}$	θ	rotation angle
		α	rotation about x_3
		β	rotation about x_2'
		γ	rotation about x_3''
Rotation about x_3	$\mathbf{R}_3(\theta) = \begin{bmatrix} \cos\theta & \sin\theta & 0 \\ -\sin\theta & \cos\theta & 0 \\ 0 & 0 & 1 \end{bmatrix}$	$\mathbf{R}$	rotation matrix

Euler angles

$$\mathbf{R}(\alpha,\beta,\gamma) = \begin{bmatrix} \cos\gamma\cos\beta\cos\alpha - \sin\gamma\sin\alpha & \cos\gamma\cos\beta\sin\alpha + \sin\gamma\cos\alpha & -\cos\gamma\sin\beta \\ -\sin\gamma\cos\beta\cos\alpha - \cos\gamma\sin\alpha & -\sin\gamma\cos\beta\sin\alpha + \cos\gamma\cos\alpha & \sin\gamma\sin\beta \\ \sin\beta\cos\alpha & \sin\beta\sin\alpha & \cos\beta \end{bmatrix}$$

Pauli Matrices

Pauli matrices	$\sigma_1 = \begin{bmatrix} 0 & 1 \\ 1 & 0 \end{bmatrix}$ $\quad \sigma_2 = \begin{bmatrix} 0 & -\mathbf{i} \\ \mathbf{i} & 0 \end{bmatrix}$ $\sigma_3 = \begin{bmatrix} 1 & 0 \\ 0 & -1 \end{bmatrix}$ $\quad 1 = \begin{bmatrix} 1 & 0 \\ 0 & 1 \end{bmatrix}$	σ_i 1 $\mathbf{i}$	Pauli spin matrices 2×2 unit matrix $\mathbf{i}^2 = -1$
Anticommutation	$\sigma_i\sigma_j + \sigma_j\sigma_i = 2\delta_{ij}1$	δ_{ij}	Kronecker delta
Cyclic permutation	$\sigma_i\sigma_j = \mathbf{i}\sigma_k$ $(\sigma_i)^2 = 1$		

Fourier Series

Real form	$f(x) = \frac{a_0}{2} + \sum_{n=1}^{\infty}\left(a_n \cos\frac{n\pi x}{L} + b_n \sin\frac{n\pi x}{L}\right)$ $a_n = \frac{1}{L}\int_{-L}^{L} f(x)\cos\frac{n\pi x}{L}\,\mathrm{d}x$ $b_n = \frac{1}{L}\int_{-L}^{L} f(x)\sin\frac{n\pi x}{L}\,\mathrm{d}x$	$f(x)$ a_n, b_n	perodic function, period $2L$ Fourier coefficients
Complex form	$f(x) = \sum_{n=-\infty}^{\infty} c_n \exp\left(\frac{\mathbf{i}n\pi x}{L}\right)$ $c_n = \frac{1}{2L}\int_{-L}^{L} f(x)\exp\left(\frac{-\mathbf{i}n\pi x}{L}\right)\mathrm{d}x$	c_n	complex Fourier cofficient
Parseval's theorem	$\frac{1}{2L}\int_{-L}^{L} \lvert f(x)\rvert^2\,\mathrm{d}x = \frac{a_0^2}{4} + \frac{1}{2}\sum_{n=1}^{\infty}(a_n^2 + b_n^2)$ $= \sum_{n=-\infty}^{\infty} \lvert c_n\rvert^2.$	$\lvert\,\rvert$	modulus

Fourier Transform

Definition 1	$F(s) = \int_{-\infty}^{\infty} f(x) e^{-2\pi i x s} dx$ $f(x) = \int_{-\infty}^{\infty} F(s) e^{2\pi i x s} ds$	$f(x)$ $F(s)$	function of x Fourier transform of $f(x)$
Definition 2	$F(s) = \int_{-\infty}^{\infty} f(x) e^{-i x s} dx$ $f(x) = \frac{1}{2\pi} \int_{-\infty}^{\infty} F(s) e^{i x s} ds$		
Definition 3	$F(s) = \frac{1}{\sqrt{2\pi}} \int_{-\infty}^{\infty} f(x) e^{-i x s} dx$ $f(x) = \frac{1}{\sqrt{2\pi}} \int_{-\infty}^{\infty} F(s) e^{i x s} ds$		

Fourier Symmetry Relationships

$f(x)$	$\leftrightarrow$	$F(s)$	**Definitions**
even	$\leftrightarrow$	odd	real: $f(x) = f^*(x)$
odd	$\leftrightarrow$	odd	imaginary: $f(x) = -f^*(x)$
real, even	$\leftrightarrow$	real, even	even: $f(x) = f(-x)$
real, odd	$\leftrightarrow$	imaginary, odd	odd: $f(x) = -f(-x)$
imaginary, even	$\leftrightarrow$	imaginary, even	Hermitian: $f(x) = f^*(-x)$
complex, even	$\leftrightarrow$	complex, even	anti-Hermitian: $f(x) = -f^*(-x)$
complex, odd	$\leftrightarrow$	complex, odd	
real, asymmetric	$\leftrightarrow$	complex, Hermitian	
imaginary, asymmetric	$\leftrightarrow$	complex, anti-Hermitian	

Fourier Transform Theorems

Convolution	$f(x) * g(x) = \int_{-\infty}^{\infty} f(u)g(x-u)du$	f, g general functions $*$ convolution
Convolution rules	$f * g = g * f$ $f * (g * h) = (f * g) * h$	f $f(x) \leftrightarrow F(s)$ g $g(x) \leftrightarrow G(s)$
Convolution theorem	$f(x)g(x) \leftrightarrow F(s) * G(s)$	$\leftrightarrow$ Fourier transform relation
Autocorrelation	$f^*(x) \star f(x) = \int_{-\infty}^{\infty} f^*(u-x)f(u)du$	$\star$ correlation f^* complex conjugate of f
Wiener-Khintchine theorem	$f^*(x) \star f(x) \leftrightarrow \lvert F(s)\rvert^2$	
Cross-correlation	$f^*(x) \star g(x) = \int_{-\infty}^{\infty} f^*(u-x)g(u)du$	
Correlation theorem	$h(x) \star j(x) \leftrightarrow H(s)J^*(s)$	h, j real functions H $H(s) \leftrightarrow h(x)$ J $J(s) \leftrightarrow j(x)$
Parseval's relation (the power theorem)	$\int_{-\infty}^{\infty} f(x)g^*(x)dx = \int_{-\infty}^{\infty} F(s)G^*(s)ds$	
Parseval's theorem (Rayleigh's theorem)	$\int_{-\infty}^{\infty} \lvert f(x)\rvert^2 dx = \int_{-\infty}^{\infty} \lvert F(s)\rvert^2 ds$	
Derivatives $\frac{df(x)}{dx} \leftrightarrow 2\pi i s F(s)$ $\frac{d}{dx}[f(x) * g(x)] = \frac{df(x)}{dx} * g(x) = \frac{dg(x)}{dx} * f(x)$		

Quantum Uncertainty Relations

De Broglie relation	$p = \frac{h}{\lambda}$ $p = \hbar k$	$p, \mathbf{p}$ h $\hbar$ λ	particle momentum Planck constant $h/(2\pi)$ de Broglie wavelength
Planck-Einstein relation	$E = hv = \hbar\omega$	$\mathbf{k}$ E v ω	de Broglie wavevector energy frequency angular frequency ($= 2\pi v$)
Dispersion	$(\Delta a)^2 = \langle (a - \langle a \rangle)^2 \rangle$ $= \langle a^2 \rangle - \langle a \rangle^2$	a, b $\langle . \rangle$ $(\Delta a)^2$	observables expectation value dispersion of a
General uncertainty relation	$(\Delta a)^2 (\Delta b)^2 \geq \frac{1}{4} \langle \mathbf{i}[\hat{a}, \hat{b}] \rangle^2$	$\hat{a}$ $[\cdot,\cdot]$	operator for observable a commutator
Momentum-position uncertainty relation	$\Delta p \Delta x \geq \frac{\hbar}{2}$	x	particle position
Energy-time uncertainty relation	$\Delta E \Delta t \geq \frac{\hbar}{2}$	t	time
Number-phase uncertainty relation	$\Delta n \Delta \phi \geq \frac{1}{2}$	n ϕ	number of photons wave phase

Quantum Wavefunctions

Probability density	$\mathrm{pr}(x,t)\mathrm{d}x = \lvert\psi(x,t)\rvert^2\mathrm{d}x$	pr ψ	probability density wavefunction
Probability density current	$j(x) = \frac{\hbar}{2\mathbf{i}m}\left(\psi^*\frac{\partial\psi}{\partial x} - \psi\frac{\partial\psi^*}{\partial x}\right)$ $\boldsymbol{j} = \frac{\hbar}{2\mathbf{i}m}[\psi^*(\boldsymbol{r})\nabla\psi(\boldsymbol{r}) - \psi(\boldsymbol{r})\nabla\psi^*(\boldsymbol{r})]$ $= \frac{1}{m}\Re(\psi^*\hat{p}\psi)$	$\boldsymbol{j}, j$ $\hbar$ x $\hat{p}$ m $\Re$ t	probability density current (Planck constant)/(2π) position coordinate momemtum operator particle mass real part of time
Continuity equation	$\nabla\cdot\boldsymbol{j} = -\frac{\partial}{\partial t}(\psi\psi^*)$		
Schrödinger equation	$\hat{H}\psi = \mathbf{i}\hbar\frac{\partial\psi}{\partial t}$	H	Hamiltonian
Particle stationary states	$-\frac{\hbar^2}{2m}\frac{\partial^2\psi(x)}{\partial x^2} + V(x)\psi(x) = E\psi(x)$	V E	potential energy total energy

Quantum Expectation Value

Expectation value[a]	$\langle a\rangle = \langle\hat{a}\rangle = \int\Psi^*\hat{a}\Psi\mathrm{d}x$ $= \langle\Psi\lvert\hat{a}\rvert\psi\rangle$	$\langle a\rangle$ $\hat{a}$ Ψ x	expectation value of a operator for a (spatial) wavefunction (spatial) coordinate
Time dependence	$\frac{\mathrm{d}}{\mathrm{d}t}\langle\hat{a}\rangle = \frac{\mathbf{i}}{\hbar}\langle[\hat{H},\hat{a}]\rangle + \langle\frac{\partial\hat{a}}{\partial t}\rangle$	t $\hbar$	time (Planck constant)/2π)
Relation to eigenfunctions	if $\hat{a}\psi_n = a_n\psi_n$ and $\Psi = \sum c_n\psi_n$, then $\langle a\rangle = \sum\lvert c_n\rvert^2 a_n$	ψ_n a_n n c_n	eigenfunctions of a eigenvalues dummy index probability amplitudes
Ehrenfest's theorem	$m\frac{\mathrm{d}}{\mathrm{d}t}\langle r\rangle = \langle p\rangle$ $\frac{\mathrm{d}}{\mathrm{d}t}\langle p\rangle = -\langle\nabla V\rangle$	m r p V	particle mass position vector momentum potential energy

a. The expectation value uses the Dirac "bra-ket" notation for integrals involving operators where the presence of vertical bars distinguishes the use of angled brackets from that on the left-hand side of the equations. For example, $\langle a\rangle$ and $\langle\hat{a}\rangle$ are taken as equivalent.

Quantum Operators

Hermitian conjugate operator	$\int(\hat{a}\phi)^*\psi dx = \int\phi^*\hat{a}\psi dx$	a ψ, ϕ	Hermitian conjugate operator normalizable functions
Position operator	$\hat{x}^n = x^n$	* x, y	complex conjugate position coordinates
Momentum operator	$\hat{p}_x^n = \frac{\hbar}{\mathbf{i}}\frac{\partial^2}{\partial x^n}$	n p_x	arbitrary integer ≥ 1 momentum coordinate
Kinetic energy operator	$\hat{T} = -\frac{\hbar^2}{2m}\frac{\partial^2}{\partial x^2}$	T $\hbar$ m	kinetic energy (Planck constant)/(2π) particle mass
Hamiltonian operator	$\hat{H} = -\frac{\hbar^2}{2m}\frac{\partial^2}{\partial x^2} + V(x)$	H V	Hamiltonian potential energy
Angular momentum operators	$\hat{L}_z = \hat{x}\hat{p}_y - \hat{y}\hat{p}_x$ $\hat{L}^2 = \hat{L}_x^2 + \hat{L}_y^2 + \hat{L}_z^2$	L_z L	angular momentum along z axis total angular momentum
Parity operator	$\hat{P}\psi(\boldsymbol{r}) = \psi(-\boldsymbol{r})$	$\hat{P}$ r	parity operator position vector

Dirac Notation

Matrix element[a]	$a_{nm} = \int \psi_n^* \hat{a} \psi_m \mathrm{d}x$ $= \langle n \vert \hat{a} \vert m \rangle$	n, m a_{nm} ψ_n $\hat{a}$ x	eigenvector indices matrix element basis states operator spatial coordinate
Bra vector	bra state vector = $\langle n \vert$	$\langle \cdot \vert$	bra
Ket vector	ket state vector = $\vert m \rangle$	$\vert \cdot \rangle$	ket
Scalar product	$\langle n \vert m \rangle = \int \psi_n^* \psi_m \mathrm{d}x$		
Expectation	if $\Psi = \sum_n c_n \psi_n$ then $\langle a \rangle = \sum_m \sum_n c_n^* m_m a_{nm}$	Ψ c_n	wavefunction probability amplitudes
Inner product between the vectors $\vert \varphi \rangle$ and $\vert \psi \rangle$	$\langle \varphi \vert \psi \rangle$		
Tensor product of $\vert \varphi \rangle$ and $\vert \psi \rangle$	$\vert \varphi \rangle \otimes \vert \psi \rangle$ or, abbreviated as $\vert \varphi \rangle \vert \psi \rangle$		
Inner product between $\vert \varphi \rangle$ and $\mathbf{A} \vert \psi \rangle$	$\langle \varphi \vert \mathbf{A} \vert \psi \rangle$ or, equivalently, inner product between $\mathbf{A}^{\mathrm{T}} \vert \varphi \rangle$ and $\vert \psi \rangle$		

a. The Dirac bracket, $\langle n \vert \hat{a} \vert m \rangle$, can also be written as $\langle \psi_n \vert \hat{a} \vert \psi_m \rangle$.

Harmonic Oscillator

Schrödinger equation	$-\frac{\hbar^2}{2m}\frac{\partial^2\psi_n}{\partial x^2} + \frac{1}{2}m\omega^2 x^2 \psi_n = E_n\psi_n$	$\hbar$ m ψ_n x	(Planck constant)/(2π) mass *n*th eigenfunction displacement
Energy levels[a]	$E_n = \left(n + \frac{1}{2}\right)\hbar\omega$	n ω E_n	integer ≥ 0 angular frequency total energy in *n*th state
Eigenfunctions	$\psi_n = \frac{H_n(x/a)\exp[-x^2/(2a^2)]}{(n!2^n a\pi^{1/2})^{1/2}}$ where $a = \left(\frac{h}{m\omega}\right)^{1/2}$	H_n	Hermite polynomials
Hermite polynomials	$H_0(y) = 1$ $H_1(y) = 2y$ $H_2(y) = 4y^2 - 2$ $H_{n+1}(y) = 2yH_n(y) - 2nH_{n-1}(y)$	y	dummy variable

a. E_0 is the zero-point energy of the oscillator.

D: RAAM Gate Pending Patent

Patent-pending description of the Routt Addressable Absolute Memory Gate™ (RAAM Gate™), the quantum computational window to the Cosmic Computer and Cosmic Switchboard, United States Patent Application Number US 2004/0078421, published by the US Patent and Trademark Office (USPTO) on 22 April 2004—*Akshaya Tritiya*—Day of Lasting Achievements, as *"Methods For Transmitting Data Across Quantum Interfaces and Quantum Gates Using Same."*

Page 1 of 30-page patent appears on page 328. The complete text is available online at http://www.uspto.gov/

US 20040078421A1

(19) **United States**

(12) **Patent Application Publication** (10) **Pub. No.: US 2004/0078421 A1**

Routt (43) **Pub. Date: Apr. 22, 2004**

(54) **METHODS FOR TRANSMITTING DATA ACROSS QUANTUM INTERFACES AND QUANTUM GATES USING SAME**

(76) Inventor: **Thomas J. Routt**, Edmonds, WA (US)

Correspondence Address:
George N. Chaclas
Edwards & Angell, LLP
P.O. Box 9169
Boston, MN 02209-9169 (US)

(21) Appl. No.: **10/637,773**

(22) Filed: **Aug. 8, 2003**

Related U.S. Application Data

(60) Provisional application No. 60/402,427, filed on Aug. 10, 2002.

Publication Classification

(51) **Int. Cl.**[7] **G06F 15/16**

(52) **U.S. Cl.** **709/201**

(57) **ABSTRACT**

Quantum gaps exist between an origin and a destination that heretofore have prevented reliably utilizing the advantages of quantum computing. To predict the outcome of instructions with precision, the input data, preferably a qubit, is collapsed to a point value within the quantum gap based on a software instruction. After collapse the input data is restructured at the destination, wherein dynamics of restructuring are governed by a plurality of gap factors as follows: computational self-awareness; computational decision logic; computational processing logic; computational and network protocol and logic exchange; computational and network components, logic and processes; provides the basis for excitability of the Gap junction and its ability to transmit electronic and optical impulses, integrates them properly, and depends on feedback loop logic; computational and network component and system interoperability; and embodiment substrate and network computational physical topology.

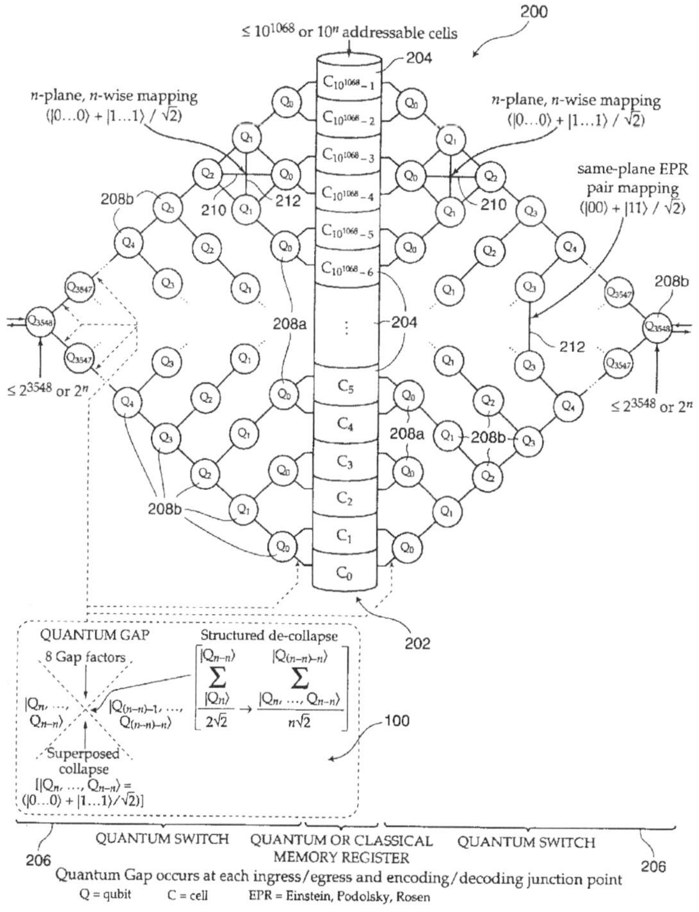

E: Maharishi's Achievements— A Glimpse of Fifty Years Around the World—1955–2005

HIS HOLINESS MAHARISHI MAHESH YOGI, founder of Transcendental Meditation and the worldwide Spiritual Regeneration Movement (**1957**), introduced research in the field of consciousness and brought to light seven states of consciousness (**1957–1967**); created a new science—the Science of Consciousness, the Science of Creative Intelligence—and trained 2,000 teachers of this new science (**1972**) [by now 40,000]; discovered the Constitution of the Universe—the lively potential of Natural Law—in Ṛk Veda, and discovered the structuring dynamics of Ṛk Veda in the entire Vedic Literature (**1975**); celebrated the Dawn of the Age of Enlightenment on the basis of the discovery of the *Maharishi Effect* (**1975**).

Maharishi created a World Government for the Age of Enlightenment with is sovereignty in the domain of consciousness and authority in the invincible power of Natural Law (**1976**); introduced the TM-Sidhi Programme and the experience of bubbling bliss in Yogic Flying to create supreme mind-body coordination in the individual and coherence in world consciousness (**1976**); formulated *Maharishi's Absolute Theory of Government, Maharishi's Absolute Theory of Education, Maharishi's Absolute Theory of Health, Maharishi's Absolute Theory of Defence, Maharishi's Absolute Theory of Economy, Maharishi's Absolute Theory of Management*, and *Maharishi's Absolute Theory of Law and Order* to raise every area of life to perfection (**1977**); brought to light the commentary of Ṛk Veda, *Apaurusheya Bhāshya,* as the self-generating, self-perpetuating structure of consciousness (**1980**); organized the millenia-old and scattered Vedic Literature as the literature of a perfect science—Maharishi's Vedic Science and Technology (**1981**).

Maharishi brought to light the full potential of Āyur-Veda, Gandharva Veda, Dhanur-Veda, Sthāpatya Veda, and Jyotish to create a disease-free and problem-free family of nations (**1985**); formulated his Master Plan to Create Heaven on Earth for the reconstruction of the whole world, inner and outer (**1988**); brought to light Supreme Political Science to introduce "Automation in Administration" and create conflict-free politics and a problem-free government in every country; inspired the formation of a new political party, the Natural Law Party, in an ever-increasing number of countries throughout the world to enrich and support national law with Natural Law, and in this way promoted a practical procedure to actualize his Absolute Theory of Government (**1992**); inaugurated Global Rām Rāj—Global Administration through Natural Law (**1993**).

Maharishi discovered the Veda and Vedic Literature in the human physiology, establishing the grand unity of all material diversity of creation—of all sciences and of all religions (**1993**). This has heralded the Dawn of the Vedic Civilization, civilization based on pure knowledge and the infinite organizing power of Natural Law—life according to Natural Law—where no one will suffer; all will enjoy the eternal glory of God—Heaven on Earth.

Maharishi has established and continues to establish Maharishi Vedic Universities, Maharishi Āyur-Veda Universities, and Maharishi Colleges of Vedic Medicine throughout the world to offer mastery over Natural Law on every level of education—from kindergarten to PhD—to every individual, and to perpetuate life in accord with Natural Law—perfection in every profession—and create a Natural Law-based problem-free government in every country—governments with the ability to prevent problems before they occur (**1993–1994**).

Maharishi introduced programs for prevention in the fields of health and security, to create healthy national life and an invincible armor of defence for the nation, by introducing new prevention-oriented programs of Maharishi Āyur-Veda—Maharishi's Vedic Medicine—for perfect health, and by introducing the programme for a PREVENTION WING in the military of every country to disallow the birth of an enemy just by training a small percentage of the military in the Vedic Technology of Defence—the Transcendental Meditation and TM-Sidhi Program including Yogic Flying (**1994**).

In **1995**, Maharishi established Maharishi University of Management in the USA, Japan, Holland, and Russia to eliminate the problems of management and improve the health, creativity, and good fortune of management everywhere.

Introduction of the knowledge of Natural Law in every field of management will actualize the evolutionary direction for every area of human concern.

Maharishi's Corporate Revitalization Program has been introduced in companies in the USA, Europe, India, and Australia to restore profitability and vitality to failing industries, and improve the performance of successful organizations.

Maharishi University of Management offers practical programs to prevent and eliminate problems of public administration, by bringing the support of Natural Law to national law.

In August **1995**, Maharishi announced a Political Leadership Training Course to present to leaders of all political parties the principles and scientifically validated programs of perfect administration through Natural Law in order to achieve the ideal of conflict-free politics and problem-free government.

Just three weeks later, the State Assembly of Madhya Pradesh, India, unanimously passed an Act establishing Maharishi Mahesh Yogi Vedic Vishwa-Vidyā-Laya (Maharishi Vedic University) in the State of Madhya Pradesh.

Maharishi Mahesh Yogi Vedic Vishwa-Vidyālaya will offer every citizen of Madhya Pradesh total knowledge of Natural Law as available in the Veda and Vedic Literature. Maharishi declared that this Vedic University will teach only one subject—*Ātmā*, the Self—and in this the University will offer the "fruit of all knowledge" to everyone.

"Fruit of all knowledge" means the total creative intelligence of the Self is fully awake on all levels of life—intellect, mind, senses, body, behavior, and environment. It means that the individual's relationship with others and also with the entire Cosmic Life—Sun, Moon, planets, and stars, which have been identified as the Cosmic Counterparts of the human physiology and quantum network architecture—is balanced and harmonious, and that the infinite organizing power of Natural Law is spontaneously available to the whole field of the individual's thought, speech, and action.

The "fruit of all knowledge" can be made available to everyone because:

1 The basic nature of *Ātmā*, the Self, is pure wakefulness—Transcendental Consciousness—pure knowledge, power, and bliss; and all streams of creation are nothing other than expressions of *Ātmā*—the unbounded ocean of the unmanifest field of consciousness—the Self of everyone.

2 Maharishi's insights into the nature of the Self, or *Ātmā*, of everyone; the emergence and evolution of Natural Law within this ocean of pure knowledge, power, and bliss; the holistic and specific structures of Natural Law available in the sounds of the Vedic Literature; Maharishi's commentary on Ṛk Veda, *Apaurusheya Bhāshya;* and the beautifully structured Vedic Science, "Maharishi's Vedic Science"—the Science and Technology of Consciousness—the most complete, fully developed, perfect science, which includes both approaches, the objective approach of modern science and subjective approach of Vedic Science, the approach of consciousness—all these beautiful gifts of knowledge for all mankind are emerging as the rising rays of the Dawn of the Age of Enlightenment, which Maharishi inaugurated in 1975.

In October **1995**, medical doctors from many nations adopted a resolution to establish Maharishi Medical Colleges in their countries in order to bring completeness to medical education, eliminate the hazards of modern medicine, and solve the current crisis in health care.

These medical colleges will offer the highest standard of modern medical training, supplemented by the latest understanding of human physiology in terms of the holistic and specific structures of intelligence available in the forty values of Vedic Literature.

To update the knowledge of practicing physicians, Maharishi Institutes of Postgraduate Medical Education are being established in conjunction with Maharishi Medical Colleges in countries throughout the world, including the USA, India, Japan, the United Kingdom, and Australia.

In December **1995**, in a two-day international celebration at Maharishi Vedic University, Holland, with the honored guest, Dr. Mukesh Nayak, Minister of Higher Education, Government of Madhya Pradesh, Maharishi appointed Ṛk Veda Salaxan-Ghan-Vidwān

Samba Dixit Agni Hotri to be the Vice-Chancellor of Maharishi Mahesh Yogi Vedic Vishwa-Vidyālaya in Madhya Pradesh.

In the first quarter of **1996**, Maharishi initiated action to establish Maharishi Vedic Universities, Colleges, and Schools in Madhya Pradesh by:

1 Training teachers of Maharishi's Vedic Science, which means those who will have the ability to impart Total Knowledge: experience of *Ātmā*, the Self, and understanding this experience through the Veda—making this experience of Total Knowledge and its infinite organizing power lively within the awareness of everyone and within the physiology of everyone;

2 Acquiring teaching facilities in every part of each city and in every large panchayat of each district.

In July **1996**, on Full Moon Day *(Guru Pūrnimā)* Maharishi inaugurated a program to establish a Global Administration through Natural Law, and on 12 January **1997** inaugurated the "Year of Global Administration," establishing a Global Administration with twelve Time-Zone Capitals around the world, in order to take full advantage of the administration of Natural Law centered in the life-giving Sun, whose influence on the earth changes from month to month, creating the different seasons, and constantly maintaining the evolutionary nature of Natural Law for all life everywhere.

This has provided a new philosophy of administration, offering new principles and programs to enrich national law in all countries with the nourishing influence of Natural Law.

Maharishi's Global Administration through Natural Law focuses on all areas of administration, but has its primary focus on the application of Natural Law in the fields of education and health—Total Knowledge, "fruit of all knowledge"—enlightenment—and perfect health for everyone. This will spontaneously make administration free from problems because all problems have their basis in lack of proper education and in ill health.

With the establishment of Maharishi's Global Administration through Natural Law, administration through national law in every country will begin to experience a lessening of problems in administration, and governments adopting the programs of Administration through Natural Law will begin to experience support of Natural Law—rise of the dignity of their sovereignty, self-sufficiency, and invincibility.

The training of Global Administrators in Maharishi Universities of Management and Maharishi Vedic Universities is under way to raise governmental administration through national law on a par with the perfect administration of the Government of Nature through Natural Law, so that every nation rises above problems, and every government gains the ability to fulfill its parental role for the whole population.

The worldwide awakening in the field of health care is due on one side to the awareness of the great inadequacy of health care and the hazards of modern medicine, and on the other side to the rise of a new system of health care—Maharishi's Vedic Approach to Health—the complete and perfect system of prevention and cure of disease, which handles health from the field of the inner intelligence of the body, from where Natural Law creates the physiology and administers it.

Maharishi's Vedic Approach to Health is being appreciated by doctors throughout the world, and the hope is rising that some day we will have a world free from sickness and suffering through Maharishi's Vedic Approach to Health and Maharishi's Vedic Science, which is the knowledge that is being imparted through Maharishi Vedic University for every individual and every nation to live life worth living—life in enlightenment.

As an achievement of the first quarter of **1997**, Maharishi established Maharishi Vedic Medical Council in India, and Maharishi Vedic Medical Association within other countries, with the participation of hundreds of eminent doctors in each country. Maharishi Vedic Medical Association is offering the principles and programs of perfect health through Maharishi's Vedic Approach to Health.

Maharishi's Vedic Approach to Health has been made available throughout the world via Maharishi Vedic Telemedicine on the World Wide Web (http://www.vedic-health.com/). This has launched Maharishi's global campaign to eliminate chronic disease as a first step to create a disease-free, enlightened world.

Maharishi also introduced a new aspect of his Vedic Approach to Health, the Instant Relief Programme for Chronic Disorders—Maharishi's Vedic Vibration Technology—a non-medical approach to enliven the body's inner intelligence and re-establish a balanced state of health.

Maharishi's Vedic Vibration Technology, using the ancient knowledge and technology of Vedic Sound—the fundamental sound values of Natural Law that structure the human physiology—has proved how quickly and effortlessly it is possible to transform the state of physiological disorder into a state of orderly physiological functioning.

Another achievement during the first quarter of **1997** was the establishment of Maharishi Global Construction Company in many countries to reconstruct the world in light of the "Vedic Principles of Construction"—building according to Natural Law (Sthāpatya Veda—*Vāstu Vidyā*), which gives importance to orientation and directionality in order to align any building (or any town, city, or country) and the activity within it, in harmony with the eternal cosmic harmony of the galactic universe.

Thus the application of all the forty areas of Natural Law has been designed and programmed, and a beautiful foundation for a healthy, enlightened world was achieved in the first quarter of **1997**.

On Full Moon Day, *Guru Pūrnimā,* 20 July **1997**, Maharishi Global Development Fund was inaugurated with the participation of the admirers and supporters of Maharishi's Transcendental Meditation Movement from many countries.

Maharishi Global Development Fund is a perpetual fund that will reconstruct the world on the basis of its invincible vitality, on the ground of the total knowledge of Natural Law, as brought to light by Maharishi.

Through its safe and creative investment policy, the Fund will attract all channels of donation and investment—private, corporate, and governmental—which will provide housing for a healthy living and working environment in all parts of the world, and will offer the knowledge and programs through which every individual can always gain the full support of Natural Law for success and fulfillment in daily life.

Maharishi Global Development Fund, incorporated in the State of Delaware, USA on 25 August **1997**, promises to improve world economy and create a better quality of life in the world. The Fund starts with a housing program in the 1000 largest cities of the world.

As the Fund is going to be inexhaustible, it will support world economy for the continued enrichment of life, generation after generation.

On 11 October **1997**, *Vijaya Dashmi Day*—Victory Day—in the midst of the largest financial community in the world in New York City, USA, Maharishi Global Development Fund celebrated the first phase of its global initiative to reconstruct the world on the basis of a projected budget of one hundred billion dollars.

During the first quarter of **1998**, in order to create an ideal, invincible India, Maharishi introduced the principles and programs of perfect administration to the people of India by introducing a new political party, the Ajeya Bharat Party, along the lines of the Natural Law Party, which has been the fastest growing political party in the family of nations.

The Ajeya Bharat Party, based on the perfect administration of Nature's Government, promotes the Vedic Approach to Administration, which utilizes the total intelligence of Natural Law to raise every area of Indian national life above problems and suffering in order to create an ideal, Invincible India.

On 6 February **1998**, Maharishi honored Professor Tony Nader, MD, PhD (His Majesty Raja Nader Rām), for his research on Veda in human physiology, which has brought to light that consciousness is the structuring intelligence and basic content of all physiological structures in creation. As a reward for his research, Professor Tony Nader received his weight in gold.

This discovery of the one-to-one correspondence between the structure of the eternal Veda and the structure and function of the human physiology has declared to the world that it is practically possible to actualize all possibilities in daily life through Vedic Education; Vedic Health Care; Vedic Administration; Vedic Industry; Vedic Economy; Vedic Management; Vedic Defence; Vedic Law, Justice, and Rehabilitation; Vedic Architecture; and Vedic Agriculture. It has proven that "individual is Cosmic," and that perfect health can be attained through the Vedic Approach to Health—the consciousness approach to health—that perfect health is realizable, suffering can be eliminated, and every nation can be raised to be healthy, wealthy, and wise; and that the family of nations can together enjoy perpetual peace on earth.

On 10 June **1998**, Maharishi inaugurated Maharishi Veda Vision—the Maharishi Channel—as the expression of the natural desire of the wise throughout the ages to create perfection in life and totally eliminate suffering—to bring the joy of "Heaven on Earth" to every individual and every nation in the world.

Maharishi Channel is a modern flow of the ancient, eternal Vedic Wisdom for perfection in life, and transformation of the stress and suffering-ridden world into a glowing world of health, wealth, and happiness.

Maharishi Channel is bringing in the timeless knowledge of Natural Law to every home, and is enlivening the reality that human life is the expression of the total knowledge of Natural Law; and that every individual can become "Cosmic" through consciousness-based education, Vedic Education; and that every individual can gain the ability to use his full creative potential and be supported by all the Laws of Nature; and that every individual can live his unbounded creativity for unbounded success and fulfillment in daily life.

Maharishi Channel very quickly expanded into a global network of eight satellite transmissions, and Maharishi Open University was inaugurated on 2 August **1998**, bringing the total knowledge of Natural Law to every country, broadcasting in twenty different languages from Maharishi Vedic University in the land of Wholeness—Holland.

Maharishi Open University introduced the total field of Vedic Wisdom in its first "Total Knowledge Course." Now, in the courses that follow, the application of this Total Knowledge will be applied to raise every profession in the world today to a higher level of perfection. Total Knowledge will be brought to light in courses on Business Management, Public Administration, Supreme Political Science, Vedic Defence, Vedic International Relations, Vedic Law (Natural Law or *Kanune Kudrat*) and Justice, Vedic Health Management, Vedic Architecture, Vedic Agriculture, and Maharishi Jyotish.

The laying of the foundation stone of the World Centre for Vedic Learning and Maharishi Vedic Vishwa Prashāsan Rājadhānī—the World Capital of Maharishi's Global Administration through Natural Law—took place at the *Brahma-Sthān* (central point of Natural Law) of India on 6 November **1998**.

This tallest building of the world will raise the Vedic Wisdom to its highest dignity, will radiate perpetual peace on earth, and will be the nourishing center of Vedic Wisdom to provide the supreme knowledge for perfection in life for all the twelve Time-Zone Capitals of Maharishi's Global Administration through Natural Law—Maharishi Vedic Vishwa Prashāsan—in order to quickly bring the benefit of Vedic Wisdom to all the people of the world.

This World Centre of Vedic Wisdom will train Vedic Scholars who will radiate an influence of peace, harmony, and happiness, bringing the support of Natural Law indiscriminately to everyone on earth for all time.

Maharishi's Programme to Reconstruct the World, inner and outer, was outlined in Maharishi's Master Plan to Create Heaven on Earth in **1988**, and now, seventeen years later (**2005**), it is literally bearing fruit—"organic fruit."

During the first quarter of **1999**, Maharishi re-established throughout India, in small villages and towns, the "one Guruji system," according to the tradition of Vedic Education, giving the opportunity to thousands of students to gain Total Knowledge and perpetuate life according to Natural Law in their family, society, and nation.

Through the "one Guruji" system, the same teacher takes the same student to higher classes year after year. The teacher and the students both rise to higher states of consciousness, and the Guruji also receives higher degrees in education from the university, with the resulting increase in professional, economic, and social status.

Maharishi's inspiration to make every country a "Country of World Peace," and his invitation to every government to declare their country the "Country of World Peace," led to the inauguration, on 20 March **1999**, of "Maharishi's Country of World Peace."

In Maharishi's Country of World Peace, the first session of the International Court of Justice will always be celebrated in the Parliament of World Peace on *Vihaya Dashami Day*—the "Day of Invincibility for Every Nation."

"Victory Day" of India, *Vijaya Dashami Day*, 19 October **1999**, was also celebrated as the "Day of Invincibility for Every Nation" in all countries where the construction of Peace Palaces began from Victory Day.

Above everything else, Maharishi's achievement of **1999** was the supreme achievement of the wise throughout the ages—an objectively derived and subjectively derived scientific formula to bring perfection to every man on the basis of Natural Law—*Veda Vani, Guru Vani, Kanune Kudrat*—the common heritage of all mankind—the eternal Constitution of the Universe, the Veda and Vedic Literature.

It is this total potential of Natural Law, the common heritage of all mankind, which is at the basis of the structure and function of the human physiology; and due to this inherent field of all possibilities within the DNA of every cell of the human physiology, and due to Maharishi's Technology of Natural Law, which, being a Technology of Consciousness, can stir the total field of human creativity within the human brain, every individual can gain the ability to know anything, do anything spontaneously right, and achieve anything through the support of Natural Law.

This vision of the forthcoming fully developed, fully enlightened perfect man and a peaceful world was the achievement of **1999**—the Third Year of Maharishi's Global Administration through Natural Law—Maharishi's Year of Invincibility to Every Nation.

The very start of Maharishi's worldwide Transcendental Meditation Movement had one verse of Ṛk Veda at is basis—one word, *"Parame Vyoman,"* of one *Ṛichā, "Ṛicho Ak-kshare parame vyoman yasmin Devā adhi vishwe nisheduḥ."*

This one timeless verse of Ṛk Veda has been discovered to be the source, or fountainhead, of intelligence—the most basic field of intelligence, Transcendental Consciousness, from where all fields of knowledge, all theories of modern science—Information Science and Technology, Quantum Network Architecture, Computer Science, Electrical Engineering, Optical Engineering, Physics, Chemistry, Mathematics, Physiology, Agriculture, Art, Astronomy, Business Administration, Economics, Education, Law, Literature, Music, Political Science, Psychology, Statistics—emerge.

This has presented the possibility of creating a perfect man, a perfect society, and a perfect world characterized by self-sufficiency and invincibility.

Maharishi inaugurated the Fourth Year of His Global Administration through Natural Law: Year of Perfectly Healthy Affluent Society on 12 January **2000**, to bring the knowledge of perfection in human life into every home and to eliminate poverty in the life of every individual so that everyone can enjoy the total cosmic creative potential of life.

Maharishi introduced the program to eliminate poverty in the world to improve the economy in the thirty-three poorest countries of the world through the development of all the unused agricultural lands using healthy organic farming principles and practice (**2000**).

On 16 July **2000**, Maharishi celebrated the *Swarṇ-Jayantī* (Cosmic Golden Jubilee) of his Master, Guru Dev, His Divinity Brahmānanda Saraswatī—50 years since he received from Guru Dev the inspiration to restore Vedic civilization to the world. Maharishi inaugurated a year-long celebration of swinging in the waves of bliss to enjoy the great blessing of Guru Dev—a Vedic world where every individual rises to their Cosmic status in higher consciousness, experiences the blossoming of noble qualities and bliss, and receives the full support of Natural Law for their every aspiration. On the collective level Vedic civilization means administration through Natural Law, creating a world free from disease and poverty, a world enjoying perpetual peace and heavenly life.

Following is an excerpt from Maharishi's Guru Purnima Address, 16 July 2000:

> The greatest blessing of Guru Dev is the perpetual, constant, all-the-time unboundedly present everywhere Constitution of the Universe, which runs the universe and maintains the unity of diversified existence. Diversified existence is eternally maintained on the level of unified wholeness.
>
> In Vedic words: *Aham Brahmasmi. Sarvam Khalu Idam Brahm*—everything is Totality. And in the state of Totality, miraculously, there is a flow, there is speed. There is least speed, least level of flow; and there is maximum speed, maximum flow.
>
> There are theories verified by mathematical conclusions that the universe is an expanding universe. It's always universe, and always an expanding universe. So these waves of time come and go in the eternal silence of the infinite and not only one infinity—infinite number of infinities. This is the vision of the ever-expanding universe.
>
> Where is the concluding point of it? This is of value to us. We are celebrating today Guru Dev's Golden Jubilee in order to bring out something most precious.

> We know gold to be most precious, shining gold, the inner aspect of the life-giving sun; the Self of everyone in terms of Veda—pure knowledge. And pure knowledge in terms of the unified wholeness of the three values: Knower, Knowing and Known. These we have understood all the time, and through Transcendental Meditation we have experienced that blissful value of our own self-referral quality of consciousness.
>
> All these years we have been telling the people about it. And those who heard it, they experienced it and they are better off today. Millions of individuals becoming better off, month after month, year after year, for all these 40-50 years.
>
> Now is the time for us to have a target of perpetual *Swarn-Jayanti. Swarn-Jayanti* means Golden Jubilee Celebration. Jubilee—the joy. The joy of what? The joy of the supreme value of life. The joy of a golden character, shining, radiating wealth, affluence and fulfillment to all mankind. We have that knowledge. It is by the grace of Guru Dev.

On 7 October, *Vijayā Dashami,* Victory Day, Maharishi inaugurated the Global Country of World Peace—*Vishwashanti Rastra*—with its Constitution in Ṛk Veda, the Constitution of the Universe, and its authority in the invincible organizing power of Natural Law, which naturally and eternally governs the evolution of all life everywhere. He invited all well-wishers of humanity to become its citizens and collectively fulfill the aspirations of the founders of every nation for permanent peace, an enlightened world, and the establishment of Heaven on Earth.

The purpose of establishing the Global Country of World Peace is to simplify administration on both levels—global and local—and bring all levels of administration in full accord with Natural Law.

The purpose of <u>Global</u> Administration is to maximize the nourishing power of Natural Law that connects our world with the ever-expanding universe around it. This Global Administration is being established along the lines of ideal administration in India—Vedic India—as available in the Vedic Literature in the Kingdom of Rām.

History records that no one suffered in the Kingdom of Rām—राम राज दुख काहु न व्यापा *Rām Rāj dukh kāhu na vyāpā (Rām Charit Mānasa, Uttar Kāṇd, 20.1)*—and no one suffered because everyone lived life spontaneously in accord with Natural Law—*Dharma*—the Will of God.

Administration of a solar system, under the influence of the life-giving Sun, is a unit of the Cosmic Administration of the galactic universe.

The administration of the solar system by the life-giving Sun, which is equally nourishing to us all, is the ideal administration on earth. It is this reality that Rām Rāj, the rule of total Natural Law, is upheld as the rule of the Solar Dynasty on earth.

Rām is portrayed in the Vedic Literature as the custodian of the total knowledge of administration—the embodiment of Unity Consciousness—Brāhmī Chetanā—राम ब्रह्म परमारथ रूपा *Rām Brahm paramārath rūpā (Rām Charit Manasa, Ayodhyā Kāṇd, 90.7, Uttar Kāṇd, 20.1-4).*

There are seven states of consciousness—waking state of consciousness, dreaming state of consciousness, deep sleep state of consciousness, Transcendental Consciousness, Cosmic Consciousness, God Consciousness, and Unity Consciousness.

Unity Consciousness is the highest state of consciousness—*Brāhmī Chetanā*—whereby the individual naturally lives mistake-free life according to Natural Law. In Unity Consciousness all the Laws of Nature spontaneously uphold every thought, speech, and action—every phase of life and living.

In Ṛk Veda this most exalted state of life is exemplified by the expression: यतीनां ब्रह्मा भंवति सारथिः *Yatīnāṁ Brahmā bhavati sārathiḥ (Ṛk Veda, 1.158.6).* Those established in Unity Consciousness—Yogic Consciousness—the consciousness of the administering intelligence of the universe—are spontaneously served by its infinite organizing power—the nourishing, evolutionary power of total Natural Law that administers the universe with perfect order.

Here is the technique for the administrator to realize ideal "Automation in Administration."

The technique of ideal administration—the technique of Rām Rāj, administration through Natural Law—is to educate and train the people to develop Unity Consciousness—*Brāhmī Chetanā*—and all their activity will naturally be upheld by total Natural Law.

Being naturally upheld by the evolutionary power of Natural Law, they will not create problems for themselves or for others. When individuals do not create problems in their lives, then the administration remains free from problems. In this way, administration is automatically maintained on an ideal level—ideal administration through ideal education—education through Veda, the total knowledge of Natural Law.

The imminent arrival of this golden Vedic age was seen by Maharishi in his coronation on 12 October **2000** of His Majesty Raja Nader Rām as *Vishwa Prashāsak,* the First Sovereign Ruler of the Global Country of World Peace. This coronation, along with the Rājyābhishek (installation ceremony) performed by the Vedic Pandits over the succeeding five days, brought to the highest level of fulfillment Maharishi's celebration of Guru Dev's Golden Jubilee.

On the sixth day of the coronation, 17 October **2000**, His Majesty Raja Nader Rām announced the establishment of his Cabinet of 40 Ministers, each upheld by the total Constitution of the Universe, and by one specific value of the 40 aspects of Veda and the Vedic Literature.

Having established ideal administration on the global level, it was necessary to establish the local units of this global administration on similar ideal principles.

In the search for establishing ideal units of local administration throughout the world it was found that tribal chiefs have been gracefully administering their people in their small kingdoms in different parts of the world for thousands of years. This level of administration has always been based on the parental love of the tribal chief for his people.

The central point from where this natural administration, based on love, draws its strength is from the natural nourishing power of Mother, which has its basis in the natural tribal language—the Mother Tongue.

The fundamental flow of communication through Mother Tongue promotes the natural evolution of life. This principle of allowing Natural Law to enrich life is again brought to light by the Vedic Literature: *Mātrī devo bhava, Pītrī devo bhava,*...etc. Uphold Mother, uphold Father, as the basic power of life—the essential power of all evolution—the fundamental power of administration.

Based on this Vedic authenticity of the natural hierarchy of life, administered through love, it was decided to acknowledge the natural tribal system of administration and restore the dignity of these units of local administration.

On 20 October, as the second step of achievement for the establishment of peace on earth, the World Federation of Traditional Kings (World Federation of Tribal Chiefs), the administrative units of the Global Country of World Peace, was formed in as assembly of tribal chiefs from New Zealand, Australia, South Africa, North America, South America, Norway, and Sweden.

Then, in a very natural, spontaneous sequence of events, tribal chiefs and traditional tribal Kings in many different countries expressed the desire to declare their small lands (their traditional kingdoms) as "Lands of World Peace."

On 12 January **2001**, while inaugurating the Year of the Global Country of World Peace, Maharishi joyfully proclaimed his satisfaction that the purpose of his Worldwide Movement had been fulfilled—a new world order of affluence and peace for the whole human race.

On 14 January His Majesty Raja Nader Rām installed the Chief Ministers of his Cabinet—those expert scientists, artists, and administrators who have insight into their own self-referral identity as *Ātmā*—their own Cosmic Self.

On 24 January **2001**, His Majesty Raja Nader Rām and his Cabinet of the Global Country of World Peace took a dip in the waters of the *Sangam*—the confluence of the holy rivers Ganges, Yamuna, and Saraswati in Prayag (Allahabad) India. His Holiness Maharishi Mahesh Yogi inspired His Majesty Raja Nader Rām to take his Cabinet for the dip, explaining that the dip in the Sangam means the dip of क् (K, the point value) into अ (A, unboundedness). Its significance is the vertical dive into the *Parame Vyoman*—the transcendental field—creating horizontal expanding waves of *Ānand* (Bliss) on the surface of life.

The founding of Maharishi's Global Country of World Peace unites peoples of all nations with a common desire for peace. It extends beyond state boundaries, beyond national boundaries, beyond continental boundaries, linking small and large territories. It unites individuals of all nationalities, cultures, and creeds—all the peace-loving people and peace-loving nations of the world—in a global initiative—in a global task—in a peaceful global unity.

With the Global Administration of the Global Country of World Peace, and with the units of this Global Administration in the local kingdoms of tribal Kings, history has taken a turn. This is the great transformation to the system of administration that will end the oppression of fear-based administration, corruption-based administration—that will end all wars and the struggle and strife of life in ignorance, and usher in the reign of perpetual peace on earth.

The Golden Jubilee Celebrations of Guru Dev were highlighted by this inauguration of Maharishi's Global Country of World Peace. We will always cherish the eternal custodians of Maharishi's Global Country of World Peace—the great Masters of the Vedic Tradition who have really blessed the world.

2002—Maharishi's Year of *RĀM MUDRĀ*

On 12 January **2002** Maharishi proclaimed **2002** to be the Year of RĀM MUDRĀ:

> Today, after doing the *puja* to Guru Dev, and after thrilling the world consciousness with the Vedic *Rashtra Gītā* of the Global Country of World Peace—we desire to proclaim the name of this year, as has been our habit to name every year of this very great transition in world consciousness from negativity to all harmony and positivity. So this year the name that comes is the Year of Rām Mudrā.
>
> Mudrā is currency, the currency of Rām Rāj, currency of that administration in which problems do not arise. And these problems not arising will be on the basis of an intense influence of global harmony and peace in the world that will prevail due to one big group of 40,000 Vedic Pandits on the holy banks of the Ganges in India—the Land of the Veda—

where throughout time traditional Vedic performances have been held in the custody of the Vedic *Pandits*.

They will be there, 40,000 at least, doing big and small *Yagyas* to awaken the divine influence in life, as prescribed by the Vedic Performances of *Yagyas* and *Mahayagyas* and *Graha Shantī*—and this system of life which requires purification year after year, called *Sānskaras*.

Sānskaras are the systems of purification of physiology, its connection with the mind, and its connection with the Self—the whole field of the transcendental Self consciousness at the basis of all different values of speech and material existence on earth. So we will organize this big group of 40,000 on the Ganges banks of India with the help of Rām Mudrā.

Rām stands for totality of Natural Law, Total Knowledge endowed with the total organizing power of Natural Law. And because this knowledge has been in the hands of the Vedic Pandits from times immemorial, now is the time that the blessings of Guru Dev, the blessings of the tradition of Vedic Masters, have aroused in us a responsibility to create this one place on Earth—preferably in the Land of the Veda—from where an intense influence of harmony and peace will radiate in all parts of the world. Due to that, it will be like the intense torchlight which will spread far and wide, and will not leave any corner of the world in darkness, in ignorance.

So that is our undertaking this year, and therefore we named this year as the 'Year of Rām Mudrā.'

Mudrā means currency, the currency of Rām. Rām is *Brāhm*, the Totality of Natural Law. Rām Mudrā is for all the marketing of our world. Our world means the world of peaceful people, not minding the other destroyers of the world who are growing in magnitude. We don't mind them. A scorpion will always sting.

But God's grace has always saved the world. So many *Rākshasas* (forces of destruction in global life) have been there in the past, and we are witnessing the *Rākshasa* opinion everywhere: 'I'll kill this, I'll kill this; bombing this, bombing this.'

So this has been continuing in the world, and it will continue. But our performance also will continue. The darkness has always existed, and the candlelights and the torchlights also have existed. So we can cope with all the destructive features of life on earth. But we will be in light.

The Vedic Tradition is an eternal Tradition of Total Knowledge in which there is no chance for any darkness to come in. Therefore, we'll create harmony and peace from one place on Earth, which we call the capital of Rām Rāj, the Capital of that administration of which the ancient records say that 'suffering belonged to no one.'

Rām Raj Dukha kahu na vyapa: 'In the reign of Rām, in the reign of Brāhm, in the reign of total Natural Law, in the reign of peace and harmony, suffering belonged to no one.'

It's not a new world. Indian history records this world to be coming and going, coming and going. Every day the sun shines, and every evening the night takes over. This light and darkness continue off and on. We enjoy both—we rest in the night, we work in the day. So we make use of both values. But we uphold the value of light, the value of harmony, of peace.

In this Year of Rām Mudrā we will have harmony in the world, and we will be concerned with ourselves, with our responsibility.

Our responsibility is to behave according to our nature. Our nature is *Sat Chit Ānanda*—bliss consciousness on an eternal continuum basis. And is this some dark patches come and go, so we have to mind ourselves. We don't mind what others do.

We will be focused during this year to establish peace on earth where such intensity of *Sāttva* will be generated—due to the daily routine of life of the Vedic *Pandits*—that it will radiate that harmony, happiness, peace and coherence in world consciousness, where problems will not arise.

So the message of today will be to centralize ourselves in our own real nature, which is divine, which is unbounded peace, which is the Unified Field as measured and brought to light by the physical sciences and the great research into consciousness at the basis of the physiology by our dear Raja Rām, who has proclaimed to the world that all physical matter is essentially the field of consciousness—the unbounded, still field of consciousness and waves of consciousness.

So here is a materialization of the age-old reality which was thought to be a field of philosophy. Now it's on the physical, material level in this scientific age. We are very well-placed in the field of knowledge, all the eternal knowledge of the 40 values of the Vedic Literature—Veda, Vedānga, Yoga, *bhākti* (devotion)—all this very great and perfect way of life. We have been giving out to the world a straight, lighted path of evolution to engage the higher states of consciousness for every aspect of our daily life.

We'll continue on those very beautiful, pleasant duties assigned by our tradition of Vedic Masters, by Guru Dev, and certified and welcomed by the scientific research in the fields of all physical sciences.

We are on a very solid ground of stability of peace perpetual on earth, and now we have conceived of a global administration that will disallow the sprouting of any problem in any part of the world. The world will be a global world of everyone concerned. And globally, the whole world family will move together on the path of higher states of consciousness, engaging higher intelligence and moving fast to achieve the supreme goal of life—realization of God, all harmony, all peace, Heaven on Earth—our beautiful target of all these years.

Now we have a global administration which will run by Natural Law—the Will of God—and which will be helped by the currency of Rām to relieve everyone from stress and strain.

The world has drifted away from the real path of peace and happiness, and we are resolved to create a Capital of World Peace, and to create from that Capital an administration of Natural Law where there is an open gate to Heaven, a direct evolutionary path of life for everyone…

There is a great jubilation today in the hearts and minds of all those who are a class of peace-loving people on earth. Today is a great starting point to launch the program of building a Capital of the World which will administer world affairs on the line of creating and maintaining Heaven on Earth.

All glory to Guru Dev, and we bow down to our Tradition of Masters which we have as a source of inspiration all the time.

All glory to Guru Dev.

Jai Guru Dev.

2003—Maharishi's Year of Ideal Government—*RĀM RAJ*

During 2003 Maharishi welcomed every government to contract with the Global Country of World Peace to create prevention-oriented problem-free administration. He pointed out that achievement of the long-sought goal of mankind—permanent world peace—would be established through the creation of 3000 Peace Palaces in the largest cities of the world, and establishment of the largest group of Vedic Pandits in India, *'permeating all time and all space values with harmony, with evenness of higher intelligence'* through recitation of the Veda and programs of *Vedic Yagya* and *Graha Shanti*.

Maharishi inaugurated the Parliament of World Peace to raise world consciousness to a high degree of coherence for all nations to enjoy permanent peace. On the auspicious Guru Purnima Day, 13 July 2003, Maharishi offered to every government to train their administrators to engage in their administrative policies and programs the intelligence and energy of total Natural Law—the Light of God—the Will of God—which governs the universe with perfect order. He explained that this training of administrators on the one hand, will make the process of administration the steps of evolution for the administrator, and, on the other hand, will render administration prevention-oriented and free from problems, and impart to it the character of *'automation in administration.'*

2004—Maharishi's Year of Peace Palaces

Maharishi inaugurated 2004 as his Year of Peace Palaces of the Global Country of World Peace on 12 January 2004, and launched a plan to immediately construct Peace Palaces in every country and train expert administrators in the knowledge of total Natural Law to create a world of peace and affluence for all times to come. He said: "We have the knowledge of total Natural Law—which administers the universe with perfect order—and we have a short, direct path to awaken this total knowledge within the awareness of every individual. With our success of the past 40 to 50 years, we begin this new year with a great momentum to perpetuate this knowledge and create a new world where no one has to face problems or suffering—now or in the future."

Maharishi said that the Peace Palaces will be constructed according to Vedic architecture in harmony with Natural Law, and will provide a proper home for the enlightened administrators of the Global Country of World Peace. "The cosmic wakefulness of total

Natural Law—the Will of God—will be the guiding feature of every Peace Palace," Maharishi said.

2005—Maharishi's Year of the Golden Jubilee

Maharishi inaugurated 2005 as his Year of the Golden Jubilee on 12 January 2005, launching a global program to establish Maharishi Vedic Universities, Colleges and Schools in 3000 cities throughout the world. Maharishi said that the new Vedic educational institutions will offer the knowledge and practical programs to actualize the Constitution of the Universe—the Unified Field—in the daily life of every individual and every nation to create permanent world peace.

"The Constitution of the Universe administers the universe with perfect order," Maharishi said. "Total knowledge of the Constitution of the Universe will create and maintain world order so that every individual enjoys enlightenment and every nation enjoys invincibility. This new knowledge will create a new human race."

Maharishi said that the new Vedic universities, college and schools will provide the total knowledge of the Constitution of the Universe through 18 faculties to make the knowledge of every area of life complete. "Great, secret details of the Constitution of the Universe—the Unified Field—to bring life into full accord with Natural Law are available only in the Vedic literature, not in the modern physical sciences," Maharishi said.

These 18 faculties are:

1. Education
2. Health
3. Agriculture
4. Management—Business and Industry
5. Architecture
6. Law and Order
7. Invincibility
8. Music and Arts
9. Science and Technology
10. Public Administration

11. Astrology and Astronomy
12. Language
13. World Peace/World Politics
14. Economics
15. Computer Science
16. Communication
17. Engineering
18. Religion

Maharishi emphasized that total knowledge of the Constitution of the Universe cannot be gained through lectures and discussions alone: "The Constitution of the Universe is beyond human intellect. It is on the transcendental level of Being. It is unmanifest, eternal, beyond relativity, and not subject to change. Vedic literature provides the practical programs, including Transcendental Meditation, its advanced techniques, and Yogic Flying, for everyone to actualize the Constitution of the Universe in daily life."

Maharishi said that the 18 faculties taken together will actualize for every student the 18 fundamental areas of the Constitution of the Universe. "These 18 fundamental areas are contained in the Vedic literature and inscribed in the human physiology—and have been discovered through scientific research by His Majesty Raja Raam," Maharishi said. "Every week, every student will go through all these areas of knowledge for their theoretical and practical values. This is how the Constitution of the Universe will become a living reality in the daily life of everyone so that the whole human race will always remain in the evolutionary direction of Total Natural Law—the Will of God."

Maharishi further stated that the study of the Constitution of the Universe will be blissful—unlike the stressful task students face in modern education. "The study and experience of the Constitution of the Universe will be in terms of the waves of bliss—not in terms of hard work. There will be no stress and no strain. Enlivening all possibilities in the Constitution of the Universe will be a joy from beginning to end."

Maharishi also said that particular emphasis will be placed on establishing Vedic universities, colleges, and schools in India: "The world needs a strong India for a strong Vedic world. A strong Vedic world will be a world of Total Knowledge—a world free from mistakes and failures."

Maharishi concluded by proclaiming a bright future for the world:

> We have the knowledge of the Constitution of the Universe, and we are establishing Vedic universities, colleges, and schools everywhere to bring this knowledge to the whole population and fulfill the Vedic aspiration: enlightenment to every individual, invincibility to every nation—and all good to everyone in the light of God. For this we say, 'All glory to our master, Guru Dev, and the tradition of Vedic Masters, and glory to the administration of this beautiful new world, His Majesty Raja Raam, First Ruler of the Global Country of World Peace.'

Figure E-1: Maharishi's Global Achievements Summarized
Spreading the Light of Enlightenment Around the World—1955-2005

Year	Name of Year	Achievement Highlights
1955		Maharishi travels from Uttar Kashi, the "Valley of the Saints," to Rameshvaram, a well known temple in the southern tip of India and later provides seven public lectures in Trivandrum, Kerala, India
1956		Maharishi continued lecturing and teaching the Transcendental Meditation technique throughout India and the region
1957		December 1957 in Madras, Maharishi addresses more than 10,000 people assembled there for the three-day Seminar of Spiritual Luminaries to celebrate the 89th birthday anniversary of Guru Dev
1958	Maharishi's Year of Spiritual Regeneration	On January 1, 1958, Maharishi formally inaugurates the Spiritual Regeneration Movement in Madras, India
1959	Maharishi's Year of Global Awakening	First world tour begins—Maharishi begins to teach the TM technique around the world
1960	Maharishi's Year of Cosmic Consciousness	Maharishi explains experiences of the TM technique in terms of Cosmic Consciousness; First 3-Year Plan inaugurated in London
1961	Maharishi's Year of Teacher Training	Second world tour begins; Maharishi decides to 'multiply himself' by training techers of the TM technique—first international course held in Rishikesh, India
1962	Maharishi's Year of Theory of the Absolute	Third world tour begins; Maharishi brings to light the Theory of the Absolute

Figure E-1: Maharishi's Global Achievements Summarized
Spreading the Light of Enlightenment Around the World—1955-2005

Year	Name of Year	Achievement Highlights
1963	Maharishi's Year of the Science of Being and Art of Living	Fourth world tour begins; Science of Being and Art of Living published
1964	Maharishi's Year of God Consciousness	Fifth world tour begins; Maharishi explains experiences of the TM technique in terms of the most refined state of Cosmic Consciousness—God Consciousness
1965	Maharishi's Year of Bhagavad-Gita	Completion of Maharishi's translation and commentary on the first six chapters of the Bhagavad Gita
1966	Maharishi's Year of Academy of Meditation	First International Academy of Meditation established in Rishikesh, India
1967	Maharishi's Year of Unity Consciousness	Maharishi explains experiences of the TM technique in terms of Unity Consciousness
1968	Maharishi's Year of Students	Students International Meditation Society founded in several countries
1969	Maharishi's Year of Supreme Knowledge	Maharishi comments on the *Brahma Sutras*, the textbook of Vedanta which provides complete knowledge of Unity Consciousness
1970	Maharishi's Year of Scientific Research	First scientific research published on the benefits of the TM technique
1971	Maharishi's Year of Science of Creative Intelligence	Maharishi formulates the Science of Creative Intelligence (SCI); Maharishi International University (MIU) founded in the United States
1972	Maharishi's Year of the World Plan	Inauguration of the World Plan to 'solve the age-old problems of mankind in this generation'; 2000 teachers of SCI trained
1973	Maharishi's Year of Action for the World Plan	More than 2000 World Plan Centers established in all parts of the world
1974	Maharishi's Year of of Achievement of the World Plan	Discovery of the Maharishi Effect—1% of a city's population practicing the TM program found to reduce crime, accidents, and sickness in society
1975	Maharishi's Year of the Dawn of the Age of Enlightenment	Maharishi travels to all six continents to inaugurate the Dawn of the Age of Enlightenment; Maharishi European Research University (MERU) founded in Switzerland
1976	Maharishi's Year of of Government	World Government of the Age of Enlightenment; TM-Sidhi program introduced, reviving the theory and practice of Yoga
1977	Maharishi's Year of Ideal Society	Ideal Society Campaign launched in 108 countries to decrease negative tendencies and increase positive trends in society

Figure E-1: Maharishi's Global Achievements Summarized
Spreading the Light of Enlightenment Around the World—1955-2005

Year	Name of Year	Achievement Highlights
1978	Maharishi's Year of Invincibility for Every Nation	Discovery of the Maharishi Effect—the square root of 1% practicing the TM-Sidhi program together in one place produces coherence in collective consciousness; Maharishi proclaims 'Invincibility to Every Nation'
1979	Maharishi's Year of All Possibilities	First Annual World Peace Assembly held in Amherst, Massachusetts, USA to create coherence in national and world consciousness
1980	Maharishi's Year of Pure Knowledge	Maharishi brings to light his timeless commentary of Rk Veda—the *Apaurusheya Bhashya*; First International Vedic Science Course for 3000 Governors of the Age of Enlightenment held in New Delhi, India
1981	Maharishi's Year of Vedic Science	Founding of two groups dedicated to gaining enlightenment; the Thousand-Headed *Purusha* program for men and Thousand-Headed Mother Divine program for ladies
1982	Maharishi's Year of Natural Law	Inauguration of Maharishi University of Natural Law in England
1983	Maharishi's Year of the Unified Field	Maharishi International University in Fairfield, Iowa hosts 8000 'Yogic Flyers'—experts in Maharishi's Technology of the Unified Field—to create the first Global Maharishi Effect
1984	Maharishi's Year of Unified-Field Based Civilization	Maharishi formulates his Unified Field-Based Integrated Systems of Education, Health, Government, Economics, Defense, Rehabilitation, and Agriculture
1985	Maharishi's Year of Unified-Field Based Education	Maharishi Vedic University inaugurated in Washington, DC; Maharishi restores Ayur-Veda to its completeness; Maharishi Ayur-Veda Prevention Centers established worldwide
1986	Maharishi's Year of Perfect Health	World Plan for Perfect Health and the Global Campaign to Create a Disease-Free Society inaugurated; Maharishi *Amrit Kalash* offered to the world
1987	Maharishi's Year of World Peace	Maharishi discovers the 21 lost *Samhitas* of *Ṛk Veda*; Global Festival of Music for World Peace introduces Maharishi Gandharva Veda music to create balance in nature
1988	Maharishi's Year of Achieving World Peace	Maharishi celebrates World Peace Day and inaugurates his Master Plan to Create Heaven on Earth through the reconstruction of the whole world, inner and outer
1989	Maharishi's Year of Heaven on Earth	Eradication of poverty and achieving an affluent society as steps to create Heaven on Earth
1990	Maharishi's Year of Alliance with Nature's Government	Introduction of the knowledge of natural law for perfection in every profession

Figure E-1: Maharishi's Global Achievements Summarized
Spreading the Light of Enlightenment Around the World—1955-2005

Year	Name of Year	Achievement Highlights
1991	Maharishi's Year of Support of Nature's Government	Group of 7000 'Yogic Flyers' established at the World Capital of the Age of Enlightenment in Maharishi Nagar, India
1992	Maharishi's Year of the Constitution of the Universe	Maharishi Vedic University inaugurated in ten countries; discovery of the Constitution of the Universe
1993	Maharishi's Year of Administration Through Natural Law—Rām Raj	Inauguration of Maharishi's Global Administration through Natural Law; *Maharishi's Absolute Theory of Government* published
1994	Maharishi's Year of Discovery of Veda in Human Physiology	Discovery by Professor Tony Nader, MD, PhD, under Maharishi's inspiration, of Veda and Vedic Literature in the human physiology
1995	Maharishi's Year of Silence	*Maharishi's Absolute Theory of Defence* published; Maharishi University of Management (MUM) established
1996	Maharishi's Year of Awakening	Construction of the Spiritual Center of America in North Carolina, USA
1997	Maharishi's Year of Global Administration through Natural Law	Inauguration of the Global Development Fund to create ideal homes for every family
1998	Maharishi's Second Year of Global Administration through Natural Law	Maharishi Vedic Instant Relief program offered to the world
1999	Maharishi's Third Year of Global Administration through Natural Law	The Year of Invincibility to Every Nation through Maharishi Open University (MOU)
2000	Maharishi's Fourth Year of Global Administration through Natural Law	Maharishi inaugurates his Global Country of World Peace to create an indomitable influence of non-violence in world consciousness, and crowns Professor Tony Nader, MD, PhD, as His Majesty Raja Nader Rām, First Sovereign Ruler of the Global Country of World Peace, for his historic discovery of the Veda and Vedic Literature in human physiology
2001	Maharishi's Year of Global Country of World Peace	Maharishi blesses the largest gathering of humanity—the *Maha Kumbha Mela*, Prayag, India—through the delegation of His Majesty Raja Nader Rām and his forty Ministers
2002	Maharishi's Year of Rām Mudra	His Majesty Raja Nader Rām establishes the Central Bank of the Global Country of World Peace in Maharishi Vedic City, Iowa, USA; Maharishi conducts special one-month Enlightenment Conferences and designs a program to construct 3000 Peace Palaces to provide every major city in the world with a powerful influence of coherence and harmony

Figure E-1: Maharishi's Global Achievements Summarized
Spreading the Light of Enlightenment Around the World—1955-2005

Year	Name of Year	Achievement Highlights
2003	Maharishi's Year of Ideal Government—Rām Raj	Maharishi welcomes every government to contract with the Global Country of World Peace to create prevention-oriented problem-free administration
2004	Maharishi's Year of Peace Palaces	Maharishi inaugurates 2004 as his Year of Peace Palaces of the Global Country of World Peace on 12 January 2004, and launches a plan to immediately construct Peace Palaces in every country and train expert administrators in the knowledge of total Natural Law to create a world of peace and affluence for all times to come
2005	Maharishi's Year of the Golden Jubilee	Maharishi inaugurates 2005 as his Year of the Golden Jubilee on 12 January 2005, launching a global program to establish Maharishi Vedic Universities, Colleges and Schools in 3000 cities throughout the world

F: Maharishi in the World Today

His Holiness Maharishi Mahesh Yogi is widely regarded as the foremost scientist in the field of consciousness and is considered to be the greatest teacher in the world today. His Vedic Science and Technology, which unfolds the full potential of Natural Law in human consciousness as the basis of improving all areas of life, is regarded as the most effective program of human development.

Maharishi's technique of Transcendental Meditation is the most widely practiced and extensively researched program for self-development in the world. More than 600 scientific research studies conducted during the past thirty-five years at over 200 independent universities and research institutes in 28 countries have validated the profound benefits of the Maharishi Transcendental Meditation program for the individual and for every area of society, including health, education, business, industry, rehabilitation, defence, agriculture, and government.

Over five million people in all parts of the world and from all walks of life practice the Maharishi Transcendental Meditation program. Forty thousand teachers of the Transcendental Meditation program have been trained so far, and more are continuing to be trained.

In addition, more than 100,000 people have learned the Maharishi TM-Sidhi program and are daily practicing "Yogic Flying," an advanced program of Transcendental Mediation that dramatically enhances all the benefits brought about by the Transcendental Meditation program for the individual, and creates a highly purifying influence in world consciousness.

Maharishi has held hundreds of World Peace Assemblies on all continents during the past fifty years, with many thousands of people coming together to create coherence in world consciousness through the group practice of the Transcendental Meditation and TM-Sidhi programs (Yogic Flying program).

In 1986, on the basis of the rising Maharishi Effect—coherence in world consciousness resulting from his World Peace Assemblies—Maharishi inaugurated his program to create world peace by establishing a permanent group of seven thousand Vedic Scientists in Maharishi Ved Vigyan Vishwa Vidya Peeth, Maharishi Nagar, India, to create coherence in collective consciousness on a permanent basis through the group practice of the Transcendental Meditation and TM-Sidhi program.

Over the past fifty years Maharishi has established a worldwide organization with more than 1,200 centers in 108 countries. Hundreds of books have been published about Maharishi's teachings. These have been translated into many languages and have been distributed globally.

Maharishi is one of the most videotaped personalities in history. There are more than 14,000 hours of video and audio tape recordings of lectures in Maharishi's international film and tape library.

Maharishi has completely restored the thousands-of-years-old scattered Vedic Literature for the total significance of its theory and practice, and has organized it in the form of a complete science of consciousness. The Transcendental Meditation program is the subjective technology of Maharishi's Vedic Science of Consciousness.

Maharishi Vedic Science and Technology is a complete science and technology of consciousness; it is the complete science and technology of life, capable of raising all aspects of life to perfection.

The practicality of creating the supreme quality of life on earth—Heaven on Earth—through Maharishi Vedic Science and Technology has been amply verified during the past thirty-three years by scientific research, which documents the benefits in every aspect of life—physiology, psychology, sociology, and ecology. It has also been substantially verified by personal experience, and by the authenticity of the ancient, traditional Vedic Literature.

The global achievements of these fifty years, on the ground of tested knowledge, prompted Maharishi to launch a global program to create Heaven on Earth—life according to Natural Law. The Heaven on Earth project calls for reconstruction of the whole world, inner and outer. The Maharishi Heaven on Earth Development Corporation has been established as a global organization to create Heaven on Earth.

Maharishi's knowledge, Maharishi's Vedic Science and Technology, Maharishi's eternal Constitution of the Universe, which is present everywhere, and Maharishi's simple approach for everyone to enjoy life according to Natural Law, are the foundation of Maharishi's global action to create Heaven on Earth and perpetuate it for all generations to come.

The revival of Vedic Wisdom through Maharishi Vedic Science and Technology, and establishment of Maharishi Vedic University, Maharishi Ayur-Veda University, and the Maharishi University of Management in many countries, provide that perfect knowledge of Natural Law which will forever continue guiding mankind on the path to perfection—daily life in accordance with Natural Law.

A review of all the scientific research on the Transcendental Meditation and TM-Sidhi programs reveals that the sequential unfoldment of pure knowledge and its infinite organizing power has brought about the experience of pure consciousness, has given rise to higher states of consciousness in the individual, and has purified world consciousness, as evidenced by the rising waves of achievement of Maharishi's Movement throughout the world over the past fifty years.

Maharishi's call to governments of the world and his offer of a practical formula for every government to come in alliance with Nature's Government, to gain the support of Nature's Government, and gain the ability to nourish everyone and satisfy everyone, is so unique and unprecedented in the thousands of years of struggling history of governments that probably the political leadership of the world, working under stress and strain, could not believe that the support of Nature could be gained in a systematic, scientific manner by all.

Having realized that it is possible to free governments from problems and develop in them the ability to prevent problems, Maharishi decided to establish a Global Country of

World Peace, with its seat in every country. The effect of the Global Country of World Peace will be to raise the administration of existing governments through national law to the dignity of Global Administration through Natural Law.

In the context of the Absolute Theory of Government it is enough to mention the ideal of government available in the Global Government of Natural Law. However, it is necessary to mention that the relationship of the government of every country with Maharishi's Global Government of Natural Law will be so elevating and nourishing to every government of the world that every Head of State will enjoy the full support of Natural Law, and his government will enjoy the ability to prevent problems and will substantiate the new definition of government provided by Maharishi's Absolute Theory of Government.

Maharishi's practical program is to quietly establish life according to Natural Law without requiring change in any area of the existing administration, which is based on the national constitution of the country. This global initiative to irrevocably change the course of time in favor of peace and happiness for all mankind places Maharishi on a supremely exalted level of rulership, which far surpasses the wisdom or administrative skill of any sovereign ruler in the world that history has ever recorded.

The establishment of Maharishi's Global Country of World Peace will lead the administrative quality of every government in the direction of perfection so that every government functions on a par with the absolute administration of the universe, the Government of Nature, which is universally nourishing. Ṛk Veda places this supreme skill of leadership in the hands of *Brahm*, the Ultimate Reality:

> यतीनां ब्रह्मा भवति सारथिः
> *Yatīnāṁ Brahmā bhavati sārathiḥ*
> *(Ṛk Veda, 1.158.6)*

Brahma, the total potential of pure knowledge and its infinite organizing power—the lively Constitution of the Universe, Natural Law—becomes the charioteer of all activity.

Ṛk Veda assigns supreme rulership to that self-referral quality of consciousness, the total potential of Natural Law—*Brahm*. The total potential of Natural Law conducts the activity of those who have identified their intelligence with the infinite organizing power of pure intelligence at the level of self-referral consciousness.

Every custodian of Maharishi's Absolute Theory of Government will have access to this enormous intelligence and power in his own self-referral consciousness—in his own Transcendental Consciousness—in his own physiology. Ṛk Veda, the Constitution of the Universe, will be enlivened in the heart of everyone, and, through a group of Yogic Flyers, an indomitable influence of harmony and peace will be generated in national consciousness, which will influence the whole collective consciousness of the world. Indomitable Maharishi Effect—positivity and harmony—will be maintained in world consciousness, generation after generation.

Maharishi in the world today is a cosmic figure caring for the well-being of all mankind and establishing a system to perpetuate life according to Natural Law, the cherished ideal of every government. Maharishi attributes his achievements to Shri Guru Dev, His Divinity Brāhmaṇanda Saraswati Jagadguru Bhagwan Shankaracharya of Jyotir Math, Himalayas—most illustrious embodiment of Vedic Wisdom in the eternal tradition of Vedic Masters.

During the past fifty years the purity of world consciousness has been steadily rising; life according to Natural Law has been steadily rising. It is satisfying that with the blossoming of this Absolute Theory of Government, the world is witnessing the signs of a new awakening in every field in the direction of fulfillment.

Now is the time for the world to witness the full glory of life according to Natural Law—to experience the full dignity of life in peace, prosperity, and happiness, with enlightenment and fulfillment in daily life.

This is Maharishi in the world today, a quiet guardian of all nations. Through his brilliance in the field of knowledge and administration, every government now has the opportunity to actualize the supreme purpose of government.

References

1 Modern Science and Ancient Vedic Science

Egenes, T. *Introduction to Sanskrit: Part One*. Delhi, India: Motilal Publishers, 1989.

Maharishi Mahesh Yogi, His Holiness. *Celebrating Perfection in Education: Dawn of Total Knowledge*, 2nd Edition. Maharishi Vedic University Press, 1997.

Maharishi Mahesh Yogi, His Holiness. *Ideal India: The Lighthouse of Peace on Earth*. Maharishi University of Management Press, 2001.

Maharishi Mahesh Yogi, His Holiness. *Science of Being and Art of Living: Transcendental Meditation*, Reissue Edition. Plume, 2001.

Nader, T., MD, PhD (His Majesty Raja Nader Rām). *Human Physiology: Expression of Veda and the Vedic Literature*, 4th Edition. The Netherlands: Maharishi Vedic University Press, 2000.

2 The Correspondence of Quantum Network Architecture to the Veda and Vedic Literature

Blahut, R. E. *Principles and Practice of Information Theory*. Reading: Addison-Wesley, 1988.

Cover, T. M., and J. A. Thomas. *Elements of Information Theory*. New York: Wiley, 1991.

Dorf, R. C., Ed. *The Electrical Engineering Handbook*. CRC Press, 1993.

Maharishi Mahesh Yogi, His Holiness. *Maharishi's Absolute Theory of Defence: Sovereignty in Invincibility*. Maharishi Vedic University Press, 1996.

Maharishi Mahesh Yogi, His Holiness. *Maharishi's Absolute Theory of Government: Automation in Administration*, 2nd Edition. Maharishi Vedic University Press, 1995.

Morrison, Philip, and Phylis Morrison. *Powers of Ten: A Book About the Relative Size of Things*. Redding: Scientific American Library, 1982.

Organisation Intergouvernementale de la Convention du Metre. *The International System of Units (SI)*. BIPM, 1998.

Tucker, A. B. Jr., Ed. *The Computer Science and Engineering Handbook*. CRC Press, 1997.

3 The Four Veda in Quantum Network Architecture

ṚK VEDA—*Holistic (Dynamic Silence)*—Cosmic Network of Consciousness: Holistic Functioning of the Cosmic Computer and Cosmic Switchboard

Cerami, E. *Web Services Essentials*. O'Reilly & Associates, 2002.

Lynch, D. C. and M. T. Rose. *Internet System Handbook*. Addison-Wesley, 1993.

Patterson, D. A. and J. L. Hennessy. *Computer Organization & Design: The Hardware/Software Interface*, 2nd Edition. Morgan Kaufmann Publishers, 1998.

Pierce, J. R, and A. M. Noll. *Signals: The Science of Telecommunications*. Scientific American Library, 1990.

RADCOM Ltd. *Telecom Protocol Finder*. RADCOM Ltd., 2001.

Ṛk Veda Saṁhitā. Translated by Swami Prakāsh Sarasvati and Satyakam Vidyalankar. 13 Volumes. New Delhi, India: Veda Pratishthana, 1977–1984.

Routt, T. J. "SNA, APPN & TCP/IP: Comparisons and Contrasts," Chapter 8 in *SNA and TCP/IP Enterprise Networking*, edited by D. Lynch, J. P. Gray, and E. Rabinovitch, 147–285. Prentice-Hall, 1998.

SĀMA VEDA—*Flowing Wakefulness*—Network Self-Referral and Feedback Systems

Sāma Veda. Translated by S. V. Ganapati. New Delhi, India: Shri Jainendra Press, 1982.

Saracco, R., J. R. Harrow, and R. Weihmayer. *The Disappearance of Telecommunications*. IEEE Press, 2000.

YAJUR VEDA—*Offering and Creating*—Network Processing Systems

Coulouris, G., J. Dollimore, and T. Kindberg. "Interprocess Communication," Chapter 4, 125–164; and "Distributed Objects and Remote Invocation," Chapter 5, 165–205; in *Distributed Systems: Concepts and Design*, 3rd Edition. Addison-Wesley, 2001.

The Yajur Veda: Sanskrit Text, 4th Edition. Translated by Devi Chand. Munshiram Manoharlal Publishers, 1988.

ATHARVA VEDA—*Reverberating Wholeness*—Nodal Input/Output Systems

Massiglia, P., Ed. *The RAIDbook: A Source Book for Disk Array Technology*, 5th Edition. The RAID Advisory Board, 1996.

4 VEDĀNGA in Quantum Network Architecture

SHIKSHĀ—*Expressing*—Dynamic Computer Network Architecture

Peterson, L. L., and B. S. Davie. *Computer Networks: A Systems Approach*, 2nd Edition. Morgan Kaufmann Publishers, 2000.

KALP—*Transforming*—Network Architecture, Design, and Implementation Process

Cheek, A., H. K. Lew, and K. Wallace. *Cisco CCIE Fundamentals: Network Design and Case Studies*. Cisco Systems, Inc., MacMillan Publishing Company, 1998.

Choi, S., D. O. Stahl, and A. B. Whinson. *The Economics of Electronic Commerce: The Essential Economics of Doing Business in the Electronic Marketplace*. Macmillan Technical Publishing, 1997.

Coulouris, G., J. Dollimore, and T. Kindberg. *Distributed Systems: Concepts and Design*, 3rd Edition. Addison-Wesley, 2001.

DeGarmo, E. P., W. G. Sullivan, and J. A. Bontadelli. *Engineering Economy*, 9th Edition. Macmillan Publishing Company, 1993.

Freeman, R. L. *Telecommunication System Engineering*, 3rd Edition. New York: John Wiley & Sons, 1996.

Hoffer, J. A., J. F. George, and J. S. Valacich. *Modern Systems Analysis & Design*, 2nd Edition. Addison-Wesley, 1998.

Jones, T. C. *Estimating Software Costs*. McGraw-Hill, 1998.

McConnell, S. C. *Rapid Development: Taming Wild Software Schedules*. Microsoft Press, 1996.

McKnight, L. W., and J. P. Bailey, Eds. *Internet Economics*. MIT Press, 1997.

Park, C. S. *Contemporary Engineering Economics*, 2nd Edition. Addison-Wesley, 1997.

Spohn, D. L. *Data Network Design*. McGraw-Hill, 1993.

Strassmann, P. A. *The Politics of Information Management: Policy Guidelines*. The Information Economics Press, 1995.

Yourdon, E. *Managing the System Lifecycle*, 2nd Edition. Prentice-Hall, 1988.

Yourdon, E. *Modern Structured Analysis*. Prentice-Hall, 1989.

Yourdon, E., and L. L. Constantine. *Structured Design: Fundamentals of a Discipline of Computer Program and Systems Design*. Prentice-Hall, 1979.

VYĀKARAṆ—*Expanding*—Redundant Network Systems

Coulouris, G., J. Dollimore, and T. Kindberg. "Replication," Chapter 14 in *Distributed Systems: Concepts and Design*, 3rd Edition, 553–606. Addison-Wesley, 2001.

Marcus, E., and H. Stern. *Blueprints for High Availability: Designing Resilient Distributed Systems*. New York: John Wiley & Sons, 2000.

NIRUKT—*Self-Referral*—Feedback Loops

Lala, P. K. *Self-Checking and Fault-Tolerant Digital Design*. Morgan Kaufmann Publishers, 2001.

CHHAND—*Measuring and Quantifying*—Dynamic Bandwidth, Load Balancing, and Content Management

Verma, D. C. *Policy-Based Networking: Architecture and Algorithms*. New Riders Publishing, 2001.

JYOTISH—*All Knowing*—Self-Aware, Massively Parallel Network Architecture

Buyya, R., Ed. *High Performance Cluster Computing: Architectures and Systems*. Volume 1. Prentice-Hall, 1999.

Cormen, T. H., C. E. Leiserson, R. L. Rivest, and C. Stein. *Introduction to Algorithms*, 2nd Edition. MIT Press, 2001.

Dowd, K., and C. Severance. *High Performance Computing: RISC Architectures, Optimization & Benchmarks*, 2nd Edition. O'Reilly & Associates, 1998.

Koniges, A. E., Ed. *Industrial Strength Parallel Computing*. Morgan Kaufmann Publishers, 2000.

Leighton, F. T. *Introduction to Parallel Algorithms and Architectures: Arrays, Trees, Hypercubes*. Morgan Kaufmann Publishers, 1992.

Lynch, N. A. *Distributed Algorithms*. Morgan Kaufmann Publishers, 1996.

Maharishi Parāśara. *Maharishi Parāśara's Brihat Parāśara Hora Śastra: A Compendium in Vedic Astrology*, Volume 1. Translated by G. C. Sharma. Sagar Publications, 1995.

Maharishi Parāśara. *Maharishi Parāśara's Brihat Parāśara Hora Śastra: A Compendium in Vedic Astrology*, Volume 2. Translated by G. C. Sharma. Sagar Publications, 1995.

Wadleigh, K. R., and I. L. Crawford. *Software Optimization for High Performance Computing: Creating Faster Applications*. Hewlett-Packard Company, 2000.

5 UPANGA in Quantum Network Architecture

NYĀYA—*Distinguishing and Deciding*—Central Processing Unit/Network Processing Unit

Hsu, J. H. *Computer Architecture: Software Aspects, Coding, and Hardware*. CRC Press, 2001.

Patterson, D. A., and J. L. Hennessy. "The Processor: Datapath and Control," Chapter 5, 336–432; "Multiprocessors," Chapter 9, 710–759; in *Computer Organization & Design: The Hardware/Software Interface*, 2nd Edition. Morgan Kaufmann Publishers, 1998.

Saha, S. *Perspectives on Nyāya Logic and Epistemology*. Delhi, India: Swantra Bharat Press, 1987.

VAISHESHIK—*Specifying*—System Configuration/Connection

Bahadur, K. P. *The Wisdom of Vaisheshika*. New Delhi, India: Sterling Publishers, 1979.

Halabi, B. *Internet Routing Architectures*. New Riders Publishing, 1997.

Perlman, R. *Interconnections: Bridges and Routers*. Addison-Wesley, 1992.

Steenstrup, M. *Routing in Communications Networks*. Prentice-Hall, 1995.

SĀṀKHYA—*Enumerating*—Arithmetic Logic Unit

Flynn, M. J., and S. F. Oberman. *Advanced Computer Arithmetic Design*. New York: John Wiley & Sons, 2001.

Gupta, A. S. *Classical Sāṁkhya: A Critical Study*, 2nd Edition. New Delhi, India: Munshiram Manoharlal Publishers, 1982.

Hennessy, J. L., and D. A. Patterson. "Computer Arithmetic," Appendix A in *Computer Architecture: A Quantitative Approach*, 2nd Edition, A-1–A-77. Morgan Kaufmann Publishers, 1996.

Patterson, D. A., and J. L. Hennessy. "Arithmetic for Computers," Chapter 4 in *Computer Organization & Design: The Hardware/Software Interface*, 2nd Edition, 208–335. Morgan Kaufmann Publishers, 1998.

YOGA—*Unifying*—Logical Network Topology and Associations

Dodge, M., and R. Kitchin. *Atlas of Cyberspace*. Addison-Wesley, 2001.

Dodge, M., and R. Kitchin. *Mapping Cyberspace*. Routledge, 2001.

Maharishi Patañjali. *Yoga Sūtras of Maharishi Patañjali*, 2nd Edition. Maharishi University of Management Press, 1998.

Swami Hariharananda Aranya. *Yoga Philosophy of Patañjali*. Calcutta University Press, 1981.

KARMA MĪMĀṀSĀ—*Analyzing*—Backbone Network System

Brandt, H., and C. Hapke. *ATM Signaling: Protocols and Practice*. New York: John Wiley & Sons, 2001.

Directory of Internet Service Providers, 13th Edition. Spring 2001.

Gray, E. W. *MPLS: Implementing the Technology*. Addision-Wesley, 2001.

Guizani, M., and A. Rayes. *Designing ATM Switching Networks*. McGraw-Hill, 1999.

McDysan, D., and D. Spohn. *ATM: Theory and Applications*. McGraw-Hill, 1999.

Maharishi Jaimini. *Karma Mīmāṁsā Sūtras of Maharishi Jaimini*. Maharishi University of Management Press, 1998.

Maharishi Jaimini. *The Mīmāṁsā Sūtras of Jaimini*. Translated by M. L. Sandal. Allahabad, India: Panini Office, 1925.

**VEDĀNT—*Lively Absolute (Living Wholeness—I-ness or Being)*—
Integrated Functioning of the Backbone Network System**

Maharishi Badarayana. *Vedānta Sūtras of Maharishi Badarayana*. Maharishi University of Management Press, 1996.

Routt, T. J. "APPN and TCP/IP: Plotting a Backbone Strategy," *Data Communications* 23 (4), (1994): 107–114.

Routt, T. J. "ATM Essentials: Switched Network Integration," *Business Communications Review*, Supplement to September 1995.

Routt, T. J. "Flexibility Is Key to Backbone Evolution," *Business Communications Review* (July 1997): 21–26.

6 UPA-VEDA in Quantum Network Architecture

GANDHARVA VEDA—*Integrating and Harmonizing*—Network/Computer Clocking and Synchronization

Coulouris, G., J. Dollimore, and T. Kindberg. "Time and Global States," Chapter 10 in *Distributed Systems: Concepts and Design*, 3rd Edition, 385–418. Addison-Wesley, 2001.

Daniels, J. D. *Digital Design From Zero to One*. New York: John Wiley & Sons, 1996.

Foster, R.G., and L. Kreitzman. *Rhythms of Life: The Biological Clocks that Control the Daily Livers of Every Living Thing*. Yale University Press, 2004.

Hartmann, G. *Maharishi Gandharva Ved*. The Netherlands: Maharishi Vedic University Press, 1992.

Kusch, P. "Some Design Considerations of an Atomic Clock using Atomic Beam Techniques," *Physical Review* 76 (1949): 161.

Major, F. G. *The Quantum Beat: The Physical Principles of Atomic Clocks*. New York: Springer Verlag, 1998.

DHANUR VEDA—*Invincible and Progressive*—Security Architecture

Anderson, R. *Security Engineering: A Guide to Building Dependable Distributed Systems*, New York: John Wiley & Sons, 2001.

Benantar, M. "The Internet Public Key Infrastructure," *IBM Systems Journal* 40 (3), (2001): 648–665.

Chapman, D. B., and E. D. Zwicky. *Building Internet Firewalls*. O'Reilly & Associates, 1995.

Cheswick, W. R., and S. M. Bellovin. *Firewalls and Internet Security: Repelling the Wily Hacker*. AT&T, 1994.

Erbschloe, M. *Information Warfare: How to Survive Cyber Attacks*. McGraw-Hill, 2001.

Hondo, M., N. Nagaratnam, and A. Nadlin. "Securing Web Services," *IBM Systems Journal* 41 (2), (2002): 228–241.

Hunt, A. E., S. Bosworth, and D. B. Hoyt, Eds. *Computer Security Handbook*, 3rd Edition, New York: John Wiley & Sons, 1995.

King, C. M., C. E. Dalton, and T. E. Osmanoglu. *Security Architecture: Design, Deployment & Operations*. McGraw-Hill, 2001.

Menezes, A. J., P. C. van Oorschot, and S. A. Vanstone. *Handbook of Applied Cryptography*, CRC Press, 1997.

Northcutt, S., and J. Novak. *Network Intrusion Detection: An Analyst's Handbook*, 2nd Edition. New Riders Publishing, 2001.

Ratha, N. K., J. H. Connell, and R. M. Bolle. "Enhancing Security and Privacy in Biometrics-Based Authentication Systems," *IBM Systems Journal* 40 (3), (2001): 614–634.

Routt, T. J., and J. A. Ketterling. "Securing VPNs: An Architectural Approach," *Business Communications Review* (October 1998): 51–56.

Rubin, A. D. *White-Hat Security Arsenal: Tackling the Threats*. AT&T, 2001.

Schneier, B. *Applied Cryptography: Protocols, Algorithms, and Source Code in C*, 2nd Edition. New York: John Wiley & Sons, 1996.

Schneier, B. *Secrets & Lies: Digital Security in a Networked World*. New York: John Wiley & Sons, 2000.

Skoudis, E. *Counter Hack: A Step-by-Step Guide to Computer Attacks and Effective Defenses*. Prentice-Hall, 2002

Singh, S. *The Code Book: The Evolution of Secrecy From Mary, Queen of Scots to Quantum Cryptography*. Doubleday, 1999.

Smith, R. E. *Internet Cryptography*. Addison Wesley, 1997.

Waltz, E. *Information Warfare: Principles and Operations*. Artech House, 1998.

Whitmore, J. J. "A Method for Designing Secure Solutions," *IBM Systems Journal* 40 (3), (2001): 747–768.

Zimmermann, P. R. *The Official PGP User's Guide*. 1995.

STHĀPATYA VEDA—*Establishing*—Physical Network Topology

Mayamata: An Indian Treatise on Housing Architecture and Iconography. Translated by B. Dagens. New Delhi, India: Sitaram Bhartia Institute of Scientific Research, 1985.

Vacca, J. *The Cabling Handbook*. Prentice-Hall, 1999.

HĀRĪTA SAṀHITĀ—*Nourishing*—Bandwidth Management, Quality of Service

Croll, A., and E. Packman. *Managing Bandwidth: Deploying QoS in Enterprise Networks.* Prentice-Hall, 2000.

Ferguson, P., and G. Huston. *Quality of Service: Delivering QoS on the Internet and in Corporate Networks.* New York: John Wiley & Sons, 1998.

McDysan, D. *QoS & Traffic Management in IP & ATM Networks.* McGraw-Hill, 2000.

Vegesna, S. *IP Quality of Service.* Cisco Press, 2001.

Wright, D. J. *Voice Over Packet Networks.* New York: John Wiley & Sons, 2001.

BHEL SAṀHITĀ—*Differentiating*—Prioritized Queueing Systems

Bolch, G., S. Greiner, H. de Meer, and K. S. Trivedi. *Queueing Networks and Markov Chains: Modeling and Performance Evaluation with Computer Science Applications.* New York: John Wiley & Sons, 1998.

Kleinrock, L. *Queueing Systems Volume 1: Theory.* New York: John Wiley & Sons, 1975.

Kleinrock, L. *Queueing Systems Volume 2: Computer Applications.* New York: John Wiley & Sons, 1976.

Kleinrock, L., and R. Gail. *Solutions Manual for Queueing Systems Volume 2: Computer Applications.* Technology Transfer Institute, 1986.

KĀSHYAP SAṀHITĀ—*Equivalency*—Availability Logic

Marcus, E., and H. Stern. *Blueprints for High Availability: Designing Resilient Distributed Systems.* New York: John Wiley & Sons, 2000.

CHARAK SAṀHITĀ—*Balancing—Holding Together and Supporting*—Network-on-a-Chip™

Caraka-Saṁhitā, Vol. I—Sūtrastahāna to Indriyasthāna. Translated by P. V. Sharma. Varanasi, India: Chaukhamblia Orientalia, 1981.

Caraka-Saṁhitā, Vol. II—Chikitsāsthānam to Siddhisthānam, 2nd Edition. Translated by P. V. Sharma. Varanasi, India: Chaukhamblia Orientalia, 1992.

Caraka-Saṁhitā: Critical Notes, Vol. III—Sūtrastahāna to Indriyasthāna. Translated by P. V. Sharma. Varanasi, India: Chaukhamblia Orientalia, 1992.

Chandrakasan, A., W. J. Bowhill, and F. Fox, Eds. *Design of High-Performance Microprocessor Circuits*. IEEE Press, 2001.

SUSHRUT SAṀHITĀ—*Separating*—Field and Gate Logic

Bolton, W. *Programmable Logic Controllers*, 2nd Edition. Reed Educational and Professional Publishing, 2000.

Laker, K. R., and W. M. C. Sansen. *Design of Analog Integrated Circuits and Systems*, McGraw-Hill, 1994.

Smith, M. J. S. *Application-Specific Integrated Circuits*. Addison-Wesley, 1997.

Sushruta Saṁhitā, Vol. I—Sūtra-Sthāna, 4th Edition. Translated by K. K. Bhishagratna. Varanasi, India: Chowkhamba Sanskrit Series Office, 1991.

Sushruta Saṁhitā, Vol. II—Nidāna-Sthāna, Śārīra-Sthāna, Chikitsa-Sthāna, and Kalpa-Sthāna, 4th Edition. Translated by K. K. Bhishagratna. Varanasi, India: Chowkhamba Sanskrit Series Office, 1991.

Sushruta Saṁhitā, Vol. III—Uttara-Tantra, 4th Edition. Translated by K. K. Bhishagratna. Varanasi, India: Chowkhamba Sanskrit Series Office, 1991.

VĀGBHATT SAṀHITĀ—*Communication and Eloquence*—Dynamic Network Modeling

Allen, A. O. *Probability, Statistics, and Queueing Theory with Computer Science Applications*, 2nd Edition. Academic Press, 1990.

Lazowska, D. D., J. Zahorjan, G. S. Graham, and K. C. Sevcik. *Quantitative System Performance: Computer System Analysis Using Queueing Network Models*. Prentice-Hall, 1984.

Payne, J. A. *Introduction to Simulation: Programming Techniques and Methods of Analysis*. McGraw-Hill, 1982.

Routt, T. J. "Network Queueing and Simulation Approaches and Tools within the Enterprise," Yankee Group Industry Report, October 1986.

Sauer, C. H., and K. M. Chandy. *Computer Systems Performance Modeling*. Prentice-Hall, 1981.

Vāgbhata's Aṣṭāñga Hṛdayam: Vol. I—Sūtrasthāna & Śārīrasthāna. Translated by K. R. S. Murthy. Varanasi, India: Krishnadas Academy, 1991.

Vāgbhata's Aṣṭāñga Hṛdayam: Vol. II—Nidāna, Cikitsita, and Kalpasiddhi Sthāna. Translated by K. R. S. Murthy. Varanasi, India: Krishnadas Academy, 1992.

MĀDHAV NIDĀN SAṀHITĀ—*Diagnosing*—Network/Systems Management

Kauffels, F. *Network Management: Problems, Standards and Strategies*. Addison-Wesley, 1992.

Leinwand, A., and K. Fang. *Network Management: A Practical Perspective*. Addison-Wesley, 1993.

Routt, T. J. "Network Management and Control: Systems Planning," Yankee Group Industry Research Report, October 1986.

Stallings, W. *SNMP, SNMP-2, and CMIP: The Practical Guide to Network-Management Systems*. Addison-Wesley, 1993.

SHĀRNGADHAR SAṀHITĀ—*Synthesizing*—Database and Transaction Processing

Bernstein, P. A., and E. Newcomer. *Principles of Transaction Processing: For the Systems Professional*. Morgan Kaufmann Publishers, 1997.

Coulouris, G., J. Dollimore, and T. Kindberg. "Transactions and Concurrency Control," Chapter 12, 465–514; and "Distributed Transactions," Chapter 13, 515–552; in *Distributed Systems: Concepts and Design*, 3rd Edition. Addison-Wesley, 2001.

Date, C. J. *An Introduction to Database Systems*, 7th Edition. Addison-Wesley, 1999.

Pascal, F. *Practical Issues in Database Management: A Reference for the Thinking Practitioner*. Addison-Wesley, 2000.

Piattini, M., and O. Diaz, Eds. *Advanced Database Technology and Design*. Artech House, 2000.

BHĀVA-PRAKĀSH SAṀHITĀ—*Enlightening*—Optical Networks

Borella, A., G. Cancellieri, and F. Chiaraluce. *Wavelength Division Multiple Access Optical Networks*. Artech House, 1998.

Born, M., and E. Wolf. *Principles of Optics: Electromagnetic Theory of Propagation, Interference and Diffraction of Light*, 7th Edition. New York: Cambridge University Press, 1999.

Cowper, R. "A View of Next Generation Optical Communication Systems—Possible Future High-Capacity Transport Implementations," Proceedings of SPIE, 3491 (1998): 575–580.

Goralski, W. J. *Optical Networking & WDM*. McGraw-Hill, 2001.

Goralski, W. J. *SONET: A Guide to Synchronous Optical Networks*. McGraw-Hill, 1997.

Hecht, E. *Optics*, 3rd Edition. Addison-Wesley, 1997.

Miya, T., Y. Terunuma, T. Hosaka, and T. Miyashita. "Ultimate Low-Loss Single-Mode Fibre at 1.55 μm," *Electronics Letters* 15 (1979): 106–108.

Mollenauer, L. F., P. V. Mamyshev, and M. J. Neubelt. "Demonstration of Soliton WDM Transmission at 6 and 7*10 Gbit/s, Error Free Over Transoceanic Distances," *Electronics Letters* 32 (1996): 471–473.

Mukherjee, B. *Optical Communication Networks: WDM, Broadcast/Multicast, Wavelength-Routing*. McGraw-Hill, 1997.

Nakazawa, M., Y. Kimura, and K. Suzuki. "Nonlinear Optics in Optical Fibers and Future Prospects for Optical Soliton Communications Technologies," *NTT R&D* 42 (1993): 1317–1326.

Ono, T., and Y. Yano. "Key Technologies for Terabit/2nd WDM Systems with High Spectral Efficiency of over 1 bit/s/Hz," *IEEE Journal of Quantum Electronics* 34 (1998): 2080–2088.

Ramaswami, R., and K. N. Sivarajan. *Optical Networks: A Practical Perspective*. Morgan Kaufmann Publishers, 1998.

Risk, W.P., T.R. Gosnell, and A.V. Nurmikko. *Compact Blue-Green Lasers*. Cambridge University Press, 2003.

Saleh, B. E. A., and M. C. Teich. *Fundamentals of Photonics*. New York: John Wiley & Sons, 1991.

Stern, M. B. "Binary Optics: A VLSI-Based Microoptics Technology," *Microelectronic Engineering* 32 (1996): 369–388.

Stern, T. E., and K. Bala, *Multiwavelength Optical Networks: A Layered Approach*. Addison-Wesley, 1999.

Willebrand, Dr. H., and B.S. Ghuman. *Free-Space Optics: Enabling Optical Connectivity in Today's Networks*. Sams Publishing, 2002.

7 BRĀHMAṆA in Quantum Network Architecture

UPANISHAD—*Transcending*—Wireless Networks, Pervasive Computing

Fletcher, R., J. A. Levitan, J. Rosenberg, and N. Gershenfeld. "Application of Smart Materials to Wireless ID Tags and Remote Sensors." Edited by E. P. George, R. Gotthardt, K. Otsuka, S. Trolier-McKinstry, and M. Wun-Fogle. *Materials for Smart Systems II*. Pittsburgh: Materials Research Society, 1997.

Gordon G. D., and W. L. Morgan. *Principles of Communications Satellites*. New York: John Wiley & Sons, 1993.

Hansmann, U., L. Merk, M. S. Nicklous, and T. Stober. *Pervasive Computing Handbook.* Springer-Verlag, 2001.

Hill, J., M. Horton, R. Kling, and L. Krishnamurthy. "The Platforms Enabling Wireless Sensor Networks." *Communications of the ACM* 47/6 (2004): 41–46.

Lee, W. C. Y. *Mobile Communications Engineering: Theory and Applications,* 2nd Edition. McGraw-Hill, 1998.

Mead, D. C. *Direct Broadcast Satellite Communications: An MPEG-Enabled Service.* Prentice-Hall, 2000.

Poor, H. V., and G. W. Wornell, Eds. *Wireless Communications: Signal Processing Perspectives.* Prentice-Hall, 1998.

Sayre, C.W. *Complete Wireless Design.* McGraw-Hill, 2001.

Simon, M. K., J. K. Omura, R. A. Scholtz, and B. K. Levitt. *Spread Spectrum Communications Handbook.* New York: McGraw-Hill, 1994.

The Principal Upaniṣads (Bṛhad-āraṇyaka, Chāndogya, Aitareya, Taittirīya, Īśa, Kena, Kaṭha, Praśna, Muṇḍaka, Māṇḍūkya, Svetāśvatara, Kauṣītakī Brāhmaṇa, Maitrī, Subāla, Jābāla, Paiṅgala, Kaivalya, Vajrasūcikā). Edited by S. Radhakrishnan. Unwin Hyman Limited, 1953.

ĀRAṆYAK—*Stirring*—Application Programming Interface

I'anson, C., and A. Pell. *Understanding OSI Applications.* Prentice-Hall, 1992.

BRAHMAṆA—*Structuring*—Network/Systems Standards and Protocols

Black, U. *OSI: A Model for Computer Communications Standards.* Prentice-Hall, 1991.

Comer, D. E. *Internetworking with TCP/IP: Principles, Protocols, and Architectures:* Volume 1, 4th Edition. Prentice-Hall, 2000.

Cypser, R. J. *Communications for Cooperating Systems: OSI, SNA, and TCP/IP.* Addison-Wesley, 1991.

Knightson, K. G., T. Knowles, and J. Larmouth. *Standards for Open Systems Interconnection.* McGraw-Hill, 1988.

Krishnamurthy, B., and J. Rexford. *Web Protocols and Practice: HTTP/1.1, Networking Protocols, Caching, and Traffic Management.* AT&T Corp., 2001.

Routt, T. J. "From TOP (3.0) to Bottom: Architectural Close-Up," *Data Communications* 17 (4), (1988): 155–170.

Routt, T. J. "SNA to OSI: IBM Building Upper-Layer Gateways," (Cover Article) *Data Communications* 16 (5), (1987): 120–142.

ITIHĀS—*Blossoming of Totality*—End-User and Application Interactions

Coulouris, G., J. Dollimore, and T. Kindberg. "Distributed Objects and Remote Invocation," Chapter 5 in *Distributed Systems: Concepts and Design*, 3rd Edition, 165–205. Addison-Wesley, 2001.

The Rāmāyaṇa of Vālmīki: Volume I—Bāla Kāṇḍa, Ayodhyā-Kāṇḍa. Translated by Hari Prasad Shastri. London: Shanti Sadan, 1992.

The Rāmāyaṇa of Vālmīki: Volume II—Araṇya-kāṇḍa, Kiṣhkindhā-Kāṇḍa, Sundara-Kāṇḍa. Translated by Hari Prasad Shastri. London: Shanti Sadan, 1992.

The Rāmāyaṇa of Vālmīki: Volume III—Yuddha Kāṇḍa, Uttara Kāṇḍa. Translated by Hari Prasad Shastri. London: Shanti Sadan, 1992.

Subramaniam, K. *Mahabharata,* 7th Edition. Bombay, India: Bharatiya Vidya Bhavan, 1988.

The Yoga-Vasishtha-Maharāmāyaṇa of Vālmīki, Vols. I–IV. Translated by V. L. Mitra. Delhi, India: Bharatiya Publishing House, 1978.

PURĀN—*Ancient and Eternal*—End-User and Application Interfaces

Coulouris, G., J. Dollimore, and T. Kindberg. "Interprocess Communication," Chapter 4 in *Distributed Systems: Concepts and Design*, 3rd Edition, 125–164. Addison-Wesley, 2001.

SMṚITI—*Memory*—Random Access Memory (RAM)/Routt Addressable Absolute Memory (RAAM)/Storage Area Network (SAN)/Network-Attached Storage (NAS)/ Hologram

Cooper, E. B., S. R. Manalis, H. Fang, H. Dai, K. Matsumoto, S. C. Minne, T. Hunt, and C. F. Quante. "Terabit-per-Square-Inch Data Storage with the Atomic Force Microscope," *Applied Physics Letters* 75 (1999): 3566–3568.

Coulouris, G., J. Dollimore, and T. Kindberg. "Distributed Shared Memory," Chapter 16, in *Distributed Systems: Concepts and Design*, 3rd Edition, 635–667. Addison-Wesley, 2001.

Dennard, R. H. *Field-Effect Transistor Memory.* U.S. Patent No. 3 387 286, 1968.

Farley, M. *Building Storage Networks.* McGraw-Hill, 2000.

Hariharan, P. *Basics of Holography.* Cambridge University Press, 2002.

Hennessy, J. L., and D. A. Patterson. "Memory-Hierarchy Design," Chapter 5, 373–483; and "Storage Systems," Chapter 6, 485–561; in *Computer Architecture: A Quantitative Approach*, 2nd Edition. Morgan Kaufmann Publishers, 1996.

Morris, R.J.T., and B.J. Truskowski. "The Evolution of Storage Systems." *IBM Systems Journal*, 42/2 (2003): 205–217.

Shor, P. W. "Scheme for Reducing Decoherence in Quantum Computer Memory," *Physical Review* A 52 (1995): 2493–2496.

8 PRĀTISHĀKHYA in Quantum Network Architecture

ṚK VEDA PRĀTISHĀKHYA—*All-Pervading Wholeness*—Quantum Computer

Adam, J.A. *Mathematics in Nature: Modeling Patterns in the Natural World*. Princeton University Press, 2003.

Abrahms, D. S., and S. Lloyd. "Nonlinear Quantum Mechanics Implies Polynomial-Time Solution for NP-Complete and P Problems," *Physical Review* 81 (1998): 3992–3995.

Adleman, L. M. "Computing with DNA," *Scientific American* 279 (1998): 54–61.

Anton, H., and C. Rorres. *Elementary Linear Algebra: Application Version*, 7th Edition. New York: John Wiley & Sons, 1994.

Arfken, G. B., and H. J. Weber. *Mathematical Methods for Physicists*, 5th Edition. Harcourt Academic Press, 2001.

Beckman, D., A. N. Chari, S. Devabhaktuni, and J. Preskill. "Efficient Networks for Quantum Factoring," *Physical Review* A 54 (1996): 1034–1063.

Benioff, P. "The Computer as a Physical System: A Microscopic Quantum Mechanical Hamiltonian Model of Computers as Represented by Turing Machines," *Journal of Statistical Physics* 22 (1980): 563–591.

Bennett, C. H. "Logical Reversibility of Computation," *IBM Journal of Research and Development* 17 (1973): 525.

Bennett, C. H. "Notes on the History of Reversible Computation," *IBM Journal of Research and Development* 32 (1988): 16–23.

Bernstein, E., and U. Vazirani. "Quantum Complexity Theory," *SIAM Journal of Computation* 26 (5), (1997): 1411–1473.

Bohm, D. *Wholeness and the Implicate Order*. Routledge, 2004.

Bohm, D., and B.J. Hiley. *The Undivided Universe*. Routledge, 1993.

Braginsky, V. B., and F. Y. Khahili. *Quantum Measurement*. Cambridge: Cambridge University Press, 1992.

Brennan, K. F. *The Physics of Semiconductors: With Applications to Optoelectronic Devices*. Cambridge: Cambridge University Press, 1999.

Byron, F. W., Jr., and R. W. Fuller. *Mathematics of Classical and Quantum Physics*. Dover Publications, 1970.

Chow, T. L. *Mathematical Methods for Physicists*. Cambridge: Cambridge University Press, 2000.

Chuang, I. L., and M. A. Nielsen. "Prescription for Experimental Determination of the Dynamics of a Quantum Black Box," *Journal of Modern Optics* 44 (11–12), (1997): 2455–2467.

Cirac, J. I., and P. Zoller. "Quantum Computations with Cold Trapped Ions," *Physical Review* 74 (1995): 4091–4094.

Close, F., M. Marten, and C. Sutton. *The Particle Odyssey: A Journey to the Heart of Matter*. Oxford University Press, 2002.

Cory, D. G., A. F. Fahmy, and T. F. Havel. "Ensemble Quantum Computing by NMR Spectroscopy," *Proceedings of the National Academy of Science* 94 (1997): 1634–1639.

Crommie, M. F., C. P. Lutz, and D. M. Eigler. "Confinement of Electrons to Quantum Corrals on a Metal Surface," *Science* 262 (1993): 218–220.

Das Sarma, S. "Spintronics," *American Scientist* 89 (2001): 516–523.

Denning, P. J., and R. M. Metcalfe. *Beyond Calculation: The Next Fifty Years of Computing*. New York: Springer-Verlag, 1997.

Deutsch, D. "Is There a Fundamental Bound on the Rate at Which Information Can Be Processed?" *Physical Review* 42 (1982): 286–288.

Deutsch, D. "Quantum Computation," *Physics World*, 5 (1992): 57–61.

Deutsch, D. "Quantum Theory, the Church-Turing Principle and the Universal Quantum Computer," *Proceedings of the Royal Society of London* A400 (1985): 97–117.

Deutsch, D., and R. Jozsa. "Rapid Solution of Problems by Quantum Computation," *Proceedings of the Royal Society of London* 439A (1992): 553–558.

DiVincenzo, D. "Quantum Computation," *Science* 270 (1995): 255–261.

DiVincenzo, D., and P. Shor. "Fault-Tolerant Error Correction with Efficient Quantum Codes," *Physical Review* 77 (1996): 3260–3263.

Drexler, K. E. *Nanosystems: Molecular Machinery, Manufacturing and Computation*, New York: John Wiley & Sons, 1992.

Drühl, K.J., "Consciousness as the Subject and Object of Physics: Towards a New Paradigm for the Physical Sciences," *Modern Science and Vedic Science* 7 (1997): 143–163.

Einstein, A. *Relativity: The Special and the General Theory*. Three Rivers Press, 1961.

Einstein, A. *The Meaning of Relativity: Including the Relativistic Theory of the Non-Symmetric Field*. MJF Books, 1922.

Einstein, A. *Einstein's 1912 Manuscript on the Special Theory of Relativity*. George Braziller, Publishers, 1996.

Farhi, E., J. Goldstone, S. Gutmann, and M. Sipser. "Limit on the Speed of Quantum Computation in Determining Parity," *Physical Review* 81 (1998): 5442–5444.

Feynman, R. P. *Feynman Lectures on Computation*. Edited by T. Hey and R. W. Allen. C.R. Feynman and M. Feynman, 1996.

Feynman, R.P., and S. Weinberg. *Elementary Particles and the Laws of Physics*. Cambridge University Press, 1987.

Fuchs, C. A. "Nonorthogonal Quantum States Maximize Classical Information Capacity," *Physical Review* 79 (6), (1997): 1162–1165.

Garey, M. R., and D. S. Johnson. *Computers and Intractability: A Guide to the Theory of NP-completeness*. San Francisco: W.H. Freeman, 1997.

Gershenfeld, N. *The Physics of Information Technology*. Cambridge University Press, 2000.

Gershenfeld, N. A., and I. L. Chuang. "Bulk Spin Resonance Quantum Computation," *Science* 275 (1997): 350–356.

Gullberg, J. *Mathematics: From the Birth of Numbers*. W.W. Norton & Company, 1997.

Grabert, H., and M. H. Devoret, Eds. *Single Charge Tunneling: Coulomb Blockade Phenomenon in Nanostructures*. New York: Plenum Press, 1992.

Greene, B. *The Elegant Universe: Superstrings, Hidden Dimensions, and the Quest For the Ultimate Theory*. W.W. Norton & Company, 1999.

Greene, B. *The Fabric of the Cosmos: Space, Time, and the Texture of Reality*. Random House Inc, 2004.

Guthrie. G.. "Vedic Computation: Redefining Computer Science in Light of Maharishi Vedic Science," *Modern Science and Vedic Science* 7 (1997): 193–223.

Gruska, J. *Quantum Computing*. London: McGraw-Hill, 1999.

Hagelin, J. "Is Consciousness the Unified Field? A Field Theorist's Perspective," *Modern Science and Vedic Science* 1 (1987): 29–87.

Hardy, G. H., and E. M. Wright. *An Introduction to the Theory of Numbers*, 5th Edition. New York: Oxford University Press, 1998.

Hausladen, P., R. Jozsa, B. Schumacher, M. Westmoreland, and W. K. Wootters. "Classical Information Capacity of a Quantum Channel," *Physical Review* A 54 (1996): 1869.

Hey, A. J., Ed. *Feynman and Computation: Exploring the Limits of Computers*. Perseus Books Publishing, 1999.

Hughes, R., D. James, E. Knill, R. Laflamme, and A. Petschek. "Decoherence Bounds on Quantum Computation with Trapped Ions," *Physical Review*, 77 (1996): 3240–3243.

IBM Research News. "IBM's Test-Tube Quantum Computer Makes History." *IBM Research News*, 2001.

Imamoglu, A., D. D. Awschalom, G. Burkard, D. P. DiVincenzo, D. Loss, M. Sherwin, and A. Small. "Quantum Information Processing Using Quantum Dot Spins and Cavity QED," *Physical Review* 83 (20), (1999): 4204–4207.

Joos, E., H.D. Zeh, C. Keifer, D. Giulini, J. Kupsch, and I.O. Stamatescu. *Decoherence and the Appearance of a Classical World in Quantum Theory*. Springer-Verlag, 2003.

Joseph, J., M. Ernest, and C. Fellenstein. "Evolution of Grid Computing Architecture and Grid Adoption Models," *IBM Systems Journal* 43/4 (2004): 624–645.

Kac, V., and P. Cheung. *Quantum Calculus*. Springer-Verlag, 2002.

Kaku, M. *Quantum Field Theory*. Oxford University Press, 1993.

Kane, B. E. "A Silicon-Based Nuclear Spin Quantum Computer," *Nature* 393 (1998): 133–137.

Kapoor, S.K. "Vedic Mathematical Concepts and Their Application to Unsolved Mathematical Problems: Three Proofs of Fermat's Last Theorem," *Modern Science and Vedic Science* 34 (1989): 75–104.

Knill, E., and R. Laflamme. "Effective Pure States for Bulk Quantum Computation," *Physical Review* A 57 (1998): 3348–3363.

Knill, E., R. Laflamme, and W. H. Zurek. "Resilient Quantum Computation," *Science* 279 (1998): 342–345.

Levi, A.F.J. *Applied Quantum Mechanics*. Cambridge University Press, 2003.

Lidar, A. A., I. L. Chuang, and K. B. Whaley. "Dechoherence-Free Subspaces for Quantum Computation," *Physical Review* 81 (2), (1998): 2594–2597.

Lloyd, S. "A Potentially Realizable Quantum Computer," *Science* 261 (1993): 1569–1571.

Lloyd, S. "Envisioning a Quantum Supercomputer," *Science* 263 (1994): 695.

Lloyd, S. "Necessary and Sufficient Conditions for Quantum Computation," *Journal of Modern Optics* 41 (1994): 2203–2520.

Lloyd, S. "Quantum-Mechanical Computers," *Scientific American* (October 1995): 140–145.

Lo, H. K., T. Spiller, and S. Popescu. *Quantum Information and Computation*. Singapore: World Scientific, 1998.

Loss, D., and D. P. DiVincenzo. "Quantum Computation with Quantum Dots," *Physical Review* A 57 (1998): 120–126.

Maharishi Mahesh Yogi, His Holiness. *Maharishi's Absolute Theory of Government: Automation in Administration*, 2nd Edition. Maharishi Vedic University Press, 1995.

Milburn, G. J. *Schrödinger's Machines: The Quantum Technology Reshaping Everyday Life*. New York: W.H. Freeman, 1997

Milburn, G. J. *The Feynman Processor: Quantum Entanglement and the Computing Revolution*. Reading, Massachusetts: Perseus Books, 1999.

Mooji, J. E., T. P. Orlando, L. Levitov, L. Tian, C. H. van der Wal, and S. Lloyd. "Josephson Persistent-Current Qubit," *Science* 285 (1999): 1036–1039.

Muehlman, J.M. "Maharishi's Vedic Mathematics in Elementary Education: Developing All Knowingness to Improve Affect, Achievement, and Mental Computation," *Modern Science and Vedic Science* 8 (1998): 37–101.

Nanotechnology: Molecular Speculations on Global Abundance, Edited by B. C. Crandall, 2nd Printing. Cambridge, Massachusetts and London, England: MIT Press, 1997.

Nielsen, M. A. "Quantum Information Theory." Ph.D. Thesis, University of New Mexico, 1998.

Nielsen, M. A., and I. L. Chuang. *Quantum Computation and Quantum Information.* Cambridge University Press, 2000, reprinted 2001.

Patwardhan, K.S., S.A. Naimpally, and S.L. Singh. *Līlāvatī of Bhāskarācārya: A Treatise of Mathematics of Vedic Tradition.* Motilal Banarsidass Publishers, 2001.

Paul, H. *Introduction to Quantum Optics: From Light Quanta to Quantum Teleportation.* Cambridge University Press, 2004.

Paun, G., G. Rozenberg, and A. Salomaa. *DNA Computing: New Computing Paradigms.* Berlin Heidelberg: Springer-Verlag, 1998.

Peacock, J.A. *Cosmological Physics.* Cambridge University Press, 1999.

Penrose, R. *The Road to Reality: A Complete Guide to the Laws of the Universe.* Alfred A. Knopf, 2005.

Peres, A. "How to Differentiate Between Non-Orthogonal States," *Physical Review* A 128 (1988): 19.

Peres, A. "Reversible Logic and Quantum Computers," *Physical Review* A 32 (1985): 3266–3276.

Peskin, M. E., and D. V. Schroeder. *An Introduction to Quantum Field Theory.* Addison-Wesley, 1995.

Platzman, P. M., and M. I. Dykman. "Quantum Computing with Electrons Floating on Liquid Helium," *Science* 284 (1999): 1967.

Price, J.F. "Maharishi's Absolute Number: The Mathematical Theory and Technology of Everything," *Modern Science and Vedic Science* 7 (1997): 165–179.

Saracco, R., J. R. Harrow, and R. Weihmayer. *The Disappearance of Telecommunications.* IEEE, 2000.

Schack, R., and C. M. Caves. "Classical Model for Bulk-Ensemble NMR Quantum Computation." *Physical Review* A 60 (1999): 4354–4362.

Schumm, B.A. *Deep Down Things: The Breathtaking Beauty of Particle Physics.* The Johns Hopkins University Press, 2004.

Shannon, C. E., and W. Weaver. *The Mathematical Theory of Communication.* University of Illinois Press, 1949.

Sipser, M. *Introduction to the Theory of Computation*. PSW Publishing Company, 1997.

Somaroo, S., C. H. Tseng, T. F. Havel, R. Laflamme, and D. G. Cory. "Quantum Simulations on a Quantum Computer," *Physcial Review Letters* 82 (1999): 5381–5384.

Strang, G. *Linear Algebra and its Applications*, 3rd Edition. San Diego: Harcourt, Brace, Jovanovich, 1988.

Taylor, J.C. *Hidden Unity in Natures' Laws*. Cambridge University Press, 2001.

Tirthaji, J.S.S.B.K.M. *Vedic Mathematics Or Sixteen Simple Mathematical Formulae From the Vedas*. Motilal Banarsidass Publishers, 1988.

Tomonaga, S.I. *The Story of Spin*. The University of Chicago Press, 1997.

Turing, A. M. "On Computable Numbers, with an Application to the Entscheidungsproblem," *Proceedings of the London Mathematical Society* 2, 42 (1936): 230.

Unruh, W. G. "Maintaining Coherence in Quantum Computers," *Physical Review* A 51 (1995): 992–997.

Von Neumann, J. "Probabilistic Logic and the Synthesis of Reliable Organisms from Unreliable Components," *Automata Studies*, Princeton University Press (1956): 329–378.

Weinberg, S. *The Quantum Theory of Fields: Volume III, Supersymmetry*. Cambridge University Press, 2000.

Williams, C. P., and S. H. Clearwater. *Explorations in Quantum Computing*. New York: Springer-Verlag, 1998.

Wilson, M., K. Kannangara, G. Smith, M. Simmons, and B. Raguse. *Nanotechnology: Basic Science and Emerging Technologies*. Chapman & Hall/CRC, 2002.

Woan, G. *The Cambridge Handbook of Physics Formulas*. Cambridge University Press, 2000.

Wolfram, S. *A New Kind of Science*. Wolfram Media, Inc., 2002.

Ye, J., D. W. Vernooy, and H. J. Kimble. "Trapping of Single Atoms in Cavity QED," *Physical Review* 83 (1999): 4987–4990.

Zee, A. *Quantum Field Theory in a Nutshell*. Princeton University Press, 2003.

Zorpette, G. "The Quest for the Spin Transistor," *IEEE Spectrum Online*, December 2001.

SHUKL-YAJUR-VEDA PRĀTISHĀKHYA—*Silencing, Sharing, and Spreading*— Quantum Algorithms, Circuits, Gates, Cryptography

Abrahms, D. S., and S. Lloyd. "Simulation of Many-Body Fermi Systems on a Quantum Computer," *Physical Review* 79 (13), (1997): 2586–2589.

Ashikhmin, A., S. Lytsin. "Upper Bounds on the Size of Quantum Codes," *IEEE Transactions Information Theory* 45 (4), (1999): 1206–1215.

Bennett, C. H. "Quantum Cryptography Using Any Two Nonorthogonal States," *Physical Review* 68 (21) (1992): 3121–3124.

Bennett, C. H., and G. Brassard. "Quantum Cryptography: Public Key Distribution and Coin Tossing," *Proceedings of IEEE International Conference on Computers, Systems, and Signal Processing*, New York: IEEE (1984): 175–179.

Bennett, C. H., and G. Brassard. "The Dawn of a New Era for Quantum Cryptography: the Experimental Prototype is Working," *Sigact News* 20 (1989): 78–82.

Bennett, C. H., G. Brassard, and A. K. Ekert. "Quantum Cryptography," *Scientific American* 267 (4), (1992): 50.

Boyer, M., G. Brassard, P. Hoyer, and A. Tapp. "Tight Bounds on Quantum Searching," *Progress of Physics* 46 (1998): 49–505.

Braustein, S. L. "Error Correction for Continuous Quantum Variables," *Physical Review* 80 (1998): 4084–4087.

Calderbank, A. R., E. M. Rains, P. W. Shor, and S. J. A. Sloane. "Quantum Error Correction and Orthogonal Geometry," *Physical Review* 78 (1997): 405–408.

Calderbank, A. R., and P. W. Shor. "Good Quantum Error-Correcting Codes Exist," *Physical Review* A 54 (1996): 1098–1105.

Caves, C. M. "Quantum Error Correction and Reversible Operations," *Journal of Superconductivity* 12 (6), (1999): 707–718.

Cerf, N. J., C. Adami, and P. Kwiat. "Optical Simulation of Quantum Logic," *Physical Review* A 57 (1998): 1477.

Chau, H. F., and F. Wilczek. "Simple Realization of the Fredkin Gate Using a Series of Two-Body Operators," *Physical Review* 75 (4), (1995): 748–750.

Chuang, I. L., N. Gershenfeld, and M. Kubinec. "Experimental Implementation of Fast Quantum Searching," *Physical Review* 80 (1998): 3408–3411.

Chuang, I. L., and D. Modha. "Reversible Arithmetic Coding for Quantum Data Compression," *IEEE Transactions on Information Theory* 46 (3), (2000): 1104.

Cleve, R., and D. P. DiVincenzo. "Schumacher's Quantum Data Compression As a Quantum Computation," *Physcial Review Letters* A 54 (1996): 2636.

Cleve, R., A. Ekert, C. Macchiavello, and M. Mosca. "Quantum Algorithms Revisited," *Proceedings of the Royal Society of London* A 454 (1969): 339–354.

Coppersmith, D. "An Approximate Fourier Transform Useful in Quantum Factoring," IBM Research Report, RC 19642, 1994.

Cory, D. G., M. D. Price, W. Maas, E. Knill, E. R. Laflamme, W. H. Zurek, T. F. Havel, and S. S. Somaroo, "Experimental Quantum Error Correction," *Physical Review* 81 (1998): 2152–2155.

Deutsch, D. "Quantum Computation Thwarts Eavesdroppers," *New Scientist* (December 1989): 25–26.

Deutsch, D., and R. Jozsa. "Rapid Solution of Problems by Quantum Computation," *Proceedings of the Royal Society of London* A 439 (1992): 553.

Diaconis, P., and D. Rockmore. "Efficient Computation of the Fourier Transform on Finite Groups," *Journal of the American Mathematics Society* 3 (2), (1990): 297–332.

DiVincenzo, D., "Two-Bit Gates are Universal for Quantum Computation," *Physical Review*, A, Vol. 51 (1995): 1015–1022.

DiVincenzo, D. P., and P. W. Shor. "Fault-Tolerant Error Correction with Efficient Quantum Codes," *Physical Review* 77 (1996): 3260.

Ekert, A. "Beating the Code Breakers,"*Nature* 358 (1992): 14–15.

Ekert, A. "Quantum Cryptography Based on Bell's Theorem," *Physical Review* 67 (6), (1991): 661–663.

Ekert, A. "Quantum Keys for Keeping Secrets,"*New Scientist* (January 1993): 24–28.

Ekert, A., J. Rarity, P. Tapster, and G. Palma. "Practical Quantum Cryptography Based on Two-Photon Interferometry," *Physical Review* 69 (31), (1992): 1293–1295.

Ekert, A., and R. Jozsa, "Quantum Computation and Shor's Factoring Algorithm," *Reviews of Modern Physics* 68 (3), (1996): 733–753.

Farhi, E., and S. Gutmann. "An Analog Analogue of a Digital Quantum Computation," *Physical Review* A 57 (4), (1998): 2403–2406.

Gottesman, D. "Class of Quantum Error-Correcting Codes Saturating the Quantum Hamming Bound," *Physical Review* A 54 (1996): 1862.

Gottesman, D. "Stablizer Codes and Quatum Error Correction." Ph.D. Thesis, California Institute of Technology, Pasadena, USA, 1997.

Gottesman, D. "Theory of Fault-Tolerant Quantum Computation," *Physical Review* A 57 (1), (1998): 127–137.

Grover, L. "A Fast Quantum Mechanical Algorithm for Database Search," *Proceedings of the 28th Annual ACM Symposium on the Theory of Computing* (1996): 212–219.

Grover, L. "Quantum Computers Can Search Rapidly by Using Almost Any Transformation," *Physical Review* 80 (1998): 4329–4332.

Holevo, A. S. "Capacity of a Quantum Communications Channel," *Problems of Information Transmission* 5 (4), (1979): 247–253.

Holevo, A. S. "The Capacity of the Quantum Channel with General Signal States," *IEEE Transmission Information Theory* 44 (1), (1998): 269–273.

Hughes, R. J., D. M. Alde, P. Dyer, G. G. Luther, G. L. Morgan, and M. Schauer. "Quantum Cryptography," *Contemporary Physics* 36 (3), (1995): 149–163.

Hughes, R. J., W. T. Buttler, P. G. Kwiat, S. K. Lamoreaux, G. L. Morgan, J. E. Nordholt, and C. G. Peterson. "Free-Space Quantum Key Distribution in Daylight," *Journal of Modern Optics* 47 (2000): 549–562.

Jones, J. A., and M. Mosca. "Implementation of a Quantum Algorithm on a Nuclear Magnetic Resonance Quantum Computer," *Journal of Chemical Physics* 109 (1998): 1648–1653.

Jones, J. A., M. Mosca, M., and R. H. Hansen. "Implementation of a Quantum Search Algorithm on a Nuclear Magnetic Resonance Quantum Computer," *Nature* 393 (6683), (1998): 344.

Jozsa, R. "Characterizing Classes of Functions Computable by Quantum Parallelism," *Proceedings of the Royal Society of London* A 435 (1991): 563–574.

Jozsa, R., and B. Schumacher. "A New Proof of the Quantum Noiseless Coding Theorem," *Journal of Modern Optics* 41 (1994): 2343–2349.

Kitaev, A. Y. "Quantum Error Correction with Imperfect Gates," in *Quantum Communication, Computing, and Measurement*. Edited by A. S. Holevo, O. Hirota, and C. M. Caves, 181–189. New York: Plenum Press, 1997.

Lidar, D. A., D. A. Bacon, and K. B. Whaley. "Concatenating Decoherence Free Subspaces with Quantum Error Correcting Codes," *Physical Review* 82 (22), (1999): 4556–4559.

Lloyd, S. "Almost Any Quantum Logic Gate is Universal," *Physical Review* 75 (2), (1995): 346.

Lloyd, S. "Capacity of the Noisy Quantum Channel," *Physical Review* A 55 (1997): 163–222.

Lloyd, S., and S. Braustein. "Quantum Computation over Continuous Variables," *Physical Review* 82 (1999): 1784–1787.

Lo, H. K., and H. F. Chau. "Unconditional Security of Quantum Key Distribution over Arbitrarily Long Distances," *Science* 283 (1999): 2050–2056.

Milburn, G. J. "Quantum Optical Fredkin Gate," *Physical Review* 62 (18), (1989): 2124.

Mosca, M. *Quantum Computer Algorithms*, Ph. D. Thesis, University of Oxford, 1999.

Monroe, C., D. Meekhof, B. King, W. Itano, and D. Wineland. "Demonstration of a Fundamental Quantum Logic Gate," *Physical Review* 75 (25), (1995): 4714–4717.

Muller, A., H. Zbinden, and N. Gisin. "Quantum Cryptography over 23 km in Installed Under-Lake Telecom Fibre," *Europhysics Letters* 33 (1996): 335–339.

Pittenger, A. O. *An Introduction to Quantum Computing Algorithms*, 2nd Printing. Boston: Birkhauser, 2001.

Plenio, M. B., and P. L. Knight. "Realistic Lower Bounds for the Factorization Time of Large Numbers on a Quantum Computer," *Physical Review* A 53 (1996): 2986–2990.

Ribenboim, P. *The Little Book of Bigger Primes*. Springer-Verlag, 2004.

Rivest, R .L., A. Shamir, and L. M. Adleman. "A Method of Obtaining Digital Signatures and Public-Key Cryptosystems," *Communications of the ACM* 21 (1978): 120–126.

Routt, T.J. *Methods For Transmitting Data Across Quantum Interfaces and Quantum Gates Using Same.* United States Patent Application Number US 2004/0078421 A1, United States Patent & Trademark Office (USPTO), 30 pages, April 22, 2004.

Shor, P. W. "Fault-Tolerant Quantum Computation," *Proceedings of the 37th Annual Symposium Foundations of Computer Science*, Los Alamitos: IEEE Computer Society Press (1996): 56–65.

Shor, P. W. "Polynomial-Time Algorithms for Prime Factorization and Discrete Logarithms on a Quantum Computer," *SIAM Journal on Computing* 26 (1997): 1484–1509.

Simmons, G. J., Ed. *Contemporary Cryptology: The Science of Information Integrity*. Piscataway: IEEE Press, 1992.

Sourlas, N. "Spin-Glass Models as Error-Correcting Codes," *Nature* 339 (1989): 693–695.

Stix, G. "Best-Kept Secrets," *Scientific American* (January 2005): 78–83.

Yao, A. C. "Quantum Circuit Complexity," *Proceedings of the 34th Annual IEEE Symposium on Foundations of Computer Science* (1993): 352–361.

ATHARVA VEDA PRĀTISHĀKHYA—*Unfolding*—Quantum Network

Barnum, H., M. A. Nielsen, and B. W. Schumacher. "Information Transmission Through a Noisy Quantum Channel," *Physical Review* A 57 (1998): 4153.

Deutsch, D. "Quantum Computational Networks," *Proceedings of the Royal Society of London* 425A (1989): 73–90.

Mattle, K., H. Weinfurter, and P. G. Kwait. "Dense Coding in Experimental Quantum Communication," *Physical Review* 76 (25), (1996): 4656–4659.

ATHARVA VEDA PRĀTISHĀKHYA *(Chaturadhyāyī)—Dissolving—* Superstring Computer

Greene, B, *The Elegant Universe: Superstrings, Hidden Dimensions, and the Quest for the Ultimate Theory*. New York: W. W. Norton & Co., 1999.

Gribbin, J. *The Search for Superstrings, Symmetry, and the Theory of Everything*, Little, Brown and Company, 1998.

Peat, E. D. *Superstrings and the Search for the Theory of Everything*, Contemporary Books, 1988.

Polchinski, J. *String Theory: Volume I—An Introduction to the Bosonic String*. Cambridge University Press, 1998.

Polchinski, J. *String Theory: Volume II—Superstring Theory and Beyond*, Cambridge University Press, 1998.

KRISHṆ-YAJUR-VEDA PRĀTISHĀKHYA *(Taittirīya)—Omnipresent—*Quantum Tunneling, Quantum Teleportation

Bell, J. "On the Einstein Podolsky Rosen Paradox," *Physics* 1 (1964): 195–200.

Bennett, C. H., G. Brassard, C. Crepeau, R. Jozsa, A. Wootters, and W. K. Peres. "Teleporting an Unknown Quantum State via Dual Classical and Einstein-Podolski-Rosen Channels," *Physical Review* 70 (1993): 1985–1989.

Bennett, C. H., G. Brassard, S. Popescu, B. Schumacher, J. A. Smolin, and W. K. Wootters. "Purification of Noisy Entanglement and Faithful Teleportation Via Noisy Channels," *Physical Review* 76 (1996): 722.

Bennett, C. H., and S. J. Wiesner. "Communication Via One- and Two-Particle Operators on Einstein-Podolsky-Rosen States," *Physical Review* 69 (20), (1992): 2881–2884.

Boschi, D., S. Branca, F. De Martini, L. Hardy, and S. Popescu, "Experimental Realization of Teleporting an Unknown Pure Quantum State Via Dual Classical and Einstein-Podolski-Rosen Channels," *Physical Review* 76 (1998): 722.

Bouwmeester, D., J. W. Pan, K. Mattle, M. Eibl, H. Weinfurter, and A. Zeilinger. "Experimental Quantum Teleportation," *Nature* 390 (6660), (1997): 575–579.

Braunstein, S. L., and H. J. Kimble. "Teleportation of Continuous Quantum Variables," *Physical Review* 80 (1998): 869–872.

Einstein, A., B. Podolsky and N. Rosen. "Can Quantum-Mechanical Description of Physical Reality be Considered Complete?" *Physical Review* 47 (1935): 777–780.

Furusawa, A., J. L. Sorensen, S. L. Braunstein, C. A. Fuchs, H. J. Kimble, and E. S. Polzik. "Unconditional Quantum Teleportation," *Science* 282 (1998): 706–709.

Gottesman, D., and I. L. Chuang. "Quantum Teleportation is a Universal Computational Primitive," *Nature* 402 (1999): 390–392.

Horodecki, M., P. Horodecki, and R. Horodecki. "General Teleportation Channel, Singlet Fraction, and Quasidistillation," *Physics Review Letters* A 60 (3), (1999): 1888–1989.

Horodecki, M., P. Horodecki, and R. Horodecki. "Mixed-State Entanglement and Distillation: Is There a 'Bound' Entanglement in Nature?" *Physical Review* 80 (24), (1998): 5239–5242.

Nielsen, M. A. "Conditions for a Class of Entanglement Transformations," *Physical Review* 83 (2), (1999): 436–439.

Nielsen, M. A., and C. M. Caves. "Reversible Quantum Operations and Their Application to Teleportation," *Physical Review* A 55 (4), (1997): 2547–2556.

Nielsen, M. A., E. Knill, and R. Laflamme. "Complete Quantum Teleportation Using Nuclear Magnetic Resonance," *Nature* 396 (6706), (1998): 52–55.

Vaidman, L. "Teleportation of Quantum States," *Physical Review* A 49 (2), (1994): 1473–1476.

Vedral, V., and M. B. Plenio. "Entanglement Measures and Purification Procedures," *Physical Review* A 57 (3), (1998): 1619.

SĀMA VEDA PRĀTISHĀKHYA *(Pushpa Sūtram)—Unmanifesting the Parts But Manifesting the Whole*—Quantum Network Architecture

Arbib, M. A., Ed. *The Handbook of Brain Theory and Neural Networks*. Massachusetts Institute of Technology, 1995.

Dayhoff, J. *Neural Network Architectures: An Introduction*. New York: Van Nostrand Reinhold, 1990.

Hagan, M. T., H. B. Demuth, and M. Beale. *Neural Network Design*. PWS Publishing Company, 1996.

Haykin, S. *Neural Networks: A Comprehensive Foundation*, 2nd Edition. Prentice-Hall, 1999.

9 Vedic *Devatā* in Quantum Network Architecture

Maharishi Mahesh Yogi, His Holiness, *Constitution of India Fulfilled through Maharishi's Transcendental Meditation*, 3rd Edition. India: Maharishi Mahesh Yogi Vedic Vishwavidyalaya, 1997.

Maharishi Mahesh Yogi, His Holiness, *Maharishi Mahesh Yogi on the Bhagavad-Gītā: A New Translation and Commentary*. Penguin Books, 1967.

Srimad Bhagavatam, Volumes I–IV. Translated by Swami Tapasyananda. Madras, India: Sri Ramakrishna Math.

The Srimad Devi Bhagawatam. Translated by Swami Vihnanananda, 3rd Edition. Oriental Books, 1989.

The Surya Siddhanta. Edited by Phanindralal Gangooly. Motilal Banarsidass Publishers, 1989.

Index

B

D

F